THE WRONG CARLOS

# The Wrong Carlos

*ANATOMY OF A
WRONGFUL EXECUTION*

James S. Liebman
Shawn Crowley
Andrew Markquart
Lauren Rosenberg
Lauren Gallo White
Daniel Zharkovsky

COLUMBIA UNIVERSITY PRESS
NEW YORK

Columbia University Press
*Publishers Since 1893*
New York    Chichester, West Sussex
cup.columbia.edu

Library of Congress Cataloging-in-Publication Data

The wrong Carlos : anatomy of a wrongful execution / James S. Liebman, Shawn Crowley,
Andrew Markquart, Lauren Rosenberg, Lauren Gallo White, and Daniel Zharkovsky.
    p.    cm.
  Includes bibliographical references and index.
  ISBN 978-0-231-16722-2 (cloth : alk. paper)
  ISBN 978-0-231-16723-9 (pbk. : alk. paper)
  ISBN 978-0-231-53668-4 (e-book)
  1. DeLuna, Carlos—Trials, litigation, etc.    2. Vargas López, Wanda.    3. Trials (Murder)—Texas.
4. Capital punishment—Texas.    5. Judicial error—Texas.    I. Liebman, James S., author.
  KF224.D45W76 2014
  364.152′3092—dc23

                                                                            2013044147

Columbia University Press books are printed on permanent and durable acid-free paper.
This book is printed on paper with recycled content.
Printed in the United States of America


c 10 9 8 7 6 5 4 3 2 1
p 10 9 8 7 6 5 4 3 2 1

COVER IMAGES: Courtesy of the author
COVER DESIGN: Marc Cohen

An earlier version of this work was published as *Los Tocayos Carlos:
An Anatomy of a Wrongful Execution*, 43 Colum. Hum. Rts. L. Rev. 711 (2012).
All rights reserved. 2013.

References to Web sites (URLs) were accurate at the time of writing.
Neither the authors nor Columbia University Press is responsible for
URLs that may have expired or changed since the manuscript was prepared.

PUBLICATION OF THIS BOOK
IS SUPPORTED BY A GRANT FROM
**FIGURE FOUNDATION.**

# CONTENTS

EXECUTION OF THE INNOCENT is the American criminal justice system's worst nightmare. But is it real? No less an authority than Supreme Court Justice Antonin Scalia doesn't think so. In 2006, he proclaimed that there has not been "a single case—not one—in which it is clear that a person was executed for a crime he did not commit. If such an event had occurred in recent years, we would not have to hunt for it; the innocent's name would be shouted from the rooftops."

This book is about two men named Carlos who lived in Corpus Christi, Texas, in the 1970s, 1980s, and 1990s. Carlos DeLuna was executed on December 7, 1989. Carlos Hernandez died in a Texas prison a decade later. Through their stories and that of a young convenience store clerk named Wanda Lopez, the book offers readers the chance to make up their own minds about the reality of wrongful executions and to decide for themselves whether there is anything about the events described here that is worth shouting from the rooftops.

In the epilogue, we offer our own thoughts about what happened and what it means for the American criminal justice system. In the meantime, we do our best to stay out of readers' way as they make up their own minds. Toward that end, we lay out the facts as fully as we can based on an intensive investigation begun in 2004, and we use a no-frills narrative to make the facts as accessible as possible to as wide an audience as we can reach. The less said here, the better.

Supplementing the book is a Web site (thewrongcarlos.net) with the most complete set of primary records and witness interviews (many of them videotaped) that has ever been compiled on an American capital case or, we believe, on an American court case of any sort. The Web site was originally compiled with the assistance of the editors of the *Columbia Human Rights Law Review* and accompanied an earlier version of this work: *Los Tocayos Carlos: An Anatomy of a Wrongful Execution*, 43 Colum. Hum. Rts. L. Rev. 711 (2012). The authors and publisher of this book gratefully acknowledge the assistance and permissions provided by the *Columbia Human Rights Law Review*, which made this book and the supporting Web site possible. The main purpose of this preface is to list a number of resources available in the book and on the Web site that can speed the reader's journey from the known facts to a conclusion about what happened. In addition to the prologue, which provides some geographic and historical context, seventeen chapters presenting the narrative itself, and the epilogue with our reflections on the case, we offer the following guides and resources. Some of these materials are available in the book; others are on the Web site.

MAPS AND VIDEOTAPES SHOWING KEY LOCATIONS OF IMPORTANT EVENTS IN CORPUS CHRISTI

- Map of key locations in Corpus Christi (in prologue)
- Interactive map of Corpus Christi (on Web site)
- Map of the area around the Sigmor Shamrock gas station (figure 2.3)
- Video tour of the Sigmor Shamrock gas station (on Web site)
- Video tour of Carrizo Street (on Web site)

TIME LINES OF IMPORTANT EVENTS

- Time line of important events, 1954–1999 (on Web site)
- Minute-by-minute time line of events at or near the Sigmor Shamrock gas station on February 4, 1983 (on Web site)
- Detailed time line of events, 1951–1999 (on Web site)

PEOPLE WHO APPEAR IN *THE WRONG CARLOS* AND THEIR RELATIONSHIPS TO ONE ANOTHER

- Alphabetical list of key people and their role in the case (appendix and on Web site)
- People listed by categories based on their relationship to Carlos DeLuna and Carlos Hernandez (appendix and on Web site)

- DeLuna and Hernandez family trees (on Web site)
- Chart tracing associations among key actors (on Web site)
- Chart displaying key legal actors (on Web site)

## COLOR VERSIONS OF PHOTOGRAPHS OF PEOPLE AND PLACES, MAPS, AND DIAGRAMS (ON WEB SITE)

## PRIMARY AND SECONDARY SOURCES SUPPORTING FACTUAL AND LEGAL STATEMENTS

- Nearly four thousand reference notes keyed to specified passages in each chapter, with the sources for each factual and legal claim made, and with hyperlinks to otherwise unpublished primary sources (on Web site)
- Bibliography of sources used in each chapter (at end of book and on Web site)
- Bibliography of all sources, listing the chapters in which each source was used, with hyperlinks to the primary source (on Web site)
- Collections of important primary materials, including law-enforcement files; crime photographs; court records; newspaper and television reports (including videotapes); and notes, transcripts, and more than two dozen videotapes of witness interviews (on Web site)

In addition to enabling readers to check our work as they go and compare their ultimate conclusions with our own, the Web site should provide a powerful resource for academic and student readers using the book as a tool for understanding the workings of the nation's criminal justice and capital punishment systems, and for all readers interested in the anatomy of a criminal and capital case.

## ACKNOWLEDGMENTS

WE ARE DEEPLY GRATEFUL for the assistance on this project by friends who at the time of our investigation were at the Gulf Region Advocacy Center (especially William Belford, Reid Pillaphont, and, most especially, Danalynn Recer), the Innocence Project (especially Nina Morrison, Peter Neufeld, and Barry Scheck), and the NAACP Legal Defense Fund (especially Miriam Gohara and George Kendall); Michael Banks and colleagues at the Morgan Lewis law firm in Philadelphia; private investigators Peso Chavez, Lauren Eskenazi, Scharlette Holdman, Ron Lax, Susan Montez, Mort Smith, Sita Sovin, Tamara Theiss, and Bruce Whitman; Columbia law-student research assistants Alexandra Blaszczuk, Natasha Bronn, Leslie Demers, Douglas Jaffe, Abshir Kore, David Mattern, Kate McCoy, Laura Lynn Noggle, Jonathan Waisnor, and Kate Weisburd; *Columbia Human Rights Law Review* editors Derek Borchardt, Gudrun Juffer, Laura Mergenthal, Aerin Miller, Alison Moe, Adam Shpeen, and Caitlin Smith; Columbia Law School support staff Luis Bello, Meredith Cowan, Margaret Symuleski, and especially Frantz Merine; and Allan Bayle, Chuck Blitz, David Bradford, Rhonda Brownstein, Jody Buckley, Peter Davies, Morris Dees, Betsy Fairbanks, Michael Fellner, Stephen Foster, Ruth Friedman, Chris Gomez, Joshua Gray, Wade Greene, Sam Gross, Jamie Guggenheim, Reed Hastings, Mysti Hillis, Mark Horowitz, Henry Liebman, Nick McKeown, David Menschel, Greg Minshall, Rick Perez, Andy Rappaport, Deborah Rappaport, Herbert Sandler, Susan Swanson, Marge Tabankin, Martha Toll, and Scott Wallace.

*THE WRONG CARLOS*

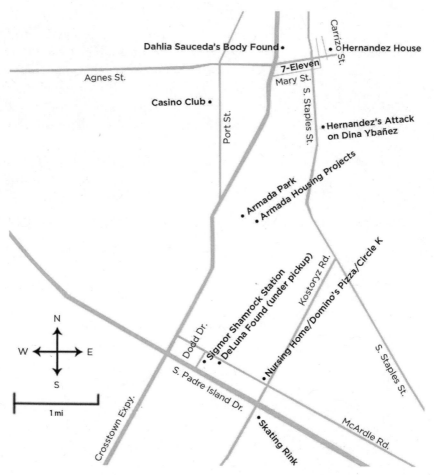

Key locations in Corpus Christi.

ON FRIDAY, NOVEMBER 13, 1863, lawmen hanged Chipita Rodriguez from a mesquite tree near Corpus Christi, Texas. Less than a week earlier, a jury had found her guilty of killing a trader for his gold. Both the trader and the sheriff were Anglo, and the sheriff handpicked the jury. Rodriguez was poor and of Mexican descent. She had little in the way of a defense lawyer, who presented even less in the way of a defense.

The sheriff's story about what happened never added up because the trader's gold was found near his body. It was rumored in the Mexican community that Rodriguez took the blame for someone else. Years later, the story goes, another man confessed on his deathbed to killing the trader.

Rodriguez's last words were "*No soy culpable*," I am not guilty. In 1985, the Texas Legislature and governor absolved her in what remains the only posthumous exoneration in the state's storied history of capital punishment.

A witness to the execution said that Rodriguez survived the hanging and moaned from inside the coffin as lawmen lowered it into an unmarked grave. Legend has it that Rodriguez's ghost haunts the river bottoms north of Corpus Christi whenever Texas executes one of its many death row prisoners.

If ghost stories are true, Rodriguez's spirit still walks. After the courts lifted a moratorium on executions that began in the 1960s, Texas resumed executing people in 1982. Since then, Texas has executed more than 500 people, four times more than any other state.

.    .    .

On December 7, 1989, Texas executed Carlos DeLuna. His death marked the state's thirty-third legal killing since renewing the death penalty in 1982 after an eighteen-year hiatus. DeLuna's barely noticed execution was also the thirty-third time that Texas Death House chaplain Carroll Pickett had eased a prisoner through his last day and onto the gurney where he was injected with poison until dead.

DeLuna was executed for stabbing Wanda Lopez to death with a 7-inch lock-blade buck knife in a 1983 Corpus Christi robbery. Shortly after the killing, police found DeLuna cowering under a pickup truck, arrested him, and took him to the Sigmor Shamrock gas station and store where Lopez had been working alone that night. There a lone Anglo eyewitness, who briefly saw a Hispanic man running out of the store, identified DeLuna as the killer.

During their hours together, Pickett found DeLuna "childlike." The young man was as simple and inconsequential as the case itself, which hardly compared with the more elaborate and horrifying crimes that usually brought men to the Death House in Huntsville, Texas, to be readied for execution. DeLuna was terrified that the lethal injection would hurt, and Pickett read the twenty-third psalm to calm him. The scripture confused DeLuna, and he asked what it meant. "We're in the valley of the shadow of death, Carlos," Pickett explained.

After years of dealing with the worst kinds of criminals, Pickett was struck most by a detail of the case in a newspaper clipping he read as he prepared to meet DeLuna. "The average convict," the Death House chaplain said later, "will not stop a block away and hide underneath a truck. If [you're] going to run, you keep running and running and running. You get as far away from the scene as possible. . . . Carlos DeLuna goes and hides under a truck a block away. That's childlike."

Aside from some reporters, only DeLuna's sister Rose and a few other relatives traveled to Huntsville in East Texas to attend the execution. Wanda Lopez's parents and brother stayed away.

Pickett officiated at sixty-two more executions, ninety-five in total. Only DeLuna's led him to seek psychiatric help. Partly, Pickett was moved by De-Luna's claim that he was innocent. Unlike most of the men whom Pickett ushered to their deaths, DeLuna didn't confess to the crime. Pickett was

also haunted by his belief that the anesthetic in the mixture of drugs injected into DeLuna's vein had failed, so the terrified young man was awake
as the other drugs paralyzed him and slowly suffocated him to death. Reverend Pickett has since become an outspoken critic of the death penalty.

•   •   •

On a scorching day in August 2004, Fernando (Freddy) Schilling, a Corpus Christi man serving time in the Jester III Unit of a Richmond, Texas,
prison, received a visit from a private detective. The investigator showed
him a picture of a handsome young Hispanic man, 5 feet, 8 inches tall,
160 pounds, with heavy eyebrows and dark, wavy hair. Without hesitation,
Schilling identified the man as his brother-in-law, Carlos Hernandez, from
twenty years earlier.

Schilling still bore scars from his fights with Hernandez, whose brutal
life was punctuated by sometimes deadly violence, much of it directed toward poor, young Hispanic women in Corpus Christi, often with a lock-
blade buck knife.

The detective told Schilling that the man in the photograph was not
Carlos Hernandez. It was Carlos DeLuna. The detective was investigating
DeLuna's claim that he had been mistaken for another man he had seen
struggling with Wanda Lopez inside the gas station. The claim was ignored
at the time, and DeLuna was convicted and executed. The man DeLuna
named was Schilling's brother-in-law, Carlos Hernandez.

"Man, he's a ringer [for] Carlos Hernandez," Schilling said. "That gives
me the goose bumps." Tears welled up in Schilling's eyes.

•   •   •

Carlos Gonzales Hernandez, Jr., was born in Corpus Christi in 1954. He
spent much of the next forty-five years committing crimes for which he was
barely or never punished.

In 1971, he was convicted of negligent homicide for killing his sister
Paula's fiancé in a car wreck. He was drunk at the time and driving over
100 miles per hour. Paula was severely injured in the accident but recovered. Hernandez's sentence was suspended. He spent no time in jail.

In 1972, Hernandez received a twenty-year sentence for each of three
armed holdups of Corpus Christi gas stations. Texas paroled him after five
years.

Hernandez escaped punishment for one crime twice. In 1979, Corpus Christi detective Eddie Garza and his partner Paul Rivera, the two most celebrated Corpus Christi detectives of their generation, arrested him for killing Dahlia Sauceda in her custom-model "Happy Time" van. Someone had beaten and strangled her to death in front of her two-year-old daughter and carved an $X$ on the back of her nude body. Hernandez talked prosecutor Kenneth Botary into releasing him and going after another man, who was eventually acquitted. Garza and Rivera arrested Hernandez for the murder of Sauceda again in 1986 after new information surfaced, but Botary had misplaced key evidence, and the charges were dropped.

In 1989, Hernandez assaulted Dina Ybañez with a 7-inch lock-blade buck knife. He received a ten-year sentence. Texas paroled him in a year and a half.

Hernandez went back to prison in 1996 for assaulting a neighbor with a 9-inch kitchen knife, his thirteenth arrest while carrying a knife. He died three years later in a prison in northeastern Texas. The cause was cirrhosis of the liver and other complications from too much drinking and smoking. His mother, Fidela Hernandez, collected on an insurance policy that she had taken out on her son, but she refused to pay to bring him home to be buried. He was put in a pauper's grave on prison grounds. "Dirt is dirt," she later explained.

# PART I

# The Death of Wanda Lopez

# 1

# Murder

WANDA JEAN VARGAS LOPEZ DIED AT WORK at a Sigmor Shamrock gas station in Corpus Christi, Texas, on February 4, 1983. She was twenty-four. Wanda's only brother, Richard Vargas, would hear her utter her last words, but they gave him no solace or peace. They just made him angry.

Richard was at his parents' house that Friday night, waiting for Wanda to get off work so they all could go out to celebrate. Wanda had insisted. She had good news to share.

Wanda worked the 3:00 to 10:00 P.M. shift alone at the small gas station and store in a poor part of town. She stood behind an 18-inch counter with a lift-top entryway. Unlike at some other stations, no glass or barrier separated her from the customers. To her right was a single cash drawer. Beside it sat the console used to regulate the gas pumps. Above the cash drawer and console, a window looked south over the pumps and beyond to South Padre Island Drive, a controlled-access highway that people call "SPID." Behind Wanda, another window faced west, across a dark, narrow street to a "gentlemen's club" named Wolfy's.

Wolfy's was a landmark back then. Its giant cutout of a buxom, scantily clad woman loomed over SPID. The club attracted a rough crowd of bikers and men from the area. The bar's customers often stumbled across the street to the Sigmor to buy cheap cigarettes or beer. Wanda dealt with them as best she could on her own. She warned her brother more than once that she'd better not catch him in a place like Wolfy's.

North of the station, to Wanda's left as she faced the counter, was a poor residential neighborhood, a warren of narrow streets and shabby frame houses with front and backyards open to each other or bounded by rotting slat fences.

Wanda was a divorced high-school dropout with a young daughter to support. Her husband left when she was four months pregnant, and she hadn't heard from him since. To support herself, she took whatever work she could get, while her parents minded the baby. She was a good worker, cheerful and reliable, and she followed the rules. She had been at the station for only a few months and already was an assistant manager.

Richard and his parents worried about Wanda, trapped in that 4- by 6-foot space, with only a counter separating her from whoever came in the door. They told her that she needed a safer job in a better neighborhood. Sometimes her father would sit in the Sigmor parking lot in his pickup truck until her shift ended. Robert Mayorga, a police officer whom Wanda went out with now and then, also checked on her when he could. They worked out hand signals for when he was too busy to leave his patrol car.

·   ·   ·

Neither Wanda's father nor Officer Mayorga was at the gas station on the night of February 4. Richard and his father were at home watching television, waiting for Wanda to finish work and for her mother to come home from her weekly bingo game. Earlier in the week, Wanda had told them that she wanted to celebrate that Friday night after getting off work and sharing her good news.

At first, Richard had declined Wanda's invitation. He worked late himself most nights and had the month's bills to pay. But when Wanda said she'd do Richard's paperwork for him so they could all go out, Richard laughed and agreed to join the celebration.

Wanda was excited about a new boyfriend. After her husband left, she sometimes went to clubs and parties on the weekend, but she never dated anyone for long, and never anyone she wanted the family to meet. Now, though, Wanda had found someone she was proud of and wanted to bring home. She called him Green Eyes. They say the man came to Wanda's funeral to pay his respects, but Richard never met him.

Sometime after 8:00 P.M., a kid from across the street crashed his bicycle onto the Vargases' driveway and ran to the door. He was breathless, yelling. He said that something had happened at the gas station. Wanda was hurt. They'd better get there fast. Richard recalls the boy saying that it didn't look good.

Richard left alone, telling his father that he'd report back as soon as he could. His father drove over to the bingo game to get his wife.

When Richard arrived at the Sigmor, he found chaos. There were patrol cars and officers everywhere, emergency lights flashing, police radios blaring. An ambulance, a fire engine, and television trucks were parked in the gas station lot. Fifty or sixty people from the neighborhood were milling around.

Richard rushed toward the store. His little sister was lying on a backboard on the sidewalk just outside the door. She was soaked in blood, and so was the sidewalk. A firefighter stood over her with an IV bag. She had a tube in her mouth and was hooked to a large plastic machine with more tubes that went into her chest. Paramedics were lifting her onto a stretcher on wheels.

"That's my sister," Richard yelled. "Let me through." The cops held him back, telling him to meet the ambulance at the hospital. He asked what had happened, but all they would say was that there'd been a tragedy.

Richard looked inside the store for clues. It was lit up, and people in plainclothes were rushing around, looking worried. There was blood everywhere. Immediately, something caught his eye. He thought that he was imagining things, but he looked closer and it was real: two people were scrubbing the floors as fast as they could. He couldn't understand why they were cleaning up the crime scene already.

The ambulance left, headed east on SPID toward Mercy Hospital. Richard followed in his car. Once inside the emergency room, he heard the words that he had dreaded since he saw his sister on the sidewalk: "Your sister is dead."

Richard called his parents, and they met him at the hospital, bringing Wanda's five-year-old daughter with them. They learned that Wanda had been stabbed once through the left breast with a knife. The blade went most of the way through her lung. She bled to death within minutes. No one told the family how it had happened, only that someone had stabbed her.

Later they heard more, in Wanda's own words and screams.

They were at home with the television going when the news came on. There was a report about the robbery-murder at the Sigmor Shamrock station on SPID. Reminding viewers that Wanda Vargas Lopez, a store clerk, had been stabbed to death, the reporter turned excitedly to a new development. It turned out that the store clerk had been on the phone with the police when she was killed. Police had the crime on a 911 tape.

The television station played the tape. Wanda's words were typed out at the bottom of the screen. At the first sound of Wanda's frightened voice, Richard's mother rushed his niece out of the room. Both were crying. They didn't have to hear this. Both started counseling soon after Wanda died and continued receiving it for years.

Richard didn't move. Wanda was pleading with the 911 dispatcher: "[C]an you have an officer come to 2602 South Padre Island Drive? I have a suspect with a—a knife inside the store. . . . He's a Mexican. He's standing right here at the counter."

Richard heard fear in his sister's voice. But he heard something else, too: expectation, even confidence. She believed that help would come soon.

What came instead was a litany of questions that the dispatcher directed back at Wanda. The longer Richard listened, the angrier he got. "What's he doing with the knife? Has he threatened you or anything? Huh? Ma'am? Where is he at right now?" "What does he look like?" And again, "What does he look like?" "Is he a white male?" "Black? Hispanic?" "Tall? Short?" "Tall?" "Does he have the knife pulled out?" "Is it in his pocket?"

Even before Wanda whispered that the Mexican man was "standing right here at the counter" and then said, "Can't talk," Richard could tell that the man was right there, buying an 85-cent pack of cigarettes. He could hear Wanda telling the man, "Okay. This? Eighty-five." Her voice quivered a little, but she managed to keep the pitch and volume normal.

When she tried to answer the dispatcher's questions, her voice went low and her words were clipped. Her lips must have been barely moving, answering, "I don't know." "Not yet." "Por qué?" "Can't talk." "What?" "Right here." "No." "No." "Yes." "Un-huh." "Yeah." Richard could hear his sister's poise collapsing, along with her confidence that there was a lifeline out that would save her.

When the 911 operator asked a second time whether the knife was out, Wanda's voice for the first time rose in fear and exasperation: "Not ye-et!" she said again. Every muscle in Richard's body tightened. "Stop asking questions!" he wanted to shout. "Send out a squad car. There's time!"

Then it was done. Wanda gave up on the 911 operator and spoke directly to the man, begging for her life. "You want it? I'll give it to you. I'm not gonna do nothing to you. Please!!!!" Then she screamed. Six unbearable seconds of wordless scuffling followed. The phone dropped. Wanda moaned.

Then came an incessant dial tone, as the killer hung up the phone.

Why, Richard wondered, didn't they send out a cruiser first thing? And why did the guy stab her? She didn't do anything to him. He didn't even have to ask for the money. Wanda just offered it to him. It must have been all the questions, Richard thought. The man must have realized that she was on the phone with the cops and gotten mad. But if he knew that the cops were on to him, why not just run? Why take the time to hurt Wanda, scuffle with her, and *then* run? It made no sense.

•     •     •

Forty minutes after Wanda's call, the police closed the case with an arrest. They caught Carlos DeLuna in a residential neighborhood a few blocks east of the Sigmor. Sometime later, police officials gave television stations the 911 tape, dramatizing the cops' quick work.

The stations played the tape over and over for days. And for months, they played it again every time something new happened in the case. Richard heard it twice more, alongside the jury, at DeLuna's trial. That was five months after the crime.

Richard was infuriated that he first learned of his sister's last words on television, without warning, along with everyone else in Corpus Christi. When he showed up at the Sigmor station, the police wouldn't tell him what "tragedy" had befallen his sister. But before he knew it, they were telling everyone else, in her own words. And for months afterward, every time he turned around it seemed, the tape was being played again, with no concern for the pain it brought him and his family.

The police, the television stations, and everyone in town had a good story. A 911 tape captures the chilling sounds of a young woman pleading for her life and her brutal murder. The community is safe, though, because the cops acted fast, made an arrest within minutes, and solved the case.

For Richard and his family, Wanda's last words were a monument to their unspeakable pain and a boundary between the lives they lived before Wanda's death and the ones they struggled through after. But Richard couldn't see what the tape had to say to everyone else. Not who killed his sister. Not why. Not even much about how. For them, Wanda's last words, played over and over again like that, were just a cheap piece of entertainment.

# 2

# Manhunt

KEVAN BAKER WANTED TO FORGET Wanda Lopez's final moments. He didn't know Wanda, but her last conscious act before dying was to collapse in his arms, begging for help. Seconds before, he'd wrestled with his own conscience as he watched her through the window wrestling with her attacker.

For a second or two, the smallish, blond, bespectacled car salesman, who trained as a medic in the navy, had debated whether to go to the woman's aid or leave. When he decided to go to her, he came face to face with the fleeing attacker, who threatened to pull a gun on him.

Even worse for Baker was his starring role at the criminal trial, five months later. By turns soft-spoken and profane, the thirty-three-year-old newlywed had no desire for attention except when he was at the wheel of his souped-up '67 Mercury Cougar. He didn't relish being the sole eyewitness at a trial for a man's life.

The months from the murder to the trial were bad all around for Baker. Right after the murder, his three-month-old marriage unraveled. Soon after the trial, he left Corpus Christi.

•   •   •

Baker finished work at 8:00 P.M. on that cool Friday evening. He was in a rush. He'd gotten off work an hour late, and his wife was waiting for him to pick her up so they could hit the clubs. Ten minutes later, he pulled his Cougar into the Sigmor for gas.

As he put the nozzle in the tank, Baker heard a bang on the inside of the store window. "Aw, shit," he thought, imagining that the clerk was telling him to pay before pumping. Baker squeezed the grip anyway, knowing that he was good for the few bucks and wanting to get out of there quickly. When no gas came out, Baker turned to look through the window at the clerk.

That's when he saw the wrestling. A Hispanic man was behind the counter, tussling with the female clerk.

"I thought they were playing at first," Baker said later. "That was my first impression—boyfriend and girlfriend. But the more seconds I stood there—I realized they weren't playing." They were "fighting." "It was a struggle."

Baker recalled that "the gentleman had the lady and was trying hard to get her into the back of the store." There was a back room that the man was trying "to carry the clerk into," and she was doing everything she could to hold herself back. At one point, the attacker grabbed her hair and jerked so hard with both hands that Baker was sure her hair must have come out.

"Oh fuck," Baker thought. "I don't want to be here. Get in the car and leave."

But he didn't have it in him to desert the struggling woman. "As an American," he said later, he felt he "should do the right thing. . . . To me it seemed like the right thing to do was go walk towards the door." So he did.

"The gentleman apparently knew I was there," Baker recalled. "As I started towards the store, he throwed the clerk to the floor and met me at the door." The man came out of the door, holding it open as he stood looking at Baker, about 3 feet away.

The assailant's greeting froze Baker in his tracks. "Don't mess with me. I got a gun," the man said. Baker saw nothing in the man's hands, no gun or any money, but he stopped anyway and looked the man in the eye. "My main thing," he explained, "was eye-to-eye contact, to make sure he didn't use the gun on me if he actually had one."

After a second or two, the man turned to his left, showing Baker his right profile. Then he "sprinted" the few steps to the corner of the building and took another left, running north behind the gas station store. When the first officers arrived, several bystanders described a man running behind the gas station and north up Dodd Street, the narrow street between the gas station and Wolfy's (figure 2.1).

Later that night and again at the trial, Baker described the man he saw grappling with Wanda. He was Hispanic; had dark hair; stood 5 feet, 8 or

FIGURE 2.1  Aerial photograph of the Sigmor Shamrock gas station in February 1983. Wolfy's is at the bottom across Dodd Street from the station. Standing a few feet outside the station store, Kevan Baker watched the assailant exit the store, turn left (east), and then left again (north) behind the store. Bystanders saw a man running behind the store and north up Dodd Street.

9 inches tall; and weighed about 170 pounds. Baker guessed that he was twenty-four to twenty-six years old. Years later, he described the man as a little older, "young thirties, probably, maybe late twenties."

At a court hearing, Baker described the man as a "transient," someone who looked as though he had "been on the street and was very hungry." His clothes were shabby and unclean. He had quite a bit of facial hair: a full mustache and whiskers all over his face, like he "hadn't shaved in, you know, ten days, a couple weeks." He wore a long-sleeved flannel shirt or jacket with red in it, which Baker thought may have covered a gray or light-colored sweatshirt.

•    •    •

Baker didn't move until he was sure that the man was gone. He wasn't taking any chances. The attacker "didn't seem like he was on drugs or anything or like he was drunk," Baker said. "He knew what he was doing."

After the man ran off behind the station, Baker took a few stunned steps back toward his car, not knowing what to do. A vehicle pulled in from the west. The driver rolled down his window, and Baker yelled for him to call the police.

Then Baker noticed the clerk. She had staggered to the front door, barefoot, dripping a trail of blood. Baker went to her.

"Th[e] young lady was coming out . . . and I met her at the door. . . . She just kind of come against me, and then fell back into the building, and started sliding down the side of the window right by the front door." As he helped her down onto the concrete sidewalk, Wanda smeared blood on the window and all along the doorframe. There was blood all over her left side, front and back. Wanda was hysterical, pleading "Help me, help me" and trying to get up. Baker gently held her to the ground, telling her to "lay down, get calm."

Baker's navy training kicked in, and he looked for a wound. He pulled up Wanda's sweater and found a slit in the left side of her bra. "A woman has an artery that goes to the breast," he explained. "[T]hat's what [the attacker] sliced." Baker knew that the clerk would bleed to death unless he could stanch the flow, and he went inside the store for something to use.

As he took a few steps inside, he was stunned by the mess. There was "blood and money and stuff all over the place." He grabbed a handful of windshield towels and ran out, ready to pack them on the wound.

As Baker knelt down, he heard sirens, and "the cops just started flying in." He told the officers where the man he'd seen had run off. Then he stood back and let the officers do their job. A sergeant told Baker to wait by the ice machine on the east wall outside the store. Soon he was joined by other people who told police they had information (figure 2.2).

.       .       .

George Aguirre came first. Aguirre had purchased gas at the Sigmor several minutes before Baker, around 8:00 P.M. While filling his tank, he had noticed a Hispanic man standing by the ice machine and drinking beer. Police later found three empty beer cans in the area that Aguirre indicated. As Aguirre watched, the man slowly took a lock-blade knife out of his right front pants pocket, opened it, and put it back in his pocket.

Aguirre later described the Hispanic man as in his mid-twenties; maybe 5 feet, 10 inches, and 175 pounds; with dark hair, "blue pants," and a "white,

FIGURE 2.2 Photographs taken from a television news videotape of the Sigmor Shamrock gas station on the night of the stabbing: (*left*) medical technicians work on Wanda Lopez in front of the store (visible over the hood of the police car) while some of the witnesses (visible over the top of the white car) look on from near the ice machine; (*right*) close-up of (*from left*) George Aguirre, Julie Arsuaga, and John Arsuaga.

long-sleeved t-shirt." A police account of Aguirre's initial description reported "tennis shoes, a T-shirt, and blue jeans."

Aguirre tensed as the man approached him and asked for a ride to the Casino Club, a Latino nightclub a couple of miles away. The man offered Aguirre "money, beer, dope, whatever." Aguirre refused, and then went inside to pay.

He told the young woman behind the counter that there was a man outside with an open knife in his pocket. Aguirre offered to call the police, but the clerk said she'd call herself. He waited until she was on the phone with the 911 operator, and then returned to his van and drove off.*

Ten minutes later, standing outside a nearby bowling alley, Aguirre heard sirens and saw police cars heading toward the Sigmor.† He followed

---

*George Aguirre would later testify that he had seen the man with the knife enter the store just as Wanda Lopez called 911 in response to Aguirre's warning, and just as Aguirre was leaving. As we explain in chapter 13, however, it is almost certain that several minutes elapsed between the time Aguirre left and the time the man with the knife entered the store. For reasons explained later, if the man had entered the store at the moment Aguirre first warned Wanda, just as she was calling 911, the police probably would have saved her. Aguirre never explained why he took the trouble to warn Wanda and to offer to call the police himself but then left her alone and drove off when he saw the man enter the store.

†We have omitted Aguirre's claim to have seen the store clerk struggling with an assailant after he left the gas station, got onto SPID, and drove eastward past the station in the right lane (the lane farthest from the gas station). Our review of the aerial photographs introduced at trial revealing the relationship between SPID and the gas station, and our visual observation of the same while driving on the freeway past the gas station, reveal that it would have been impossible for someone in the far-right lane on the east side of the freeway—even someone standing still, not to mention someone driving at freeway speeds—to look past the three other eastbound lanes, then the three

the squad cars and, when he reached the station, approached an officer to explain what he'd seen earlier. Police corralled him with Baker near the ice machine.

. . .

Julie and John Arsuaga were the final additions to the group of witnesses by the ice machine. They had run over from Phase III, a nightclub 115 yards east of the Sigmor, along the SPID frontage road. Between the club and the gas station, along the same strip, stood two other businesses: Ziebart's car-detailing garage and a Harley-Davidson repair shop. Like the Sigmor and Phase III, these businesses were flanked on three sides by parking areas, with an alleyway behind and the frontage road in front.

Minutes earlier, as the Arsuagas were pulling into a parking spot in front of Phase III, they noticed a man running east along the walkway between them and the club. John put the time at "about five minutes after 8:00 P.M." The jogger passed through their headlight beams and, once past the club, cut diagonally across a field between the club and Lebowitz Furniture, the next building farther east. He disappeared into the backyard of a home across the alleyway behind Lebowitz.

The couple described the man as Hispanic; about 5 feet, 8 inches; 170 pounds; with wavy, medium-length dark hair. He wore "dark slacks," pressed "uniform"-style, and a white, button-down dress shirt.

Of the witnesses, Julie had the best eye for details of coif and clothing. Her description of the shirt was typical: "The sleeve was rolled up, it was a white, you know, blouse-style shirt, you know, something like what you [a lawyer in court] have on." It "was open, you know, because I could see the side of it, kind of flapping back a little bit—might not have been completely unbuttoned, but close to the bottom it was."

The man whom the Arsuagas saw was "not running fast, just a self-set pace—you know, jogging, kind of." He struck John and Julie as comical. They joked about someone out for a leisurely jog in dress clothes at night.

---

westbound lanes, over the edge of the freeway, and down to, and inside, the Sigmor store. Additionally, Aguirre gave inconsistent accounts of what he did after he left Wanda and drove away from the Sigmor. While conversing with Kevan Baker when the two were corralled together near the ice machine, Aguirre claimed that, when he left the gas station, he drove to a pay phone and succeeded in reaching the police by telephone but didn't mention seeing the struggle between the store clerk and the assailant from his car on the freeway. At trial, Aguirre said he did view the struggle from his car but didn't reach the police by phone.

After the man disappeared, the Arsuagas heard sirens and noticed some commotion at the Sigmor station. John could see a man there helping someone down onto the ground in front of the station's store, followed by the arrival of two or three police cars. What had seemed silly suddenly looked serious. John flashed his headlights and honked his horn to get the cops' attention. When that didn't work, the two drove west past the Harley-Davidson shop to Ziebart's garage, parked their car, and ran next door to the Sigmor to tell the police what they'd seen.

·   ·   ·   ·

The witnesses' recollections are not the only firsthand accounts of what happened that night. Two police audiotapes also tell a story. The first is the 911 tape of Wanda's call about a man with a knife inside her store at 2602 South Padre Island Drive—the tape that ends with Wanda's scream, the scuffle, and someone hanging up the phone. Police evidently gave this tape to the television stations to use. It is the only tape that the police disclosed to the public after Wanda's death.

The other tape contains forty-two minutes and thirty-one seconds of telephone and radio calls to and from Jesse Escochea, the Corpus Christi Police Department's untrained, twenty-one-year-old radio dispatcher. It was police practice to record over the master tape of 911 calls and radio dispatches every forty-five days or so, but the police made a copy of this 911 call and the forty-plus minutes of radio traffic that followed it during a massive manhunt for the attacker. Although Escochea went over the manhunt tape with a state's attorney several months later, the tape's existence was unknown to anyone outside law enforcement until private investigators tracked it down twenty-two years later in Escochea's possession in Los Angeles.

Not long after Wanda's murder, Escochea had left Corpus Christi for Los Angeles, where he worked for a time as a police dispatcher. Later he took occasional roles as an actor in cops-and-robbers television shows and made a living tracking and filming police emergency runs and turning them into reality videos for foreign markets. He kept a copy of the manhunt tape from the Sigmor stabbing as a souvenir of what he told a news reporter was one of his most memorable moments as a dispatcher.

The manhunt tape begins with Wanda's 911 call, which Escochea answered by happenstance. As the dispatcher, he wasn't supposed to pick up the telephone, but he did because the incoming-call light had been flashing for a long time, and neither of the regular operators had answered it. The remainder of the tape records radio traffic between Escochea and police officers in the field during the chaotic manhunt for Wanda's attacker. It ends with Carlos DeLuna's arrest.

. . .

Escochea took Wanda's call at 8:09 P.M. Immediately she said what she needed: "Yes, can you have an officer come to 2602 South Padre Island Drive? I have a suspect with a—a knife inside the store." Escochea didn't like the caller's tone of voice. Listening to the tape years later, he recalled thinking that Wanda had "a little bit of an attitude."

For well over a minute, Escochea questioned Wanda about the "Mexican" man inside the store—what he looked like and what he was doing. Then he heard Wanda try to give the man the money from the cash drawer: "You want it? I'll give it to you. I'm not gonna do nothing to you. Please!!!"

It was only then, seventy-seven seconds into the call, that Escochea broadcast his first "armed robbery in progress," giving the gas station address.

Seconds later, Wanda screamed. Scuffling and moaning could be heard in the background. Then the phone went dead.

A minute later, Escochea broadcast another bulletin: "It's going to be a Hispanic male with a knife. I had the chick on the phone. There's going to be an assault in progress, also."

Escochea initially dispatched Officer Thomas Mylett to the scene. Mylett didn't answer, and a second call went out a minute later at 8:11 P.M. Responding to that call, Sergeant Steven Fowler reached the scene in just over a minute. If Fowler had been dispatched when Wanda first called, he would have arrived before she screamed.

Fowler found Wanda on the sidewalk, covered in blood, and radioed— inaccurately—that she had been shot. He bent over Wanda to ask what had happened but immediately saw that she couldn't answer. Forty seconds after arriving, exactly two and a half minutes after Wanda screamed, Fowler called for an ambulance.

If Escochea had called for an ambulance when he first heard Wanda scream, it would have arrived at about the time Fowler called for it.

. . .

Officer Bruno Mejia was the second officer on the scene. He corralled witnesses at the ice machine as they arrived and took descriptions of the suspect. He broadcast the descriptions over the police radio frequency as "BOLOs"—alerts to "be on the lookout."

The first BOLO reported Kevan Baker's description of a "Hispanic man, about 5 foot 9, wearing a flannel shirt and a gray sweatshirt," who was "north-bound on foot, to the rear" of the Sigmor. Baker's statement that the assailant had headed north behind the station was confirmed by police fanning out in that area who heard reports from others of a "person [seen] running to the rear of the store." Four versions of this BOLO went out over the course of a minute, all within about three minutes of when Wanda first screamed.

After getting Baker's description, Mejia spoke next to George Aguirre and John and Julie Arsuaga. Like Baker, they all saw a Hispanic man, twenty-five years old, about 5 feet, 8 inches, 170 pounds, with black hair. Someone—probably Julie Arsuaga—described the man's hair as "medium" or "ear-length" and "slightly wavy, just a tiny bit, not real curly."

The twenty-two-year-old Mejia struggled, however, to make sense of other details the three new witnesses provided, especially the Arsuagas. Unlike the light-colored sweatshirt Baker described and the white, long-sleeved T-shirt Aguirre saw, the Arsuagas were sure that the man they had seen in their headlights running past the Phase III nightclub wore a white dress shirt. The Arsuagas described the shirt in great detail: the sleeves were rolled up, and it was unbuttoned near where the shirt reached the man's dark, well-pressed, "uniform-type" slacks.

These were not the slovenly clothes Baker described, nor the blue jeans Aguirre initially recalled. And unlike the unshaven and mustachioed man whom Baker saw at the gas station, the man who jogged east past the Arsuagas was clean shaven.

The witnesses' reports about location and timing also conflicted. The Arsuagas were at the Phase III, more than a football field *east* of the Sigmor along the SPID frontage road, when the man in the dress shirt jogged past at a leisurely pace. John Arsuaga gave the time as "shortly" or "five minutes" after 8:00 P.M.

This didn't jibe with Baker's observation—confirmed by the manhunt tape—of Wanda Lopez's attacker still in the gas station door six minutes later. And it conflicted with Baker's statement that the man sprinted in a completely different direction, heading *north* "behind" the gas station. That put the suspect near Dodd Street, and cops swarming the area received reports from "several" people of a man running north and slightly behind the gas station to Dodd Street and farther north along that street (which turns into Dodd Drive) toward McArdle Road.

Baker and the other witnesses gathered near the ice machine noticed the inconsistencies, too, and struggled to "sort [them] out." "We were all together," Baker later recalled, "collaborating," trying to make sense of what everyone saw.

.     .     .

All nine of the BOLOs that Mejia broadcast over a twenty-minute span that night included Baker's description of a man in a *flannel jacket and gray sweatshirt*. The officer wavered, however, in broadcasting the information he got from Aguirre about the *long-sleeve T-shirt*—occasionally including it in his BOLOs, but usually omitting it. Mejia never felt comfortable enough about the Arsuagas' report of a *button-down dress shirt* to include it in any of the BOLOs.

At first, in fact, Mejia included descriptions of any sort from Aguirre and the Arsuagas only along with expressions of doubt or a warning that they might refer to a different person. Not until his final BOLO, which guided the final eighteen minutes of the search, did Mejia give up trying to keep the witnesses' accounts separate and merge them into a single description.

In that description, the assailant's clothes were a confusing blend of all the witnesses' recollections, while the assailant's facial hair tracked what the Arsuagas recalled ("clean shaven") and contradicted what Baker had seen ("mustache," ten days' growth of beard). In this and all his BOLOs, Mejia left out precious bits of information.

The first time one of Mejia's BOLOs tacked on information from Aguirre and the Arsuagas was at 8:16, P.M. about six minutes after Wanda screamed. In this new bulletin, Mejia collapsed the Arsuagas' description of a white, partially unbuttoned *dress* shirt into Aguirre's description of a white, long-sleeved *T-shirt*. Aware of the discrepancies between what he was hearing from the Arsuagas and the other witnesses, the officer cautioned that the new information might describe someone different from the rest of the BOLO:

"About 5 feet, 9 inches, should have a flannel shirt and gray sweatshirt." *"Also, witnesses are saying he had a white untucked T-shirt. I don't know if it's another suspect."*

In his next two BOLOs a few minutes later, Mejia seemed to have settled on the description from Baker: "Hispanic male, 5–9, gray sweatshirt, flannel shirt. *No other information.*" And then: "Gray sweatshirt and a flannel shirt."

Later, however, dispatcher Escochea added back in the other witnesses' information, emphasizing that it contradicted the rest of the BOLO, and that he was uncertain about it. For example, twelve minutes after Wanda screamed, the BOLO said:

"Hispanic male, 5–9, wearing a flannel shirt and gray sweatshirt. Suspect last seen heading northbound on foot to the rear of the Shamrock. May possibly be wearing a white, long-sleeved T-shirt. That's may *possibly* be."

Seven minutes later, the dispatcher asked Mejia for more information, and the officer again queried the witnesses. Julie Arsuaga can be heard in the background on the dispatch tape, pressing her case. Mejia reported "some people" saying that it was "a white shirt, possibly a white shirt." Then came a trickle of grooming descriptions from the Arsuagas: "Clean shaven," "medium-length curly hair," then, nearly a minute later, "slightly wavy just a tiny bit."

Mejia's final BOLO was broadcast at 8:32 P.M., twenty-two minutes after Wanda screamed. This time Mejia combined the various details into what sounded like a consistent description of a single individual:

"A Hispanic male, 5–9, with flannel shirt, possibly a gray sweatshirt. It may possibly be a white T-shirt, also, long-sleeves. Clean shaven, medium, wavy, ear-length hair. He was out there earlier looking for a ride to the Casino."

The first sentence was from Baker. The second and last were from Aguirre. The facial and head hair information was from Julie Arsuaga.

Adding to the sense that the description was of a single person, Mejia never broadcast Baker's information that the attacker he saw sprinting *north* behind the gas station had a full *mustache* and *ten days' growth of beard* and the *unkempt look and shabby clothes* of a derelict or homeless person. Nor did he mention the Arsuagas' information that the white-shirted, clean-shaven man who jogged past them at a leisurely pace had disappeared behind Lebowitz Furniture over a football field in length *east* of the Sigmor and wore a *button-down dress* shirt and dark, *well-pressed* pants.

For the last eighteen minutes of the search, the police hunted a ghost, with features picked almost at random from three conflicting portraits, and not matching any actual account of the suspect's clothes, grooming, velocity, or direction of travel (see table on p. 24).

.    .    .

After dispatcher Escochea signaled to patrol cars that a robbery and assault had occurred and that the attacker had escaped to the north of the Sigmor on foot, cop cars flooded the area. Within minutes after Wanda collapsed just outside the store, Escochea had every available unit in the city limits— over twenty—looking for the man who had stabbed her.

One of the first to the scene was a sheriff's department constable, Ruben Rivera. He and his partner, Carolyn Vargas, were driving back downtown after serving papers in a civil case. They detoured to the Sigmor after hearing Escochea's emergency call. Rivera remembered a mosaic of officers: wildlife rangers, sheriffs' deputies, city police, and state highway patrolmen, as well as plainclothes vice squad officers in unmarked cars: "[T]here was everything out there . . . combing the neighborhood."

As police converged on the area, officers and residents radioed and called in information from the warren of dark narrow streets, shabby wood-frame houses, interlocking yards, and alleyways. Mixed up with Mejia's BOLOs on the tape were a jumble of clipped and urgent reports coming from many directions, including some from places so far outside the neighborhood that, in retrospect, they were beyond the reach of a man fleeing the Sigmor on foot.

Among the din of one-off calls were three intense bursts of radio traffic, each concentrated in time and place. The first flurry of sightings by officers came from the two blocks of Dodd Street and Drive that run north from the Sigmor station in the direction Kevan Baker saw the assailant headed (figure 2.3, points A1, 2, and 3). The calls peaked where Dodd intersects the more heavily trafficked McArdle Road (point 3).

The second set of sightings rolled east along McArdle for fourteen blocks, past a city park with ball fields, a middle school, and a nursing home (points 3–6 and 7). The sightings became especially intense around the

Each Observer's Description of the Man Near the Gas Station

| WITNESS | HEIGHT, WEIGHT, HAIR | AGE | STYLE | SHIRT | PANTS | MUSTACHE | BEARD | LOCATION |
|---|---|---|---|---|---|---|---|---|
| *(legend)* | ● Hispanic male, 5'8"–5'10", 160–170 lbs, dark, wavy hair | ▲ Mid- or late 20s  ■ 20 years old | ▲ Shabby clothes  ■ Dress clothes | ▲ Gray, long-sleeve T-shirt or sweatshirt  ▲ Same and red flannel shirt  ■ White dress shirt | ▲ Blue jeans  ◇ White pants  ■ Dark, pressed slacks | ▲ Mustache  ■ Clean shaven | ▲ Beard or ten-days' growth  ■ Clean shaven | ▲ Sprinting north behind Sigmor  ■ Jogging east and behind Phase III  ■■ Arrested behind Phase III |
| Steven Fowler at Circle K (2/3/83, earlier in evening) | ● | | ▲ | | ◇ | | | |
| Kevan Baker (2/4/83, 8:11 P.M. and afterward) | ● | ▲ | ▲ | ▲▲ | | ▲ | ▲ | ▲ |
| BYSTANDERS AT SIGMOR (2/4/83, 8:15 P.M.) | ● | ▲ | ▲ | ▲ | | ▲ | ▲ | ▲ |
| Bruno Mejía's initial BOLO (2/4/83, 8:15 P.M.) | ● | | | ▲▲ | | | | ▲ |
| GEORGE AGUIRRE (2/4/83, 8:15 P.M.)* | ● | ▲ | | ▲ | ▲ | ▲ | | |
| JOHN AND JULIE ARSUAGA (2/4/83, 8:15 P.M. and afterward) | | | ■ | ■ | ■ | ■ | ■ | ■ |
| Bruno Mejía's final BOLO (2/4/83, 8:32 P.M.) | | | | ▲▲, | ■ | ■ | ■ | |
| GEORGE AGUIRRE (6/20/83 and 7/20/83)* | ● | | ■ | ■ | ■ | | | |
| CARLOS DELUNA at time of arrest (2/4/83, 8:50 P.M.) | ● | ■ | ■ | ■ | ■ | ■ | ■ | ■■ |

Note: Shading indicates two sets of descriptions (the first five and last four) that largely overlap each other and are generally inconsistent with the other set.

*George Aguirre's descriptions evolved between February and June and July.

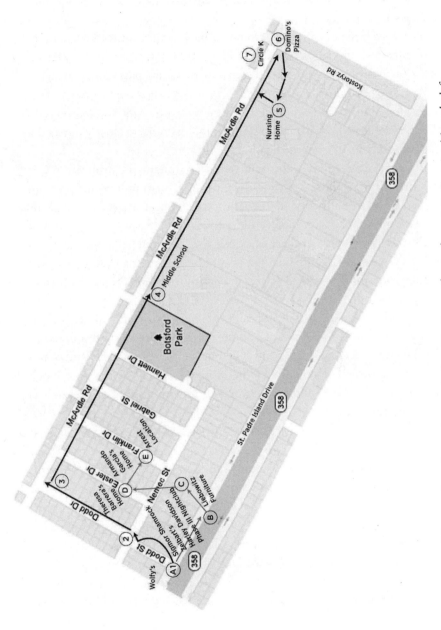

FIGURE 2.3  The area where the manhunt took place. The Sigmor Shamrock gas station is point A1 on the left.

intersection of McArdle and Kostoryz Roads, where there was a Domino's Pizza on one side of McArdle and a Circle K convenience store on the other side (points 6 and 7).

The third burst of calls came from way back west toward the Sigmor, in the bungalows and yards behind the Phase III Club and Lebowitz Furniture store where the Arsuagas had seen a man jogging past (points B–E).

At Carlos DeLuna's trial, dispatcher Escochea called the first burst of activity along Dodd "a hectic situation as far as radio traffic was concerned." "Units were just throwing out [radio] traffic" as officers closely pursued a man running north from the Sigmor.

The first officers to join the hunt were two unnamed patrolmen in Car 155. Then Officer Thomas Mylett, the Corpus Christi police officer whom Escochea had initially tried to dispatch to the Sigmor, arrived at the scene. He was followed by Constables Ruben Rivera and Carolyn Vargas, as well as Corpus Christi police officer Mark Schauer. They all had been told to go where eyewitness Kevan Baker had pointed when the first officer reached the Sigmor—in "the immediate area in back of the store," "the area north of the station down Dodd Street."

Constable Rivera remembered pulling into the driveway of the gas station just behind the ambulance. "Someone came forward and pointed in the direction of Dodd Street and hollered 'he ran that way.'" Rivera and his partner turned right onto Dodd, stopped the car at the next block (point 2), and started off on foot to search for the suspect where the witness had indicated.

Soon Escochea received reports from several units of a person seen running in the same Dodd Drive area (see figure 2.3, points 2 and 3). At 8:16 P.M., less than six minutes after Wanda screamed and three minutes after the first BOLO, an officer in Car 155 radioed that a civilian witness "just saw the suspect in the 4900 block of Dodd." That's the block of Dodd Drive that ends at McArdle (point 3), as one travels from the south. Escochea called all units there, reporting that the "suspect [was] last seen by a witness running through the yards." Within minutes, twenty patrol cars converged on the intersection.

For several minutes, officers tracked the assailant through the yards. With many cops out of their cars, the radio chatter died down. At one point, officers driving on McArdle radioed in a request for help stopping a dark blue Mercury with two Hispanic men in it. An unnamed officer responded urgently, "No, he was on foot. We need somebody to try and stop him." Officers chased the Mercury anyway, stopping it a few minutes later and confirming that it was a false lead. Gradually, the cops lost track of the suspect.

The next burst of radio traffic began around 8:23 P.M., thirteen minutes after Wanda screamed and eleven minutes after Mejia began broadcasting BOLOs. This burst was even more chaotic than the first, and it was tinged with a sense of danger as the dispatcher desperately tried to reestablish contact with officers in hot pursuit of the suspect on foot. The volley of reports concentrated on several points along McArdle Road east of Dodd (points 3–7) and peaked where McArdle meets Kostoryz (points 6 and 7).

Sergeant Fowler, the first cop at the Sigmor, was also the first to direct attention to the intersection of McArdle and Kostoryz, where he had stopped a man earlier that evening. At 8:23 P.M., he asked the dispatcher if he had any police units near the intersection. Until then, Fowler had been attending to Wanda. When the ambulance arrived and the EMTs took over, Fowler started listening to the radio traffic and realized that the man described in the BOLOs might be the same one he had questioned earlier that night at a Circle K at McArdle and Kostoryz (point 7).

The Circle K was the competing convenience store nearest to the Sigmor. About an hour earlier, Fowler had seen a man loitering suspiciously outside it. When Fowler asked the man what he was doing, the man said that he was waiting for a ride. Fowler may have figured that if the Sigmor attacker had initially planned to rob the Circle K before being spooked by a cop, he might now be heading back to that store for his car or a ride.

Conversing with Escochea over the radio frequency recorded on the dispatch tape, Fowler described the man he'd seen: "Hispanic male, about 5 foot 9, white T-shirt or heavy T-shirt, almost a sweatshirt-type. . . . Beard and mustache." Fowler thought the man was wearing white pants.

Escochea immediately saw a connection to Wanda's description of her attacker on the phone and also to eyewitness Kevan Baker's description of the man he saw fleeing the Sigmor. "OK," he said over the radio, "sounds like the description the chick was trying to give me on the phone. She said he was out there trying to bum a ride, armed with a knife. Possibly could be the same one." Still on the radio, Escochea asked Mejia to repeat the BOLO. After Mejia repeated Baker's description—the eighth of Mejia's nine descriptions of the assailant's clothing—Escochea said that it "[s]ounds like the same guy [Fowler] was looking at earlier."

In the middle of this discussion, reports began coming in of a suspect running along McArdle toward Kostoryz. Constable Rivera recalled that "an officer had broken the frequency [radioed in] and said there was a subject over in the . . . ballpark area" (point 4), along McArdle about halfway from Dodd to Kostoryz.

Midway through Escochea's exchange with Fowler about the man at the Circle K, the dispatcher got a call for backup at 3131 McArdle, still farther along McArdle between a nursing home (point 5) and a Domino's Pizza outlet. Domino's (point 6) was also at McArdle and Kostoryz, across the street from the Circle K (point 7). An intruder had set off a business burglar alarm in the area, and plainclothes vice officers were responding.

Two minutes later, uniformed officers in Car 139 pulled into the Domino's and spotted a suspect running "up behind" the store. The officers gave chase, prompting an urgent call for backup: "Anyone near Kostoryz and McArdle?" The dispatcher wanted "somebody else out there with 139."

Units raced to the intersection. Undercover vice squad officers were the first to join the Car 139 cops. Four minutes later, patrolmen on foot saw a suspect in the alley connecting the back of Domino's to the back of the nursing home (between points 6 and 5). He "just left the nursing home here, just south of McArdle heading north," came one urgent call.

Other sighting reports followed in quick succession: "He jumped the fence heading towards McArdle." "On Kostoryz and McArdle, near the nursing home, [we] got a suspect just jumped the fence to the rear, with an officer on foot." After being cut off at the Domino's, the suspect seemed to be doubling back toward the nursing home and possibly trying to cross McArdle to the Circle K. Police thought they were closing in.

Three minutes after Mejia's final BOLO, and twenty-two minutes after Wanda screamed, the dispatcher called every available unit to the area around Kostoryz and McArdle between the nursing home (point 5) and Domino's Pizza (point 6). Seconds later, an urgent call for emergency assistance came in from the area, followed by a signal requiring the channel to be kept clear of all traffic unrelated to the emergency.

Frantic calls went out from the dispatcher to the cops swarming dark alleys looking for an armed suspect to "be advised we do have several vice units in the area, plainclothes." For two minutes, the dispatcher desperately tried to regain contact with officers in Car 155, who had been among the first responders at each step of the chase and had suddenly gone silent.

Call piled on top of call, one every few seconds at the peak. Where they overlap on the tape, some are hard to hear. One sounds like "Too far. He got away." In the confusion, one event took steam out of the McArdle–Kostoryz search, then another event brought it to a halt.

The first event was Julie Arsuaga's insistent description of the man she saw jogging past the Phase III nightclub, which prompted Mejia to broadcast Julie's stream of grooming details about the man she saw. After Escochea got Fowler's report of a 5-foot, 9-inch Hispanic male loitering at the Circle K earlier that evening with a light sweatshirt, beard, and mustache who said he was looking for a ride, and after realizing it "sounds like the description the chick was trying to give me on the phone," the dispatcher pressed Mejia for a better description of the Sigmor suspect's face.

On the tape, Mejia can be heard talking to the witnesses, with a female voice prominent in the background. Then, instead of Baker's description of the mustachioed man with a couple of weeks' worth of whiskers who sprinted away to the north, Mejia gave Julie's description of the "clean-shaven" man she saw jogging east of the station past the Phase III. Soon thereafter came Mejia's final BOLO, complete with the facial-hair details from Julie Arsuaga.

The urgency drained from dispatcher Escochea's voice. Clearly, the clean-shaven man at the gas station whom Mejia was describing was not the mustachioed and unshaven man whom Sergeant Fowler had questioned earlier that evening at the Circle K. Reverting to his usual monotone, Escochea repeated the new information: "OK. You got that he's clean shaven?"

What abruptly ended the McArdle–Kostoryz search, however, was the onset of a third burst of radio traffic. It came from a dilapidated residential area way back to the west on Nemec, Easter, and Franklin Streets behind the Phase III and Lebowitz Furniture, a few blocks from the Sigmor.

The radio traffic began with a 911 call from neighborhood resident Theresa Barrera at 8:39 P.M., just three minutes after officers had chased the suspect over the fence behind the nursing home near McArdle and Kostoryz, and seven minutes after Mejia's final BOLO. The 911 operator transferred Barrera to Escochea, whose dispatch tape recorded their conversation:

BARRERA: Hey, there's a guy . . . there's police going up and down Nemec and Easter Street, you know what I'm talking about?

ESCOCHEA: Yes ma'am, we had an armed robbery in the area.

BARRERA: Huh?

ESCOCHEA: We had an armed robbery in the area, they're checking for the armed robber.

BARRERA: Yeah, there's a guy hiding under my truck.

ESCOCHEA: Ma'am?

BARRERA: I live on Easter Street, 4-9-4-9 Easter Street.

ESCOCHEA: 49, 49.

BARRERA: Get that [*inaudible*], get it on 49 Easter. He's hiding under the [*inaudible*] truck. [*And then, almost immediately*] He just got up and ran on Easter Street.

ESCOCHEA: Which way did he run, ma'am?

BARRERA: He ran down Nemec Street toward Gabriel and Franklin.

Barrera couldn't give the dispatcher any kind of description of the man under her pickup truck. A month later, however, she described a white shirt, pants of unknown color, and white tennis shoes.

After ending the call with Barrera, Escochea put out a new emergency call for all units, which were then swarming the eastern edge of the search area near McArdle and Kostoryz, to go back toward the western edge of the area behind Phase III and Lebowitz Furniture (see figure 2.3, points B and C): the "suspect was laying underneath a truck" on Easter (point D), and then was seen "heading eastbound on Nemec" (parallel to points D–E, on Nemec).

Almost as one, the fifteen or twenty patrol cars that had rushed to McArdle and Kostoryz (points 6–7) headed about a mile back west to Easter and Nemec Streets (point D). In a flurry of broadcasts, units reported new positions, including at a staging area on Nemec just behind Lebowitz.

Nine minutes later, just before 8:50 P.M. and about forty minutes after Wanda screamed, the first report of an arrest came in. Constables Ruben Rivera and Carolyn Vargas initially spotted the suspect. He was lying in a puddle under a second pickup truck on Franklin Street off Nemec (point E). He had no shirt, shoes, or socks on, just black "slacks," and no mustache, just a day or two's worth of stubble on his face.

The man begged the constables not to hurt him. "Don't shoot me! You've already got me!" Rivera noticed that he reeked of alcohol.

Officers Schauer and Mylett showed up at the end and helped Rivera pull the suspect sideways from under the truck and over a cement curb onto a grassy area next to the street where they handcuffed him. Although Rivera and Vargas from the sheriff's department first sighted and caught the man, Schauer and Mylett took credit for the arrest for themselves and the police department.

Twenty seconds later, Schauer confirmed their prize over the radio frequency: "Okay, we got one suspect in custody." Mylett, who moonlighted weekends as a bouncer at the Casino Club, immediately recognized the suspect as someone who frequented the Casino. He was twenty-year-old Carlos DeLuna. Mylett remembered DeLuna well. Two weeks before, he had arrested DeLuna for being drunk and disorderly in the Casino Club parking lot. The dispatcher confirmed that DeLuna had a "28"—a criminal record.

The truck DeLuna was under (point D) was parked exactly a block east of Barrera's truck (point E). The most direct route between the two was to cross Easter Street from Barrera's home, pass through the front, then the back, yard of Barrera's neighbor Armando Garcia, and then pass through the back and front yards of the house behind Garcia's.

On Sunday, two days later, Garcia cut his lawn along that route. As he did, he found a trail of discarded clothes. Two white tennis shoes were on the side of his house between the front and backyards. In the rear corner of his backyard, Garcia found a white dress shirt. The shoes and shirt were put into evidence against DeLuna at his criminal trial.

.      .      .

After Mylett and Schauer arrested DeLuna, they were so sure they had the right man, they never bothered to ascertain his height, weight, or age or to compare them to the information from eyewitness Baker. Their commanding officers never requested that information, either. In fact, DeLuna was 5 feet, 8 inches tall and 160 pounds (consistent with Baker's description) and twenty years old (younger than the man Baker described).

Mylett and Schauer revealed their confidence that they had the Sigmor stabber in another way as well: with their broadcasts blaring on the dozens of police radios in the area and at the gas station, the two officers proposed "bringing the suspect *back* to the [crime] scene" for identification.

"Anyone see the armed robbery?" Mylett asked his superiors at the gas station, who had set up a field command post there. The answer was affirmative and that Schauer and Mylett should "go ahead and take him back to the scene."

A minute later, at 8:51 P.M., forty-one minutes after Wanda screamed, the manhunt tape ends.

# 3

# Show-up

ON A LATE NOVEMBER EVENING, twenty-one years after Wanda Lopez collapsed in his arms, Kevan Baker was in the living room of his rural southern Michigan home. A middle-aged African American man in an overcoat and tie appeared at the front door, introducing himself as a private investigator from Chicago.

Baker wasn't surprised. "This is about that case in Corpus Christi, isn't it?" he said.

The former car salesman had been expecting this visit for years, maybe even hoping for it. He'd left Corpus Christi soon after testifying, under oath, that Carlos DeLuna was the man he'd seen taking the life of Wanda Lopez. He knew that DeLuna had been on trial for *his* life. Baker had a lot to get off his chest. Even after forty-five minutes of talking, he made the investigator keep his tape recorder running so he could come back one more time to the question that most weighed on his mind.

Had he done the right thing that night at the gas station?

"It's just," he said, "I wish this never happened, you know what I'm saying." His voice trailed off. Then, seeing himself at the Sigmor that night, he continued. "I don't want to be there.... I'm going, 'God, this sucks, it really does.' But I tried to do the right thing. I walked towards the store, and I tried to help her out. That's basically what it was about."

And that, Baker told the investigator, was how it went for him at every step of that chilly Gulf Coast night. It was Friday and he was ready to party, but it didn't happen. At every turn, he thought, "Oh fuck, I don't want to be here. Get in [the] car and leave." But instead, he ended up staying and doing what he decided was the right thing, ignoring what his instincts were telling him.

When he heard the Sigmor clerk bang on the window, he was late to pick up his wife and head out to the clubs and was rushing to pump gas. He ignored the thump on the window and tried to pump the gas anyway, but the nozzle was dry and he had to look at the store clerk. That's when he saw her wrestling with a man.

They must be horsing around, he remembered thinking. Lovers' play. None of his business. But when he looked again, he realized that she was in trouble. He wanted to leave, but he knew that the right thing was to go to the door.

That's what he did, and he got his life threatened in return. Then Wanda was in his arms, bleeding to death.

When the cops came, they wanted to know what the guy looked like, but he and the other witnesses standing together near the ice machine couldn't agree. Baker gave his description and then stayed out of it. It mattered more to the others to have it their way.

Then, Baker recalled, the cops put him through what they called a "show-up identification." Instead of lining up different people at the police station and asking if he could pick someone out through a one-way mirror, they wanted him and the other witnesses to go face-to-face with the guy at the scene of the crime and see if someone could identify him right there.

At first Baker refused, along with the other witnesses; everyone was terrified. But the police lieutenant pleaded with them—it was important for witnesses to come forward—so Baker agreed to do what the lieutenant asked.

The cops surrounded Baker and walked him over to the patrol car. They had a young man in the backseat of a squad car without a shirt, his hands cuffed behind his back. "Is this the guy you seen?" the lieutenant asked. "It was really tough, you know," Baker recalled, "saying yes or no." But the police were waiting, the crowd was watching, and "it seemed like the right guy." So he said it was.

It was tough later on, too, when they asked him to identify DeLuna in court. "But," as Baker told the private eye, the guy in the squad car "was Hispanic," like the man he'd seen running out of the store. "Whether I was right or wrong . . . ," he began. Then his voice trailed off.

"But it just seemed right," he said, finally. "That's kind of the way I went."

· · ·

Twenty-four-year-old Mark Schauer was the officer who had arrested and handcuffed DeLuna and driven him over to the Sigmor station. It was 8:49 P.M. when Schauer reported that he had the stabbing suspect in the rear seat of his squad car and "was transporting him back to the crime scene." At the time, Schauer's car was at Nemec Street and Franklin Drive, near the police staging area for the last part of the manhunt, and only 875 feet from the Sigmor along Nemec and Dodd Street.

For reasons Schauer never fully explained, it took him fifteen minutes to arrive. He reached the gas station at 9:05.

During the ride to the gas station and thereafter, Schauer reported, De-Luna "was not silent even for a moment." The suspect asked what he was being charged with. He said, "'Hey, man, you take care of me and I'll take care of you.' He said this over and over."

· · ·

For the preceding forty minutes, the cops had made Baker, Aguirre, and the Arsuagas remain at the ice machine outside the east wall of the store.

The machine was a few feet from the front corner of the store. For the first half hour, they stood there with a direct view of Wanda on the sidewalk outside the door, maybe 25 feet away. They watched the medics work on her.

To their left, as they watched, were the gas station parking lot, the frontage road, and the highway, South Padre Island Drive, beyond. To their right was a narrow passageway between the brick eastern wall of the store and a storage shed. The passageway led past the ice machine to a grassy area behind the store. The temperature was in the mid-fifties, cold by Corpus Christi standards. An eighth of an inch of rain had fallen that morning, and there were some damp stains on the pavement. Most of the moisture had evaporated, though, and the grass was firm.

Patrol cars were scattered around the station, lights flashing. Officers roamed the area. Joel Infante, a police photographer, arrived, followed by Olivia Escobedo, a police detective dressed in a fashionable white raincoat and high-heeled leather boots. The two waited in the parking lot while the medics worked on Wanda, blocking access to the store.

Trucks from the local television stations pulled into the southeast side of the parking lot and started filming. Traffic slowed on the frontage road, and people were gawking. Some parked and got out to look. There were several dozen onlookers, many in the Wolfy's parking lot across Dodd. They watched the techs work on Wanda and wondered how a clerk behind the counter could have gotten stabbed. If she died, it would be the first convenience store killing in Corpus Christi that anyone could remember.

Officers kept abreast of the manhunt on their car radios and walkie-talkies. The witnesses and onlookers listened, too.

Sigmor area supervisor Pedro (Pete) Gonzalez was among those at the gas station. He'd received a call about an unexplained emergency and was told to go to the store. When he got there, he found the place swarming with police. His employee Wanda Lopez was on the ground, drenched in blood, and paramedics were frantically trying to revive her. Scuttlebutt in the crowd was that the techs got her back to consciousness a couple of times, but only briefly.

Recollections differed about whether police put up crime scene tape. There was none in the police photos taken outside the store and in the gas station lot, and Escobedo, the lone detective on the case, recalled much later that the department didn't use police tape to secure crime scenes at the time. "We just had to yell at people to stay back and not step on our crime scenes," she explained.

Gonzalez and station manager Robert Stange were able to wander between the frontage road and gas pumps and into the wing lots on either side of the store. They picked up information from brief conversations with police officers and chatter on police radios. The first thing they heard was that it was a robbery.

The ambulance left for the hospital around 8:40 P.M., and Escobedo and the police photographer were able to get inside the store.

Ten minutes later, information about a suspect began flying around the parking lots at the gas station and Wolfy's. "It started as a rumor," store manager Stange recalled. Police car doors were open, and windows were down. "Radio transmissions were coming back that they had somebody under a car they were going to bring back to the location for identification."

Stange heard that police had found a suspect a few blocks away hiding under a car. Someone said that they found a bloody shirt near the suspect.

Although Stange didn't know it, the first statement was true, but the second was not. No shirt was found until the next day, and police needed lab tests to see if Wanda's blood was on it.

•        •        •

Lieutenant Eddie McConley was the second-ranking police officer at the gas station. Looking through the windows, he had immediately noticed a bloody scene inside the store and disarray from a violent struggle. Even after Escobedo and Infante went inside, he kept an eye on the doorway to be sure no one else entered and spoiled the scene. He positioned himself midway between the door and the witnesses at the corner of the building near the ice machine, remaining about 10 to 12 feet from each (figure 3.1).

On his walkie-talkie, McConley heard Schauer's broadcast about the arrest. He told Schauer to bring the suspect "back" to the Sigmor for a show-up identification.

Eventually, Schauer arrived with DeLuna in his squad car. He navigated the potholes on the western edge of the Sigmor lot and parked parallel to

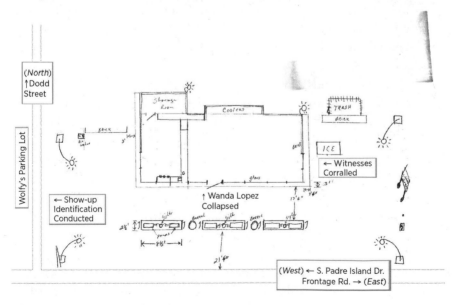

FIGURE 3.1   The police diagram of the Sigmor Shamrock gas station on the night of the murder of Wanda Lopez, with typewritten additions by the authors.

Dodd Street, directly across from Wolfy's. People pressed forward to see the suspect sitting in the rear seat on the gas station side.

Sigmor supervisors Gonzalez and Stange made their way to the sidewalk on the west side of the car, 2 feet from the vehicle. They traded places every once in a while so each could get a better view inside the car. The gas station lighting was poor. It was hard to see the man inside the car.

•     •     •

When McConley saw the squad car pull in with the suspect, he walked over to the ice machine to talk to the witnesses. They already knew that the police had caught someone.

"Here comes a cop," Baker recalled, reliving the scene and replaying the cop's words. "'We found him. Is this the gentleman? He was hiding underneath a car.'" Julie Arsuaga later remembered being told the same thing by the officer.

McConley asked the four witnesses to go over to the man to see if they could identify him.

Immediately, all the witnesses got upset. Everything they'd seen and heard—the man opening a long knife and putting it in his pocket, the threat to shoot Baker, the wound in Wanda's chest, her lifeless body being lifted into the ambulance—told them they didn't want to be anywhere near the guy.

Julie said what they all were thinking: "No, I don't want to see him." It was too dangerous and scary. John refused, too. Baker said he just wanted to get his gas and go. He remembered thinking that he was lucky to be alive and didn't want to take any more chances. The next day, he clipped an article from the newspaper and sent it home to his folks in Michigan with a note saying, "thank God, I didn't die." Aguirre also demurred.

After some coaxing, however, Lieutenant McConley convinced Baker and Aguirre to go over to the man. McConley promised that he and the other cops would shield the witnesses from the suspect. The Arsuagas still refused.

Baker went first. Led by McConley, cops surrounded him and walked him to the car. Officers shined flashlights through the windows directly into the suspect's eyes to blind him—so "there would be no revenge kind of thing," an officer said.

Store manager Stange watched from a few feet away. He remembered Baker "standing at the front of the car. . . . [H]e didn't want to get any closer. He was terrified, he just did not want to be involved."

Accounts differed about what happened next. Some witnesses at the trial testified that officers stood DeLuna up outside the squad car, shirtless and shoeless in the cold air. Officer Schauer, who had driven the suspect to the gas station and stayed with his squad car the whole time, testified that De-Luna remained inside the car: the "[suspect] was in the back seat of the car and somebody was flashing the light in his eyes." That was also what Robert Stange remembered: DeLuna "never got out of the car. He was sitting in there with no shirt" while Baker "looked through the windows." Baker told the private investigator the same thing.

By all accounts, Baker stood behind McConley. At 5 feet, 6 inches, Baker had to look over the cop's shoulder. He never got a full view. "Keep the light in [the suspect's] eyes," someone said.

Baker told the private investigator that the suspect looked "distraught"—"like, 'I'm in the back of the police car. I'm fucked,' " "whether . . . innocent or guilty, you know, 'I'm fucked.' "

Again, Baker found himself wishing he wasn't there. There was so little to go on. He'd seen the man for only a few seconds as he ran out of the store, and right away the guy had said he had a gun. At the mention of a gun, Baker told the Chicago detective, "I was on 110 percent hype." He had locked eyes with the man, willing him not to pull a weapon: "[T]here was other more important things to worry about" than how "long [the guy's] sideburns" were.

Now, peering at the man from behind the police lieutenant, Baker tried to focus. The man had his shirt off. He was Hispanic, dark hair, dark complexion. "Okay," Baker thought, "it might be him; it might not be." The cops were watching and waiting. So were the people in the crowd. Baker took a few seconds, "five, ten," he had said at the trial, "fifteen at the most." "Yeah, that's the guy," he told the tall cop. Then he got the hell out of there.

Police repeated the process with Aguirre. He, too, identified DeLuna.

Later that night at the police station, Detective Escobedo showed John and Julie Arsuaga mug shots of six men, including Carlos DeLuna. Both eventually identified DeLuna as the man they'd seen taking a leisurely jog in his dress clothes east of the gas station, before disappearing into the yards along Nemec Street near Franklin Drive.

. . .

Asked at the trial about his identification of DeLuna, Kevan Baker described two differences between the man he saw wrestling with Wanda and the man he saw in the squad car. One was obvious. The man who ran out of the store had a gray sweatshirt and a flannel jacket on. The man in the patrol car was naked from the waist up.

Baker puzzled over the other difference. The man he came eye-to-eye with outside the Sigmor had no marks or scratches on his face. The man in the squad car had a "scarred up" face with blood on it.

Although Baker didn't know it, Julie Arsuaga had noticed something similar. At a pretrial hearing, she examined a black-and-white photo of Carlos DeLuna, who she then said was the jogger who'd passed in front of her car that night near the Phase III. She noted, however, that DeLuna had a fatter face in the photo than did the jogger she'd seen and speculated that DeLuna must have lost weight since the picture was taken. After being told that police took the photo at the police station on the night of the crime, Julie admitted that DeLuna's puffy face in the picture was "different to a degree" from the face of the man she had seen jogging by.

Years later, when Wanda's family sued the Sigmor Shamrock for damages, another—color—set of photos of DeLuna came to light, also taken at the police station on the night of the murder. The new photos confirmed Baker's and Julie Arsuaga's observations, especially when compared with other photos of DeLuna from around the same time. After his arrest, DeLuna had a cut on the bridge of his swollen nose. There were bruises on his right cheek and under both eyes. He had a fat lower lip.

Shown the color photos twenty years later, DeLuna's sister Rose wept at the sight of her brother's banged-up face (figure 3.2). She recalled the first time she had visited him in jail while he was waiting to go on trial for killing Wanda Lopez. He told her that the cops had beaten him after they pulled him out from under the truck. One of them said he recognized DeLuna as a smart-ass drunk he'd arrested at the Casino Club a couple weeks earlier.

Aguirre also had a problem in court when asked whom he'd seen at the gas station. At the same pretrial hearing where Julie had testified, a prosecutor named Steven Schiwetz asked Aguirre to point out the man he'd seen

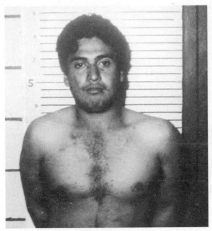

FIGURE 3.2   Carlos DeLuna at the police station immediately after his arrest for the murder of Wanda Lopez (*left*) and in July 1983 (*right*).

with a knife. DeLuna was sitting between his two lawyers at a table a few feet away. Schiwetz asked, "Do you see him in the courtroom today?"

AGUIRRE: I'm not too sure. I can't—

SCHIWETZ: I want to direct you to the man sitting in between the two lawyers over here. Do you know whether or not that's the man you saw that night?

AGUIRRE: It's been a while. I couldn't—

SCHIWETZ: Can't say?

AGUIRRE: I can't say.

SCHIWETZ: Fair enough.

In the end, only Baker testified in court that he had seen DeLuna at the gas station that night.

In his testimony, Baker noted another discrepancy between DeLuna—in this case, as he looked in court—and the man who had tussled with Wanda at the Sigmor. "I would say the gentleman on your left," Baker pointed to DeLuna, wearing a button-down dress shirt and dress pants, "looks very much like a lawyer or a doctor." The man Baker had seen coming out of the Sigmor store had looked different—like "someone who had been on the street and was very hungry." His clothes were dirty and disheveled. He looked "like a transient."

* * *

At his home in Michigan twenty-one years later, Baker told the private detective that he was 70 percent positive that the man in the police car was the man he'd seen wrestling with Wanda.

"[S]eventy percent is not 100 percent," the detective said.

"Right. It's not," Baker agreed.

Baker explained. "I'm going, 'God that looks like him, you know, it really does.'" Then he reflected, "[I]t goes back to, I'm a [short] white guy. . . . [T]o you," he said to the black detective, "which one of these five blond short guys is it?" Baker didn't mince words. He had trouble recalling Hispanic names; they were all "Julio" to him, he said. And he had trouble telling Hispanics apart and judging their age. "It's tough," he said, "to identify cross cultures."

He hadn't wanted to "screw anybody," he said, but at the same time, he had to make an "adult judgment," "try to connect the two together." "I wasn't all that sure," he later said to a news reporter. "But him being Hispanic and all . . . I said, 'Yeah, I think it is him.'"

There was one thing, though, that had bothered Baker at the time and had concerned him ever since. He brought it up several times to the detective and later to a news reporter: "I will say this. One of the police officers did mention to me that 'we found this guy hiding underneath a car without a shirt on, two blocks north of us or three blocks north of us.'" Baker thought that "might have tinged my—not tinged, but maybe tried to direct me that this is the guy or something [by saying] right there, 'we found him a couple blocks north.'"

And again: "The cops told me they found him hiding under a truck. That led me to believe this is probably the guy." "That's probably why I was 70 percent sure."

Would he have been less than 70 percent sure if a cop had not told him that? On the audiotape, Baker's answer is emphatic. "Yes." In that case, it would have been only "fifty-fifty."

The private detective pressed Baker on the point:

DETECTIVE: When they asked you if this is the guy, and you said "yeah, it is." Even though you said, "yeah it is," in your mind, were you 100 percent sure?
BAKER: Oh no.

DETECTIVE: You weren't 100 percent sure?

BAKER: No.

DETECTIVE: And you responded "yeah, it is," because—

BAKER: . . . I went to facial features, basically eye-to-eye contact. . . . I was waiting for a gun to come out.

* * *

Schauer and DeLuna were at the Sigmor for less than five minutes. Immediately after Baker and Aguirre identified the suspect, Schauer took him to the police station. Before he transported DeLuna, Schauer reported, "The suspect . . . said, 'I didn't do it, but I know who did. I know who did.' "

"[A]gain and again, he said 'I'll help you if you help me.' " He kept asking to speak with a sergeant, and he "kept trying to make deals."

At the police station, DeLuna answered all the questions the cops put to him. No one asked if he committed the crime, or if he knew who did.

In the meantime, the tragic news that Wanda Lopez had died came in from the hospital. Schauer booked Carlos DeLuna for capital murder.

# 4

# Crime Scene

AFTER MARK SCHAUER LEFT WITH CARLOS DELUNA, a police officer told store manager Robert Stange and his boss Pete Gonzalez to stay put and wait outside the store.

Stange had worked the morning shift at the store that day starting at 6:00 A.M. and had turned it over to Wanda Lopez at 3:00 P.M. Valentine's Day was coming up, and Stange had joked with Wanda about whether she'd gotten her valentine yet. She hadn't, she said, so Stange gave her a Tootsie Roll from the display on the counter. Wanda laughed. Stange went home and soon was asleep.

A few hours later, he awoke to a call from a police operator. There was a situation at the Sigmor. He had to go secure the store. The dispatcher wouldn't say what had happened but offered a police escort. Stange knew that it wasn't good. He drove over fast and met Gonzalez in the parking lot, just as Wanda was being put into an ambulance. No one was allowed inside the store.

As Stange and Gonzalez waited outside, they couldn't help but notice the blood—outside on the door and sidewalk, dripping down into the parking lot, and more inside that was visible through the plate-glass windows. A dense trail of blood drops and bloody prints from Wanda's narrow bare feet ran diagonally across the fake brick floor tiles from the lift-top opening in the clerk's counter to a red carpeting mat inside the door. The scene was horrifying, and Stange wasn't looking forward to cleaning it up whenever the police finished looking for evidence.

Stange had managed the 2602 SPID Sigmor location for a year before Wanda was killed, and he ran it for eight years afterward. Then he was promoted to auditor, and later to area manager, of several gas stations.

In Stange's line of work, it was common knowledge that a holdup and a dead body added up to capital murder—the crime at the top of the food chain for cops. As Stange waited, he could tell that the police thought they'd buttoned up one of those. After the squad car carrying the suspect drove off, nearly all the other police cruisers left as well, and the crowd broke up.

The female detective and police photographer were the only ones inside the store. They'd been there for half an hour and were working fast. The detective never even took off her raincoat.

To Stange, it seemed like police were thinking, "We got a robbery, and now we got a death, so we got a capital case. And we got somebody under an automobile, and an identifier out in the parking lot. . . . We got the guy, and it's done."*

For Stange, though, a piece was missing. He couldn't figure out why the guy had stabbed Wanda.

Stange liked Wanda (figure 4.1). She was always happy, always talking about her young daughter. And she was conscientious in the store—careful and great with the customers.

She had transferred from another store, where she'd gotten cross-wise with the manager. He was a ladies' man who'd slip away afternoons with a woman who came by in a car. He told Wanda that if his wife came looking for him, she should lie for him. Wanda wouldn't. Sure enough, his wife appeared one afternoon, and the manager was in big trouble. After that, he wanted Wanda out of the store.

Stange felt lucky to get Wanda. For him, the incident at the other store said something about her character. He made her assistant manager right after she came. Best of all, Wanda could handle the store alone. Other employees got scared and called Stange to come over, but Wanda didn't; she knew what to do. She followed the rules.

*Lead detective Olivia Escobedo acknowledged later that she had used her police radio to follow events outside the store, including the manhunt and capture of Carlos DeLuna and his identification by Kevan Baker and George Aguirre.

FIGURE 4.1   Wanda Lopez in high school (*left*) and within months of her death (*right*).

When it came to robberies, Sigmor had one simple rule, which Stange explained to the investigators years later, linking it to a robber's psychology. Robbers know, Stange pointed out, that they won't get much from a convenience store. They just want to surprise the clerk, grab whatever cash is on hand, and leave fast without a lot of people seeing them. What they want, Stange explained, is "to get in, get out before anyone knows what happened, and go, and disappear."

Sigmor's one rule was to give the robbers what they want.

Stange described the drill: "[S]omebody comes in—a knife, a gun. They stand on the other side of the counter and ask for the money. The employee opens the cash drawer and gives it to them. They leave. They're gone."

Wanda knew the drill. Stange jokingly acted it out with her. "This is a robbery, I want your money." She put the money on the counter. "Take it." Stange was positive that Wanda wouldn't put up a fight. Everything she did was for her daughter. She wanted to do her job and go home. She wouldn't take chances.

Besides, Sigmor took care of itself by limiting how much cash was in the drawer. It had a Rules and Regulations card with twenty rules on it. Employees had to initial each one of the rules. When Wanda's folks sued for damages, a lawyer put the initialed card in evidence.

Rule 2 said: $75.00 SHALL BE THE MAXIMUM AMOUNT OF MONEY NECESSARY TO OPERATE THE CASH DRAWER. DROPS OF $20 WILL BE

MADE. THIS MEANS THERE SHALL NEVER BE MORE THAN $75 IN THE DRAWER AT ANY TIME. THERE ARE NO EXCEPTIONS TO THIS RULE.

Stange explained that every store had two other places for money besides the cash drawer. One was a "key safe" with a few extra $5 and $10 bills, in case the clerk had to make change on a $50 bill, and some rolls of coins. Clerks had a key to that safe. Just above the key safe was a drop-slot safe. Clerks couldn't open that one, but whenever the cash drawer went over the $75 limit, or they got a $20 bill or higher, the money went into the slot. "There were times," Stange said, when "you couldn't make change. You didn't have it."

"You were especially careful at night," he said. The later it got, the less was kept in the drawer. If anyone saw a lot of money in the drawer, the clerk was a target. At 8:00 or 8:30 P.M. in winter, Stange said, Wanda would have had only $60 in bills in the drawer, maybe less.

* * *

Stange is a watcher, a quiet guy who takes everything in and files it neatly in his memory. And his memory is good. Years later, he remembered the Tootsie Roll display on the counter the day Wanda was killed, and the location of the spark plugs and flashlight batteries. Police photos that Stange had never seen confirm the details.

Stange also remembered the potholes and bad lighting in the parking lot that night, and the look of terror on Kevan Baker's face when police coaxed him over to the squad car to look at the suspect.

What Stange most vividly recalled was the scene inside the store when the police let him in. "It's awful to say," Stange admitted later, but he was curious to get inside. He thought that Wanda could handle herself in a robbery. He wanted to figure out why she got stabbed.

When Detective Olivia Escobedo let Stange and Gonzalez in, she held the door for them and told them to step around the blood and not touch anything. Stange scanned the familiar store. It was laid out in a narrow rectangle, with the long side facing out onto the gas pumps and parking lot. That side was all glass, with the front door in the middle. To his right as he entered the door were two aisles of merchandise, which seemed to be intact.

Six feet to the left of the front door, running the width of the store, was the clerk's counter. It had butcher-block veneer and a painted plywood apron down to the floor. At the far end, pieces of the countertop and apron were cut out and hinged to cabinets along the back wall, forming a lift-top in the counter and flap door through the apron. In the backmost corner of the clerk's area behind the counter was a storeroom that jutted out into the alleyway behind the store. Stange noticed that the storeroom door was open.

The whole side of the store to Stange's left, from the front door to the counter and behind it, was in disarray. The lift-top and flap door were supposed to be secured shut by a hidden slide bolt, but police had found them open. Outside the opening, crashed into a rack of hats, was the clerk's chair on rollers with Wanda's sweater hung on the back. The chair was supposed to remain behind the counter.

Escobedo brought Stange and Gonzalez behind the counter. They could see cash bills in the open cash drawer and on the floor, and she wanted to know how much was missing.

The trail of Wanda's bloody footprints in front of the counter was sickening enough, but Stange was stunned by what was behind the counter. There was blood everywhere. Not just drops and streaks, but puddles and mists of it. Whole sections of the floor were smeared with it.

This was nothing like any robbery Stange had ever heard of, and he worked hard to reconstruct what had happened.* On the counter, on a laminated sales-tax chart taped next to the clerk's adding machine, was an unopened pack of Winston cigarettes. The cigarette case sat on the counter, flush against the window to the clerk's right as she faced the customers. Between the case and the adding machine was the "Tootsie [Roll] I love you" Valentine display.

Stange guessed that after entering the store, the man must have turned left between a stack of generic cigarettes by the window and the rack of hats farther inside the store, and headed straight for the name-brand cigarette case on the counter—and for Wanda.

To make the sale, she would have been standing behind the counter and adding machine, in the corner of the clerk's area where the counter met the front window. Below the counter to her right was the telephone. Above it, on a shelf running along the front window, sat a white plastic console controlling the gas pumps. Just to its right, underneath the same shelf and behind the clerk, was a black metal cash drawer where she could make change.

---

*The description that follows is based partly on Robert Stange's account in his videotaped interview and partly on police photographs and reports describing the scene he surveyed when Detective Escobedo brought him into the store.

The location of the cigarette pack put the man on the customer side of the counter at the adding machine. But Stange could see that a fierce struggle had taken place *behind* the counter as Wanda bled to death. "The gentleman," Stange decided, must have "jumped over the counter" to get at Wanda. She would have had the flap door closed and latched from the inside, underneath the counter.

There was no blood on the counter near the adding machine. Wanda had apparently started bleeding at the gas-pump console on her right. There were drops of blood on its keyboard, and blood had cascaded down its front to the shelf. A thicker pool had collected along the edge of the shelf, evidently transferred directly from Wanda, and had dripped onto packs of spark plugs in a box on the floor below the shelf and onto the floor itself.

Blood also had caked on the front of the black metal cash drawer. Cash bills, flecked with blood, were strewn on top of the open drawer and on the floor beneath it.

Stange couldn't tell whether the man had stabbed Wanda across the counter as she stood near the gas console, or whether he'd stabbed her after jumping the counter. The store manager was sure of two things, though. Wanda would have given the man the money the instant he asked for it, and she *did* try to give him money from the cash drawer *after* she'd been stabbed. To Stange, that meant the money wasn't the reason for the attack—another inkling that this was no ordinary robbery.

Most ghastly of all were Wanda's bloody handprints on the window above the cash drawer, as if she'd tried to reach outside for help. Stange would never forget wiping the prints off the window.

.     .     .

Although Stange didn't know it, police also found a large, brown, lock-blade buck knife with gold metal trim underneath the cash drawer (figure 4.2). The blade had blood on the tip and flesh on the rest of it.

Years later, a forensic expert from England looked over the police photos. It was his opinion that Wanda pulled the knife out of her breast while standing at the gas console and cash drawer, causing the blood to gush.

.     .     .

It looked to Stange as though Wanda had next tried to escape through the flap door. The only part of the floor without much blood on it began

FIGURE 4.2 Police photographs of the southeast corner of the clerk's area behind the counter of the Sigmor Shamrock store, taken around 9:00 P.M. on February 4, 1983. The knife is under the cash drawer in the bottom photograph. (Color versions of these and the other crime-scene photographs in this chapter are on the Web site, thewrongcarlos.net.)

1 or 2 feet from the cash drawer and ran back toward the counter opening. Wanda must have rushed quickly across that space, shedding her left sandal—another rare item with no blood on it. But the attacker evidently grabbed her at the passageway and wrestled her back toward the middle of the clerk's area. Wanda obviously resisted, grasping at anything she could get her hands on, hemorrhaging blood.

The countertop and apron near the opening were smeared with blood, and the apron was spattered with it along the bottom. In her desperation to find a handhold, Wanda had swept pens, typing paper, napkins, a calendar, a box of sugar packs, and a Sigmor bag onto the floor, which she and her attacker had then kicked all over the place. Everything on the floor was wet with drops and puddles of blood (figures 4.3 and 4.4).

The First National Bank calendar hit the floor near the flap doorway, stuck on the just-ended month of January. On the calendar was a pool of light-colored blood with rays of spatter emanating out from a wad of pink chewing gum. Next to the calendar were large dark drops of blood on the floor, and several even darker pools were on the Sigmor bag next to that. It looked like Wanda coughed up blood onto the calendar as her wound leaked blood onto the floor and bag.

Wanda wasn't strong enough. She had nothing to hold onto and slipped in her own blood. Her attacker dragged her back from the flap door to a stack of Coke and Mr. Pibb cases partway between the front windows and the back room, on a line with the flap door.

It was then that the fiercest struggle began, as the man steered Wanda toward the storeroom and she fought back. The soft-drink cases there were partially toppled, and big drops of blood had pooled at their base. From there to the threshold of the storeroom was a gruesome 3-foot trail of blood drops, spatter, and smears. The trail ended at the largest pool of all, next to the open back-room door. Between the soda cases and the pool were two pairs of parallel, crescent-shaped skid marks in a wave pattern, surrounded by large blood drops and a downpour of droplets.

The skid marks showed where Wanda, rapidly losing blood, had planted her feet in a desperate effort to stop her momentum, as the attacker gave her two vicious yanks toward the back room. Then, abandoning the effort, the attacker must have violently thrown Wanda to the ground, causing the large pool of blood near the back-room door and a vast mist of drops

FIGURE 4.3 Police photographs of the northern half of the clerk's area: (*top left*) the First National Bank calendar on the floor, and the passageway through the counter with one or two bloody shoe prints (*arrow*); (*top right*) the large pool of blood just outside the back room, and the blood smudge on the back-room floor; (*bottom*) the area detailed in the other two photographs.

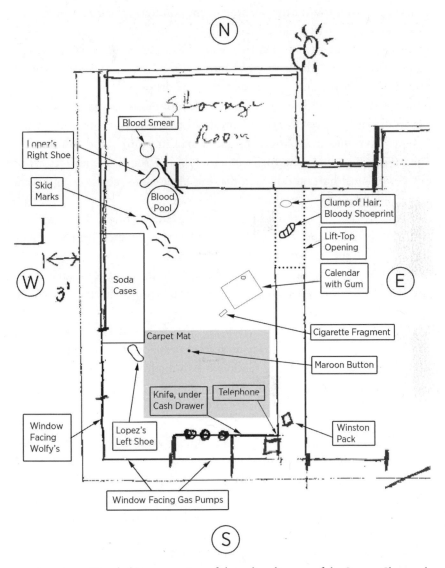

FIGURE 4.4 The clerk's area portion of the police diagram of the Sigmor Shamrock store (see figure 3.1), with additions by the authors, including the typewritten labels and drawings of the button, cigarette fragment, calendar, gum, bloody shoe print, and clump of hair.

radiating from it toward the opening in the counter—the direction the attacker must then have headed.

It was there, on the ground, that Wanda lost her right sandal. It lay upside down between the large pool and the back room, soaked dark with
blood at the instep and surrounded by large drops of blood on the floor
and smaller drops and streaks on the back-room door. Most of the blood
stopped two tiles away from the threshold to the back room, but on the
concrete floor just inside the room was a lone smear of blood a few inches
square in size, where the man—Wanda's blood staining the bottom of
his shoe—must have stood when making his last unsuccessful tug before
throwing Wanda to the ground.

Then, as quickly as the struggle had started, it ended. The man fled
through the flap door, leaving behind a bloody right-shoe print—or perhaps two—in the passageway through the counter.

Whether it was Wanda or the man who raised the lift top, unlatched the
flap door, and knocked the roller chair out from behind the counter, Stange
couldn't tell.

Wanda must have pulled herself up and followed her attacker out.
Stange and Gonzalez had already noticed the trail of her bloody footprints
and blood drips from the counter opening to the front door where she collapsed, streaking the doorframe with blood.

•    •    •

Stange could see what had happened. But he couldn't understand why.
What kind of robber would do this?

The money the detective had asked about was another thing that confused Stange. Bills and rolls of change were scattered around. Stange knew
that they had come from the cash drawer because the key and drop-slot
safes were locked and untouched.

Everyone was thinking robbery, but when Stange got inside and saw all
the money available and untaken, he was "awestruck," as he later put it. It
wasn't a robbery.

Stange described his thinking to the private investigators: "When you
enter a crime scene and the cash drawer is open and there's money lying
around behind the counter, and when the individual has come over the
counter and the area behind it is in disarray from a struggle, what part of
that is a robbery?" The man stabbed Wanda *while* she was trying to hand
him the money and then didn't take it. It wasn't about the cash, Stange con-

cluded. The man went over the counter to get *her*. It was an "act of anger or violence," but why?

Afterward, Stange recalled, there was a lot of talk around the Sigmor. Rumors swirled. Maybe the man was hoping to rob her and got angry when he realized she'd called the cops. But why not just leave? At that point, he hadn't done anything wrong. And if he was determined to get the money, then why didn't he just take it and leave?

There were also rumors about someone having it in for Wanda. Some said it was her former husband. "Supposedly," Stange said, "there was a connection with the Mexican mafia, in relation to the perpetrator and to her husband through a jail contact."

Others thought it was some other ex-lover, someone more recent. Stange himself wondered if Wanda and the attacker had been together at some point. She had dated in the past, and lately there had been a new young man. Someone was jealous, people speculated, someone who didn't want to let her go, who watched her from across the street at Wolfy's. It was revenge. There were a lot of rumors, Stange said, but the police never looked into them.

Stange and his boss told the detective that there was too much money lying around to say if any had been taken. They had to do an inventory. The detective sent them back outside.

·     ·     ·

Later that night, Stange did an inventory, but it didn't clear things up. Inventories were a simple process back then. Stange did one every week. His first step was to calculate the total value of all the merchandise on hand: gasoline, candy bars, windshield fluid, and the rest of it, plus all the cash in the cash drawer, key safe, and drop-slot safe. The last step was to see whether this week's amount was the same as last week's.

In between, Stange added to this week's amount the total of all bank deposits and credit card sales since the last inventory. That way, if he sold a loaf of bread or a tank of gas during the week, the loss in merchandise was made up for by the money received. He also subtracted the value of all *new* merchandise that came in and Sigmor was billed for that week. That way, if Pennzoil delivered twenty-four cans of motor oil the previous day, his count of all the merchandise would square with the amount on hand when he had done the previous inventory.

Every once in awhile, the adjusted total this week would be *greater* than last week. That might happen if the Coke truck driver accidentally dropped off one more case of Sprite than he was supposed to, and one more than Coca-Cola billed the Sigmor for.

Usually, though, the total this week would be *less* than last week. That happened for a lot of reasons. Customers pumped gas and drove off without paying, which was common in those days. And there were shoplifters. Or the Coke driver delivered one too *few* cases of Sprite. Or, most likely, a clerk gave too much change, or slipped a fiver into his or her own pocket now and then. The store could also come up short from a robbery.

The one thing you could *not* tell from the inventory, Stange explained to the investigator, was whether you came up short because someone took some money from the cash drawer or because someone shoplifted something or a deliveryman shorted you on merchandise. The station didn't use a cash register with a paper tape record of all sales, and there was no other way of tracking the flow of cash. The clerks made change in their heads or with an adding machine.

Years later, an accounting professor from Chicago reviewed the papers that Stange had put together when he did his inventory that night. The professor confirmed Stange's explanation. Given how the Sigmor kept its records, "they can't know how much cash was missing . . . because they can't know how much cash was there" before the attack.

Stange found that the store was short $166.86 since the last inventory. That wasn't an unusual amount. For that time period, Stange recalled, it was an acceptable loss.

For Stange, the more important facts were that he found $55 in loose cash at the store when he cleaned up, and that Wanda made her last drop-slot deposit about a half hour before the attack. Since Wanda wouldn't want to have more than $60 in the cash drawer after dark on a Friday night, he guessed that the robber couldn't have left with more than a couple of $10 bills.

Stange remembered staring at the numbers. "You've got to be kidding," he thought. For $20—for the minuscule amount that was gone—it wasn't about a robbery. The cash was available to Wanda's attacker. It was there. And she had tried to give it to him. "I just don't believe he ever actually took any cash," Stange told the investigator.

Stange told district supervisor Jim Manning the same thing when he arrived at the gas station that night. Stange couldn't understand it as a robbery, because it wasn't. The money was still there. It didn't make sense. "Was [Stange] ever asked . . . by anybody in law enforcement" what he thought had gone down? "No." After that night, the police talked only to Manning and Gonzalez, never to the store's actual manager, Stange.

.     .     .

A few minutes after the detective sent Stange and Gonzalez back outside of the store, she and the photographer announced they were done. "It's all yours," they said, and left.

It was 10:00, the store's usual closing time, barely an hour after the detective got inside the store, and less than two hours after Wanda was stabbed. Stange and a manager from another store scrubbed the place down, put everything in order, and ran the inventory. Although Stange didn't get much sleep, he opened the store the next morning at 6:00, the usual time.

He was astonished by how quickly the investigation had ended. "It's like, 'we got the pictures, we got the guy, let's just get out of here. We're done.'" If it was his life at stake, Stange thought, he wouldn't like it done that way.

# 5

# Suspect

NOT LONG AFTER CARLOS DELUNA'S ARREST FOR CAPITAL MURDER, his mother, Maria Margarita Martinez, became ill. According to her daughters, she'd always been a healthy woman, but her youngest son's arrest brought on kidney problems and other complications. Doctors operated on her three times. Two weeks before Carlos's trial was set to begin, heart problems developed, and she went into intensive care.

Margarita was supposed to be Carlos's star witness, but the judge wouldn't postpone the trial until she was well enough to testify. Margarita clung to life while the trial went on, with her daughters shuttling back and forth between the hospital and the courthouse. She died two weeks after the trial ended, at age sixty-one.

Margarita had ten children, the first of whom was born when she was only thirteen. According to family lore, she left the father of her first six children, Francisco Conejo, after she couldn't take the beatings anymore. At the time, Becky, the youngest of the six, was just a baby.

In the 1950s, Margarita moved her family from San Antonio to the La Armada housing project in Corpus Christi. Her children remember the "Mexican projects" as not so bad back then. Everyone was poor, but they didn't know any better and were thankful for a place to live. The government kicked in part of the rent and sent Margarita a check once a month for groceries and school clothes. The older children remember her working hard to raise them herself and be "like a mother and dad to all of us."

After moving to Corpus, Margarita started seeing Joe DeLuna. Joe made a decent living hauling scrap metal to Mexico and selling it. Within a few years, they had three children together—Manuel in 1961, Carlos on the Ides of March in 1962, and Rose in 1963. Joe and Margarita never married, and Joe carried on a relationship with another woman that produced three sons. He left Margarita when she was pregnant with Rose.

Rose DeLuna Rhoton is the family historian. In a conversation at a North Houston McDonald's in 2004, and in several that followed, she shared what she knew with the investigators looking into her brother Carlos's case.

According to the stories Rose heard, her mother first caught the eye of the much younger Joe DeLuna in a bar soon after moving to Corpus Christi. From then on, she hid her age from Joe. He walked out for good, the story goes, when he found out that she'd lied to him—that she had six children by Conejo, not the four still at home. The two eldest boys were already grown.

Rose heard that her father, Joe, was a "momma's boy" and that his momma thought he was too good for Margarita. The older siblings remembered Margarita and Joe fighting all the time.

Rose, short for Rosemary, was named after her grandmother Rose DeLuna and her mother Maria Margarita. She never met her grandmother and namesake, though, or her father. She heard that Carlos once went over to their grandmother Rose's house looking for his dad, but the old lady sent him away. She didn't want to have anything to do with her grandson or any of Joe's other children by Margarita, and Joe never did either.

None of the Conejo or DeLuna kids knew the father of Margarita's tenth child, or the baby boy himself. "She gave him away," Rose told the investigators. "So I never met . . . that brother. [But] she did keep us three."

When Rose was about four years old, Margarita met Blas Avalos, and the two were soon married. Rose rated Blas "okay" as a stepfather. Every once in a while, he'd spank one of them, but only when Margarita made him do it. It wasn't in his nature to hit them, Rose believed. Mostly, Blas stayed on the sidelines.

Blas's big problem was his drinking. Rose called him a "weekend alcoholic." Starting on Friday night, after he came home from his job laying asphalt, and through Sunday night, Blas would drink at home or at an older neighbor's house nearby. "The two of them would just sit and drink until they passed out," Rose recalled.

.   .   .

Rose understood why her mother let the tenth child go. Her mom was already too exhausted to raise her second set of kids. As Carlos DeLuna himself wrote to a news reporter in 1989, briefly describing his childhood, "My mother she was 40-years-old when she had me. And she was old, and I guess she was tired of raising kids."

The job of rearing Manuel, Carlos, and Rose fell to their three older half-sisters. Each older girl took responsibility for one of the DeLuna kids—dressing them, feeding them, and buying them clothes. Vicky Conejo chose Manuel, Mary picked Carlos, and Becky took Rose.

When the older girls were dating, they couldn't leave the younger kids home and had to bring them along. Mary Conejo Arredando laughed when she described the arrangement years later. It wasn't so bad, she said. She liked taking Carlos. He was a "good boy"; he behaved.

Margarita also made the older girls get jobs while they were in junior high and high school. At "paycheck time," Vicky recalled, "we would buy [the younger kids] . . . clothes. That's the way we were raised. . . . [E]very paycheck, we had to go buy something for our brother . . . like he was our responsibility." The rest of the paycheck went to Margarita to help with the rent.

Margarita wanted the older girls to stay home from school to look after the younger kids, as well as hold down paying jobs. The principal and teachers tried to get after Margarita about this, but she ignored them. Mary recalled being summoned to the principal's office and asked why she was absent all the time. She explained that her mother needed money and had to work outside the house. Someone had to stay with the littlest children. The school gave Mary a job in the school cafeteria, but her sister Vicky quit school to be at home with the DeLuna kids.

.   .   .

For eight of the nine children she raised, Margarita viewed her role as a parent in a narrow and practical way: get them to a point where they could take care of themselves and send them on their way. She loved them, Vicky said, but once they could support themselves, her job was done. Rose remembers a home without love, hugs, or "good mornings." Her mother just wanted the kids grown and out of the house. It didn't bother her that Vincent, the oldest, left as a teenager and never came back. Margarita was just happy that he could get along on his own.

Becky, the youngest of the Conejo kids, got pregnant when she was fourteen, a year older than her mother had been when Vincent was born. Margarita had no sympathy. Her attitude was, "Hey, I didn't tell you to get pregnant," so Becky left home.

Manuel, the oldest of the three DeLuna children, quit school when he was in junior high and left home after that. He followed his half-sister and surrogate mom Vicky Conejo Gutierrez to Garland, Texas, near Dallas, where she and some of the other half-siblings had moved with their young families to work in a Kraft Foods plant. Manuel traveled back and forth between Garland and Corpus Christi, and in and out of trouble with the law—starting with a car theft as a teenager that ended when he backed the vehicle into a police cruiser at the Casino Club and tried to flee the scene.

Rose was still little when Becky, her surrogate mom, left. The other girls had married and left home by then, so it fell to Rose to cook and clean for her older brothers. It was "normal [for] the Mexican generation," Rose explained, that the mom was harder on the girls than the boys. Rose and her sisters had to do exactly as they were told or they "got the crap beat out of [them]." Manuel and Carlos did "pretty much . . . whatever they wanted."

Rose recalled getting up at 4:00 A.M. If she wanted to go to school, she had to make sure the house was cleaned and breakfast was made for the boys. When school got out, she had to go straight home to make dinner and finish cleaning. Rose started running marathons when her own children got older. She always felt bad that she wasn't allowed to participate in sports after school. She pointed out that Margarita had no problem when her two sons joined the football team in junior high.

School was an annoyance for Margarita because it meant extra expenses for clothing and supplies. The only reason she let the kids go to school, Rose said, was "the . . . [law]. If that law wasn't in place, we wouldn't be going to school." After Blas came on the scene, the family moved to a tiny house in a new subdivision. The move made it harder for Rose and her brothers to get to school—they had to take a city bus to the school bus stop, and then another bus to school.

"You have to understand," Rose explained, Margarita herself "never went to school." She couldn't read or write, or speak any English. She worked her whole life cleaning people's homes. "I don't blame her," continued Rose.

"That's just the way she was brought up." For "a lot of old generation . . . Mexicans, that's how it [was]. You don't go to school. . . . When you are old enough to get a job you should be out . . . working."

                                                 •        •        •

For Carlos, however, Margarita was a different kind of mother. All her other kids noticed it. "Oh, God, she loved Carlos," Vicky recalled. "He was her pride and joy. She would do anything for Carlos, anything." He was her favorite, her "*consentido*." "I don't know why," Vicky said, but for Carlos her mother's love "was more."

Some of the siblings thought that Margarita cared more for Carlos because he looked like his handsome father, Joe. Vicky believed that it was a mother's nature to defend a child who couldn't seem to stay out of trouble.

But Rose, who was closest in age to Carlos, knew that it was something else. More outspoken than her siblings, Rose came right out and asked her mother. Carlos was always doing things he wasn't supposed to do. Why didn't she get mad and hit him like she did the others? Why was it that any time he messed up, she was there, helping him?

Margarita's answer weighed on Rose, another burden to shoulder for a mother too worn out to bear it herself anymore. Margarita believed that there was something wrong with Carlos. She told Rose that Carlos was like a "little bird with [a] broken wing. The other little birds can take care of themselves; they've flown out of the nest. . . . I don't have to worry about them." But this one couldn't make it on his own.

"My mom raised nine kids," Rose explained. "[W]hen you have that many kids . . . you know [when] there's something wrong with one." Although Margarita was too uneducated to know how to say it, Rose believed her mother could see that "Carlos had a disability."

"He was slow," Rose said reluctantly, shying away from more clinical words. "My mom . . . knew that he was slower than the others. . . . She knew he wasn't learning the way he should be."

"Could [Carlos] talk to you like we're talking right now?" Rose asked. "Yes. If you look at him and talk to him, do you think there is something wrong with him? No." And when it came to manual work, Carlos could watch you do something and pick it up, she said. But if you gave him a task where he had to make sense of something he read or heard, then "you would see he had an issue." He "couldn't do it."

.   .   .

That's why Margarita paid more attention to Carlos than the others—"always getting him out of the situations that he got himself into. Because she knew he had an issue." And "that's what killed my mom," Rose believed. That's why she "gave up" and died, because she "let Carlos down." She didn't help him in his greatest hour of need.

Rose explained. Shortly before Wanda Lopez was stabbed, Carlos had called home from a skating rink and bowling alley a mile from the Sigmor Shamrock gas station to ask for a ride home. By then, the other children had moved out, and it was just Margarita and Blas. Carlos had moved in only a few weeks before, on parole from prison. Blas got Carlos a job at the paving company he worked for, but beyond that he and Margarita weren't used to taking care of a twenty-year-old. Only an hour before Carlos had called, they had dropped him off at the skating rink. Now he wanted to come back home.

But it was Friday night, and even before taking Carlos to the rink, Blas had started drinking. When Carlos called for a ride home, his stepfather was too far gone to take the car out again. Margarita demurred as well. She couldn't see well at night and didn't want to drive by herself.

As Blas testified at Carlos's trial, Margarita told Carlos to find a ride home or use the pay he received earlier that day to get a cab home. Carlos had been counting on Margarita, not his barely communicative stepfather, to be his star witness at trial: to explain to the jurors that her son, begging for a ride home, a week's pay in his pocket, wasn't bent on robbing anyone.

But Margarita didn't testify. Maybe if the judge had postponed the trial, she could have dragged herself out of the hospital and into the courtroom, but Rose wasn't sure.

Her mother "didn't know how to get [Carlos] out of it," Rose told the investigators. "If she could, she would." Carlos had called her to pick him up from the skating rink, and Margarita "blame[d] herself for that, for not going out there and trying to get him. . . . She believe[d] she let him down." It was after that, Rose continued, that her "mom gave up." She "was tired, and she gave up."

Even after he was arrested, Carlos couldn't reach his mother to tell her. He called his oldest half-sister, Toni Peña, and told her that "he had been

arrested, and they were not going to let him go." Toni told the investigator
that "[h]e did not seem to understand what had happened to him."

If Margarita "would have just went for him," Rose reflected. "If she
would have just got in that car and went and picked him up [at the skating
rink], he would not have been in the situation that happened."

"That's what killed my mom."

·    ·    ·

For a long time, Rose admitted, she, too, blamed Margarita. And she
blamed herself.

"I believe it was in February of '83 that they claimed that Carlos committed this crime," Rose recounted for the investigators. "My mom passed
away in August of '83." Rose saw Margarita just before she died. She asked
Rose one thing. "I want you to do something for me," Margarita told Rose.
"Promise me that you'll always look out for Carlos. Promise me that."

"I told her, 'Okay, I'll look after him,'" Rose said. She knew that her
mother asked her and not any of the other siblings because Carlos was especially close to her.

A precise and dignified woman, Rose is not given to shows of emotion.
But when she recalled the promise she had made to her mother, she broke
down and cried. "I couldn't help him," she sobbed. "I did not know how to
help him. . . . And I blame myself."

·    ·    ·

Rose believed her brother when he told her and others in the family that he
hadn't killed Wanda Lopez. "My brother Carlos could not do such a crime,"
Rose told the investigators firmly. "Could he steal? Yeah, he stole. Could
he do drugs? Yeah, he did drugs. I know all that. But he could never . . . kill
anyone."

"Growing up as kids," she explained, "my brother was afraid of the dark.
That tells you something. . . . He was afraid of the dark."

"[Carlos] and I had a paper route," she recounted. "We rolled up papers
and we would go throw them out early in the morning." On their morning route, there was "a Chihuahua [dog] this big," Rose said putting her
hands about a foot apart. And Carlos "was afraid of that Chihuahua. . . .
Thirteen-year-old boy afraid of a Chihuahua this big. So I know my brother
couldn't commit such a crime. . . . I know dead in my heart that he couldn't

commit such a crime. And I feel horrible that I could not help him in any way."

All the siblings were shocked when they heard about Carlos's arrest for murder. They knew he'd been a wild teenager, but they couldn't believe he'd knife a woman to death. Carlos's half-sisters remember him as a good kid— "well behaved," in Vicky's recollection, "gentle and loving," in Mary's.

Rose remembered Carlos as "a follower. Carlos followed people." If one of the DeLuna siblings was up to no good, it was Carlos's older brother, Manuel. Manuel was always the instigator, and Carlos did what Manuel said.

One Christmas, Margarita bought bicycles for Manuel and Carlos (figure 5.1). Soon after, off Carlos went on his bike, following Manuel, who said he would lead them from their Gulf Coast home to North Texas, where their older brothers and sisters lived. They were quickly caught and punished by the authorities for skipping school.

That was Carlos, Rose recalled: doing whatever Manuel said—including taking the rap when his older brother misbehaved. Manuel would blame Carlos, Rose explained, and her younger brother would never defend himself. "It was always Carlos taking the blame for Manuel," agreeing that he was the one at fault. Although not one to admit his own failings, Manuel agreed with his sister about Carlos. "My brother was not a leader," he

FIGURE 5.1 The DeLuna children in the 1970s: (*left, clockwise from top left*) Manuel, Mary Conejo, Rose, and Carlos; (*center, from left*) Carlos and Manuel; (*right*) Carlos.

told the investigators, "he was a follower. He could be brainwashed to do anything."

At Carlos's trial, the prosecution called Eddie Garza, the celebrated Corpus Christi police detective, to testify that Carlos had a "bad character" as a teenager. Garza worked the city's Hispanic neighborhoods and knew all the troublemakers. Rose despised Garza for what he said about her brother at the trial. But Garza's assessment of Carlos in an interview at his detective agency years later was not so different from Rose's.

Garza remembered Carlos as "a slow thinker," not completely retarded, "he wasn't that. He was just a slow thinker, a follower, not a leader." He was someone whom the others "would tell . . . 'Go do this' or 'Go do that' and the guy would follow what someone else told him. He wasn't a person that would stand up and think on his own what he was going to do."

Carlos's elementary-school teachers referred him to Special Services for evaluation because he was so far behind in class. A sixth-grade teacher wrote, "He can read but can't comprehend. He is lost on abstract concepts such as fractions. He does pretty well one-to-one but can't function in even a small group. His attention span is extremely short."

Medical and psychological tests revealed that the twelve-year-old had a "language learning disorder." He had the mental functioning of a ten-year-old, the expressive vocabulary of an eight-year-old, and the small motor coordination (for "pencil and paper tasks") of a child "between 7½ and 8½ years old." He was two years below grade level in reading and three years below in math. He could understand words in isolation, but he used few of them in his own speech and had trouble with phrases and sentences.

Carlos's comprehension and memory were abnormal. When it came to understanding things in the moment, he could make a lot more sense of visual than of auditory cues—what he read as opposed to what he heard. But when it came to remembering what he had just learned, it was the opposite. So, he had problems either way: Things he read, he could understand but not remember. Things he heard, he could remember if he understood them, but he rarely did.

The psychologist recommended special education classes in reading and math.

Two years later, when Carlos was fourteen and in the eighth grade, the school district's Special Education Committee put him through another round of medical and psychological evaluations. They concluded that he had "low average I.Q.," "fine-motor difficulty," possible "neurological dif-

SUSPECT

67

ficulties" or "cerebral dysfunction," and a "specific learning disability." They recommended extending Carlos's special education placement to history and science.

· · ·

One thing Carlos was good at in junior high was football. His older brother played as well. But in the eighth grade, the school kicked Carlos off the team for failing his classes. No pass, no play. That was a big deal for Carlos and the other kids. He got tired of them laughing at him for being slow and quit school without finishing the eighth grade.

Margarita was fine with Carlos quitting junior high because he quickly got a job at the Whataburger. But looking back on it, Rose saw the setback as a turning point—when Carlos lost confidence and started heading in a different direction from her. For Rose, who eventually fought her way into the middle class—obtaining a good job in accounting even as her husband prospered in the real-estate and talent-recruiting businesses—the whole focus was on doing well in school and getting away from the life she saw around her.

"I didn't want to live like that," she told the investigators. "I didn't want to have ten or fifteen kids, from all these different men and be on welfare and not be educated. So I was looking ahead." But it was different for Carlos. Rose felt that he knew he couldn't even keep up with the kids around him and decided he "didn't care" what happened to him.

Rose believed that many things frightened Carlos, including the teasing he faced in school. But he was a good-looking kid, so he adapted by being "cocky," a flashy dresser, and a "showoff."

"If you would have known Carlos [as a teenager], he was very cocky, and always played this tough guy," Rose said. But "in reality, he wasn't anything like that. When you went one-to-one with him, he was the nicest person."

· · ·

Carlos's clothes and his hair were a big part of his image (figure 5.2). "Carlos would never wear blue jeans," Rose recalled. He "would never wear . . . flannel . . . shirts, sweats, flannel jackets, never." He always wore pressed slacks and long-sleeved dress shirts. "He always looked nice, dressed nice all the time." His pants were "polyester," she said, "longer on the bottom of the legs, like bell-bottom pants." "You would never see him but with black

FIGURE 5.2   Rose and Carlos DeLuna, late 1970s.

slacks," she said. He liked black because it made him look thinner and plat-
form shoes, to make him look taller.

Describing Carlos's shirts, Rose said it was "[a]lways . . . a dress shirt,
always long-sleeved dress shirts, with the big [cuffs] around here [*points to
her wrists*] and the long collars around here [*points to her neck*]." His shirt

was "always . . . tucked" and unbuttoned "three or four buttons down." "You never saw him in a T-shirt." When he was younger he wore bright colors, but later he preferred white dress shirts—he had a closet full of them, a closet full of white shirts and black pants.

Carlos kept his wavy hair long and stylish, a comb at the ready. "Always kept" his hair "neat," Rose recalled. "Always kept his appearance neat. Always shaved and cleaned."

&bull;    &bull;    &bull;

Twice after leaving school, Carlos had more psychological evaluations. Both findings were the same: low intelligence, higher "social" functioning, and pathetically obvious efforts to con the evaluator to hide what he could and couldn't do.

Roland J. Brauer, Ph.D., ran a battery of tests on Carlos at a juvenile facility when Carlos was sixteen, noting a sharp discrepancy between Carlos's "dull-normal" intellectual functioning and stronger "social awareness and social reasoning." He reported that Carlos was "manipulative" during the exam—trying to "con" him about eye problems and headaches. Given Carlos's "dull thinking," however, the "manipulations" were "very transparent."

If not for these "obvious" manipulations, Brauer wrote, Carlos "could be a pleasant boy to be around."

When Carlos was arrested five years later for killing Wanda Lopez, a judge ordered two evaluations. Psychologist James Plaisted tested Carlos's I.Q. as 72, borderline mentally retarded. At first, Carlos answered most of Plaisted's questions by saying that he couldn't remember anything, but "after rapport had been established and Mr. De Luna had become comfortable with answering questions," he became more cooperative.

Plaisted concluded that Carlos was malingering and was smarter than tests showed, given his "obvious . . . effort to deceive me into thinking he was suffering from a psychotic process," and because of differences between what Carlos claimed to comprehend on written tests and what he understood when the same words were spoken orally.

Plaisted knew a thing or two about deception himself. The year after examining Carlos, the psychologist was caught sexually molesting children in a church youth group that he ran. After more incidents, he ended up in prison on a forty-year sentence.

Psychiatrist Joel Kutnick performed the second evaluation of Carlos and afterward asked the prosecutor, Steven Schiwetz, to provide "background information in terms of how far this defendant got in school and whether there was a question of his being retarded," as tests initially had suggested. Schiwetz said he would look but never came up with anything. Kutnick reported to the court that school records were "not obtainable" and agreed with Plaisted that DeLuna was malingering.

Twenty-one years later, investigators obtained Carlos's school and juvenile evaluations within days of routine requests to the Corpus Christi School District and Juvenile Department. Both showed that his intelligence and learning capacity had been questioned since elementary school.

•    •    •

Shortly after quitting school, Carlos met a girl named Aida or Ida Sosa at the Casino Club. Rose described Aida as "a street girl," who "lived in abandoned houses with men." "That girl was trouble," Rose said. In a letter to a news reporter in 1989, Carlos also associated Aida with trouble. "I think I was 15 years old," he wrote, "when I first got in trouble with the Law. I was going out with this girl who was about two years older than me, and she had already been in trouble with the Law before."

"I truly did love her, or . . . thought I did," Carlos continued. "But I met her brother and his friends, and that's where all the trouble started."

Carlos asked Margarita if Aida could live with them. When Margarita refused, there was a fight. It ended, Rose recalled, when Carlos said, "[I]f you don't let her come in, I'm going to move out," and he did. Ever the follower, Carlos quickly adopted Aida's lifestyle. The two lived in abandoned houses and began stealing from relatives and neighbors, sniffing paint, drinking, and getting in trouble with the police.

Rose recalled that they wouldn't see Carlos for a while, but "[a]s soon as he ended up in jail, my mom would take him out of jail, and then he would do it all over again. It was a cycle, just a turning-wheel cycle."

•    •    •

Carlos's run-ins with the law began in early 1977, when he should have been in ninth grade. He was arrested once for truancy and twice for running away.

In September 1977, Carlos went to Dallas to join his brother Manuel, and his mother reported him missing. When he returned to Corpus a week later, the authorities put him in Juvenile Hall for counseling. Noting that the fifteen-year-old had been out of school for over a year and wouldn't cooperate, the Juvenile Department concluded that "no help could be offered" and released him.

In 1978, the arrests got more serious. He was arrested in February of that year for attempted burglary and public drunkenness, but charges were dismissed for "insufficient evidence." He was back in jail in March on charges of burglarizing a used-car lot across the street from the Casino Club, but the same prosecutor again dismissed the charges because he mistakenly charged DeLuna with a crime for which juvenile proceedings were not permitted.

On the last day of May, Corpus Christi police sergeant Enrique (Rick) Garcia stopped a 1969 Ford at the Casino Club that had been reported stolen from Garland, Texas. Carlos was driving the car, Aida was in the passenger seat, and Manuel was in the backseat. According to a police report, Carlos had run away to Garland and had stolen the car there. He had also reportedly broken into his mother's house and stolen a television and other things, and not long before that he'd been caught 200 miles away in Abilene driving a car owned by the uncle of another boy in the vehicle.

No one was prosecuted for these crimes. The paperwork on the first car theft never reached Corpus Christi from Garland. And neither Carlos's mother nor the uncle who owned the other car pressed charges. Instead, Margarita bailed Carlos out of jail.

Within weeks, police had Carlos and Aida red-handed on a new rap— sneaking an elderly woman's purse out of her house after getting inside on Aida's pretext of needing to make a phone call. Aida's brother saw Carlos take a $10 bill and $30 in food stamps out of the woman's wallet and called the police. Their report describes what happened next: "[W]e received a call to 504½ Flood. . . . Upon arrival into the house we observed Ida standing by the bed looking down. There was also a very strong odor of spray paint. We asked Ida if Carlos was there and she said 'Carlos who?' We looked under the bed and found Carlos and ordered him out. . . . Carlos had silver paint on his hands and paint fumes on his breath." Carlos had a spray can of Krylon silver paint and a beer can wet with the inhalant. Police reported that he and Aida "are currently co-habitating." Carlos showed police where he and Aida had hidden the food stamps.

This was Carlos's fifth referral to the local Juvenile Department in nine months, and the department finally took action. Its predisposition investigator Al Reyna reported that Carlos had "refused supervision" from Margarita for months, had moved into Aida's apartment, and worked at odd jobs. As for Carlos's arrest, "[o]ne moment he is admitting that he is at fault and the next moment he wants to sue everyone connected with his case." Finding Carlos "completely out of control" and in need of a stable and structured environment and counseling, Reyna recommended commitment to a Texas Youth Council juvenile facility.

It was during this stay at the local Martineau Juvenile Shelter that Brauer evaluated Carlos, identifying his "dull-normal" intelligence and "transparent" manipulation. Brauer agreed that Carlos needed a structured environment where rules of behavior are reinforced: "His present living situation in which he is free to roam and do as he pleases is totally inadequate."

While Carlos waited for the Juvenile Department to decide what to do with him, he and Aida were arrested again with a can of Krylon paint. Again, their hands and mouths were smeared with the stuff, but this time they were using it on the grounds of an elementary school. This was the earliest of Carlos's arrests when police reported his possessions at the time of his arrest. They found a comb, tweezers, and a watch, but no weapon.

.     .     .

The Juvenile Department placed Carlos in the custody of the Texas Youth Council, or TYC, the state agency that handles long-term juvenile incarceration. What Carlos did in TYC custody and what its psychologist learned about him are unknown because the agency destroyed all 500 pages of his records in 2004, after twenty-five years had expired during which no one had asked for them.

Other law-enforcement records reveal, however, that Carlos was in and out of TYC programs and institutions during 1978 and 1979. Things hadn't gone as Reyna and Brauer had hoped:

| | |
|---|---|
| September 1978 | Runaway from a court-ordered Job Corps placement |
| January 1979 | Unauthorized use of an automobile to escape from the Crockett State School for Boys ($12.25 in his pockets; no weapon) |
| November 1979 | Intoxicated at the scene of a car wreck; Carlos had crashed Manuel's red Toyota through a chain-link fence, smelled |

of alcohol, and couldn't recite his ABCs (comb, billfold, money clip, keys, and traffic tickets; no weapon)

| | |
|---|---|
| December 1979 | TYC parole violation for driving a friend's car without permission and without a driver's license, ending up in a ditch |
| December 1979 | Unspecified TYC parole violation following an arrest by Sergeant Rick Garcia at the Casino Club (comb, billfold, keys, papers, and bracelet; no weapon) |
| January 1980 | Escape from a TYC facility |

Between arrests, Carlos worked at a Whataburger and as a busboy at a sit-down restaurant.

With Carlos's eighteenth birthday approaching, the TYC gave up on him in early 1980 and left him to the Corpus Christi police. By then, alcohol had replaced spray paint as his substance of choice to abuse. The Casino Club, to which Manuel, an underage regular, had introduced his younger brother a few years earlier, was Carlos's favorite place to drink.

Other customers remembered Carlos from that time as "hyper. He talked fast and drank a lot." A cop who moonlighted as a bouncer at the club said "regulars" there typically described DeLuna as "stupid or crazy."

The next few months were a revolving door of trouble, jail stints, and more trouble:

| | |
|---|---|
| February 6, 1980 | Drunk and disorderly outside his mother's home where he was loudly and profanely arguing with her and his step-father (comb and billfold with no cash; no weapon) |
| February 7, 1980 | Minor consuming alcohol at the Casino Club after being turned away and sneaking back in (comb, billfold; no weapon) |
| March 5, 1980 | Trespassing at the Casino Club, which he insisted on entering when the owner as well as police told him he couldn't; Sergeant Rick Garcia was the arresting officer (comb, billfold, cigarette lighter; no weapon) |
| March 28, 1980 | Public drunkenness and disturbance in the middle of the street outside Margarita's home (comb, billfold; no weapon) |

May 23, 1980        Public intoxication after staggering up to a police of-
                    ficer who had arrested him a month earlier and dar-
                    ing him "to do it again" (comb, billfold, papers; no
                    weapon)

                              •        •        •

It was during this period when Rose, a year younger than Carlos and in
high school, confronted Margarita about how strict and impatient she was
with the other children and how tolerant she was of Carlos.

Resentful of the latitude that Margarita gave Carlos, Rose had some
sympathy for how the Corpus police felt about her brother. Because Margarita was illiterate and spoke only Spanish, Rose often accompanied her to
get Carlos out of jail.

"When he would go to jail, my mother was there to bail him out all the
time," Rose recalled. "And he would tell police officers, 'you know I'm going to be . . . out of here in an hour. Watch my mom walk in, and she's going
to get me out.' And that's exactly what would happen." Carlos "would just
go out laughing, 'I told you I'd be out.'" Rose believed that her brother
"pissed off a lot of people in Corpus."

"I believe strongly that a lot of those officers would say, 'give him enough
rope and one of these days he's going to hang himself.' That's what I believe." Since those days, Rose has struggled with her love and resentment
for her brother and her mom, and with her sympathy and hatred for the
police and other authorities who played such a big role in bringing both of
them down.

Rose despised Carlos's constant stealing, lying, and huffing paint. But he
was also a "kind heart," always "helping you out if you needed help." Carlos
was the one who stuck up for her when Manuel blamed her for something
he had instigated; the one who brought her hamburgers from work—"a
big deal," growing up in a poor family; the one who gave her lunch money
because he knew how "embarrassing [it was], when you're a teenager, and
you have to go stand in line and get your free lunch ticket," showing everyone you're too poor to pay. Manuel worked, too, but he never did any
of that.

Looking back on it, Rose took solace in one thing: for all his showing
off as a teenager, Carlos died a humble man. Not, though, before the police
gave Carlos his comeuppance.

. . .

On June 19, 1980, sheriff's deputies arrested Carlos for attempted rape in Garland, where his older siblings lived. While on bail for that offense, he was arrested in nearby Dallas for driving a stolen car. He pleaded no contest to both charges.

In pleading to the first charge, Carlos admitted that he had followed the seventeen-year-old victim into a YWCA parking lot where he tore off her clothes and threatened to kill her if she didn't stop resisting. He had no weapon.

Two witnesses approached and scared off DeLuna. The victim went home and got her brother, and they went looking for her attacker. They found Carlos, still at the YWCA, but he ran away, shedding his shirt and shoes.

The victim and her brother followed Carlos but lost sight of him at 4267 Munger. They went home, where they gave a description to the police. Officers went over to the Munger address to begin a search and, to their surprise, found Carlos still there, hiding "in bushes." The victim and witnesses identified him at the scene.

Around the same time, Carlos also confessed to stealing a car from the driveway of a man named John Williams Jones. Dallas police officers caught DeLuna with the car two days later, when he ran a red light right in front of them.

Carlos was sentenced to two years minimum and three years maximum in prison for the two offenses. With credit for time spent in jail after his arrest and for good behavior while in prison, he was paroled sixteen months later, on February 23, 1982. He stayed out of trouble for nearly three months on parole, but not more. On May 14, Carlos attended a welcome-home party for Marcos Garcia, a friend from prison. Margarita and Blas left him off at the Garcia home, wearing black slacks and a blue, long-sleeve dress shirt.

Sometime after 11:00 P.M., Carlos and Marcos left the party together. An hour later, after midnight, witnesses saw Carlos return alone, and around 1:00 A.M. they saw him run out of the Garcia home with his blue shirt unbuttoned. In the meantime, Marcos's fifty-three-year-old mother, Juanita Garcia, had awoken to find a man lying on top of her. The man put a pillow over her mouth and threatened her. She thought she recognized the voice as DeLuna's and made out his silky blue shirt.

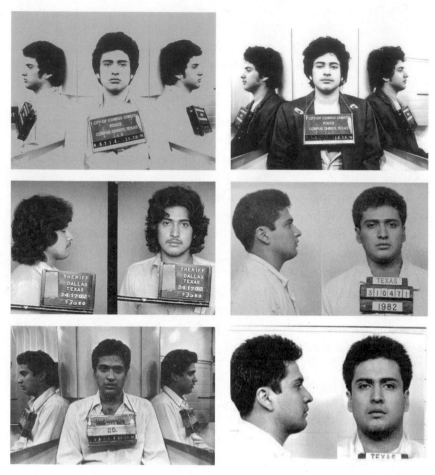

FIGURE 5.3 Booking photographs of Carlos DeLuna: (*top left*) November 30, 1979; (*top right*) December 23, 1979; (*middle left*) July 30, 1980; (*middle right*) 1982; (*bottom left*) January 21, 1983; (*bottom right*) July 26, 1983.

The man punched Garcia once in the ribs, breaking three of them; removed her clothes; unzipped his pants; and stroked and kissed her. Then he left suddenly. No weapon was used.

Police determined that there was no rape or attempted rape and charged Carlos with misdemeanor assault. They never prosecuted, however. Instead, prison officials revoked Carlos's parole because he had left Corpus Christi without permission shortly after the incident at Marcos's house. DeLuna was back in prison on June 22, 1982 (figure 5.3).

Prison officials paroled Carlos again on December 30, 1982, thirty-six days before Wanda Lopez was killed.

·     ·     ·

When Rose talked about the bridges that Carlos had burned by being cocky and "piss[ing] off a lot of the police officers in Corpus," she might have been referring to Officer Thomas Mylett.

Mylett was the first Corpus Christi cop the police dispatcher had radioed to go to the Sigmor when Wanda screamed, but he never answered. Later, though, he joined the manhunt and helped Constable Ruben Rivera and Officer Mark Schauer pull Carlos out from under the pickup truck. It was Mylett who proposed bringing DeLuna "back" to the Sigmor for identification.

Mylett was also present when Schauer radioed in that he was driving Carlos the three blocks to the filling station and then, for unexplained reasons, took a quarter-hour to get there.

When they brought Carlos out from under the truck, Mylett recognized him as the twenty-year-old he'd arrested two weeks earlier at the Casino

FIGURE 5.4 Television news shot of Detectives Olivia Escobedo and Paul Rivera escorting Carlos DeLuna through the "perp walk" outside the courthouse in Corpus Christi.

Club for drunk and disorderly conduct. The cop immediately broadcast the reason for the earlier arrest to anyone who was within radio-shot.

Mylett had been off duty, working security at the Casino Club, when Carlos, stinking drunk, stumbled up and asked if he "knew [Rick] Garcia, the police officer who was shot last year." Carlos then told Mylett that he was glad Garcia had been shot and wished that he'd been killed. Garcia had himself arrested Carlos several times at the club.

Then, according to Mylett, "Subject asked if I wanted to fight about the conversation he just had with me. I . . . had the subject step outside the night club and arrested him for public intoxication and disorderly conduct."

·    ·    ·

After pulling him out from under the pickup truck, Mylett and Schauer stood DeLuna up and checked his pockets, finding a billfold but no weapon. The police in Corpus Christi, Dallas, Garland, Abilene, and the other cities where he'd been arrested had never found a weapon on him. Detective Eddie Garza had never heard of DeLuna carrying a weapon. None of his siblings or friends had ever seen him with one. Rose was sure Carlos would never carry a gun or knife. He'd be too scared.

Still, as soon as Mylett recognized him and told the other officers who he was, they were sure that Carlos DeLuna had finally given them enough rope to hang him (figure 5.4).

PART | II

# The Lives
# of Carlos Hernandez

# 6

# Probation and Parole

IN THE 1970S AND 1980S, Corpus Christi was a city of many poor Hispanic neighborhoods. In its geographic center stood the La Armada projects, where Carlos DeLuna and his siblings grew up. Two miles south, near the Sigmor Shamrock station, sat the dilapidated neighborhood where the police hunted Wanda Lopez's killer and arrested DeLuna. Hugging the eastern edge of the city along Corpus Christi Bay, the largest of the Corpus Christi barrios ran several miles south from downtown.

The one institution in the city that regularly brought young Latinos together from all these neighborhoods was the Casino Club, on South Port Street.

Located about a mile north of the Armada Park area and a mile west of the downtown and bay-front barrios, the Casino Club was notoriously "rough" and "wild." People who hung out there in the 1970s and 1980s vividly recalled the scene played out almost every night: drinking (much of it underage), dancing, and "fights both inside and outside the club." "Sometimes, people died" there.

Yolanda Ortiz owned the club until it closed in the late 1980s. Describing it to investigators years later, she made no bones about what went on at the place.

"The club was a rough place," Ortiz said. "Stabbings were common and occurred almost weekly." Ticking off some of the more memorable crimes, Ortiz recalled a "bouncer . . . shot in the leg by a patron in the '80s. Two or three times [she] took butcher knives away from patrons." "One time a girl was stabbed or shot in the parking lot and she died." Another time, Ortiz noticed that "a patron, David Lamb, had a small spot of blood on his shirt," and she asked him "if he had been in a fight. David said, 'what?'" and then fell to the floor, dead from the wound. She hired off-duty Corpus Christi cops to keep order for $10 an hour. More than one of them was caught selling drugs.

Most of the "crowds of regulars," however, just drank and danced. "The dance floor was large with a big projector screen on the wall next to it where pictures of patrons were shown while they were dancing," Ortiz told the investigators. "Everyone wanted their picture on the screen."

Ortiz easily recalled Manuel DeLuna as a regular and dimly recollected his younger brother Carlos, who "would get drunk a lot, and they would ask him to leave." Years later, Ortiz was able to rattle off the names of the people the DeLunas hung out with at the club: Beto Vela, the Perales sisters—Linda and Mary Ann—Pedro Olivarez, and Jesse Garza.

Another Casino Club regular at the time was Mary Margaret Tapia. Margie, as everyone called her, grew up on Carrizo Street, in one of the poorest parts of the barrio near downtown and the bay front. Margie started going to the club in early 1978, around the time that Carlos DeLuna was first arrested there for being drunk and disorderly.

Margie was a rebel who did whatever her mother didn't want her to do. Although only fourteen years old at the time, she chatted up the bouncers at the Casino, and they let her inside. She spent as much time there as she could, dancing and drinking and seeing where things would go with the older guys she met. Margie, too, recalled the DeLuna brothers from the club, as well as another, more memorable, man the DeLunas sometimes associated with. His name was Carlos Hernandez.

. . .

Margie developed a crush on Carlos Hernandez in September 1978, when she had just turned fifteen and was five months pregnant.

Born on Bastille Day (July 14), 1954, Hernandez was twenty-four at the time, a lot older than Margie. But as she told the investigators in a string of interviews a quarter century later, that was part of the allure.

After getting pregnant, Margie had quit school and stopped going to the clubs. Every afternoon, she sat on the porch of her family's Carrizo Street home, hoping to catch a glimpse of Carlos Hernandez on his way from work to his mother's house kitty-corner across the street. Carlos would tease her about not being in school and urge her to come down from the porch to talk to him. Margie giggled and refused but thought that Carlos was cute, with his pipe-layer's hardhat, work clothes, and a six-pack of beer always in hand. "What did I know about guys?" she told the investigators with a laugh.

Thanks to a plot her mother, Janie Adrian, cooked up with Carlos Hernandez's mother, Fidela, to get their two children together, Margie was about to learn a lot more about this guy. Janie wanted her pregnant daughter married, and Fidela wanted someone else to look after her least-favorite son, who was recently home after five years in prison.

Attracted to her handsome neighbor, Margie went along with her mother's plan. At first, she and Carlos just went to movies and out to eat, but things developed quickly. Nine years younger than Carlos and two months shy of having someone else's child, Margie moved in with him at Fidela's house in November 1978. The arrangement lasted until July 1979.

At first, Carlos was sweet and charming. He "loved the fact that I was pregnant," she said. "[H]e did everything to make sure I ate, make sure I got food, husbandly things." After her son Eric was born, Carlos loved the boy as if he were his own. Carlos "knew [Eric] wasn't his," she recalled, "but for some odd reason, he thought he was." Even after Carlos and Margie split up, Carlos would often visit Eric at Margie's mom's house. Fidela told Margie's mom that she "even took out a life insurance policy on Eric which is now paid off."

*     *     *

What passed for a honeymoon didn't last long. After about eight months with Carlos, Margie felt her crush turn into something else entirely. Carlos had two sides, Margie told the investigators. At the flick of a switch, his sweet side would vanish, and another would replace it. "Carlos Hernandez had a mean side," she explained. "A very mean bad side. He would change from one day to the next. He would . . . be ok you know [for a] couple days, and then the next day he would be all mad." There was no way to please him.

The mean side began to dominate. When Carlos was angry, which usually meant he was drunk, Margie was in for abuse. He beat her and threatened to kill her. Once, after the baby was born and Margie had gotten her figure back, she made the mistake of dressing up nicely and waiting on the porch for Carlos to come home. When he saw her, he cursed her for being

outside the house dressed like that and came up the stairs and kicked her
with his work boots. Then he took her inside and raped and brutalized her
for hours, threatening her with a hammer if she didn't do exactly what he
said. It didn't faze him that Eric was sleeping on the other side of the bed.

Carlos had his own terrors and seemed to want to punish Margie for
them. "He hardly slept," she recalled. "If he slept he had nightmares . . . really bad nightmares." He would scream and grab Margie by the throat, or
"swing[ ] his arms and fight[ ] at nothing. He was afraid; his eyes were wide
like someone was going to hurt him." Margie tried to comfort him and
asked what he was seeing. Usually Carlos didn't want to talk about it, but
he once told her that he was fighting someone in his sleep. Margie knew
that Carlos had been to prison and figured something unspeakable must
have happened to him there.

A big part of Carlos's dark side, Margie said, was his bizarre obsession
with his knife—a long blade inside a brown fake-wood handle with gold-
colored metal trim, which opened up and locked. Carlos always carried the
knife on his right side, either in a pouch or in his pocket.

Margie sometimes felt that Carlos paid more attention to the knife than
to her. "He would sit there at night, when we were watching tv," she recalled. He had a stone, and he'd "[p]ut water and just be sharpening it."
Then he'd clean it. Then he "would say something to it and put it under
where he slept." He treated it like it was "a real person or something," she
said, "just . . . like you would put a kid to bed."

·    ·    ·

As Carlos grew more violent toward Margie, he also demanded more control over her life. He didn't even want her crossing the street to her mother's
house. Soon he wouldn't let her go out at all without him. If Margie defied
him, he would beat her. She was a prisoner, she told the investigators much
later. She didn't see a way out.

It eventually took the police to get her out of Fidela's house. She begged
her older sister Mary Jane and her brother-in-law Richard Garcia for help.
The two called the cops, telling them an underage girl and baby boy were
being held captive. The police, Margie recalled, showed up at the Hernandez home and "asked me 'do you want to go.'" She said she did. "Carlos was
standing at the door. They said get the baby's things."

Recalling the incident much later, Richard Garcia described Carlos's reputation for abusing women. Carlos was a "coward who beat women to make them do what he wanted" and make them "his slave," Garcia said. But when Carlos wanted to attack men, "he got others to fight his fights for him." The husband of another of Hernandez's victims described him similarly: "a coward," who "took his frustration out on women," who "only attacked women, not men."

Margie felt lucky to have gotten out of Fidela's house alive.

* * *

There were a lot of things about Fidela's house that frightened people. Rita Hull, a close friend of Carlos's older sister Paula who nursed Paula as she died of cervical cancer, described Fidela Hernandez as a mean, evil woman. A "*bruja*," Rita called her. A witch.

Fidela wanted Paula to die so she could collect the insurance. Rita recalled Fidela saying this right to Paula's face: "Just . . . die so I can collect." When Paula did die, at age forty-two, Fidela got her money and wouldn't use any of it to pay for Paula's funeral. Rita made the arrangements herself. The county buried her in a pine box.

Paula's son John Michael Schilling described his grandmother as a "mean lady." He struggled for words to describe her, finally settling on "very bad— no good—she didn't like any of us."

Fidela worked at a dry-cleaning store on Staples Street, but for years, according to Rita, she made most of her money from men who came to her house for sex. Margie saw this, too, when she lived there—Fidela's "sugar daddies," as the older woman called them, constantly shuffling into and out of the house. Years later, Fidela told investigators that her mother had encouraged her to prostitute herself from a young age because she had a nice body that could make her good money.

Always looking for ways to make a dime, Fidela also told the investigators about her scheme to carry life-insurance policies on all her children. Just as she expected, trouble and early deaths seemed to run in the family.

Her first child, Arelia, died at eleven months. Fidela was seventeen, and her husband at the time, Santiago Ramos, wouldn't provide food, so the baby starved to death. The doctor "put something else down as the cause of death," Fidela told the investigators, so the authorities wouldn't inquire.

After Santiago and Fidela split up, their other daughter, Margarite, was raped and impregnated by Fidela's second husband, Carlos Hernandez, Sr. In the fall of 1960, when Carlos, Jr., the oldest of the couple's four boys, was six, his father went to prison for a different rape. When the elder Carlos was released, he moved to Dallas and had nothing more to do with Fidela and their children.

Family welfare officials later reported that Fidela was "bitter" because Carlos, Sr., had left her for prison and never came back. Fidela "has tended to take out her frustrations on the children and particularly on Carlos [Jr.]."

For a year after their father went to prison, Fidela sent Carlos and the next oldest brother, Gerardo (Jerry), to live in a state home for orphans, claiming she couldn't support them. The local welfare department was involved with the family for years.

Fidela told juvenile officials that "she and [Carlos, Jr.,] could not get along." According to Rita, Fidela favored Javier, the third oldest of the Hernandez boys, and tormented Carlos by making her preference known.

Javier had his own problems. His troubled life ended with his death in a fire at the home of his longtime girlfriend. The police thought that he had committed suicide. No one ever knew whether Fidela collected on Javier.

Another of the Hernandez children to die a premature and violent death was Efrain, or Frankie, the youngest of the Hernandez boys. In 1979, at age twenty-one, Frankie was beaten, stabbed with a broken bottle, and left to die in a park where his body was dumped. Someone had carved out one of his eyes, and he choked to death on his own blood. Police never solved the crime, but Fidela and others in the family said that Frankie had gotten too close to a woman who was in a lesbian relationship, and her jealous lover and the lover's brother killed him. The main thing for Fidela, though, was that she collected on that insurance policy.

Only Jerry escaped Fidela and Corpus Christi. "Jerry disowned the family," Rita Hull said, "and left the house after graduating from high school. He was the only one [of the five siblings] who graduated."

                              •      •      •

Rita Hull described Carlos, Jr., as the worst of the Hernandez family. Paula Hernandez's husband, Freddy Schilling, saw it the same way. Freddy got a special dose of Carlos's mean streak because Carlos couldn't stand him or pretty much any man who was with his sister Paula.

"Carlos was very violent," Freddy told an investigator a long time later. "He threatened my life many, many times. . . . He would pull clubs, or he would pull a knife. He . . . picked up trash cans and tried to hit me with them. He always threatened me."

"I'll be honest with you," Freddy said. "I was really scared of this dude. I fought him off for a long time." For years, Freddy believed that "one of us was going to hurt [the other] real bad. But I wasn't looking forward to it."

By all accounts, Carlos Hernandez was an alcoholic and a mean and violent drunk. Something about alcohol set him off, made him aggressive and "constantly mad at the world," as a neighbor recalled. He would get trashed on Schlitz or another brand of cheap beer and then go off without warning, from calm to exploding with rage. When Carlos drank, Freddy said, you didn't want to be around him. He'd literally "stab you in the back."

Carlos "looked like the demon when he was under the influence," Diana Gomez said, describing the man she lived with for several months in 1985. When he was sober, he "was totally the opposite," she said. He would go off and do a day's job. But at night, when he drank, he became "an evil person." And drinking was an everyday thing.

Hernandez wasn't physically imposing—5 feet, 7 inches, and about 160 pounds—but he scared a lot of people. He had a violent charisma.

"[W]e were all afraid of Carlos," his nephew John Michael Schilling told an investigator much later when he was interviewed in prison. "I was scared of him," a lawyer who represented Hernandez acknowledged in an interview around the same time. Carlos was "dangerous, very dangerous." He "talked shit."

"That guy brought a lot of fear in other people," Freddy said. His wife, Paula, was scared of her brother Carlos. Their brother Javier was afraid of him, too, and for good reason. Javier once showed up at Paula's house covered in blood after Carlos ended a dispute by stabbing his younger brother in the leg. That incident was John Michael Schilling's most vivid recollection of his uncle Carlos, but not the only one. He also recalled his mother telling him that his uncle "had carved an X on someone's back" with a knife.

Even people who didn't know Carlos were afraid of him. Partly it was the look in his eyes. He had "a look of real hatred," recalled Paul Rivera, a well-known Corpus Christi detective who arrested Carlos several times. Partly it was Hernandez's violent reputation.

Everybody around the neighborhood knew what Carlos was like, his brother-in-law Schilling said. "He'd come around, [and] everybody would be real quiet. No one would say nothing. They didn't even want to start a conversation with him."

Carlos's longtime lawyer, Jon Kelly, remembers walking with him into a boisterous bar in the Hispanic part of Corpus. Suddenly, Kelly said, everyone got quiet. The guys playing pool gave up the table to Carlos. "You knew . . . people were saying, 'That's Carlos Hernandez,'" the criminal defense lawyer recalled with a touch of admiration.

Another time, Kelly witnessed a confrontation between Hernandez and another man at a bar. "I beat up his girlfriend," Carlos told Kelly, explaining why the man was hostile. There were fists and knives, and ugly things were said. "I knew it was time to leave," Kelly recalled.

Kelly told Hernandez not to come around his home. It scared people, the lawyer said. "It wasn't how he acted, but how he looked. You could sense the evil."

•      •      •

As Margie Tapia had quickly learned, Carlos directed his double-edged charisma mainly toward women. Freddy Schilling was another expert on Carlos's treatment of women. He'd observed up close Carlos's violent protectiveness of his sister, Paula, and his relationship with Paula's close friend Gloria Licea (later Sanchez), and especially what happened to Dahlia Sauceda. Both Freddy and Carlos had dated Sauceda at the same time—an arrangement that ended badly for everyone but Carlos.

Carlos had a knack for avoiding the consequences of the trouble he made for himself and others. He bragged about it and believed he had a special karma. Things would go poorly for the others, usually women, but not for him. He would escape. He was untouchable, a cat with nine lives.

At first, Freddy explained, Carlos was loving toward women. But then he became "jealous, very constantly haunting them. [They] couldn't go there, couldn't do this. His sexual toy." Women feared him, Freddy said. "He would actually scare them to the point to where they couldn't leave him. That's the way he was."

Rosa Anzaldua was the exception. She fought back. Rosa was with Carlos as far back as 1980, two years before they married in May 1982. Like other women before and after her, she was the object of his abuse. Eventually, though, she got tired of the black eyes and swollen lips. One night when Carlos was complaining about dinner being late, Rosa grabbed a pot of boiling water off the stove and threw it on her husband, scalding him badly. Rosa left Carlos in October 1983, about six months after Wanda Lopez died.

A month after Rosa left, Carlos went to her house with an axe. Threatening to kill Rosa and her children, he shoved the axe handle into her chest. Before leaving, he smashed a window with a metal bar, shattering glass over the sleeping children, one of whom was his own son Jesus. The next day, Rosa filed for divorce and a restraining order, citing Carlos's "violent and ungovernable temper."

.      .      .

Hernandez's knife was an important part of his violent aura. Carlos always carried a knife, Freddy recalled. "I can't ever recall him not having one. . . . [If] he thought something was going to happen, he'd pull a knife out."

It was a "pretty big knife . . . that he carried around all the time," Carlos's niece Pricilla recalled. "It wasn't just a small little pocket knife. It was a pretty good sized, thick knife." "It was real big," one of the Hernandez neighbors agreed. "It was one that you could just hit it like that and it would open right away." Although Hernandez was on parole from prison his entire adult life and was not allowed to carry a weapon, even his mother described him as always having a knife.

Shown the photograph of a knife (figure 6.1), Carlos Hernandez's lawyer Jon Kelly had the same reaction as others: "Yes. He had that all the time." Even in the presence of his lawyer, "he had that on him quite often, I'd say."

People remember Carlos obsessively "sharpening his buck knife," "sitting out there on the sidewalk and playing with it or showing it off," "throwing it at trees," "brandish[ing] it . . . in front of [his nephews]" and showing them how fast he could "flip it out," talking to it, even cutting his own chest and stomach with it "like a rooster getting ready to fight."

In this and in other ways, Carlos Hernandez was oddly a man of regular habits. He always carried a knife, always kept it on his right side, and it was always the same kind and color: a lock-blade buck knife with a brown fake-wooden handle and with brass-colored rivets and trim on the top of the handle and the bottom near a lever that locked the blade open or closed.

Shown the photograph of the knife without knowing its source, several former girlfriends, relatives, neighbors, knifing victims, and other associates of Carlos Hernandez during the 1970s to 1990s identified it in interviews many years later as the kind Carlos always carried. "Yeah, that's the knife," was how his nephew John Michael Schilling put it.

Asked if she'd seen the photograph before, Margie Tapia answered immediately: "No, but I can tell you what it is. . . . Carlos Hernandez's knife," she said. The one she used to see all the time, the one Carlos obsessively sharpened and put to bed at night. She was sure of it.

Margie and the others didn't know it, but they were looking at a police photograph of the weapon used to stab Wanda Lopez to death.

•      •      •

Carlos's regular habits extended to his clothes and grooming, which, most agreed, were not the source of his charisma (figure 6.2). "Carlos used to dress real ugly," a former girlfriend told the private investigators years later. "He looked more like a hobo." "He looked homeless." When asked to de-

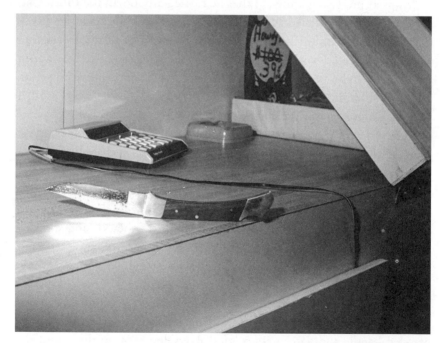

FIGURE 6.1  The knife shown to associates of Carlos Hernandez in interviews in 2004 and 2005. The photograph was taken by the police at the Sigmor Shamrock gas station on February 4, 1983. (Color versions of this and other knife photographs are on the Web site, thewrongcarlos.net.)

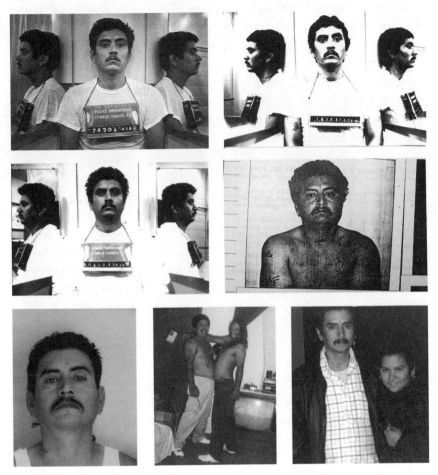

FIGURE 6.2  Carlos Hernandez: (*top left*) after his arrest in April 1985 for public intoxication; (*top right*) after his arrest in July 1986 for murder; (*middle left and right*) after his arrest in April 1989 for aggravated assault; (*bottom left*) after his arrest in March 1994 for heroin distribution; (*bottom center*) with brother Javier, early 1990s; (*bottom right*) in his "winter uniform"—flannel checked overshirt, gray undershirt, and blue jeans—with an unidentified woman, late 1980s.

scribe what Carlos always wore, she said, "[a] white T-shirt. Jeans. His beer. . . . And in cold weather he would wear a flannel jacket" with "squares, plaid," and tennis shoes. "He was real sloppy."

Others elaborated, describing Carlos's summer uniform as a white T-shirt or muscle shirt with blue jeans. In winter, it was a white or off-white sweatshirt or thermal shirt and sometimes a "blue- or red-checked flannel shirt" or "coat-shirt." Carlos was never one for dress shirts. Asked where Carlos bought his clothes, whether he went to the J. C. Penney's at the mall, another former girlfriend laughed. The thought of Carlos Hernandez in a department store didn't compute.

The same girlfriend described Hernandez's facial hair: "He never did sport a full beard, I don't remember that, but the mustache, yes . . . always." He kept his thick, wavy hair medium length.

•   •   •

Carlos's jealous devotion to his sister Paula was another feature of his behavior that associates often recalled. Rita Hull saw a connection between that behavior and the events of December 30, 1970.

That night, Carlos wrecked a car belonging to Paula's fiancé's family. Sixteen at the time, Carlos was drunk and driving over 100 miles per hour on a city street when he slammed on the brakes, skidded nearly 500 feet into the oncoming traffic lane, turned the car on its side, and skidded again until the car crashed into another vehicle.

Only Carlos walked away unharmed. Paula and the people in the other car were badly injured. Paula's fiancé, Louis Sissamis, was dead. Sissamis was nineteen and in the air force. He'd met the seventeen-year-old Paula while on leave, and they were quickly engaged. Described as "sweet" and "kind-hearted" by family members, Louis was from a middle-class Greek family that owned a restaurant in town. He was the closest Paula ever came to escaping the life that Fidela had predestined for her children.

That night, Carlos had shown up uninvited at a party that the Sissamis family was giving on its yacht in the Corpus Christi harbor, evidently to celebrate the upcoming wedding of Louis and Paula. Carlos was drunk, and Louis's father was angry at Louis and Paula. Louis borrowed the keys to his father's car to get Carlos away. The next thing the family heard, their son was at Memorial Hospital in a coma. He never awoke, and his parents never got over the death of their son.

Carlos pled guilty to negligent homicide. After convincing probation officials that he was "sobered quite a bit by the effects of the recent accident," and that the shock would mitigate the "character disorder" his prior record had indicated, Juvenile Department officials recommended probation instead of time in Juvenile Hall. This was the first of many convictions and charges Carlos ducked without serious consequences.

People who knew Carlos said the accident did have one lasting effect on him—the guilt he felt toward Paula. He thought he owed her something. He would later find his own way to repay her.

.     .     .

A few months after the accident, Fidela sent Carlos to live in Fremont, California. The move wasn't because of the accident, juvenile authorities concluded, because Fidela had always "minimized" the car wreck and Sissamis's death. Instead, her own difficulties with Carlos led her to ship the boy out of town.

The trouble had started a year before the accident. After getting all Ds and Fs in his first semester of high school, Carlos dropped out in early 1970. He "was unable to relate effectively to his classmates and the school work," the juvenile report notes. In quick succession, Corpus Christi police arrested Carlos for truancy, running away from home, traffic violations, disturbing the peace, public drunkenness, and sniffing lacquer. Each time, police called Fidela to bail him out of jail. Frequently she refused, letting the sixteen-year-old remain inside for a week at a time.

What put her over the edge, however, was an incident in March 1971, a month into Carlos's probationary period following his conviction for negligent homicide. Late one night, Fidela called the police to her home. When they arrived, Carlos was cursing and throwing punches at his mother and brothers. He was high on glue or paint, the arresting officer wrote, and had to be restrained. Fidela "insisted" that the police put Carlos "in jail for safe keeping." The next day, he was moved to a juvenile shelter, his probation revoked.

Three weeks later, Carlos enrolled in Irvington High School in Fremont, California. Romeo Solis, his mother's brother, was listed as his guardian. Carlos's juvenile probation officer worked out the arrangement. Forced to choose between Fidela and Carlos, he decided the mother was to blame. Fidela was "constantly on Carlos's back about anything he did" and held her husband's rape conviction and departure from home against her son and the other kids. In addition, friends of Louis Sissamis were threatening to kill Carlos.

Solis agreed to the arrangement on condition that his sister have no control over the boy.

For a time, Carlos seemed to be making some progress. Although he continued to earn Ds and Fs in some of his tenth- and eleventh-grade classes, he got As and Bs in English and physical education, as well as in a summer jobs program, and there were no unexcused absences from school. He played on the school softball team.

In the fall of 1971, Carlos asked to stay in California, which his parole officer thought was his "best bet." Given Fidela's "inability to provide proper supervision," the officer wrote, Carlos "will be better off in another environment."

By this point, however, Carlos was seventeen, and the department considered him an adult. It released him from his juvenile sentence and parole eight months after they began.

.    .    .

At first Carlos remained in California, but he soon grew tired of his uncle's supervision. By January 1972, Carlos was back in Corpus Christi and back in trouble. That month police arrested him for stealing a woman's car out of the Memorial Hospital parking lot and driving it without lights or a driver's license.

A few weeks after being released on bond for the felony theft, he was picked up for "sniffing." His face was smeared with gold paint, and police found a rag doused with the substance, as well as some bullets in his pocket.

A week later, things got more serious. Corpus Christi police officers arrested the slender teenager for a two-hour robbery spree, in which he and partners knocked off two Circle K gas station convenience stores and a Humble Oil station at gunpoint. One of the robbers entered the store and pretended to purchase cigarettes. Another came in and distracted the store clerk by asking to use the restroom, at which point the first shoved a .38-caliber pistol in the clerk's back, grabbed the money, and escaped in a car driven by a third accomplice.

Eyewitnesses quickly described the car and gave its license plate number to the police. Within an hour of the third robbery, police had the three teenagers in custody. One of the store clerks identified Carlos as the robber, and all three confessed. In his intake interview for prison, Carlos admitted to being the gunman in all three robberies.

On September 28, 1972, Carlos pled guilty to one count of felony theft of a car and three counts of robbery by firearm. A judge sentenced him to ten years in prison for car theft and a hefty twenty years for each robbery because each was committed "by firearm." The sentences were made "concurrent."

Almost five years to the day later, the Texas Board of Pardons and Parole voted to release Carlos on parole, effective on January 4, 1978. Nine months later, his relationship with Margie Tapia began (figure 6.3).

*   *   *

Although everyone feared Carlos after he returned to Corpus in 1978 on parole, that wasn't the case during his five-year stint behind bars. According to Freddy Schilling, when his young brother-in-law was first arrested for the Circle K jobs and locked up in the local jail, "they raped him." "I know he was sexually abused."

Schilling heard that Carlos then spent the duration of his time in the state pen as "what they call a punk. . . . I don't know how true it is, or what,"

FIGURE 6.3 Photograph of (*left to right*) Carlos Hernandez's youngest brother, Frankie; fifteen-year-old Margie Tapia; and twenty-four-year-old Carlos Hernandez. The picture was taken in the fall of 1978, ten months after Carlos was paroled from prison, six months into Margie's pregnancy, and seven months before Frankie was murdered.

continued Schilling, "but this is what I heard." The intake report at the time Carlos was first admitted to prison describes him as "weak" and says that he "may easily be taken advantage of by older and/or more aggressive inmates."

Clearly, prison made an impression on Hernandez. Two years into his parole, while in jail being interrogated about the murder of Dahlia Sauceda, he was taped on a jail phone pleading with Fidela to get him out of custody. At the trial of a man subsequently charged with the crime, Carlos was asked why he had been so upset during the call. The twenty-five-year-old admitted being on the verge of tears and begging his unsympathetic mother in Spanish to "remember what they did to me."

"I was referring to when I was in the penitentiary," Carlos explained. He said that he was "afraid to go back to the pen" and would "lie to the police" if necessary to stay out.

Judging from this rare window into a private moment of weakness, and from Hernandez's public behavior after leaving prison, he adopted three strategies for staying out of the penitentiary and avoiding what had happened to him there. Use a knife, not a gun. Never again leave any witnesses. Exploit every weakness of others, but don't expose your own.

•   •   •

Between his parole on the armed robbery convictions in 1978 and his final trip to prison in 1996, Carlos Hernandez was arrested about two dozen times. At no point was he ever found with a gun or bullets or charged with using them in a crime.

Over half the time, however—starting with his first postprison arrest in July 1978 for public drunkenness and a second in August 1978 for assaulting someone in a bar—Carlos was carrying a knife or had used one to commit the crime.

Typically the weapon was a "lock-blade buck knife." Asked at the Sauceda murder trial to explain how that kind of knife worked, Hernandez described a long blade lodged inside a wooden handle that automatically locks into a fixed-blade buck knife when it's opened. The reason he preferred it to a pocket knife, Carlos testified, was that it doesn't fold over and cut you when you use it to cut something else.

Carlos's arrests in July and August 1978 were typical in another way. Although his possession of a knife, use of alcohol, and commission of crimes

all violated his parole conditions, the parole board let him off with a reprimand and didn't send him back to prison. In October 1978, he was "continued on parole" again after police arrested him for "evading arrest."

The next time police arrested Carlos—in February 1979, for driving under the influence and disorderly conduct at the emergency room, following
the accident he caused—the police didn't even bother to report him to the
parole board. Instead they fined him and released him after he called Fidela
to bail him out.

*       &#8226;       &#8226;

Soon after making parole and returning to Corpus Christi, Hernandez surrounded himself with a circle of younger guys attracted by the power and
coiled rage he exuded—by the charisma of an ex-con who was expert with a
sharp knife and was not to be messed with.

Like others, Lina Zapata, a Carrizo Street neighbor and longtime friend
of Hernandez, used the Spanish word *pachuco* to describe him. A "gang-
ster type from the old school," she translated, someone who "carried knifes
[and] had to show everyone they were macho."

In late 1979, private investigator Eddie Cruz made it his business to get
inside Hernandez's gang on assignment from a criminal defense lawyer. Cruz
made a study of Hernandez. He was both attracted to and repelled by him.

Long afterward, he remembered Hernandez as "a leader-type person"
with a bunch of young guys and a lot of attractive girls around him. He
"knew he was good," Cruz said, and liked the spotlight. He knew he "could
go into the Casino Club and score any time [he] wanted to." He had the
"balls" to work the night shift in the toughest all-night bodega in town and
not show fear.

Hernandez built his style around his habits. He "loved to smoke," Cruz
remembered, and made a show of it, either Marlboros or "Winstons in
the red pack." He was constantly flipping open his knife, snapping it into
place. He carried a "chicano-type" bicycle chain—a *"pachuco"* thing, Cruz
explained. Carlos talked with his hands, making "all kinds of demanding
gestures."

The younger guys would be there with Carlos, Cruz recalled, "talking
until four, five in the morning," drinking beer, smoking marijuana. "Then
for some reason," Carlos would "give some kind of a signal, and they'd just
take off, just go."

Over time, Cruz found that Carlos "was really a mean guy"—someone you didn't want "to cross in any way." He was very violent. "The guy can just blow up and he'll come at you. Maybe not himself, but he'll put someone after you." If Hernandez told his guys he wanted somebody beat up, he'd just have to say, "go get this guy, he's a *cólero*," a crazy guy, "or he's putting the make" on one of Hernandez's girlfriends, and "the other guys would go out and [do it]."

Paula's good friend Gloria Licea was one of Hernandez's girlfriends at the time. Once, while she was seeing Carlos, she made the mistake of complaining about how badly her estranged husband had treated her. Not long afterward, a bunch of young guys stabbed her husband on the street, saying it was "to punish him for how bad he had treated" Gloria. Gloria suspected that Hernandez was behind it. When she later broke off relations with him, he threatened and stalked her.

Police detective Eddie Garza also kept an eye on Hernandez and the young guys around him. He, too, remembered that Hernandez would "have [his] people beat the crap out of [other] people. . . . They looked to him as a leader." The group "wasn't a gang, like today," Garza told investigators in 2004, but a "group that hung around with him."

They gathered at a bunch of places in the Hispanic neighborhoods in the old part of Corpus near downtown and the bay. Friday and Saturday nights, they'd be at the Casino Club on South Port where it intersected Marguerite Street. Other times, it would be a rough bar a mile south on Marguerite at Staples, or at Fidela's house on Carrizo Street a few blocks farther south, or else in nearby South Bluff Park. Or it might be Carlos's apartment in the Six Points area farther west along Staples, or at the nearby Maverick Market where he worked.

Garza recalled that during Hernandez's first years out of prison in 1978 and 1979, one of the teenagers around him was Carlos DeLuna, eight years his junior. Eddie Cruz also met DeLuna in Hernandez's orbit, as did several of Hernandez's neighbors. Margie Tapia and her sister Beatrice saw the two Carloses together as well.

It was in describing the connection between Hernandez and DeLuna that Garza called DeLuna a "follower" and drew a sharp contrast with Hernandez. Summarized in the investigators' notes from the 2004 interview with Garza, the former police detective elaborated on the differences between the two. Hernandez, the notes read, was a "bad ass. Terror of [the] neighborhood. Everyone was afraid of him." Carlos DeLuna was "a slow thinker." Garza "never knew [DeLuna] to be violent."

"If anyone was violent or mean," the retired police detective had said, "it was Carlos Hernandez. He would stare right through you." He was "cold." He had "no feelings." Carlos DeLuna, by contrast, "had feelings." He was a "follower, not [a] leader." "If Carlos Hernandez said 'take [the] rap for me,'" Garza continued, "Carlos DeLuna would."

.     .     .

One person who wasn't prepared to do Hernandez's bidding—and paid for it—was Freddy Schilling, the husband of Carlos's much-revered sister Paula (figure 6.4).

Freddy was handsome and often unfaithful to Paula. Sometime after Carlos returned from prison, Freddy started noticing Dahlia Sauceda at the Casino Club and at one point offered her a ride home. At first, they just talked about problems she was having with her husband and a boyfriend she was also seeing. But "one thing led to another, and before you know it," Schilling said, "me and her started doing things."

Soon Freddy was spending more time with Dahlia than with his wife and two sons, and Paula was angry. He told Dahlia that their relationship had to end, and she told him something that suddenly set her apart from the other women he messed around with: she had "a lot of money," Freddy said.

A couple of years before, a city truck had backed into her driveway to turn around in the cul de sac where she lived and had killed her baby playing there. "To be honest with you," Freddy says, "I don't know how much she got" in her settlement with the city. "All I know was I was able to spend it."

The settlement explained the customized "Happy Time" van that Dahlia drove around in, with detail and large windows on the outside and carpeting, soft chairs, and a sound system in the back.

Right after Dahlia told him about her money, Freddy recalled, the two were "driving down the road . . . right here on Staples" past a used-car lot. "I see this little '72 Mustang Mark One," and he and Dahlia stopped to admire it. Dahlia "said, 'You like that.' I said, 'Yeah.' . . . She says, 'Do you want it?' and I say, 'Who wouldn't?'" The following day, she went in with a cashier's check and bought the car for him.

Freddy and Dahlia ran off to Houston together. While there, Dahlia supported Freddy and gave him money to send to Paula and the kids in

FIGURE 6.4  Paula Hernandez Schilling; her husband, Freddy Schilling; and their two sons, Freddy and John Michael, circa 1983.

Corpus Christi. "I just kept living that life," Freddy recalled, "spending and having and enjoying it." Something like that "comes once in a lifetime," he said. "That's the way I looked at it at the time."

It wasn't too long, however, before Freddy returned to his family in Corpus Christi. His conscience got the better of him, he said. "My wife . . . was upset, worried, crying," he recalled. "She said she needed me. . . . My little kids were crying, too." Paula took him back.

Her brother Carlos, however—always aware that he'd taken another man out of Paula's life—was not so forgiving. Soon after returning from Houston, Freddy was relaxing in a chair at a friend's house when Carlos entered the room, walked directly toward him, and sucker-punched him in the face, knocking him off the chair.

Freddy bounced up, and the two wrestled their way into the kitchen, exchanging blows until Freddy lost his footing and slipped on the linoleum floor. While he was on the ground, Carlos grabbed a hot frying pan off the stove and began beating Freddy over the head with it. Freddy was on the verge of blacking out when Frankie Hernandez rushed in and broke up the fight. Freddy didn't see much of his former girlfriend after that.

•     •     •

Some months later, on the morning of November 20, 1979, a couple of boys came across a customized van parked in a vacant lot overrun with high weeds. The site—near the C. C. Egg Company, at the intersection of Mexico and Mussett Streets—was a third of a mile away from the rough bar where Carlos and his group hung out, and about the same distance to Fidela's house.

Thinking the eye-catching van might be stolen, the boys decided to check it out. In the back of the van they found a dead body. On a soft chair nearby lay a two-year-old baby girl, asleep. The boys covered the victim's nude body with a yellow blanket from the van and called the police.

The lead detective on the case was Olivia Escobedo. When she arrived at the scene, she identified the victim as Dahlia Sauceda. The back of the van was a wreck, junk strewn everywhere. In the mess were several cans of Schlitz beer. Semen collected from the victim revealed that Dahlia had recently had sex. What appeared to be her clothes were tossed to the side of the van. Near the body was a pair of men's plaid boxer shorts.

The medical examiner concluded that the cause of death was strangulation and blows to the victim's body, chest, and abdomen that broke three ribs on her left side, damaging her lung. She had bruises and scratches all over her face and body. There was a bite mark on her hip, and her left little toe was badly cut. Whoever had killed her had carved a large X on her back with a sharp knife.

# 7

# Acquittal

ON NOVEMBER 29, 1979, Corpus Christi police arrested nineteen-year-old Jesse Garza for the murder of Dahlia Sauceda.

· The police had an eyewitness who had seen Garza beat, rape, and murder the young woman. Pedro Olivarez told them that his friend Garza strangled Dahlia with her blue jeans before using a rusty kitchen knife that police found on the floor of the van to mark a large $X$ on her back.

Detectives also had a statement from Roger Fuentes, Garza's stepbrother and roommate. Fuentes said Garza wasn't home between 1:00 and 3:00 A.M. on the night of the killing. This matched Olivarez's claim that Sauceda had pulled up in her van around 1:30 A.M. and asked them to go "cruising" and that Garza killed her not long after that. Garza had no alibi.

Olivarez and Garza were friends from the Casino Club. The twenty-three-year-old Olivarez almost never missed a night there. Pudgy and cheerful, he was sort of the club mascot. He hung around with everyone but never really made it with any of the young women.

Garza was handsome and a flashy dancer and dresser. He got a lot of attention from the women.

·     ·     ·

If there was any good news for Jesse Garza following his arrest, it was that the court appointed an ambitious young criminal defense lawyer named Albert Peña to represent him. The case was a tough one, and its outcome helped to establish Peña's reputation as one of the top criminal defense lawyers in Corpus Christi.

Describing the challenges he faced to investigators looking into the case years later, Peña said that at first he felt his biggest problem was his client, who swore he had nothing to do with the crime. To show how adamant he was, the young Garza had even bloodied his knuckles punching out a cinderblock wall during an interrogation, insisting that he was innocent. Police had pictures of Garza's injured hands and the dents in the wall.

Garza's resolve complicated the usual endgame in a case like this, which was a deal for a guilty plea in return for a lesser charge like manslaughter. But as Peña reviewed the physical evidence from the crime scene, he started to think that his client might just be telling the truth.

To begin with, the size 34 plaid boxer shorts found in the van were too big for the 5 foot, 4 inch, 135-pound Garza. Someone else had undressed in the van. Although recognizing the risk, Peña decided to go all in on Garza's claim of innocence.

Peña's next problem was that an innocence investigation cost money for a private eye, and Garza didn't have any. But Jesse Garza was lucky again. His uncle Eddie Cruz worked as a fraud investigator for an insurance company and agreed to help out for free.

The name Carlos Hernandez came up early in the investigation. People who knew Dahlia Sauceda told Cruz and Peña that she and Hernandez had been sleeping together for months. It was even more complicated than that, however. Hernandez had a gripe with Dahlia. She'd dated his brother-in-law Freddy Schilling, luring him away to Houston, and Carlos was angry about the heartache this had caused his sister Paula.

The lead was promising. Although Peña didn't have proof that Hernandez killed Dahlia, he did have something against Hernandez that the police didn't have against Jesse Garza—a motive.

On Peña's orders, Cruz infiltrated Hernandez's circle of young acolytes and attractive women. Cruz already had an in: he moonlighted as an early-morning newspaper distributor, and Hernandez sometimes worked the graveyard shift at a Maverick Market store on one of Cruz's routes. Cruz occasionally shot the breeze with Hernandez and his young guys on the sidewalk in front of the market while Hernandez had a smoke.

Cruz learned where Hernandez and his group hung out and started showing up for a beer or a joint. They knew him as the newspaper guy and didn't think anything of it. In the meantime, Cruz reported what he learned to Peña.

●　　●　　●

Peña took his suspicions about Hernandez to the police. He spoke to Paul Rivera, a hard-charging detective who was helping on the case. Rivera already had doubts about the case against Garza. Detective Olivia Escobedo had asked him and his partner, Eddie Garza (no relation to Jesse), to take Olivarez out in a squad car to confirm the route that Dahlia's van had taken the night he saw Jesse kill her. Olivarez was clueless about where the van had gone.

After hearing from Peña, Rivera asked the department's fingerprint expert to compare Hernandez's prints on file with ones found in the van, which police hadn't yet matched to anyone. Sure enough, the print on a Schlitz can found in the back of Sauceda's van matched Hernandez's.

That same day, December 10, 1979, three weeks after the killing, Rivera arrested Hernandez on suspicion of murder and brought him in for questioning. At the time, Rivera found a locking buck knife with a blade several inches long in Carlos's pocket. While arresting Hernandez at his home, Rivera asked him for a pair of his undershorts. The plaid undershorts Carlos provided matched the pair in the van—same brand, color, and size.

Rivera didn't immediately tell Hernandez that they had matched his fingerprints to one found on a beer can in the back of the van. Nor did he mention the undershorts discovered in the van. Instead, Rivera asked Hernandez about his relationship to Dahlia Sauceda and where he was the night she was killed. In answer, Hernandez lied. He hadn't seen Sauceda in three months, he said, and was with a girl named Yolanda Rodriguez the whole night. Hernandez admitted these lies when he later testified at Jesse Garza's trial, explaining that he believed he had to mislead the police to keep from being sent back to prison.

Rivera brought in a technician to run a lie-detector test on Hernandez. The examination indicated deception on five questions: Do you know who killed Dahlia? Were you with Yolanda Rodriguez that night like you said? Did you kill Dahlia? Were you with Dahlia the night she died? Was your fingerprint in Dahlia's van? Carlos's story was so incoherent overall—he'd been smoking pot all day, he said—that the technician recommended another examination later on.

Rivera then confronted Hernandez with the truth. Police had his fingerprint on a Schlitz can from the van, and the plaid boxer shorts found there matched the pair Rivera had picked up at Hernandez's house. Carlos was lying when he said he hadn't seen Dahlia in months. He had been in the van that night, and everyone knew it.

Right away, Hernandez said that he wanted to make a phone call, which he did, speaking in Spanish, to his mother Fidela. The jail's tape-recording system caught Hernandez, on the verge of tears, begging Fidela to help get him out of jail. He reminded her of his fear of going back to prison and "what they did to me" the last time he was there.

When police recovered and translated the tape some weeks later, they also learned that Carlos admitted to Fidela that he'd been with Dahlia that night but said he was too drunk to remember what had happened. Ever the practical one, Fidela told her son to tell the police that he had been with Dahlia earlier. That's what he did.

When Rivera reinterviewed Hernandez later the same day, Carlos admitted to having sex with Dahlia in her van the night she was killed and leaving Schlitz cans and his undershorts behind. But he said he'd last seen her alive, hours before she was killed.

He'd run into Dahlia twice that night, Carlos told Rivera. Both times he'd gone to the 7-Eleven on Staples and Mary Streets near Fidela's house to buy some beer. The first was around 10:00 P.M. When he came out, Dahlia was sitting in her van with her baby and offered him a ride home. When he got in, they talked about having sex, and she made a detour to an alleyway behind the Old Apache Bar on Tancahua Street.

Carlos said they had sex in the back of the van for fifteen or twenty minutes, and then she drove him home. Not long afterward, he went back to the 7-Eleven for more beer, and there was Dahlia again, outside in the van with her baby. This time, she took him straight home. It was around midnight.

Rivera called in the polygraph technician again, and again Carlos's statements indicated deception on several questions: Do you know who killed Dahlia? Were you the person who killed Dahlia? Do you know Jesse Garza? (Hernandez said he didn't.) Did you kill Dahlia? Again, "evaluation of this subject's polygrams [was] professionally impossible due to the inconsistence of the responses."

Hernandez never explained why he left his undershorts in the van the first time or why he didn't retrieve them when he was in Dahlia's van a little later.

When the private investigators asked Fidela in 2004 about the Sauceda killing, she wouldn't say whether Carlos killed Dahlia, although she had repeatedly told friends that he did. Fidela did tell the investigators that Carlos came home that night about 4:30 A.M., long after he said Dahlia had dropped him off the second time.

. . .

The decision whether to charge Hernandez with the murder or stick with Garza lay with lead detective Olivia Escobedo and Assistant District Attorney Kenneth Botary. Escobedo knew that Hernandez's fingerprint had been found in the van, had seen reports from Detective Rivera and the polygraph technician on Hernandez's shifting statements, and had listened to the tape of Carlos's phone call to Fidela. But she never brought him in for questioning.

Botary knew that Garza's lawyer Peña would try to blame the crime on Hernandez and told Carlos to come in to talk. Carlos came in with a tape recorder and demanded to record the interview. Botary let him and made his own recording and transcript of the interview. There were references to the transcript at Garza's trial—Carlos apparently asked Botary during the interview if he could lie to the jury—but the full contents are unknown. Whatever Carlos said convinced the assistant D.A. to take Garza to trial and leave Hernandez out of it.

Escobedo's and Botary's unwillingness to change course didn't surprise Peña. Police and prosecutors don't like to admit mistakes, he said later. Besides, the story was getting a lot of press: a naked woman discovered raped and murdered in the back of her van, her two-year-old child nearby. People wanted quick action. Escobedo and Botary had no interest in looking indecisive or letting the investigation drag on.

Escobedo and Botary had already charged Garza, and they had a trump card that beat whatever Peña had on Carlos Hernandez—eyewitness Pedro Olivarez, Jesse Garza's friend, who said he had seen Jesse Garza kill Dahlia Sauceda (figures 7.1 and 7.2).

. . .

Unfortunately for Escobedo and Botary, Olivarez wasn't the witness they'd hoped for. Their short, overweight, slightly goofy-looking star witness had never finished high school and had trouble expressing himself in English. Some people said he was slow-witted.

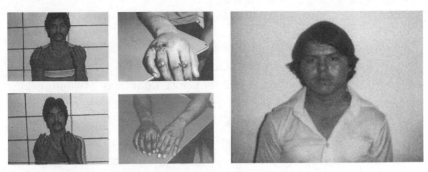

FIGURE 7.1 Police photographs of Jesse Garza's bruised hands after he punched the wall while being interrogated about the murder of Dahlia Sauceda (*left*) and Pedro Olivarez after his arrest for the murder (*right*).

FIGURE 7.2 Jesse Garza (*top left*) and Pedro Olivarez (*top right and middle left*) in happier times at the Casino Club; (*middle right and bottom*) Casino Club patrons in the late 1970s and early 1980s.

Initially, Olivarez told police that he didn't know who had killed Sauceda. Only after being interrogated by Sergeant Sidney Smith and being told he was a suspect himself did he say Garza did it. Smith was notorious among defense lawyers in town for his many methods of getting suspects to talk. They called him "the Reverend" because he once obtained a confession by posing as a minister and convincing the suspect to bare his soul.

Olivarez almost lost Botary's case before it even started. He walked up to defense lawyer Peña in a courthouse hallway the day trial was to begin and said that his father wanted him to tell the truth, that Garza didn't kill Dahlia. Peña took the frightened young man upstairs to repeat his claim to Botary and a court stenographer.

The prosecutor quickly cloistered Olivarez with Smith, and the master interrogator soon had Olivarez back to his story that Garza killed Sauceda.

Botary told the judge that the state was ready to present its case. But when Botary called Olivarez to testify, the young man was tongue-tied and struggled to get a story out. The judge brought in a Spanish translator to see if that would help.

Olivarez testified that Dahlia approached him and the handsome Garza outside the Casino Club and offered them a ride. After cruising around all night and into the next afternoon, with other people coming and going, Dahlia dropped Olivarez and Garza off at Garza's house.

As did other witnesses who testified about Dahlia's travels in the van that night, Pedro mentioned a sullen man with a mustache sitting in the front seat of the van who was hostile to Dahlia and everyone else. Dahlia told at least one person that she was scared to be left alone with the man.

Olivarez testified that early the next day, around 1:30 or 2:00 A.M., Dahlia returned to Garza's to get them. She let Garza drive, and he drove the van into a lot overgrown with brush.

According to Olivarez, Garza said he wanted "to rape [Dahlia] and all that crap." Olivarez said he didn't want to watch and left the van. He then watched Garza sexually assault, beat, and strangle the young woman to death using her own blue jeans. And he watched Garza carve an X on her back with the rusty steak knife from the van. Garza and Olivarez walked to the freeway and hitched a ride to Garza's place.

The medical examiner put the time of death between 1:00 and 3:00 A.M.

After Botary finished asking Olivarez questions, Albert Peña got his chance. He soon had the young man locked in a chain of confusions and contradictions.

Olivarez had testified that Garza parked the van head-in to a fence, but police photographs showed it parked parallel to the fence. He said they stopped for gas at the 7-Eleven on Staples and Mary, but that store had no gas pumps.

At first, Olivarez told the jury that there were Schlitz cans in the van, but later he swore there were none. He said he talked to his brother the night Dahlia was killed, and then admitted that was a lie. He said the group in the van had stopped at a bar for forty minutes to watch the entire first half of a *Monday Night Football* game, but that part of the game actually lasted twice as long. Shown a map, he couldn't mark the route the van took or any of the places it went.

      ●     ●     ●

After a day of testifying, with still more cross-examination left to go, Olivarez had had enough. He didn't show up in court the next morning. The judge sent the marshals to get him and demanded an explanation. Olivarez explained that he was afraid that someone "might beat me up or kick my ass or stab me or something" for testifying. The judge held him in contempt and sentenced him to thirty days in jail.

Back on the witness stand, Olivarez's confusion grew. He admitted that he had lied to police when he first said he didn't know anything about the killing.

Olivarez gave five or six different explanations for his flip-flop on the day the trial was about to start. He first said that, weeks earlier, he'd been beaten up at the Casino Club by some guy named "David and a couple of friends of somebody else." But Olivarez admitted that he had no idea whether Garza had sent the guys or whether the beating had to do with the case.

Olivarez said he had recanted his claim that Garza was the killer (only, then, to recant his recantation) to get Peña off his back. His testimony about this second explanation gives a flavor of how hard it was to understand what he was saying:

PEÑA: And you told [prosecutor Botary] that Jesse had not killed Dahlia?
OLIVAREZ: I didn't told him that.
PEÑA: You didn't say that?
OLIVAREZ: No.
PEÑA: Do you see that lady [pointing to the court stenographer, who had observed Olivarez tell Botary just before the trial was to start that Jesse hadn't killed Dahlia]?

OLIVAREZ: Yes, because I wanted to get rid of you because I didn't want nothing against you.

PEÑA: In other words you . . . lied to me?

OLIVAREZ: Yes.

Later Olivarez abandoned his initial reasons and offered others—at one point saying that he lied because he was mad at his girlfriend:

PEÑA: You were mad at your girlfriend. That's why you told me that Jesse had not killed Dahlia last Thursday?

OLIVAREZ: Yes, sir.

PEÑA: Is that why you also told the lady [the court stenographer] that Jesse had not killed Dahlia, because you were mad at your girlfriend?

OLIVAREZ: Yes, sir.

PEÑA: And you also told Kenneth Botary that Jesse had not killed Dahlia because you were mad at your girlfriend?

OLIVAREZ: Yes, sir.

Olivarez finally said he didn't know why he lied and had no idea what it meant to be under oath when you testify.

•     •     •

Prosecutor Botary next called Detective Olivia Escobedo to testify about the police investigation she'd been assigned to lead. Peña again used his cross-examination of the state's witness to undermine its case against Jesse Garza. The wily lawyer had gotten wind that the other detectives were going behind Escobedo's back, and he used the information to make her look foolish.

Escobedo admitted, for example, that when she decided to push the charges against Garza and let Hernandez off the hook, no one had told her that Hernandez had been arrested with a large lock-blade knife in his pocket and with boxer shorts matching those in the van.

"I don't feel that I was kept informed throughout the whole investigation," she told the jury, tearing down her own case.

Escobedo admitted that she never asked the state crime lab to test the undershorts in the van to see if they were stained with Dahlia's blood—an "oversight," she called it. She acknowledged paying little attention to Hernandez's jailhouse phone call to his mother when she listened to it.

"I guess I was hearing it, but was not listening," she explained, when asked how she missed the importance of Carlos's statement that he'd been with Dahlia that night, and of Fidela's advice to say he had been with Dahlia "earlier."

Things got even worse for Botary's case when he questioned Roger Fuentes, Garza's stepbrother and roommate, who had told police that Garza didn't come home the night Dahlia was killed. Surprising Botary, Fuentes testified to the jury that Garza *was* at home the night Dahlia was killed. Fuentes had said something different to the police, he explained, only after four intimidating interrogators had made him think he had to say something or he'd be charged with the crime himself.

Prosecutors don't usually call a witness to give the defendant an alibi, but that is exactly what Botary did, based on the investigation Escobedo led.

.    .    .

Peña wasn't content, however, simply to poke holes in the state's case. He wanted the jury to know exactly who committed the crime that the state was trying to pin on his client. The only sure way to free his innocent client, he believed, was to "prosecute" Carlos Hernandez.

The defense lawyer began with the best evidence the police themselves had of who was with Dahlia in the back of her van before her bloodied and naked body was found.

Through a police expert, Peña showed that Hernandez's fingerprint was on a Schlitz can in the back of the van. Through other witnesses, he showed that the pair of distinctive red plaid boxer shorts found near the victim's body didn't match the style or size of underwear worn by Jesse Garza but were the same as boxers found at Carlos's house when Detective Rivera arrested him on suspicion of killing Dahlia.

Peña also homed in on the weapon the killer used.

After casting doubt on Olivarez's testimony that a dull, rusty steak knife, without any blood or flesh on it, was the source of the precise $X$ carved into Dahlia's back and the mutilation of her toe, Peña repeatedly reminded the jury of the large lock-blade knife found on Carlos Hernandez. Several witnesses, including Hernandez's own mother, confirmed his fondness for buck knives and his expertise in their use.

Dr. Joseph Rupp, the medical examiner Botary called to testify about the cause of death, helped Peña establish a motive. Based on Rupp's lengthy experience with homicide cases, he believed that the single $X$ carved into

Dahlia's back was not the random act of a "casual pickup," such as Garza, but of someone who knew the victim, had a "sadistic" intention, and wanted to send a message.

The $X$ "has a meaning," Rupp testified. "The exact meaning, I'm not sure of, but . . . this was just not a random thing. This was a mark on her to show [her] something or him something or someone else something."

Peña then called Freddy and Paula Schilling to testify about Freddy's affair with Dahlia, how badly it tore up Paula, and Carlos's angry reaction to his brother-in-law's desertion of his sister and Dahlia's disrespect for her. Freddy testified that Carlos was constantly violent toward him, saying, "I did this to his sister and that he is going to do this to me and do that." It wasn't just running off to Houston with Dahlia, Freddy said, but "because I mess around . . . generally" with a lot of women.

That, Peña suggested to the jury, was the meaning of the $X$. It was a message to Freddy and his girlfriends about what happens to people who make trouble for Carlos Hernandez's sister.

Freddy then revealed another way that he believed his brother-in-law had nearly taken him down. Everyone in the neighborhood knew about Freddy's affair with Dahlia and about her confrontations with Paula outside the Schilling home. The last of those had occurred just two days before Dahlia was killed, when Dahlia called Paula a bitch, and Freddy warned her that he "was going to knock the hell out of her if she came around" again.

Freddy was the first person arrested by the Corpus Christi police on suspicion of killing Dahlia. Without an ironclad alibi from the boss at his night job and a clean bill of health from a lie-detector test, Schilling himself might have been in the dock at that trial. Years later, Paula's illegitimate daughter Pricilla, who lived at Fidela's house with Carlos, recalled an angry fight in which Freddy accused Carlos of setting him up to take the blame for Dahlia's death.

●     ●     ●

The best witness for Peña's defense, however, was Carlos Hernandez himself.

Peña began his examination by asking Hernandez to repeat to the jury his last story to the police: that he had had sex with Dahlia in the van earlier that night but last saw her when she left him off at Fidela's house, hours before she was murdered.

Ruthlessly, then, Peña took Hernandez's story apart, making sure everyone in the courtroom knew how much he enjoyed showing Carlos up.

Peña repeatedly asked Carlos why he lied to Detective Rivera about not seeing Dahlia for months and came clean only when confronted with his fingerprint on the beer can and his shorts in the back of the van. Peña repeatedly answered his own question, accusing Carlos of murdering Dahlia.

When Hernandez wavered in explaining why he lied—he didn't want to get involved; he was afraid of having his parole revoked for drinking with Dahlia and carrying a knife; he was afraid of going back to prison where he'd been brutalized; he couldn't think of anything else to say—Peña demanded that he pick his favorite excuse.

When Hernandez did—claiming he'd forgotten about the sexual encounter until his fingerprint and undershorts reminded him—Peña pressed him on how, then, he was able to recall in such detail what "really" happened. Carlos, for example, pinpointed the time he left the 7-Eleven and ran into Dahlia the first time as 10:40 P.M. Where, Peña asked, did that certainty come from, after not remembering the incident at all?

Hernandez answered that the details came flooding back after he'd reflected on them overnight. Peña pointed out that Hernandez gave Rivera both statements within hours on the *same* day. Indeed, according to police records and Detective Rivera's testimony, only two events occurred between the contradictory statements: Hernandez more or less flunked a polygraph test, and he was coached by Fidela on the phone to say he'd been with Dahlia "earlier" than when she was killed.

Armed with that last bit of information, Peña then accused Carlos of crying to his mother for help in fabricating a story. The best Carlos could come up with in response was that Fidela hadn't really helped because she'd meant "earlier" in the year, not earlier that night.

Peña also repeatedly used Hernandez's habits and pride against him. The lawyer demonstrated Carlos's facility with knives by using him as an expert to explain how a buck knife is different from a pocket knife (it has only one, longer blade, which locks) and why he preferred buck knives over others (less chance of cutting himself).

Radiating contempt, Peña mocked Hernandez for his low scores on the pinball machine at the 7-Eleven, for watching cartoons (part of Carlos's alibi on the night of the crime), and for twice running out of the van without his underwear.

When Hernandez struggled with a question, Peña asked him if he wanted to consult his mother before answering. When Hernandez couldn't suppress a smile, the lawyer pressed him about what was funny at a murder trial. The lawyer got the witness to mark on a map where the van with Dahlia's body was left and where Carlos and his mother lived a few blocks away, and then made an aside about how well Carlos drew *X*s.

"I got him real angry," Peña said later. Carlos's "hot temper . . . played right into my hands."

.    .    .

The jury found Jesse Garza not guilty of killing Dahlia Sauceda. After the trial, some of the jurors approached Peña and asked him why Hernandez hadn't been charged in place of Garza. Having wondered that himself, Peña gave his opinion: Botary and Escobedo, he told the jurors, "had already narrowed in on one guy, and they were not going to go off that road, come hell or high water." That's "the nature of the beast," Peña explained. Law enforcement "will not admit that they're wrong, especially when they already had a person in custody."

.    .    .

Peña won his case without playing every card he had. He didn't call Gloria Licea to testify.

Licea was Carlos's former girlfriend and a close friend of Paula's. At one point after Dahlia was killed, Paula walked out on Freddy and moved in with Gloria. Carlos was often at Gloria's house wanting to talk to his sister. Gloria overheard their conversations, and Paula confirmed what Carlos had said—"they were never going to be able to prove it, but he had been the one that killed [Dahlia]."

Paula wouldn't give the information to Peña's investigator when he came by to interview her, so Gloria went to Peña herself. The lawyer sent her to the police, who recorded her statement but never followed up.

Out of concern for Gloria's safety and that of her young daughters, Peña decided to leave her out of the trial. Gloria had reason to be afraid. She believed that Carlos had gotten some of his guys to stab her estranged husband with an ice pick as payback for treating her badly, and she knew that Carlos had stalked her after she broke up with him. She didn't want to think about what he would do to her or her daughters if she testified against him.

•   •   •

In 1986, six years after Jesse Garza was acquitted, police arrested Carlos Hernandez for the murder of Dahlia Sauceda. The case had gone unsolved, and the arrest was big news. The *Corpus Christi Caller-Times* printed a picture of Detectives Paul Rivera and Eddie Garza taking Carlos into custody.

Years later, Fidela gave investigators a copy of the *Caller-Times* photograph from her scrapbook where she kept it as a memento of her son Carlos. Someone had drawn an *X* across Paul Rivera's face (figure 7.3).

•   •   •

Another of Hernandez's girlfriends gave Rivera and Garza the evidence they needed for the arrest. Diana Gomez was in a relationship with Carlos during her wild years in the mid-1980s. At the time, she lived mainly on the

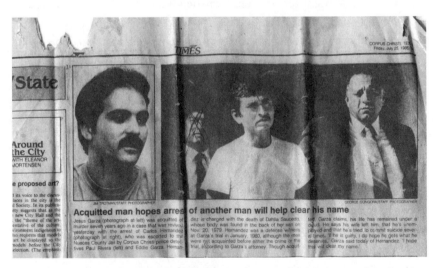

FIGURE 7.3 The *Corpus Christi Caller-Times* photograph of the arrest of Carlos Hernandez in July 1986 for the murder of Dahlia Sauceda. At left is Jesse Garza, who had been acquitted of the crime. The arresting officers are Detectives Paul Rivera (with an *X* drawn on his face) and Eddie Garza.

beach, donating plasma at the blood bank and collecting aluminum cans for money. She needed a place to stay and found one with Carlos.

Almost twenty years later, sitting in her tidy home on the north side of Corpus where she ran a quilt-making business, Gomez told investigators that it hadn't taken her long to see there was little future—maybe none at all—with Carlos.

Early on, she'd noticed the same two Carlos Hernandezes others had observed. One was sober, attractive, and able to support himself; the other was drunk and dangerous. When Carlos drank, she recalled, his forehead would "crinkle," his eyes would get bloodshot, and she knew she'd better look out. One time, they got into an argument when she wanted to stay outside and drink some more and he wanted her to come inside with him to go to sleep. He pushed her down hard, hurting her. Then he locked her out of the house, while her baby was still inside.

At that moment, she knew that she'd have to move on soon, and it didn't take long for Carlos to give her even more reason to do it.

·    ·    ·

Carlos often had night terrors that disturbed his sleep. He never wanted to talk about it with Diana, until one night he did.

Hernandez, she recalled, was tossing and turning in bed, sweating badly. She wanted to help, asking, "What's going on, what's going on, Carlos?" Carlos surprised her by answering.

He started out slowly, saying that "he had done something wrong, something bad." Little by little, he told Diana what he had done and why. "And it was very scary for me," she said, "very scary for me, what he did." Her hope that he'd finally let her comfort him gave way to horror.

Carlos said he had murdered a girl inside a van. Her name was Dahlia. "And he told me, detail by detail . . . how he went about it": "how he came about to get her alone, in her van, how he had had sex with her and choked her, choked her until . . . he said he saw her eyes roll back. He flipped her over and cut a cross from shoulder blade to buttock. A cross, like that, he told me that."

The woman's baby girl was there in the van with them, Carlos told her. Diana remembered shaking. "This can't be right, he's having a bad dream." But then Carlos offered terrifying proof.

He cut off Dahlia's toe, he told Diana, "for a, like, souvenir's sake. He asked me if I wanted to see it." No, Diana told Carlos in tears. She didn't want to see that.

·    ·    ·

Carlos told Diana why he did it, too. His sister's husband, Freddy, was "messing around with that girl." By killing Dahlia, he stopped her from "causing problems on the marriage of his sister." Diana remembers Carlos saying that he carved an *F* where the lines of the *X* crossed.

Although Diana said she didn't want to hear more, Carlos couldn't stop himself now that he'd gotten going—and besides, he was proud of his work. He told her that he had killed Dahlia and meant to, but he also made sure he wouldn't get caught. He described how he used his undershorts to clean out the van—"fingerprints, steering wheel, lights, everything." He even cleaned Dahlia's fingernails, where she'd fought him.

He left the van next to some bushes near the C. C. Egg Company off Mexico Street and ran home. It was near dawn. His only mistake, he told Diana, was leaving his shorts behind.

Lucky for Carlos, Olivia Escobedo—by "oversight"—never asked the crime lab to check the shorts for evidence of foul play. Carlos was good. He was crafty and sly. But he was also lucky.

One thing fixed in Diana's mind. "That little girl?" she asked Carlos. Carlos replied that the baby was asleep when he ran away. "He just . . . left them like that," Diana fretted, just "left them like that." Diana's own baby was asleep in the next room.

·    ·    ·

Soon afterward, Diana left Hernandez. Whatever Dahlia had done to his sister, Carlos had done something worse. "That wasn't right to do," she recalled thinking. "I mean, how can you take a human being like that and— nobody's got that call."

Back on her own, Diana struggled to keep the information to herself. Eventually, she contacted Detective Paul Rivera, a friend of her family's. What Rivera and his partner, Eddie Garza, told her after she recounted what she knew surprised her—made her shake again, as she did twenty years later when she described the events once more.

"It was all true," the detectives assured her. Carlos hadn't made it up. "They'd been hunting him for a while." They had just needed more proof to catch him. Now they had it. Rivera and Garza took Diana's statement in April 1986. That was the last she heard from either of them. Until the private investigators came by her tidy home eighteen years later, no one else had expressed interest in what Carlos Hernandez had told her.

.    .    .

Rivera and Garza didn't sit by, however. They tracked down the old police files on the killing and assembled a case against Carlos Hernandez for the district attorney. The report lays everything out:

- Hernandez's fingerprints on a Schlitz can in the van
- The size 34 red plaid undershorts Rivera picked up at Hernandez's home shortly after the killing that matched the pair found near the victim's body
- The buck knife Rivera found in Hernandez's possession at the same time
- The semen in the victim, which Hernandez admitted was his
- Hernandez's initial lie about not having seen Dahlia for months and spending the night she died with another woman
- His phone admission to his mother that he had been with Dahlia that night, and her advice to say—as he then did—that he'd been with Dahlia earlier that night
- His confession to Diana Gomez, tightly tracking the known facts of the crime
- The explanation for the mutilated toe—a detail never mentioned in the newspaper, which only an insider to the crime would know

In July 1986, six and a half years after the death of Dahlia Sauceda in the back of her "Happy Time" van, the district attorney indicted Carlos Hernandez for murder. Paul Rivera and Eddie Garza arrested him. They had their best game faces on when they performed the perp walk for the press. They looked like they were sure they had their man.

His forehead visibly crinkled in the news photo, Carlos Hernandez looked like he just might agree. But that was before Assistant District Attorney Kenneth Botary unwittingly teamed up with defense lawyer Jon Kelly to change Carlos's luck yet again.

．　　．　　．

Sitting in jail for months waiting for something to happen, Hernandez became increasingly anxious. Things had gone badly for him the last time he'd spent more than a few days in the county lock-up. And going from there to the state pen had been even worse.

Bail was set at $25,000, far more than Carlos could afford or Fidela would risk on the promise that her least favorite son would show up in court when he was supposed to.

The lawyer assigned by the judge to represent Carlos didn't do much work on the case. When the court finally set a trial date in September 1986, the attorney asked for a delay.

Carlos knew well enough from past experience what would come next: an offer to plead guilty in return for a few years off the usual life sentence for murder. And he knew that the years he still owed the state on the car theft and armed robberies would be tacked on, because parole would surely be revoked.

From the drubbing he took and the end result at Jesse Garza's trial, he also understood the difference a good lawyer like Albert Peña could make. When nothing had happened by November, Carlos sent the judge—Jack Blackmun—a handwritten complaint stating that his lawyer had come to see him only three times since July, listing all the requests he made of the lawyer, without results, and demanding that the judge appoint "a proper counsel."

Luckily for Carlos, he got one. In mid-November 1986, a few days shy of the seventh anniversary of Dahlia Sauceda's death, Judge Blackmun appointed Jon Kelly to represent Carlos Hernandez.

As Kelly told the investigators who came around years later asking about Carlos Hernandez, he wasn't one of those criminal defense lawyers who wants his client to tell him everything. He could learn all he needed to know about the bad things they'd done from cops and witnesses. The less he knew from his clients, he said, the more aggressively he could represent them.

Kelly scrupulously followed this rule with Carlos Hernandez. One of the most active defense lawyers in town, Kelly was fully aware of Hernandez's reputation as an "extremely violent . . . extremely dangerous person." He'd heard the cops talk about the knives, drunken rages, and violent crimes, especially against women. When the judge appointed him to represent Carlos, people in the courthouse warned him to be careful. They said that Hernandez had committed other killings and bragged about it, and he didn't doubt all that was true. But when Carlos tried to confess his crimes to Kelly, whether in a law office or a more public place, the lawyer always cut him off.

Kelly also experienced the man close up. He described Hernandez to investigators years later: "Relatively thick Hispanic accent. Could be somewhat charming. Extremely violent temper. I'm sure you've heard that. Ungovernable temper after consumption of large amount of alcohol."

"He would drink to excess and make mistakes," Kelly continued. "I imagine he could be violent, merciless. People gave him a wide berth."

He had good qualities, too, the lawyer said. When he wanted to be, and was sober, he was a good worker. "For a street thug, he was very dependable."

Overall, the defense lawyer concluded, Hernandez "was not that bad. He took a bath before court and kept his mouth shut, just like a lawyer would ask."

In any event, Kelly knew what the police claimed Hernandez had done to Dahlia Sauceda. The last thing he needed was to hear more details from Carlos. Instead, Kelly began filing papers demanding that the prosecutors give him all their evidence in the case, from Escobedo and Botary's indictment of Jesse Garza years before to everything gathered by Rivera and Garza in 1986.

After reading the transcript of the earlier trial, Kelly was particularly interested in two pieces of evidence: the tape recording of Carlos's conversation with his mother from the police station, and the transcript of Carlos's conversation with Botary that had convinced the prosecutor to go to trial against Jesse Garza and let Carlos Hernandez alone.

•     •     •

On New Year's Eve 1986, Judge Blackmun dismissed the case against Carlos Hernandez. Too much time had passed, Blackmun concluded, and the prosecutors had not come up with the evidence that Kelly needed to prepare an effective defense.

. The tape-recorded conversation with Fidela and the transcript of Carlos's conversation with Botary were essential pieces of evidence in the case, and the D.A.'s office never produced either one.

Hernandez's release was big news. Local newspapers and television stations covered it. The case was notorious, and Carlos had been waiting for a trial to happen for a long time, with no action. Asked by the press to explain his victory, Kelly explained, "It's Christmas."

Hernandez got lucky. Although they had him dead to rights with his fingerprint, boxer shorts, semen, lies, and confession, it turned out that Kenneth Botary had taken custody of the tape and transcript and somehow lost both. Carlos Hernandez was a free man. No one would ever be punished for murdering Dahlia Sauceda and carving an *X* on her back.

      &bull;    &bull;    &bull;

Carlos knew a good thing when he had it, and he stuck by Jon Kelly, doing odd jobs and putting up signs for the lawyer when he ran for office. When Kelly needed someone to persuade a recalcitrant witness to come forward, Carlos had a talent for getting it done. Carlos could be "convincing," Kelly said with a chuckle.

Once, when Kelly was involved in a highly political prosecution involving the city council, someone broke into his house. Carlos said the cops wouldn't be able to do anything and offered to find the guy himself and take care of it. Kelly had a pretty good idea of what Carlos meant. He took the offer as a gesture of respect but turned it down.

Kelly returned the favors—representing Carlos in his continuing run-ins with the law and getting Fidela a protective order to stop her son Javier from beating her.

Hernandez and Kelly became close. They drank beer and smoked pot together, frequenting some notorious local cantinas. Something about the way Carlos carried himself, and the way others feared and respected him, appealed to the lawyer. Through all of it, though, Kelly stuck by his rule. Whenever Carlos started to talk about the bad things he'd done, the attorney would shut him down. There were some things, Kelly said later, he didn't want to know.

      &bull;    &bull;    &bull;

Others, however, couldn't stop Hernandez from telling them what he knew. He told both the son of his mother's friend and the son of a girlfriend that he had killed Dahlia—providing details in the latter case. His niece Pricilla heard Carlos talk about hurting a woman in a van. There was a little girl there, too. Pricilla would run inside her grandmother's house when she heard Carlos say things like that.

When Carlos fought Freddy Schilling, he would threaten "to kill you just like I killed that bitch of yours." Freddy also heard from Paula that Carlos had confessed to killing Dahlia. Paula told Rita Hull the same thing as she was dying of cancer: "Carlos felt guilty for killing Louis in the car accident and was trying to make it up to Paula by killing Dahlia." Paula even told her teenage son that his uncle Carlos had carved an $X$ on a woman's back.

Dina Ybañez got the worst of it, however. She was Hernandez's neighbor in the years after Kelly sprung him. There were things that Carlos was proud of, she told investigators—things he thought defined him as a man. One was his ability to kill and get away with it.

Dahlia Sauceda was his first victim, Hernandez told Dina. He'd killed her in the back of a van, in front of her baby girl. He almost killed the baby as well but didn't. There was another woman, too, he said. And Dina just missed being killed herself.

.    .    .

Still, there is the question of Pedro Olivarez, who claimed to have seen Jesse Garza kill Dahlia Sauceda.

Almost twenty-five years after Dahlia's murder, Olivarez agreed to set the record straight—urged on, again, by his elderly father. Initially, however, Pedro refused to discuss the matter. He changed his mind only after being told that Carlos Hernandez was dead, and then only after being shown the man's death certificate.

Olivarez admitted to the investigator what twelve jurors in Jesse Garza's case had long since figured out: he'd made up the story about Garza killing Dahlia. Dahlia had, in fact, picked up Garza and Olivarez outside the Casino Club and invited them to go cruising with her and some others. And there was, in fact, a brooding mustachioed man with Dahlia—the man Olivarez and everyone one else in the van knew, but were afraid to say, was Carlos Hernandez.

When Garza and Olivarez climbed into the back, Hernandez occupied what in Dahlia's "Happy Time" world counted as the place of honor: the front passenger seat next to her. But Dahlia had her eye on flashy Jesse Garza, and she made Carlos move to the rear, so Jesse could sit next to her.

Carlos was pissed. His fury at Dahlia for messing with his sister hadn't kept him from carrying on a relationship with her for months, and Carlos didn't like it a bit when Dahlia displaced him in favor of the handsome Garza.

As they all drove around for hours drinking beer and smoking pot, and as Dahlia and Jesse grew more intimate in the front seat, Carlos grew increasingly enraged in the back. Finally, he challenged Jesse to fight.

Hernandez had a reputation, and Jesse and Pedro decided that they'd better get out of there. They made Dahlia drop them off in downtown Corpus Christi. Before they left the van, however, Carlos told Pedro that he was going to hurt Dahlia, and that if Pedro ever said anything to anyone, he would kill him and his family. Until he saw Carlos's death certificate, Pedro never did tell anyone besides his mother and father.

The next day, Pedro heard that Dahlia had been beaten to death and carved up with a knife. While not the sharpest person around, Pedro knew that Carlos Hernandez had killed Dahlia.

A few weeks later, three young men jumped Pedro outside the Casino Club. They told him the beating was from Carlos Hernandez. If Pedro said anything, they'd finish him off and go after his family.

Pedro wouldn't risk it, not coming from Carlos Hernandez. The beating that Olivarez suffered wasn't his only exposure to Hernandez's violent side. On another occasion, Carlos had forcibly sodomized Pedro. He had no interest in ending up like Dahlia on the other side of Carlos's knife.

So when Sidney "the Reverend" Smith interrogated him and told him that they were about to charge Pedro himself, along with Jesse Garza, for murdering Dahlia, Pedro pointed the finger at Jesse. He knew that Jesse hadn't killed Dahlia Sauceda. He knew that Hernandez had killed her, just as he said he would. But he also knew that Hernandez would kill him if he ever talked. Until he was sure that Hernandez was dead, Olivarez wouldn't say a word against his brutal tormentor.

# 8

# Confession

PRICILLA HERNANDEZ GREW UP at her grandmother Fidela Hernandez's house on Carrizo Street. For Pricilla, the street was a sinister backwater cut off from the rest of the world.

Carrizo Street is only two blocks long, in the heart of the Corpus Christi barrio. It starts at Blucher Street on the north, passes Kinney Street, and dead-ends at a weedy embankment just before Laredo Street on the south. Because the street jogs at Kinney, the dead-end block where Pricilla lived is cut off from even the other block with the same street name.

Fidela's house was at the very end of the cul-de-sac, farthest from the outlet on Kinney, on the west side of the street. Like the other structures on the block, it was a ramshackle, wood-frame affair. But it sat apart from the others up a little hill from the street.

The Tapias' and other dwellings across the street backed onto an empty lot abutting Blucher Park, across Kinney Street. The neighbors called the lot "the park," but it was just an open space, strewn with litter and shaded by a few trees. People hung out there, drank, and used drugs. There wasn't much else to do on Carrizo Street.

. . .

Pricilla was Paula Hernandez's first child, conceived out of wedlock. Soon after leaving the hospital following the car wreck in which her brother Carlos killed her fiancé, seventeen-year-old Paula had slept with Beto Vela. Beto was a force at the Casino Club, known for his one-night stands with many of the young women there. He was in his first of several marriages at the time.

Paula was ashamed of her illegitimate daughter. When she married Freddy Schilling, she wanted a fresh start, so she left Pricilla behind on Carrizo Street with Fidela and her three uncles: Carlos, Javier, and Frankie. Pricilla lived there until she was thirteen, when she walked out.

.    .    .

Life was hard for the young girls on Carrizo Street. When Margie Tapia was only fifteen, her mother arranged for her to move in with Pricilla's uncle Carlos, even though he was a lot older and not the father of her child. As Margie and Carlos turned the tiny Hernandez living room into a bedroom, Pricilla couldn't help but notice that Carlos's new "wife" wasn't much older than Pricilla herself or her playmate Beatrice Tapia, Margie's sister. Then there was the pregnant twelve-year-old down the street who was forced by her mother to have sex with men to raise money for an abortion. The problem went away, however, when the girl miscarried while playing basketball.

Years later, Pricilla told the private investigators that she couldn't wait to leave Carrizo Street and, especially, to put behind her the things that happened at Fidela's house. Asked why, she answered through tears: "A lot of violence. A lot of hurt." Carlos and her other uncle Javier would fight, knives would come out, and soon someone was bleeding. There was "always blood" at Fidela's house. One time, Pricilla saw Carlos stab Javier in the shoulder. Lucky for Javier, he was wearing a coat, or it would have been worse.

One of the most vicious fights Pricilla remembers was between Carlos and her stepfather, Freddy Schilling. Carlos was arguing with Freddy about a woman named Dahlia. The fight ended in a stabbing, and an ambulance came. Freddy wasn't a violent man, Pricilla said. Unlike Carlos, Freddy didn't carry knives.

.    .    .

As far as Pricilla was concerned, however, it wasn't her uncles but her grandmother Fidela who caused most of the trouble in the family. "A witch," Pricilla called her, who never showed love to anyone. No hugs. No kisses. None of the normal things a grandmother does.

Thanks also to Fidela, Pricilla's home was permeated with sex. It was "ugly" and "dirty," and it was constant. Everyone in the neighborhood knew that Fidela had men in and out of her home for money. When he was a kid, Javier told neighbors he watched his mother having sex with one of them. She didn't hide it.

Fidela's appetite was also directed at her granddaughter. She made Pricilla take showers in front of her, as she previously had done to Pricilla's mother, Paula. Sometimes Fidela forced Pricilla to sleep in a bed with her and her uncle Carlos.

Worst of all, in the Hernandez household, sex and violence went hand in hand.

When Pricilla was nine, Carlos started molesting her—exposing himself at first, then forcing her to perform oral sex, then worse. He raped her repeatedly until she was a teenager and left the house.

Nobody did anything to stop it. Carlos told her not to tell anyone, because no one would believe it. Once, Javier walked in on Carlos unzipping his pants in front of Pricilla. After a fight with Carlos, Javier told his niece that he would protect her, but he never did. When Pricilla told her mother what was happening, Paula just cried. When Pricilla told Fidela, she called Pricilla a liar and told her granddaughter to keep her mouth shut. The best Pricilla could do was to stay around other people and avoid being alone with her uncle.

Carlos was "sick," she told the investigators, and did nothing but harm her and everyone else.

·     ·     ·

Carlos molested other children. His younger brother, Frankie, told neighbors that Carlos raped him all the time. When he went to Fidela for help, she told him to "fight like a man."

The abuse reached outside the family as well. Pricilla heard from one of Carlos's lady friends that he molested a little girl on Seventh Street. He was twice caught molesting another girlfriend's five-year-old niece but was never reported. Carlos tried to rape the daughter of a next-door neighbor who was at Fidela's house playing with Pricilla. He pulled her behind the house, but she was able to kick him and get free. She ran home and told her mother, but no one called the police. Just six months before the private investigators came to Marcella Brown's house to ask about Carlos, a friend from years before, she learned from her adult son that Carlos had molested him in the 1980s.

That's how Carlos was, Pricilla said. "He thought he was untouchable." He didn't think the rules applied to him. He scared people and got away with things. Carlos was arrested for many crimes in his day—armed robbery, grand theft, dealing heroin, assault with a deadly weapon, attempted burglary, murder, and attempted murder—but he almost never went to prison for them. When he committed crimes in the neighborhood, no one ever turned him in, not even for abusing their own children.

For Freddy Schilling, it was Carlos's brazen abuse of his own niece Pricilla and other young girls that summed up his brother-in-law best. Carlos Hernandez, Freddy said, was

> no good, man. The dude was no good, no good. And it wasn't just my daughter [Pricilla], believe me, because I've seen him. He used to hang around this laundry right there on Park and Staples. . . . It used to be kind of the hangout for the neighborhood there. And he would constantly hang out there [and] try to make passes at . . . girls 13, 14 years old. He was always trying to get them. In fact, some of them were my daughter's friends. My daughter could tell you that, that Carlos tried to put his hands on them. The dude was sick, man. He was throwed off, he was throwed off, believe me. [H]e used to scare the shit out of me.

.    .    .

It wasn't just the abuse that made Pricilla decide to run away, however. There was something else.

She was eleven or twelve at the time, around 1983. Carlos and Javier were sitting outside on the porch, talking and drinking beer. She and a friend were playing on the grass near steps that ran down the slope from the porch to the street (figure 8.1).

Carlos was playing with his buck knife and bragging about it to Javier. He said he'd hurt someone with a knife, stabbed her. Her name was Wanda, he said, and Javier knew her.

"Nah, you didn't do that," Javier said. "Yes," Carlos said, he did. But he didn't think anyone would find out.

.    .    .

In 2004, investigators also visited Beatrice Tapia, Margie's younger sister, asking about their former neighbor Carlos Hernandez. Bea hadn't seen her childhood friend Pricilla Hernandez in years, but she remembered the same terrifying conversation that Pricilla had overheard.

The two girls were on the steps going up to the Hernandez porch talking to each other and listening to Carlos and Javier, who were drinking beer on

FIGURE 8.1 The Hernandez house on South Carrizo Street where it dead-ends near Laredo Street: (*top*) steps up from Carrizo Street, where Pricilla Hernandez and Beatrice Tapia were sitting when they heard Carlos and Javier Hernandez talking on the porch; (*bottom*) the porch.

the porch. Bea heard Carlos tell his brother that he had done something wrong, and he mentioned the name Wanda. He said he'd hurt her—he'd killed her—and he felt sorry about it.

Carlos's admission scared Bea. Like Javier, she knew who Wanda was. She remembered Carlos talking about a woman by that name who worked at a gas station near Wolfy's. Carlos seemed to be sweet on this Wanda and talked about going over to the station to see her.

Later Bea got really scared when she heard on television that a woman named Wanda Lopez had been stabbed to death at the Sigmor Shamrock on SPID.

After Carlos had said what he'd done to the woman, Bea looked at Pricilla, who put her finger to her lips. Bea kept the secret until investigators came around twenty years later, after Carlos Hernandez had died in prison. Until then, no one had ever asked questions about Carlos Hernandez and Wanda Lopez.

·     ·     ·

Bea and Margie's mother, Janie Adrian, had her own memories of Carlos around the time of the killing at the Sigmor Shamrock. Those days, she was friendly with Fidela. They went out drinking and dancing together.

Janie told the investigators that she remembered Carlos Hernandez coming to her house one night looking for Margie. The two had broken up years before, and although Carlos still came by to see Margie's son Eric, this was different. He said he really had to talk to Margie.

Carlos pulled up in a car and honked for Janie to come over.* He didn't get out of the car but opened the door and hung halfway out of it. He was nervous and agitated. Janie told him that Margie wasn't there, and he left.

Janie recalled Carlos coming by not long before she heard on the news that Wanda Lopez had been stabbed at the Shamrock station. At the time, she didn't think much about Carlos's anxious visit. That changed, however, when she overheard Carlos talking in the "park" behind her small

---

*Carlos Hernandez only rarely had regular access to a car. One period when he did, however, was in 1983, when he commandeered Rosa Anzaldua's 1975 Mercury. Anzaldua and Hernandez were married in 1982. In November 1983, after Hernandez attacked her and her children with a baseball bat, Rosa sued for a divorce and also asked for an order of protection and an order requiring Hernandez to return her Mercury. In early 1984, the court granted all three requests.

apartment. The guys who hung out there often gabbed loudly enough for her to hear, and Janie didn't mind keeping track of the goings on.

Worried to this day that she's in trouble for not telling the police—and angry at Carlos for breaking the neighborhood code by saying things he should have kept to himself—Janie haltingly told the investigators what she heard Hernandez say.

Misspelling the Spanish word, the investigator recorded Janie's statement in his notes:

> Bragging. . . . He said it, he hurt Wanda, and he said (Janie Adrian is crying now) Carlos DeLuna took the fall. Wanda Lopez. My *tocallo* took the blame. When he was drinking he didn't keep his mouth shut.

Carlos Hernandez, she later elaborated, said "he stabbed this girl." Her name was Wanda. His "stupid *tocayo* took the blame for it."

"*Tocayo,*" Janie explained, means "namesake" or *cuate* (twin). She volunteered that she had seen Carlos Hernandez and Carlos DeLuna together on Carrizo Street before. They "look the same," she said.

Janie recalled that Hernandez sounded proud as he talked to the other guys. If he hadn't used Wanda's name, she said, he might as well have been talking about "kill[ing] a dog or something."

Janie made a connection to the night Carlos had come by desperately looking for Margie. She wondered whether maybe he hadn't felt so proud then, before they got DeLuna for the crime.

Asked whether she called the police, Janie was at once indignant and defensive. That's not the type of person she is, she said. In her world, when "you hear something, you just shut up and that's it. You don't know nothing, you didn't hear nothing." No one wanted to be seen as a "stoolie." It was a running joke, she said, between her and Fidela. "I'm not going to make it easier" for the cops, they'd repeat to each other. "Let them do their job."

That's why Janie was irritated at Carlos for running his mouth. It was dangerous to learn "more than what we were supposed to have known"— especially when it was Hernandez himself you knew something about. Hernandez "would really really remember stuff that people would do to him," Janie recalled, "and he would go back" for them.

Luckily, Janie said, the police never came around asking if anyone knew anything about Hernandez and Wanda Lopez. Although Carlos was bragging about it up and down Carrizo Street, they never came around. It was decades before anyone did.

"Maybe I should have said something at the time," Janie said, "but we're not like that. We're not."

Asked her opinion, twenty years later, about who killed Wanda Lopez, Janie said "Carlos Hernandez," because that's what had "come out of his mouth. . . . There was a stabbing and her name was Wanda Lopez." When she heard that, she said, "It came into my head, how could this be?" But she decided it was none of her business. "I mean, he shouldn't be saying nothing like that."

$$\bullet \quad \bullet \quad \bullet$$

When Pricilla Hernandez was thirteen, she left Fidela's house on Carrizo Street to live with her mother, Paula. When that didn't work out, Pricilla moved in with her father, Beto Vela, and his wife, Linda Perales Vela (later Ayala).

Beto told Linda that he didn't even know that Paula had a daughter by him until Pricilla showed up on his doorstep once when she was twelve years old. Pricilla remembered Fidela pointing Beto out to her as her father and encouraging her to go live with him.

Beto and Linda took Pricilla in, but that didn't work out either. Pricilla's new parents discovered that she was pregnant and believed the father was their own fifteen-year-old son, Pricilla's half-brother Paul. Beto and Linda kicked both of them out after catching them in bed together. Linda ended up raising Pricilla's daughter and maintained an on-again, off-again relationship with Pricilla herself.

Over the years, Pricilla told Linda a lot about what went on in Fidela's house on Carrizo Street and what her uncle Carlos Hernandez did to her. That helped Linda make sense of her stepdaughter. Knowing that Pricilla had seen men going into and out of the house for sex with her grandmother, and that the young girl had been raped by her own blood relative, Linda figured that Pricilla was bound to end up doing something like that herself.

Strangely, Linda Perales Vela was also connected to Carlos *DeLuna's* family. She met Manuel DeLuna in church when she was ten, around 1970. In the mid-1970s, they began dating and hanging out at the Casino Club. Linda met Manuel's brother Carlos at the club. He was "real hyper," she remembered—"not a fighting person," she said, but "he talked fast and drank a lot."

In 1983, Linda heard that her name had come up in connection with the killing of Wanda Lopez at the Sigmor Shamrock gas station. Carlos DeLuna had been arrested for the crime, and he had said something about running into Linda and her sister Mary Ann at the skating rink that night. Linda heard about this from Mary Ann, who went to court to testify about it.

No one had contacted Linda at the time. Reflecting on it later, she doubted she saw DeLuna at the skating rink that night, but she wasn't sure. She used to go to the rink a lot, but by 1983 she was probably home with her children.

Years later, right after Linda divorced Beto Vela, she reconnected with Manuel DeLuna, and they were married for a short time in 1998. That's what brought the killing of Wanda Lopez and the two Carloses together for Linda.

Manuel told her that his brother was innocent and that Carlos Hernandez was the killer. Manuel had heard that from another guy in prison, who'd heard it from Hernandez himself.

What really made Linda pay attention, though, was what her stepdaughter, Pricilla, told her after learning that Linda had married Carlos DeLuna's brother. Pricilla had overheard her uncle Carlos Hernandez saying it was he, not Carlos DeLuna, who had killed Wanda Lopez.

·   ·   ·

Others heard Carlos Hernandez say things as well. Lina Zapata first met Carlos in the 1980s, when her family moved to Carrizo Street. Lina's father told her to stay away from him because he'd been in prison and was violent.

Lina got to know Carlos better in the early 1990s, when she moved into an apartment complex on Hancock Street, where Carlos lived with his girlfriend, Cindy Maxwell.

One time, she and Carlos were drinking together, and out of the blue he said he'd killed before, as if that was a normal thing to say in the middle of a conversation.

"No shit, you killed someone?" Lina asked. "Yeah," Carlos said. He didn't elaborate. Asked later if she ever heard Carlos talk about Dahlia Sauceda, Lina said the name wasn't familiar. She did remember him talking about a woman named Wanda.

Carlos Hernandez met Cindy Maxwell in 1979, and he lived with her on and off into the 1990s. An African American woman with a mental disability whose parents acted as her legal guardians throughout her adult life, Cindy was working as a custodian at a public library when she met Hernandez.

Although Carlos had relationships with many other women in those years, he always went back to Cindy. She took care of him. She paid for everything. She bought him beer—a twelve-pack a day—and whatever else he wanted. She loved Carlos in spite of his drinking problem and the violent incidents she sometimes reported to the police. On one occasion, he threatened to "cut her," and on another he "accidentally" cut her son.

According to Cindy's niece, Cindy knew more than just that Carlos drank and had a temper. Cindy told her that Carlos had killed a woman during a robbery. Cindy didn't offer details. Around the same time, Hernandez told Cindy and a friend, Michelle Garza, "that he had killed a lady in a van." Garza later told the investigators that she "thought [Hernandez] was just making it up, until Cindy told me he had stabbed some other lady," too.

When the investigators came around, Cindy had nothing bad to say about Carlos. She'd heard from a friend that he killed a lady in a robbery, and she heard Carlos say a lot of things himself over the years. But when Carlos talked like that, Cindy said, she wouldn't listen.

* * *

At some point between 1987 and 1989, when Manuel DeLuna was in state prison, he ran into a young kid from Corpus Christi he remembered as Ortiz—"Carlos" Ortiz, he thought, but he wasn't sure.

"I was walking down the hallway at the Old Clemens Unit," Manuel told the investigators, "and ran into him in the classification [office, when] he was just coming in from the chain [the bus for new inmates]." Ortiz "asked me if my name was Manuel DeLuna from Corpus Christi and if Carlos was my brother."

Ortiz said he had something to tell Manuel, and they agreed to meet in the rec yard. When they did, Ortiz started talking about Carlos Hernandez and Carlos DeLuna.

Ortiz said he met Hernandez at Armada Park in Corpus Christi, where a bunch of guys were drinking beer. Hernandez "started bragging about all his killings"—three of them, all women. There was one in a van, one at gas a station, and one under a bridge.

"I killed this chick, this chick, this chick," is how Manuel remembered Ortiz describing the conversation. Hernandez was a "woman killer," Ortiz had said, someone "who actually liked to hurt women."

The main reason Ortiz wanted to talk to Manuel, however, was something that Hernandez said about the "gas station" killing he had committed. On that one, Hernandez had bragged, "Carlos DeLuna took the fall." "DeLuna" took "Hernandez's rap."

"Everyone knows that your brother was not guilty," Manuel remembers Ortiz saying.

For months, the private investigators looked in vain for a Carlos or Charles Ortiz from Corpus who'd been in prison fifteen years earlier. Near the end of their work on the case, they homed in on a detail Manuel had given. He and Ortiz had taken the same plumbing course in the Old Clemens Unit. A search of prison records identified a *Miguel* Ortiz from Corpus Christi, several years younger than Manuel, who was in the same prison and plumbing class.

News reporters later caught up with Miguel Ortiz in Corpus Christi. It was a short conversation. Ortiz said that he and Carlos Hernandez "were drinking in a park when Hernandez talked about a clerk he had 'wasted' at a gas station. 'I just let that go,'" Ortiz told the reporters.

*     *     *

Even Jesse Garza's lawyer, Albert Peña, heard the rumor that it was Carlos Hernandez, not Carlos DeLuna, who had murdered Wanda Lopez.

Speaking about it years later, the accomplished lawyer choked up at the thought of someone facing the death penalty for a crime another person had committed. "I heard through police sources and through people at the courthouse, people in the know, that Carlos Hernandez was suspected of doing it," Peña said. But they put "blinders on."

In Peña's mind, everything went back to what happened in 1980. They should have put Carlos Hernandez away then for killing Dahlia Sauceda. If Olivia Escobedo and Kenneth Botary had done their jobs, Wanda Lopez would still be alive. And maybe others, too.

# 9

# Mistaken Identity

EDDIE GARZA LEFT THE AIR FORCE and joined the Corpus Christi Police Department in 1964. After several years as a patrolman, he became a sergeant with the Criminal Investigations Division in 1970, working theft and burglary, and then major crimes and homicide.

As Garza told the out-of-town investigators, he had learned in his years on the beat and as a detective that a cop doing investigations "[is] only as good as [his] informants."

"You don't get it out all on your own," he explained. You have to develop rapport in the community, find people who trust you to help them when they need it, and not get them in trouble when they help you with information.

By 1983, Garza had developed a strong network of informants. After working hundreds of cases and making many arrests, he also had a good idea of who in the community was capable of what kinds of crimes. A teenager in the Hispanic community could hardly steal a pack of cigarettes in Corpus without Eddie Garza hearing about it.

· · ·

Within a few weeks of the murder of Wanda Lopez, Garza began to hear from his informants about it, and they were all naming the same person. It was a name Garza and his colleagues in the department knew well, but not the name of the man they had arrested and charged with capital murder.

Word was that Carlos *Hernandez* was boasting on the street that he had killed Wanda Lopez and had gotten someone else to take the fall.

Garza wasn't surprised. The longtime cop had known Hernandez since he was a kid and had arrested him several times. Hernandez was always getting into trouble. He was always getting into fights, especially near his house on Carrizo Street.

Decades after the fact, Garza immediately remembered Hernandez's crime of choice ("assaulting women"), his weapon of choice ("a buck knife" with "a retraction button at the rear of the deal" to unlock the blade), and especially his "look." It was the look of a "cold, cold person," Garza vividly recalled, who "could stare straight through you"—a "frightening, mean look" that made you "feel a threat there."

.        .        .

By 1983, Carlos Hernandez believed that he could beat almost any rap, and he pretty much did.

Of course, he had several convictions under his belt—negligent homicide in 1970, a grand theft and three armed robberies in 1972. Somehow, though, he'd gotten off with only probation in the 1970 case and served only five years for the four 1972 felonies combined.

In late 1979, less than two years after returning to Corpus Christi on parole, he'd even walked out of the police station a free man after his fingerprint and boxer shorts were found next to Dahlia Sauceda's battered body in the back of her van. After that, Hernandez grew bolder. He had reason to think that he couldn't be touched and let the cops know he didn't fear them.

One time, Garza's partner, Paul Rivera, was working security at the annual Buccaneer Days Festival along the waterfront when Hernandez, drinking as usual, made an obscene gesture at the cop. A large man with a commanding air, Rivera understood the gesture as a reprisal for the officer's arrest and interrogation of Hernandez in the Dahlia matter, prompting Carlos's desperate call to Fidela for help. This time, however, having escaped the Dahlia affair unscathed, Carlos responded to Rivera's threat to arrest him for public intoxication by challenging the cop to a fistfight.

Paul Rivera had a strong opinion of Hernandez, which he had no problem expressing years later. A "no good son of a bitch," he called him. "[C]razy," "a mean motherfucker." But on that occasion in front of the Buccaneer Days crowd, facing Hernandez "with that hate look" in his eyes, the tough cop decided to let it go. He didn't arrest Carlos.

.    .    .

Carlos Hernandez spent his entire adult life on parole from the serious crimes he committed as an eighteen year old. Throughout the time, he was arrested constantly—over two dozen times—for the sorts of crimes that parolees are told they cannot commit if they want to remain out of prison: public intoxication, disorderly conduct, making threats, assault with a deadly weapon, murder. Worse, he openly violated the cardinal rule of parole: no weapons. He was arrested at least thirteen times while carrying a knife.

Yet despite these arrests, Carlos's parole was revoked only twice, both times in the 1990s.

In 1981, he was arrested for threatening his girlfriend with a knife, and then refusing to leave the premises. No charges were filed, and the parole board didn't even hold a hearing to consider ending his parole.

On February 23, 1983, less than three weeks after the Sigmor Shamrock killing, the Bureau of Pardons and Paroles found that Hernandez had violated two parole conditions. He had lied about his whereabouts and had failed to get permission to change residence. As usual, the penalty was a reprimand rather than the withdrawal of parole.

In November 1983, Hernandez was arrested for assaulting his wife, Rosa Anzaldua, with an axe handle and spraying broken glass all over her sleeping children. This time, he was convicted of a misdemeanor—causing bodily injury—and sentenced to thirty days in jail. But again, his parole wasn't revoked. He was back on the street in a month. The judge who let him off easy was Hector De Peña, Sr., father and namesake of the lawyer who represented Carlos DeLuna at his July 1983 trial for killing Wanda Lopez.

In 1994, Carlos Hernandez was caught with twenty-four grams of heroin packaged for sale. Narcotics detectives had executed a search and arrest warrant at a room in a sleazy hotel on the waterfront. They found Hernandez's friend Mary Ellis with heroin and a large sum of money. As they were searching the room, Hernandez showed up in his car. Police arrested him as well and found several clear plastic bags of heroin and Valium pills in his car and clothes. The evidence of dealing couldn't have been stronger, but Hernandez was never charged. His parole was left in place.

People wondered about Hernandez's good fortune.

At times it seemed like just that: dumb luck. No one knows exactly what Hernandez said to Assistant District Attorney Kenneth Botary in 1980 to talk his way out of charges in the Dahlia Sauceda murder. But when attorney Jon Kelly relied on Botary's misplacement of the transcript of that conversation to spring Hernandez from the same murder charges in 1986, it looked like the luck of drawing a good defense lawyer. Who knows?

But Hernandez may have had more than luck working for him.

Eddie Garza had known as early as 1983 that Hernandez was working as a confidential informant for the police. Kelly, who used Hernandez to get information from the community for his own criminal cases, had heard the same.

"If I needed information in the community," Kelly said, Hernandez "could get it. People didn't lie to him. . . . People told him things because they were scared." In two or three cases, Kelly recalled, Carlos brought him information he wouldn't have gotten otherwise.

It stood to reason that Hernandez was informing for the police. For someone with the criminal record he'd amassed to remain on parole required serious special treatment.

●    ●    ●

If Hernandez knew how to play the informant game, so did Eddie Garza. Based on what his informants told him about Hernandez in late February and March 1983, he believed that "the person that had actually committed the crime" at the Sigmor "was Carlos Hernandez."

It wasn't just the informants who led Garza to that conclusion. Given Hernandez's history of gas-station robberies, his skill with a buck knife, his temper, and his tendency to pick on women, the Wanda Lopez killing exactly fit his m.o.

Garza knew both Carloses, and, as he told news reporters years later, he didn't think DeLuna "had it in him to do something like this and stab somebody to death." This was Hernandez's kind of crime: "Hernandez was a ruthless criminal. He had a bad heart. I believe he was a killer."

This wouldn't be the first time the Corpus police suspected Hernandez of killing a Latina woman. There was Dahlia Sauceda back in 1979. And Garza's partner, Paul Rivera, had talked to his informants and Hernandez's lawyer, Kelly, about other unsolved murders he suspected Hernandez of committing, including that of a woman named Hortencia Mata, whose nude and beaten body was found under the south end of the Harbor Bridge on April 21, 1982.

In March 1983, Garza took the information he was getting from his sources to Olivia Escobedo. A sex crimes specialist, Escobedo was just learning the ropes as a homicide detective and thought of Garza as her mentor. He told her that Carlos Hernandez was "out on the streets boasting that he had gotten someone else to take the fall for him" in the Wanda Lopez killing and urged her to take a hard look at the man.

There could be no confusion as to the Carlos Hernandez whom Garza meant, he said later. This particular Carlos Hernandez was notorious among police, prosecutors, and others at the courthouse. From their own personal experience investigating cases and making arrests, Garza explained, most of the detectives in the criminal investigation division knew of Carlos Gonzalez Hernandez.

Detective Escobedo knew who Carlos Hernandez was, too, from the Dahlia Sauceda case. She'd sat in court and watched as defense lawyer Albert Peña took apart her first big homicide case, humiliating her with questions about why she'd gone after Jesse Garza without first investigating Hernandez, and then masterfully using Hernandez's own testimony to convince the jury that it was he and not Jesse Garza who had killed Dahlia in her van.

Garza was also certain that the police could find Hernandez if they wanted to bring him in. The patrol division knew his hangouts and the people around him. If someone had told Garza to find Carlos Hernandez in connection with a crime like this, the old detective said, he would've gone straight to Carrizo and Laredo Streets just east of Staples and Mary and had him in custody in minutes. It was only ten blocks from the police station.

Jon Kelly agreed. "Carlos Hernandez was easy to find at the time." He was a "known quantity" in the Mary Street area. "There was no question he could have been found."

Janie Adrian, Carlos Hernandez's Carrizo Street neighbor, said the same. "Everybody knew Carlos Hernandez around there, everybody. If you asked the dogs, the dogs would probably tell you."

.     .     .

Garza never knew what Escobedo did with the information he gave her. He remembered her saying that she had all the evidence she needed to convict Carlos DeLuna, and he recalled backing off to "let her work her case."

What Garza didn't know was that, soon after he alerted Escobedo that Carlos Hernandez was taking credit for "hurting" Wanda Lopez, police took Hernandez into custody.

Late on April 2, 1983, two months after Wanda's death, Corpus Christi police officer L. Serna found a man "lurking" behind a 7-Eleven on Brownlee Boulevard and Agnes Street with a knife in his pocket.

The man was Carlos Gonzalez Hernandez. He was seven blocks from his Carrizo Street home, eleven blocks from the police station. He had a criminal record a mile long.

Serna arrested him on "suspicion of attempted robbery" but listed Hernandez's violation of an outstanding traffic warrant as the formal reason for the arrest. Hernandez had failed to pay a traffic ticket.

Although Garza never learned of it, soon after he urged law-enforcement colleagues to take a hard look at Carlos Hernandez, they decided to do just that.

．　　．　　．

Hernandez's traffic warrant had been outstanding for months and had never been enforced. Traffic warrants were rarely enforced in those days, unless there was another reason to get the person in custody. As Carlos Hernandez (and DeLuna, for that matter) knew from experience, standard procedure on arrests like this was to release the person within a few hours after paying a minor fine. Moments after being booked, Hernandez made a phone call to someone named "Raul," possibly a bail bondsman.

In this case, however, the Corpus Christi police didn't release Hernandez within hours. They kept him locked up for four days and kept him a lot busier than the usual traffic-ticket scofflaw.

The only police officer to join Olivia Escobedo inside the Sigmor convenience store on the night Wanda was killed was Joel Infante, an Identification Division technician. Infante took the crime-scene photographs and field-tested for fingerprints. At the scene, Infante had recovered partial prints from the front door, the telephone, and one of the empty cans of cheap beer found outside where George Aguirre had seen a man lurking with a knife. None of the prints matched those of Carlos DeLuna.

Because Carlos Hernandez was a known quantity to police, they also had his "major case prints"—all ten fingertips, the palm side of all three joints of his fingers, and the palm of each hand. They had two sets, one from 1972, when he was arrested for armed robbery, and one from October 26, 1981, when he was arrested at Staples and Mary for threatening his girlfriend with a knife.

Of course, fingerprints played no part in the incident triggering Hernandez's arrest on April 2 for violating a traffic warrant, and failing to pay a traffic ticket was hardly a "major case." Yet on April 4, Infante retrieved Hernandez's existing fingerprint cards from the Identification Division to make fingerprint comparisons. Not content with the full sets of prints he already had, Infante took Hernandez out of lockup and took additional impressions to allow better comparisons.

On the same day, April 4, 1983—a day and a half after his arrest, when mug shots usually are taken—officers put Hernandez in the three-way mirror at the police station and took his picture.

Although Hernandez was dressed in his usual "wife-beater" undershirt, his appearance was unusual in one respect. This is the only known photograph of him between 1978 and his death over twenty years later in which he didn't have a mustache. For some reason, he'd decided to change how he looked during the same period when, just as suddenly, he'd changed his residence without telling his parole officer.

Years later, a former Scotland Yard fingerprint expert examined the prints that Infante had recovered at the Sigmor Shamrock crime scene. Most were too fragmentary for comparison. The few that could be compared, from the front door and phone receiver, matched neither Carlos Hernandez nor Carlos DeLuna.

On April 6, police released Hernandez without comment after he paid $67 on the traffic fine. He'd proved to be untouchable again.

•    •    •

During Hernandez's four days in police custody in April 1983, he just might have run into Carlos DeLuna, who was being held on charges of murdering Wanda Lopez.

This was not the first time the Corpus police had the two Carloses in custody at the same time. A review of local police records many years later revealed that at least twice before, on January 12–15, 1979, and May 23–24, 1980, the two were or may have been at the police station or a local lockup at the same time.

•    •    •

Although Carlos Hernandez was out of immediate police sight after April 6, 1983, he was not out of mind.

The district attorney's file in the prosecution of Carlos *DeLuna* for the murder of Wanda Lopez, recovered twenty-one years later on a Public Records Act request, contains the rap sheets of Carlos DeLuna and seven other Corpus Christi men in their twenties with police records, all seven of whom were named Carlos *Hernandez*.

The rap sheets indicate that Detective Escobedo provided them to the district attorney's office on May 2, 1983, a few weeks after Garza told Escobedo that Carlos Hernandez was making admissions on the streets and after the police had Hernandez in custody for several days. It was two months before Carlos DeLuna dared say the words "Carlos Hernandez" to his lawyers.

The "Hernandez" rap sheets show that they were reviewed on May 2, 1983, by someone with the initial *S*, probably Assistant District Attorney Steven Schiwetz, who, along with Kenneth Botary, had been assigned to prosecute Carlos DeLuna.

Among the seven Carlos Hernandezes that Escobedo and the prosecutors scrutinized, only one fell in the same 5 feet, 7 inch, to 5 foot, 9 inch, 160- to 175-pound range as the man whom Kevan Baker had seen at the Sigmor station on the night Wanda Lopez was murdered.

Only one of the seven had a record of convenience-store armed robberies. Only one had a record of any robberies at all, and only one had been arrested with a knife on suspicion of an attempted robbery of a 7-Eleven within weeks of the Lopez killing.

And only one had been arrested and interrogated on suspicion of murder: the killing of a young Hispanic woman in which the weapon was a knife.

These were all the same man: Carlos Gonzalez Hernandez, born in July 1954, who was listed at 5 feet, 7 inches, and 175 pounds and resided most of his life at 217 South Carrizo Street. The same Carlos Hernandez whom Detectives Eddie Garza and Paul Rivera had known for years and arrested many times. The Carlos Hernandez whom Albert Peña had blamed for the murder of Dahlia Sauceda as he dismantled Olivia Escobedo and Kenneth Botary's case against Jesse Garza three years earlier.

•    •    •

Reached years later in Florida where she was working as a real-estate agent, Olivia Escobedo said she didn't run a field investigation of Carlos Hernandez or question him about the stabbing of Wanda Lopez because his name never came up in the case. She didn't know that the investigators had found Hernandez's rap sheet in her old files on the matter.

Escobedo acknowledged that she knew Carlos Hernandez from the Dahlia Sauceda affair. If he was under suspicion for killing Lopez, she said she definitely would have followed up. "Wanda Lopez reminded me of myself," the former detective explained, "a single mother, on her own, working a night shift to make ends meet." That's why, Escobedo claimed, she investigated the killing of Lopez as thoroughly as possible and ran down every piece of information she had.

She also said flatly that if Hernandez's name had come up in the Lopez investigation, prosecutor "Ken [Botary] would have made sure that I followed that lead."

Eddie Garza's former partner, Paul Rivera, also had no recollection, years later, of Hernandez's name coming up in connection with the Lopez killing. Rivera, who by then had switched over to the county sheriff's office, took an interest in the private investigators' reexamination of the case. He checked in with them when he saw them at the county building looking for records and talked to witnesses they interviewed.

One day he summoned two members of the investigating team to his office to meet another sheriff's department employee, Elmer Cox. Cox said he'd once been detailed to transport Carlos DeLuna from one facility to another in the early 1980s. He said DeLuna blurted out that "I've been stabbed 100 times and I only stabbed that bitch one time and she died."

Cox recalled turning to his transport partner, David Petrusaitis, and asking, "Did we just hear a confession?"

During the period Cox described, DeLuna was deep in court proceedings and adamant that he was innocent. Any hint of a confession would have been a momentous event, as well as a coup for the cop who got it. Yet no word of any such confession was ever mentioned in court or in the press. Additionally, a close physical examination by corrections personnel at the time revealed no knife-wound scars on DeLuna, and other details Cox gave were inconsistent with the known facts.

Investigators tracked down Petrusaitis, then a deputy sheriff in Cleburne, south of Fort Worth. Petrusaitis made a notarized statement denying Cox's claim. He was sure he'd never been involved in transporting a capital prisoner like DeLuna.

"If I had been and I had overheard a res gestae admission from an inmate to a murder during the course of the transport," he added, "I would have written down exactly what was said and documented it with a date and time and filed a follow up report with the Sheriff's Office." He also would have made sure the report was sent to the prosecuting attorneys in Corpus Christi. "This was then and still is standard police procedure."

Inquiry and Public Records Act requests with the Nueces County Sheriff's Department and district attorney's office turned up no sign of any such report.

Rivera's effort fizzled at that point. A year later, news reporters spoke to him about the case; he took issue with things his former partner, Garza, had told them, but he didn't mention Elmer Cox.

·     ·     ·

At the time of Carlos DeLuna's arrest on January 21, 1983, for drunk and disorderly conduct at the Casino Club, when he had made a coarse remark about the shooting of Sergeant Rick Garcia, and after Carlos Hernandez's arrest on April 2, 1983, behind the 7-Eleven on Brownlee and Mary, the police took mug shots of both men in the same three-way mirror at the police department (figure 9.1).

The images were made ten weeks apart, just before and after the killing of Wanda Lopez at the Sigmor. DeLuna was in his usual white, long-sleeved dress shirt, his face shaven, his thick, wavy hair kempt. Carlos Hernandez was in a tank-top T-shirt, his face unshaven, his thick, wavy hair uncombed.

When Detective Eddie Garza saw pictures of the two Carloses mixed together without identifying information, he was struck by how similar the men in the photos looked. He identified a photo of DeLuna as Hernandez at a younger age. After studying the pictures for a while, he thought he saw a slight difference in the eyes. Even then, he couldn't say for sure that he was looking at more than one person.

The resemblance between Hernandez and DeLuna is especially striking in profile. Kevan Baker, the sole eyewitness to the crime, got a close look at the assailant only as the man turned left and fled, exposing his right profile.

Garza wasn't the only one who had trouble telling the two Carloses apart. Shown photographs by the private investigators years later, a number of friends and family members of the two men mistakenly identified pictures of one Carlos, whom they'd never met, as those of the other.

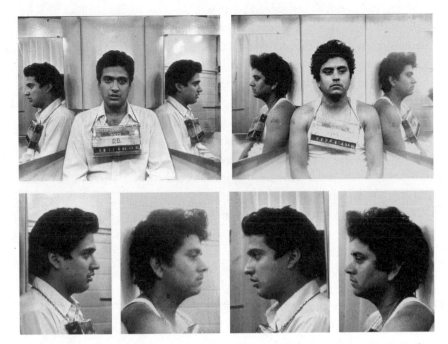

FIGURE 9.1  Three-way-mirror mug shots of Carlos DeLuna on January 21, 1983 (*top left*), and Carlos Hernandez on April 4, 1983 (*top right*), and close-ups of DeLuna's and Hernandez's left profiles (*bottom left*) and right profiles (*bottom right*).

Rose Rhoton, Carlos DeLuna's sister, misidentified a picture of Carlos Hernandez as her brother. When Freddy Schilling, Hernandez's brother-in-law, was first shown pictures of the two men side by side, he thought they were both Hernandez. Schilling later described his reaction when told that one of photographs was of Carlos DeLuna, who'd been accused of a crime he said another man committed:

> Like I said, it sent chills through my body when I seen it. Then when he told me that this (*points to photo on left*) was Carlos DeLuna and this (*points to photo on right*) was Carlos Hernandez, I said, "God damn, I can believe that, that's probably where the mistake was made." 'Cause it really, really looked like Carlos [Hernandez] (*holds up the photo to the camera*). You can see, right there, the resemblance. I really, really thought it was Carlos [Hernandez] when I first seen these pictures here. I didn't know anything about Carlos DeLuna, I've never met the man.

When Hernandez's lawyer Jon Kelly was shown a picture of DeLuna, he initially thought it was Hernandez without a mustache. Shirley Currie, a friend of Hernandez, misidentified a picture of DeLuna as being Hernandez at a younger age. Mary Ellis, Hernandez's friend who was caught up in the same heroin bust with him, similarly mistook a picture of DeLuna as Hernandez.

Linda Perales, who knew the DeLuna brothers as a teenager and married Manuel years later, mistook a picture of Hernandez as DeLuna. Karen Boudrie, a television reporter who covered the DeLuna case over six years and spoke to DeLuna often, did the same, as did Robert Veregara, a police officer who had arrested both men.

When shown pictures of the two men, Gloria Licea Sanchez, a former girlfriend of Hernandez, shook her head and said she could see why people could easily mistake one for the other.

The consequences of being mistaken for Carlos Hernandez were not lost on his niece and frequent victim, Pricilla Hernandez. Shown pictures of the two men, she pointed to a photo of DeLuna and asked, "[W]ho is this? This is my uncle. Oh my God that's crazy. This is creepy. This guy looks like my uncle. God forbid."

# PART III

# The Prosecution of Carlos DeLuna

# 10

# Investigation

DETECTIVE EDDIE GARZA was a good soldier.

When Olivia Escobedo was assigned the Carlos DeLuna case, the respected detective had his doubts. He felt that the case required a more seasoned investigator.

"If you're convicting somebody of a capital murder," he told the out-of-town investigators, you'd better be "sure you have enough evidence that that person was at the crime scene." He wasn't convinced that Escobedo was up to the task.

Escobedo was green and didn't have the reputation for good work that some of the other detectives had. She'd just been promoted to investigator, and her specialty was rape.

In rape cases, the main evidence comes from the victim. In homicide, detectives don't have that luxury. You have to dig deeper. That's why Garza liked to work in teams of two or more homicide detectives, with three identification techs to process evidence, especially in capital cases.

"Just to have one detective in charge" of a capital case, "I don't think that that's right." Escobedo's single identification tech was a converted patrol officer, reputed to have a drinking problem, who thought of himself as a photographer and fingerprint guy, not a full-fledged identification technician.

Still, when the chief of homicide let Escobedo go it alone, Garza didn't object.

Although he had dozens of homicide investigations under his belt, after he told Escobedo what his informants had heard Carlos Hernandez say about the Wanda Lopez stabbing, he let her decide what to do about it. It was her case.

And when prosecutors Steven Schiwetz and Kenneth Botary asked him to testify to Carlos DeLuna's bad reputation, he did that, too. Still, Garza worried that the police might have arrested the wrong man.

Years later, the private investigators reexamining the case asked Garza to look over Escobedo's case file and the crime-scene photos and give his opinion about how her scene investigation had gone. He concluded that the crime scene had not been gone over correctly. Clues were overlooked, and the evidence Escobedo had come up with didn't prove that DeLuna committed the crime. The evidence probably proved that he didn't. The Corpus police had gotten the wrong man, he feared.

                              •       •       •

There were a lot of things about the case Escobedo put together that didn't add up for Garza. Why, for starters, Carlos Hernandez would go around saying that he stabbed Wanda Lopez, if it was DeLuna who committed the crime.

The witnesses' descriptions of the man they saw around the crime scene didn't square either. Some saw a derelict with a mustache and shabby clothes sprinting west and north; others saw a clean-shaven man in dress clothes jogging east.

Nobody explained why the killer had gone behind the counter, yet left without taking most or all of the cash.

George Aguirre told police at the gas station that he had warned Lopez about a guy with a knife by the ice machine east of the store. Lopez couldn't see the man because the store's east wall was solid brick, and she couldn't see anyone unless he or she was at the pumps or the front door. So when she called 911, how did she know that this particular man—who she said didn't have a weapon out yet and was asking to buy cigarettes—was a bad guy with a knife?

Garza also didn't like the way the police had gotten Kevan Baker and Aguirre to identify DeLuna at the Sigmor—all by himself, at night, with his hands cuffed behind his back, spotlighted in flashlight beams. "You don't identify a person by just [asking] somebody, 'Hey, look at this person, is that the one you saw?'" Garza explained. That just invites the witness to say, "'Yeah, that's the guy,' because you've got him in custody [and] take it for granted." That's the wrong way to do an identification.

The investigating officers should have held a lineup at the police station, mixing up the suspect with others and having them all stand behind a one-way mirror. That way, the witnesses wouldn't have been afraid and wouldn't have been forced to make an anxious up-or-down decision on one particular suspect. Having Baker and Aguirre view a bunch of people to see if any one of them stood out as the perpetrator—the way John and Julie Arsuaga did with photographs before selecting DeLuna out of the bunch—would have been a lot more reliable.

But the out-of-town investigators wanted Garza to focus on Escobedo's scene investigation, and that's what he did.

•       •       •

The first thing you look for in a scene investigation, the former homicide detective explained, is whether the suspect has something on him that you know came from the crime scene—property he ran off with or blood from the victim.

Examining the file and photos with that in mind, Garza focused immediately on the knife wound through the victim's left breast and the struggle between her and the stabber as she hemorrhaged blood.

The autopsy showed that the wound was deep. The knife had pierced the victim's left lung and caused "a great deal of . . . very rapid bleeding." Multiple liters of blood had oozed from the wound. Some may have "spurted" from severed arteries in her breast and between her ribs.

Baker had seen the two "wrestling" as the attacker tried "to carry the clerk into the back room of the store" and she furiously resisted. Then the man "released the girl and walked out." One photo showed bruising around her right eye. Others showed several feet of scuff marks in blood where the man viciously yanked her toward the back room.

The scene was about as bloody as it could be from a single wound. There were large pools of standing blood, and as drops rained down from the victim's chest wound and hit the floor, they rebounded upward in a mist of droplets. Everything near the victim that rose above the floor—cabinets, doors, boxes—was coated with spatter several inches off the ground, and in some places a couple of feet (figure 10.1).

Garza reasoned that any person standing near the victim—not to mention wrestling with her—had to have the same coating of spatter on the sides and tops of his shoes and pant legs.

In the struggle near the back-room door, drops of blood had flown onto an 18-inch cabinet top along the back wall of the clerk's area and over it onto the back wall, about 4 feet off the ground.

From the thick pools of blood on the floor and the scuff marks and footprints in blood, Garza was also convinced that the perpetrator left the store with a coating of blood on the bottom of his shoes. Large portions of the bottom of the victim's sandals were darkly discolored with blood. A close-up of the right shoe showed blood soaked well into the rubber sole and staining the sandal's leather sides and straps.

The victim's white Sigmor smock, beige pullover top, and bra were soaked through with blood, and her body was covered with it. She had evi-

FIGURE 10.1   Detail of blood spatter on the floor and nearby surfaces inside the Sigmor store: (*top left and center*) blood soaked into Wanda Lopez's right sandal and dripped on cash found at the scene; (*top right*) smudges of blood on surfaces that she or the assailant touched; (*bottom right*) six packs of soda bottles stacked three cases high, with blood spatter on the top layer. (Color versions of these and the other crime-scene photographs in this chapter are on the Web site, thewrongcarlos.net.)

dently pulled the knife from her wound and dropped it, bloody and slick with flesh, below the cash drawer. After that, the victim transferred large quantities of blood to the gas pump console, cash drawer, and countertop near the cash drawer.

On the 911 tape, she was overheard trying to give the assailant the money, and the location of the murder weapon under the cash drawer— and the thick blood caked on the drawer and cascading down the pump console—revealed that the earliest and some of the worst bleeding had oc- curred right where the money was kept. The loose bills strewn about nearby were stained with it.

Baker had heard the store clerk banging on the window, and the em- ployee who cleaned up found bloody palm prints on the window above the cash drawer. Detective Escobedo and her assistant missed the palm prints on the darkened window at night. Their reports didn't mention them.

When the attacker saw Baker heading for the door, he threw the blood- soaked victim to the floor and fled.

Detective Escobedo found "blood smeared on the door handle on the inside of the door," which must have come from the hands of either the killer or his victim.

Garza was sure that the victim's hands were blood-soaked as she fought off the attacker. She'd pulled the bloody knife out of her chest, and there was blood on the front-door handle and frame where she'd opened it. Her clothes also were soaked in blood, and every surface she'd touched bore streaks and smudges of it—thigh, waist, and chest high. All this convinced Garza that Wanda must have bloodied the assailant's shirt and possibly his pants as she struggled to escape his grasp, and that the killer must have got- ten blood on his own hands and under his fingernails as he punched and wrestled with Wanda and threw her to the floor.

.    .    .

There was talk when they pulled DeLuna out from under the pickup truck that he had blood on his shirt, a detail that was reported as fact in at least one news article on the case.

When Eddie Garza reviewed the file, he discovered that wasn't true.

After police arrested DeLuna at Franklin and Nemec at the end of a forty- minute manhunt, they retrieved his canvas sneakers, white long-sleeve shirt, and black slacks; seized $149 in cash bills that were rolled up in his pants pocket; and examined and photographed his body, naked from the waist up.

There was no blood on him, his clothes, or the money. Not a drop.

Several days after the arrest, Escobedo sent the pants, shirt, shoes, and paper money to the state crime lab for testing with a chemical called luminal that can find even the tiniest trace of blood. There was none. At the police station, an officer had even swabbed DeLuna's skin for traces of blood. The swabs went to the lab as well, and they too came back negative for blood.

Those negative results were enough, by themselves, to convince Garza that DeLuna was not the killer. There was no way, the longtime detective flatly said, that someone could have left the blood shower the culprit caused with no blood on his shoes, clothes, hands, face, or any contraband from the scene. If DeLuna had been at the crime scene, Garza believed, there "definitely . . . would have been a transfer of blood" to each of those things, and especially the "soles," "sides," and "laces" of DeLuna's shoes.

The shoe sides and laces were important. Although the weather was "clear" at the time of the crime, it had rained an eighth of an inch in the morning, and scene photos revealed some moisture on the ground (figure 10.2). In Garza's opinion, however, what little standing water that was left wouldn't have been enough to dissolve bloodstains in porous cloth on shoes, as well as pant cuffs, pants themselves, and a shirt. To remove bloodstains from fabric requires scrubbing and bleach—not something a fleeing suspect had access to. Yet the state lab techs couldn't find even a microscopic speck of blood on the sides or laces of DeLuna's shoes or on the rest of his clothing.

Garza was also adamant about the shirt. "If a person with a white shirt would have been at this crime scene [there] would have been a transfer of blood somewhere or another to that white shirt."

The same, he thought, was true of the cash in DeLuna's pocket: "[I]f any money came from that crime scene, there should have been some speck of blood on [it]."

"There had to be one stain of blood somewhere, as much blood as was at that crime scene, there had to be one speck of blood that . . . could have connected DeLuna to the crime scene. And that was not there."

•     •     •

There were other mismatches between what police found on DeLuna when they arrested him and what had to be true of any man fleeing that particular crime scene.

FIGURE 10.2 Detail of photographs taken outside the Sigmor store documenting moisture conditions on the pavement and grassy areas between 8:16 and 8:40 P.M. while medics worked on Wanda Lopez (barely visible in top photo). DeLuna was arrested at 8:49 P.M.

Kevan Baker had described the assailant yanking the victim by her thick, shoulder-length hair before throwing her to the ground and fleeing. Although Olivia Escobedo and Joel Infante, her lone technician assistant, didn't notice it, one of their photographs shows a horrifying clump of longish, frizzy hair in the passageway out of the clerk's area—where the attacker must have flung it as he fled. In cases involving close contact between victim and assailant, routine police practice includes a scan of the suspect's fingernails, garments, and body for foreign hair. No hair was found after police scanned and swabbed DeLuna's body and lab techs analyzed his clothes.

Another mystery involved the cash found in DeLuna's pocket when he was arrested. In store manager Robert Stange's estimate, no more than $20 or at most $40 was missing. Officer Mark Schauer reported that, after arresting DeLuna, he searched the suspect's pockets for a weapon. He found none but did find $149 in "a wad of paper currency rolled up in [DeLuna's] right pants pocket." After arriving at the police station, Schauer put the "rolled up" bills on a table and noticed that all "the twenties were observable on the bottom of the roll." He left the bills "rolled up into a . . . bunch" until he "started unflapping it to count it" but was interrupted and "rolled it back up" so he could count it later.

In the middle of a bloody and chaotic stabbing, struggle, and escape, with blood-stained bills flying everywhere, how would the stabber have had time to "roll up" twenty-five bills, organizing them by denomination and not getting any blood on them before placing the bundle in his pocket?

•   •   •

The evidence that Escobedo and the lab techs looked for and didn't find on DeLuna pretty much excluded him as the perpetrator in Garza's opinion, but no less concerning to the longtime homicide detective were important items of evidence that the killer probably left at the scene but Escobedo didn't even bother to look for.

In an incident involving a knife and a physical struggle, it is almost as likely that the assailant left some of his own blood at the crime scene as it is that he escaped with some of the victim's blood on himself. In her report on the scene, Escobedo listed nineteen distinct locations where she observed blood.

The investigating officer's most basic step, Garza explained, is to "obtain swabs from every area of blood, whether it be on the wall, whether it be on the floor or doors," and send it to the lab "for testing blood type" and enzymes. (Garza put aside DNA testing, which in 1983 was a few years from being invented.)

Unbelievably, however, Escobedo and Infante did not take a single swab or blood sample from the scene. Although they found blood at numerous locations where the killer might have left it—the knife, the handle of the door through which he escaped, the floor, and numerous crumpled and stained napkins and paper towels—they tested none of them for an attacker's blood.

As for the paper towels, Garza was dismayed to see that, instead of preserving and testing them, Detective Escobedo was photographed standing on one of them. Next to her is a roll of fingerprint tape that she or Infante had carelessly dropped, further "contaminat[ing]" the scene.

Escobedo even forgot to have technicians scrape the victim's fingernails for traces of the attacker's skin and blood that may have collected there as she fought him with the only weapon she had. "Somebody dropped the ball," Garza lamented.

In a single-perpetrator case like this, if there was a drop of blood at the crime scene that didn't match the A-B-O type of the victim or Carlos De-Luna, or one of their enzymes, that would have been as good as DNA in ruling out DeLuna as the killer. And it would have provided an important clue to who the killer was.

By failing to take this most rudimentary of investigative steps, Escobedo passed up any chance of finding out whether the perpetrator left traces of himself at the crime scene. Given how little Escobedo and Infante looked for, Garza said, it was not surprising that they found no physical evidence at the scene to use to identify the perpetrator.

"It probably was there to be found," Garza believed. "It just was overlooked."

"The case wasn't put together right."

.    .    .

Garza didn't have to speculate about some of the evidence left behind by the killer. He could see it in the photographs. But, somehow, Escobedo and Infante flat-out missed most of it.

Next to Escobedo, in the picture of her standing on evidence, is part of a cigarette (figure 10.3). The fragment is burned on one end and either unfiltered or broken off on the other. Although the floor around the fragment is

FIGURE 10.3 Detail of photographs taken inside the Sigmor store: (*top left*) Detective Olivia Escobedo standing on items knocked to the floor during the struggle; a maroon button is in the bottom left of the frame (*arrow*); (*top right*) close-up of a cigarette fragment with a black, possibly charred, spot but no red blood on it; (*bottom*) detail of calendar and (*clockwise from calendar's left edge*), a wad of pink chewing gum, a roll of fingerprint tape, and the cigarette fragment.

blanketed with tiny red droplets of blood, the cigarette paper has none on it. It had to have fallen after the blood spilled. It must be the killer's.

Escobedo noticed the cigarette fragment but, incredibly, never tested it for saliva (where a person's blood often secretes) or other telltale signs of its owner. She never had it examined for fingerprints.

Not far from the cigarette was a wad of pink chewing gum. It, too, must have fallen during the fracas, because it lay on top of the First National Bank calendar, which itself probably fell to the ground during the struggle.

Escobedo and Infante missed the gum entirely. They never tested it for saliva or secreted blood.

Behind Escobedo was a maroon button that didn't come from DeLuna's or Lopez's clothing and may have come from the reddish flannel jacket the attacker wore. Escobedo noticed the button but never tested it for prints or blood.

She also spotted a comb under a counter but didn't bag and save it or test it for hair or fingerprints not belonging to the victim that could have been compared with DeLuna's.

She didn't even test the beer cans discarded where Aguirre saw the man drinking to see if they had traces of the killer's saliva and secreted blood.

If any saliva, hair, or prints on the cigarette, gum, button, comb, or beer cans didn't belong to DeLuna, Escobedo would have known she had the wrong man. She never looked.

·        ·        ·

The killer left behind something more telling than a button and a cigarette butt.

In their photographs and reports, Infante and Escobedo focused on a bloody trail of small, bare footprints from behind the counter through the flap-door to the front door (figure 10.4). From the size of the feet and presence of Wanda's upturned sandals behind the counter, it's clear that the footprints record her tortured exit from the store before collapsing into Kevan Baker's arms just outside.

But the photos record someone else's steps as well.

Two photographs taken inside and one taken outside the store appear to record the stabber's bloody trail as he fled the scene, including a complete print of a right shoe stamped in thick blood heading from behind the counter and toward the front door.

FIGURE 10.4 Detail from police photographs of a trail of bare footprints and blood drops from just outside the passageway through the clerk's counter to the front door.

Another photo, taken outside the Sigmor, shows what may be two bloody prints of a man, on the balls of his feet, sprinting along the sidewalk away from the front door—exactly the escape route that Baker saw the fleeing killer use (figure 10.5). There was little that Garza could say about those marks. Because Escobedo never investigated the killer's flight path outside the door, she never spotted these marks, or measured or photographed them close up. She didn't even cordon off the sidewalk where Baker said the killer had fled, and other photos show police officers trampling the site. No one will ever know whether the reddish smudges are shoe prints—and, if so, whose.

Eddie Garza, however, had a lot to say about the shoe prints inside the store, where only Wanda and the killer had been.

Clearly visible in one of the color photographs is a bloody smudge on the concrete floor of the back storeroom where the attacker tried to pull Wanda Lopez as she resisted. The skid marks on the floor show that Lopez had planted her feet near the stacked soda cases and that the attacker held her and gave her three violent tugs toward the back room (figure 10.6).

The smudge may be a print the killer left while standing inside the storeroom and pulling Wanda toward him. Between that smudge and Wanda's skid marks is a large pool of blood and Wanda's right shoe, evidently where Baker saw the attacker "thr[o]w [Lopez] on the floor" and "start[ ] toward the front door."

FIGURE 10.5 (*Left*) The sidewalk outside the Sigmor store after Wanda Lopez was taken to the hospital. To the left are blood stains, bandages, and debris left by the victim and medics. Barely visible in the bottom right-hand corner are two reddish stains along the assailant's escape route that may be partial shoe prints. (*Right*) Detail of the two stains.

FIGURE 10.6 (*Left*) The northern end of the clerk's area, including (*foreground*) Wanda's skid marks; (*on and near back-room door*) blood spatter, Wanda's right shoe, and a large pool of blood; and (*inside back room, as indicated*) a reddish smudge on the concrete floor. (*Right*) Detail of the reddish smudge.

The full print of a right shoe cast in blood is in the passageway through the clerk's counter, about where someone would stand after raising the countertop to unlatch the half-door through the counter. The possible heel print is just behind it. Both are near where the killer dropped a clump of the victim's hair and face away from the clerk's area on a path to the front door (figures 10.7 and 10.8).

The "footprint is very noticeable," Garza observed. Its maker must have stepped in a pool of blood, because this later step "squashed the blood over to the side."

The person who left the print, Garza said, "would have to be the of-fender" because Wanda wore straight-bottomed sandals or was barefoot, and this print has "a heel print from a shoe."

Unlike the foot marks that Wanda made that so fascinated Escobedo and Infante, these shoe marks were crucial to the investigation, Garza said. They were an "imprint" of himself that the killer had left behind. They could rule in or out any suspect whose shoes did or did not match the marks.

"That should have been measured," he said, and there "should have been a better quality picture made of this, with a ruler laying beside it."

"[I]f I were the investigator, I would be looking very, very closely to match the heel print right there to the shoes that the offender would have been wearing."

Escobedo and Infante, however, never mentioned the shoe print in their reports or testimony. Although they had done so with one of Wanda's

FIGURE 10.7  (*Left*) The passageway through the clerk's counter, with a full shoe print (*midway through passageway, as indicated*) and (*bottom edge, center, as indicated*) possible heel print. (*Right*) Detail of the shoe print and possible heel print.

FIGURE 10.8 (*Top left*) The route from the back room through the passageway. (*Top right*) Detail of the clump of hair that Escobedo and Infante failed to notice. (*Bottom*) The relationship of the clump of hair (*center left*), full shoe print (*top right*), and possible partial shoe print (*bottom right*).

footprints, they made no close-up or cast of the shoe print and didn't measure it. They made no effort to see whether DeLuna's shoes, which had no blood on them anywhere, nonetheless matched the print.

In all probability, Escobedo and her technician never even noticed the blood-soaked present the killer had inadvertently left for them (figure 10.9).

* * *

Among other things, the Sigmor Shamrock crime scene was a jumble of surfaces that human hands had recently touched.

Natural oils from hands leave behind imprints of the profusion of ridges and valleys in the skin on bits of their fingers and palms. Garza saw several

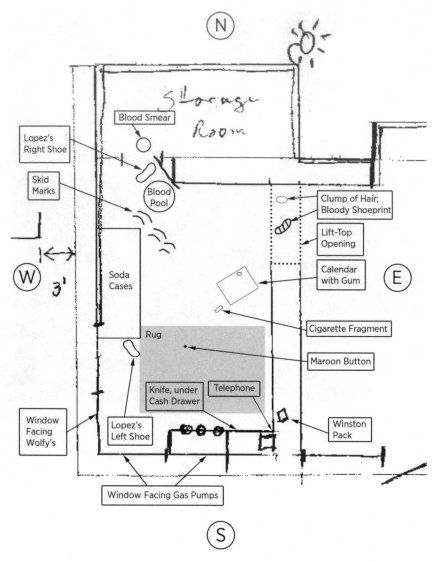

FIGURE 10.9  The clerk's area portion of the police diagram of the Sigmor Shamrock store (see figure 3.1), with additions by the authors (see figure 4.4).

surfaces in the photos that the stabber—and in some cases, many other people—must have touched. Many of the surfaces, he said, could have yielded fingerprints: more presents, perhaps, that the killer had left behind.

The trick was to use the right method to recover the prints from each type of surface. Dusting with graphite powder was the method the Corpus

Christi police typically used to collect prints at a crime scene, especially from surfaces they couldn't carry to a laboratory. Superglue and ninhydrin were better for moist, greasy, and other difficult surfaces, especially when the evidence could easily be confiscated at the scene and sent to a police lab for analysis.

You have to choose your method carefully, Garza explained. Once you use black graphite powder on a surface, it fouls the prints, and other methods won't work.

Garza saw many surfaces in the photos that he would have tested for prints:

- The empty cans found where Aguirre saw the killer drinking beer near the ice machine
- The ice machine
- The front door
- The cigarette case and display
- The Winston cigarette pack the attacker plunked down on the counter
- A large pen and a penny next to the cigarette pack
- The Formica counter itself, which the killer probably jumped over
- The telephone receiver he hung up
- The cash drawer
- The money bills strewn around the floor
- The key to the safe where money was stored
- Items the killer and victim probably swept onto the floor while they struggled, including napkins and paper towels, the cigarette fragment, the maroon button, the calendar, a plastic Sigmor bag, coin wrappers, a piece of typing paper, and a box of Sigmor sugar packs
- Cardboard soda cases that were knocked over during the struggle
- A comb found under a counter
- A "Kool Tube" on the floor next to Wanda's sandal just outside the storage room
- The open door, door knobs, and frame to the back room where the attacker tried to drag the victim
- The lift-top part of the passageway through the counter where the killer probably exited
- The latch that secured the half-door through the counter, which he had to unlatch to escape
- The half-door itself

- The clerk's roller chair, which someone had pushed out from behind the counter
- The buck knife

Garza was astonished that, from all these surfaces, Escobedo and Infante came away with usable fingerprints from only two—a beer can (one partial fingerprint) and the front door (three partial fingerprints in a clump and one partial palm print).

Worse, the department's fingerprint examiner found that the prints lifted were so fragmentary or damaged that he couldn't use them to make comparisons. Asked at the time about the quality of the prints Infante produced, the expert responded that they were "very bad." "[I]n effect," prosecutor Schiwetz explained to the jury, "there are no fingerprints in the case."

Infante didn't even try to look for prints on most of the promising surfaces. He limited his attention to the beer cans, the front door, the Winston pack (no luck), a portion of the Formica counter (also negative), the telephone receiver (same), and the knife (too greasy). That was it.

Besides one $5 bill, *nothing* was confiscated at the scene for fingerprint analysis under lab conditions—not the bloody handle to the front door, the phone receiver, the cash drawer, the paper towels or calendar, the cigarette fragment or button, the comb, the flip-top counter, or the half-door latch and the half-door itself. Items like that, which the killer almost certainly touched, "should have been taken off and taken to the laboratory and tested further."

But Escobedo seems to have believed that if Infante, doubling as a scene photographer and working with inferior equipment at night, couldn't lift a print at the scene, then it wasn't worth looking further at a laboratory.

Relying on Infante, a converted patrolman with little training, was itself a mistake, Garza felt. From what Garza could see, the man didn't do things right.

Garza pointed out that Infante came up empty even when he dusted surfaces that people were touching all day long. "The counter was made of Formica," Garza pointed out. "There should have been . . . prints from people that patronized the business." "If none were lifted," Infante's technique must have been "improper" (figure 10.10).

A former Scotland Yard expert who reviewed the fingerprints much later agreed. The effort to find latent prints, and the crime-scene examination in general, he concluded, "appear to be full of mistakes from start to finish."

FIGURE 10.10 Photograph taken from a television news video of Joel Infante attempting to obtain fingerprints from the clerk's counter in the Sigmor Shamrock store.

The biggest shame was the handling of the lock-blade buck knife. Its metal blade, brass trim, and locking lever were ideal surfaces for fingerprints. There was a "great possibility" that the killer left his calling card there. But when Infante found the weapon under the cash drawer, he could see that it was wet with blood and flesh. He said so in his report, and his photos plainly show it. Right there, he should have known that the graphite powder in his field kit wouldn't work.

He should have known either to bring the knife to the local lab or to "package it up and send it to the Department of Public Safety [in Austin] or even the FBI laboratory [in Washington, D.C.]" so experts could process it with the right equipment. Instead, Infante spread graphite powder all over the weapon on a counter at the Sigmor store, spoiling it forever for proper fingerprint and blood analysis.

No wonder Escobedo never asked a lab to go over the knife for the stabber's prints or blood. Infante had ruined it. A present of his own for the killer.

·    ·    ·

To Garza, everything about the scene investigation suggested haste and a rush to judgment: failing to set up a perimeter to keep onlookers away, overlooking clearly visible evidence, neglecting to test many promising surfaces for fingerprints and fouling those that were tested with the wrong materials, contaminating the scene, flying solo instead of bringing in a team of detectives and technicians, ignoring the absence of blood on DeLuna.

Escobedo even forgot to obtain a set of reference fingerprints from the body of Wanda Lopez, to rule out the victim as the source of the few prints that Infante *had* recovered. Although the prosecutor assigned to the case discovered the mistake a day before Lopez's funeral, by the time an officer dispatched by Escobedo arrived at the funeral home, Wanda had already been buried.

Garza worried that his inexperienced colleagues had simply quit when they heard over their radios that a man found under a truck was identified by witnesses. "Just because he's arrested under" a vehicle, the veteran detective said, "they thought it was open and shut. But where's the evidence?" There was no way they should have finished the field investigation in barely an hour.

"Just let [the] investigation take, whether it be one day, two days, or three days," he said. The scene was perfect for finding evidence that the killer had left behind. The crime was violent and chaotic, and an eyewitness chased off the perpetrator before he could cover his tracks. Whatever he left behind was right there in a small space "no more than about ten by ten." With time and some natural light, there was no telling what would be found.

If Escobedo had let the crime scene see the light of day instead of letting store employees scrub it down and reopen before dawn, "the results of this case would have been totally different."

The crime scene "was not gone over," Garza concluded. The people assigned "did not do a proper job, especially on a capital case." The detective assigned to the case "didn't have the proper experience of how to investigate a major crime," and the "identification person did not have the proper experience" and "the proper training [and] knowledge of what to look for at a crime scene." Together they "ignored and overlooked" the most promising evidence. Top to bottom, it was "a screwed-up damned case."

. . .

Eddie Garza didn't mince words. Asked to consider all the evidence that Olivia Escobedo did and didn't find, the longtime detective said that if he were sitting on a jury, "there is no way I could convict somebody of capital murder."

Factoring in what he knew from his own sources, Garza believed that "we had the wrong person." "Carlos Hernandez [was] the one that I felt . . . had committed this particular crime."

# 11

# Defense

HECTOR DE PEÑA, JR., was the first lawyer assigned to defend Carlos De-
Luna against charges that he had killed Wanda Lopez. Long afterward, De
Peña recalled the case as a series of disturbing discoveries, each coming a
little later than he would have hoped.

Carlos DeLuna and his family couldn't afford a lawyer, so Judge Jack
Blackmun assigned him one who would be paid by the state. Blackmun was
the same judge who three years later would appoint Jon Kelly for, and then
free, Carlos Hernandez in the Dahlia Sauceda murder case.

Why Judge Blackmun picked De Peña for the job—and not, for example, Kelly—was a matter of some discussion at the time. As is true for police
detectives and prosecutors, murder cases are at the top of the food chain for
criminal defense lawyers. And murder cases where the prosecutor asks for
the death penalty are the most noteworthy of all.

Fighting murder charges is tough work. Jurors feel responsible for providing some kind of payback or justice to the deceased victim and the
surviving family. This is especially so when the victim, like Wanda Lopez,
didn't "have it coming" in any way—and most especially when the jurors
didn't have to imagine the victim's hellish suffering because it was recorded
on a 911 tape. Albert Peña, the lawyer who got Jesse Garza acquitted in the
1980 Sauceda murder trial, understood this well. When he decided to go all
out for a not-guilty verdict for Garza, he knew that the jurors would never
let his client off unless they were sure of two things: that Garza didn't do it,
and that they knew exactly who did.

Fighting *capital* murder charges is even more difficult. With the defendant's life at stake, the case is sure to be discussed in the newspapers and

on television, and anything short of a conviction and death sentence is an embarrassing loss for the district attorney's office. Prosecutors fight capital cases hard, using every weapon at their disposal, including an entire police department to chase down witnesses and leads.

Defense lawyers are also on display in capital cases. Every move they make is analyzed and second-guessed by other lawyers and the press. If their client has no money, they're sure to be outgunned by the D.A. and police department. Courts don't have to agree to fund even a single defense investigator, and when they do, the amounts provided can be laughably low. In Corpus Christi at the time, the maximum available for a defense investigator was $500—enough for twenty-five hours total from someone willing to work at rock-bottom rates.

One reason capital murder cases are so demanding is that they're actually two trials in one. In other cases, there's one full-blown trial in front of a jury to decide if the defendant is guilty. If the jury finds the defendant guilty, the judge decides on a sentence after a short hearing. But in a capital case, if the jury finds the defendant guilty, there's a second full trial, at which the same jury decides whether to sentence the defendant to death or life in prison. At that trial, the prosecutors get to put on more evidence—of "aggravating" factors, or every reason they can find why the crime or the criminal is especially bad. Then the defendant is allowed to put on "mitigating" evidence—reasons why the crime wasn't as bad as some others, or why the defendant is a better person than the crime suggests or has a good excuse for what happened.

Making things even more difficult, the second, sentencing trial was a new concept in 1983. Courts had started using the procedure only a few years before Carlos DeLuna was arrested, and Texas had carried out its first execution under the new procedure only two months before. Even experienced capital murder lawyers were still getting used to the new rules in 1983.

"Let's be honest," Carlos Hernandez's lawyer, Jon Kelly, said while explaining to the private investigators how things went in capital cases in 1983. Most capital murder verdicts were challenged—and more than a few were overturned by appeals courts—because of "incompetence" of defense lawyers trying to deal with all the complications and difficulties of a capital trial with few resources to draw on.

It was understood that lawyers assigned to represent "indigents" in capital murder cases were "going to be under pressure" from prosecutors, the court, the client, and the press and had to be able "to handle a myriad of things." That's why, Kelly said, the assumption in Corpus Christi at the time was that you'd be assigned to represent someone threatened with death only if the judge thought you had "enough brains" and experience to "make sure that basic rights are protected" despite all the difficulties you faced.

"In those days, it was an honor to be an attorney in a capital murder case," Kelly explained—a sign that the judge "thinks you're good," that you're in the highest echelon.

•    •    •

When Judge Blackmun appointed Hector De Peña to represent Carlos DeLuna, the criminal defense lawyers in town were shocked and a little resentful. It wasn't just that De Peña was not the high-caliber criminal defense lawyer usually tapped for that kind of assignment; it was that De Peña wasn't a criminal defense lawyer at all. He was a small-time general practitioner, the kind of lawyer who takes whatever comes in the door: wills, bankruptcies, contracts for the sale of a home, speeding tickets, you name it.

Lawyers like that didn't usually handle a lot of major criminal cases, let alone ones that ended up in actual trials in front of a jury. De Peña was no exception. When he was assigned the DeLuna case, he had never represented a criminal defendant in front of a jury on *any* kind of serious criminal charge, let alone a capital murder charge. As Jon Kelly told the investigators, with all due respect for a Corpus colleague who later became a pretty good judge, Hector De Peña, Jr., wasn't on anyone's mental list of lawyers to consider for a capital murder case in 1983.

Other opinions were blunter: De Peña was incompetent to handle a capital case. He was out of his league. He may not have been "up to a capital murder [case]."

No one knew for sure why Blackmun appointed De Peña to represent DeLuna, but there was talk. It was rumored that De Peña was having trouble making ends meet. His father, Hector, Sr., was a longtime local judge who had some clout with voters (judges are elected in Texas) and other judges. Lawyers in town speculated that Blackmun's assignment was a favor to Hector, Sr., on behalf of a son who was short on cash. "You could make $15–20,000 in a month on a capital case," Kelly pointed out. "That was a nice piece of change."

At least part of the speculation was true. In 1984, a year after representing Carlos DeLuna for capital murder, De Peña represented himself in a bankruptcy filing. His papers said that he had almost $50,000 in unpaid debts going back as far as 1969, with only $8,000 in assets consisting mainly of a 1982 Saab.

De Peña opened his law office in 1978. From the start, the bankruptcy papers show, his practice generated too little money to cover his rent, credit card bills, and car payments. For a time, he survived on loans from six different banks and credit unions, but by the early 1980s he began defaulting on the loans, and his creditors were hauling him into court. Every cent that De Peña earned from assigned cases like DeLuna's went directly to the IRS for unpaid taxes. Adding to his problems, De Peña faced a malpractice suit claiming that he had failed to file a routine mechanic's lien to secure payment on a service contract he negotiated for a mom-and-pop refrigeration company.

●     ●     ●

De Peña himself acknowledged years later that the trial for Carlos DeLuna's life was one of his first jury trials of any sort, civil or criminal, minor or major.

Because he was a solo practitioner, he had no other lawyers in his office to help out. "My wife helped me," he volunteered. She was a "motivator . . . on a big case."

Not being a lawyer, however, De Peña's wife got emotionally involved in the case in a way Hector didn't, he recalled with a chuckle. She got mad at the games she thought the prosecutors played—making Hector look bad in front of the jury and that sort of thing. She couldn't believe that her husband would go out for a cup of coffee with the younger of the prosecutors, Steven Schiwetz, during breaks in the trial. Hector told her not to take it personally. The prosecutors were just doing their job. Lawyers could advocate inside the courtroom and be friends outside.

Later on, though, De Peña saw some wisdom in his wife's less trustful view. When he was handling DeLuna's case, he thought of prosecutors as "trying to find truth," as colleagues who would tell you whatever they knew about the case on a "handshake and gentlemen's agreement." Over time, though, he realized that some of them were simply looking for "notches in their belt" for every conviction they could get. "Rambo tactics," he called it. "Ends justify the means."

De Peña thought he saw that distinction at play between the two prosecutors in Carlos DeLuna's case. "There was Ken Botary," he told the investigators, "the older . . . prosecutor, and then [Steven] Schiwetz, who was
his second chair." "My opinion was that Mr. Botary was basically trying to
make a name for himself"—he "was out to get a conviction." Schiwetz, De
Peña believed, "was trying to see that justice was done."

                              •        •        •

The difference between the ideal and the real when it came to prosecutors
was one of De Peña's belated discoveries in the DeLuna case.

    Another was that, as much as he needed the money, he was in no posi-
tion to handle a capital case himself, even with his wife's moral support.

                              •        •        •

Carlos DeLuna was arrested on Friday, February 4, 1983. De Peña got the
assignment to represent DeLuna on February 7. The trial was scheduled to
start on March 28 (it was later postponed), which didn't give him much
time to come up with a strategy for both parts of the capital trial, get ready
with questions for the State's witnesses, and prepare his own witnesses and
physical evidence.

    The lawyer's first task was to learn from Carlos himself, other witnesses,
and the physical evidence whether the police had arrested the right guy.
If there was any chance they did, De Peña also had to figure out if his client had any legal "excuses" (mental problems, say) that might reduce any
crime to a less serious one, or at least persuade a jury to impose a sentence
other than death. Getting that done required De Peña to interview all the
witnesses and file written requests with the judge for at least three things:
money for an investigator, a mental examination of DeLuna, and an order telling the prosecutors to share their information in the case, including
about other suspects.

                              •        •        •

De Peña worked on the case for five days—Monday, February 28, to Friday,
March 4, 1983. He requested and examined police reports and evidence.
He met with Carlos once or twice, with the second or only meeting occur-
ring on Tuesday, March 1.

    The results baffled the inexperienced lawyer. From the police reports, he
knew that George Aguirre had fingered Carlos as the man he saw outside

the Sigmor Shamrock gas station with a knife and that Kevan Baker had identified him as the man he saw grappling with the bloody victim before throwing her down and rushing out of the store. He also knew that the police had arrested his client nearby underneath a pickup truck.

From DeLuna, he heard a different message—the same one the young man had given to the arresting officer and then or later had repeated to his family and girlfriend, the prosecutors, the jury, news reporters, a prison pastor, and anyone else who would listen. He had not killed Wanda Lopez.

What brought De Peña up short was what Carlos said about who *did* kill the store clerk.

At first DeLuna claimed he didn't know who had killed the clerk. Then he admitted that he did know. He'd seen another man commit the crime, someone he knew. But he wouldn't provide a name because it would be suicide to rat the man out. "I'm dead whether I'm out [of jail] or in if I identify him," DeLuna told his lawyer.

"I believe [Carlos] was truthfully afraid of this individual," De Peña explained to the investigators years later. "He felt this individual had [the] ability to see that he was silenced" if he talked or revealed a name.

No matter how hard De Peña pleaded, Carlos wouldn't give up a name.

*     *     *

De Peña came away convinced but stumped. After "working with this young man for the period of time that [I] did," De Peña said, "I didn't feel he was capable of killing someone." "I honestly believe to this day that Carlos didn't do it" and that "his friend killed her."

But De Peña was in a bind after only a week of work. If his client had said, "I'm innocent, and here's what I was doing at the time," De Peña could have tried to prove it. And if he couldn't prove it, he could come back to his client to say his story didn't check out and he'd be a fool to try to snow a jury with it.

If his client had *not* denied any involvement, De Peña could have searched for a legal excuse to lessen the crime or "mitigating factors" to justify a lower sentence. More likely, he would have worked out a deal for Carlos to plead guilty in return for a life sentence.

In fact, Assistant District Attorney Schiwetz came to De Peña before the trial—and again during the trial—with an offer to withdraw the request for a death sentence if Carlos would plead guilty. "[T]hroughout this thing," De Peña said, Steve Schiwetz "tried real hard to get my client to accept a life sentence rather than the possibility of the death penalty." De Peña thought that twenty-year-old DeLuna's tender age weighed on the prosecutor.

But Carlos refused a deal. He was adamant that he was not involved in the girl's killing, De Peña explained. He was adamant that he was not guilty, and he wanted his day in court.

Carlos's "mind-set," the lawyer recalled, was that because he was innocent, the prosecutors wouldn't be able to come up with evidence of his guilt. "They wouldn't find him guilty" because "there wouldn't be enough facts."

●   ●   ●

His client's simple way of thinking was another part of De Peña's problem.

"From a standard education perspective, you might say [Carlos] was retarded," De Peña said later. The young man could survive well enough on the streets, but he was "from [a] clinical point of view, maybe retarded."

De Peña didn't, however, expect Joel Kutnick, the psychiatrist assigned to look into DeLuna's mental state, to say that DeLuna was impaired. "Kutnick always found them competent if they were minimally oriented in time and space," the lawyer recalled.

De Peña had higher hopes for James Plaisted, the psychologist assigned by the judge. Plaisted was a member of De Peña's Baptist church and active with the youth group. It was only later that De Peña realized tht Plaisted was no saint. He was "preying on little kids," De Peña said. Their church referred kids to him for counseling, and he molested them.

●   ●   ●

New to big criminal cases, De Peña hadn't bargained for a client whose intelligence he doubted, who insisted that he was innocent and refused to take a deal or argue excuses, but who was too scared to name the man he saw committing the crime.

His client, De Peña realized, wanted *him* to find the guy on his own, or else get the police to do it. Faced with this state of affairs, De Peña stewed for a month without doing anything. Word went around among the experienced criminal lawyers that De Peña was floundering.

On April 6, De Peña called for reinforcements. In the first of two requests to Judge Blackmun that day, he asked for a psychiatrist to examine Carlos. His client, he said, had exhibited "symptoms of severe disorder or mental defect for many years" and couldn't help with his defense. It was this request that led the judge to assign Kutnick and Plaisted to take a look.

De Peña's other request was for a second lawyer on the case. Two months in, De Peña realized he couldn't go it alone.

.    .    .

On April 15, Judge Blackmun assigned James Lawrence to work with De Peña. He also pushed back the date for trial to June 20 (figure 11.1).

When the trial took place, Lawrence pretty much ran it for the defense. Of the thirty-five witnesses called by the State to testify, Lawrence cross-examined twenty-four. De Peña cross-examined one—a minor witness at that. No one cross-examined the ten remaining witnesses. Of the five witnesses the defense presented, Lawrence prepared two—including the single, main witness, Carlos DeLuna himself—and De Peña prepared three minor witnesses. De Peña happily took a back seat.

The two lawyers didn't coordinate their work very well. Years later, De Peña said he was upset by Lawrence's all-important final argument to the jury, which De Peña felt was insulting to the jurors. "But I couldn't control that part of it," De Peña said. "I didn't know just how [Lawrence] was going to present his final argument."

.    .    .

There were complaints, as well, about how De Peña delivered his own argument to the jury. He was so anxious about making his first ever "closing statement" to a jury in a big case that he couldn't keep his voice up. The court reporter, whose job it was to take down everything the lawyers and witnesses said, couldn't hear De Peña. Neither, it seemed, could the jurors.

Later the court reporter joked that the only thing she heard De Peña say clearly during the entire trial was "Oh shit!" That was De Peña's reaction from his seat when the prosecutor brought out some damaging information the defense lawyers hadn't known about, because they had failed to interview several people on the witness list the prosecutor had given them before trial. The inexperienced lawyer took the court reporter seriously when she twitted him about having to include his profane remark in the official transcript of the case.

FIGURE 11.1   Images from television newscasts in July 1983 of (*top, from left*) prosecutors Steven Schiwetz and Kenneth Botary, (*bottom, from left*) defendant Carlos DeLuna, and defense lawyers James Lawrence and Hector De Peña.

•     •     •

Unlike De Peña, James Lawrence was an experienced criminal defense lawyer, one who prided himself on how many criminal cases he could handle in a year. His cases came mostly on assignment from the courts to represent people who couldn't pay, like DeLuna.

There were some in Corpus Christi who didn't think much of Lawrence as a defense lawyer. Detective Eddie Garza said that Lawrence would meet his clients for only a "few minutes," get them to plea bargain, and "collect his fee." Others thought his experience counted for a lot, rating him honest and "excellent."

When the private investigators first asked Lawrence about DeLuna, he said he didn't remember the capital murder case at all. It was lost in the shuffle of the hundreds of cases the courts had appointed him to handle that year. He showed the investigator a log book listing all his cases. There indeed were hundreds each year.

Assistant District Attorney Steven Schiwetz was able to refresh Lawrence's memory. Schiwetz approached Lawrence because he was "hot under the collar" that investigators were looking into the case so many years later.

Even after talking to Schiwetz, however, Lawrence said he couldn't remember much. The police found his client hiding under a truck, he recalled, which didn't look good. DeLuna told him "he ran because he was on parole. He saw what was going on [inside the Sigmor station] and then heard sirens [and ran] away."

Lawrence also brought up "the money thing": that convenience store clerks don't keep nearly as much money in the cash drawer as DeLuna had on him.

Lawrence especially remembered that the police had no physical evidence linking DeLuna to the crime, which was odd given all the blood at the scene. The lawyer also recalled that the witness who saw the killer coming out of the store gave a description of another person, not DeLuna. "Hell, if that isn't reasonable doubt I don't know what is," he said.

.    .    .

After Lawrence was assigned the case in April, De Peña breathed a sigh of relief and went on with the rest of his struggling practice. At a hearing on June 10 at which the judge considered DeLuna's request for a postponement of the trial because his lawyers weren't ready, the judge asked De Peña why he hadn't worked on Carlos's case or met with his client since early March. De Peña admitted knowing that "there was leg work that needed to be done" on the case but said that he hadn't done it "because of trying to maintain my own practice and my own cases." No one asked De Peña to explain why his appointment to represent DeLuna on capital murder charges didn't count as one of his "own" cases.

Lawrence had also been busy with other matters. Late April and much of May had gone to another murder case the local court had assigned to him. Lawrence did file a written request, repeating De Peña's earlier one, to view the police evidence on DeLuna, and he did take a look at the evidence. But he had no time for his own investigation into what happened.

It wasn't until early June that Lawrence finally could focus on DeLuna's case. He filed several motions, including one to have the judge throw out John and Julie Arsuaga's identification of DeLuna after being shown a group of photos by Detective Olivia Escobedo. It was then that Lawrence first met Carlos—on June 1 or 2 to tell his client what was in the State's file, and again on Saturday, June 4, to hear DeLuna's side of the story.

Lawrence had hoped that his client would accept a plea bargain. But Carlos "wasn't going to take a deal because he said 'I am innocent,'" Lawrence explained later. "He told me from the beginning that [he] saw something, heard sirens and [thought the] cops wouldn't believe him, so he ran." Carlos was "reluctant to give up a name," Lawrence recalled. "He wanted to be sure he would be protected if he gave [a] name."

●　　●　　●

Although the prosecutors discussed the possibility of a plea bargain with DeLuna and his lawyers, no one mentioned that possibility to Wanda Lopez's brother, Richard Vargas.

Not long after Wanda died, four Corpus Christi law-enforcement officers in suits came by to pay their respects to Richard and his parents. They assured the family that they had caught the killer and would prosecute him to a death sentence.

Richard told them they'd better finish the job, because if they didn't he would. "You don't need to get involved," they told him. "We'll see it through."

Decades later, Richard said he had meant what he said. Everything until that visit—how the police operator had interrogated his sister instead of sending someone to save her, how the store manager washed down the store before anyone knew what happened, how the police gave the television stations the 911 tape without letting the family know—had made him wonder how seriously the police were taking the case. At the time, Richard recalled, he couldn't get DeLuna out of his head. He dreamed about sneaking into the jail to "kill the bastard" himself.

•    •    •

At the end of May, a retired judge from Houston named Wallace "Pete" Moore was assigned to run the trial in DeLuna's case. Moore liked to take a case in Corpus now and then. It was a good way to pick up a little extra income. If he stayed in the good graces of the local judges, the assignments might keep coming.

Or at least that's how Jon Kelly had Moore figured. Kelly didn't like to have visiting judges in the criminal cases he handled because they're "getting paid" and "don't want to cause trouble for the judge whose bench [they're] sitting on. That's number one." A visiting judge is "there not to make waves. And the way to do that is to rule for the State and against the defendant. Because he ain't going to be asked back if he does it another way."

"Number two," Kelly continued, as a visiting judge "you don't really care, do you? Because you're not going to be here when this is over."

Because De Peña and Lawrence weren't ready to go to trial when Moore got his first two-week assignment on the case, the local judges extended his assignment twice—and his fee.

•    •    •

On June 9, with the trial set to begin eleven days later, Lawrence finally obtained permission from the court to spend the maximum $500 on an investigator. The next day, Lawrence asked Judge Moore to postpone the start of the trial because he had not had time to investigate or prepare. In an unusual move, his typewritten motion asked the judge to kick De Peña off the case for not doing enough work and to assign a new lawyer to replace De Peña.

Somewhere along the way, the sentence asking for De Peña to be replaced was crossed out in ink, and the judge never ruled on it. But Lawrence's statements criticizing De Peña's lack of diligence remained in the document as a reason for a postponement. That's what caused the judge to ask De Peña why he did no work on the case between March and June.

Lawrence then explained his own failure to get going on the case—and why he hadn't yet talked to De Peña to find out what his cocounsel knew. Still displaying an unusual amount of public candor about a fellow lawyer, Lawrence excused his failure to talk to his co-counsel by saying that he was pretty sure that even after months on the case, De Peña knew "even less" about it than Lawrence did after only a few weeks.

The judge refused to postpone the trial.

A week later, DeLuna tried to take matters into his own hands, scribbling a statement entitled "Ineffective Counsel" and sending it to the judge. The words Carlos strung together were gibberish: "Conflict and the relationship of client and attorney can not be reached, therefore, the Defendant cannot go safely to trial and have this said attorney [De Peña] prepare his defense." But the gist, and DeLuna's desperation, were clear enough. He couldn't safely place his life in De Peña's hands. Or, as he wrote in another letter to the court, "Mr. De Pena Jr. was not doing nothing to help me so I filed a motion to have Mr. De Pena remove [sic]."

DeLuna's second handwritten document requested a delay in the start of the trial because his mother was in the hospital and couldn't testify for him on June 20.

Judge Moore ignored DeLuna's "Ineffective Counsel" statement and rejected his plea for a delay. On June 20, however, the day on which the trial was supposed to start, Moore "reset" the trial for July 5 "at request of Defense."

•   •   •

Lawrence was finally able to begin investigating what had happened to Wanda Lopez on Friday, June 9, the same day the judge gave him $500 for an investigator. On Tuesday, July 5, the lawyers began selecting a jury.

Between those dates, Lawrence had three weeks and the July Fourth weekend to figure out what had happened to Wanda Lopez and how to defend Carlos DeLuna against murder charges and the death penalty.

•   •   •

After quickly settling on a culprit, the police and prosecutors had worked steadily from February to July to prepare a case against him.

It took law enforcement only about a half hour on the evening of February 4 to decide who had killed Wanda Lopez. Everything became clear to them between 8:50 P.M., when they pulled DeLuna out from under a pickup truck, and 9:20 P.M. or so, when they got Kevan Baker and George Aguirre to identify DeLuna in the back of the police cruiser at the gas station.

Carlos DeLuna, they concluded, had robbed, knifed, and wrestled with Wanda Lopez before throwing her to the ground, rushing out of the store, and hiding in neighboring yards until he was found underneath the truck. Thirty or forty minutes later, Detective Escobedo shut down her investigation at the store and let Robert Stange wash down the crime scene.

Detective Escobedo and three prosecutors—initially a man named Jack Hunter, who later turned the case over to Kenneth Botary and Steven Schiwetz—spent the next five months preparing witnesses, questions, and evidence to prove DeLuna's guilt and shoot down any possible contrary theory. Assisting them were at least twenty-seven different local and state law-enforcement officers and evidence technicians who helped prepare the case for trial.

The process began immediately after the killing, when Escobedo showed John and Julie Arsuaga a set of photos and John identified DeLuna as the man they saw jogging near the Phase III nightclub. Escobedo also asked for an autopsy of Wanda Lopez by the county medical examiner, who collected evidence according to Escobedo's instructions.

Over the next few days, Escobedo ordered officers to get written statements and evidence from witnesses Kevan Baker, George Aguirre, John and Julie Arsuaga, police dispatcher Jesse Escochea, Theresa Barrera (who first spotted a man under her pickup truck and watched him run in the direction of the truck where DeLuna was found), and Armando Garcia (whose house was on a bee-line between the trucks and who found DeLuna's shirt and shoes in his yard).

Escobedo also collected written reports from police officers involved in the manhunt and arrest. There was Steven Fowler, who was first on the scene, and Bruno Mejia, who was second and handled the witnesses and BOLOs. Then there were Thomas Mylett and Constable Ruben Rivera, who helped take DeLuna into custody, and Mark Schauer, who led the arrest and drove DeLuna to the gas station, witnessed the show-up identifications, and found $149 rolled up in the suspect's pocket. Last, there was a report from Joel Infante, who photographed the crime scene and helped with the investigation there.

On Monday, February 7, 1983, Escobedo spent the morning reviewing the police file with prosecutor Jack Hunter, who evidently discovered gaps in Escobedo's work. Soon after the meeting, Escobedo ordered subordinates to obtain elimination fingerprints from Wanda Lopez's body (which, however, they failed to do before Lopez was buried). She also ordered all officers who took part in the arrest and show-up identification to type up new, more detailed reports for the prosecutors to use to make the case against DeLuna. Using all the reports and witness statements as references, Escobedo prepared a long memo for the prosecutors summarizing all aspects of the case against DeLuna.

Escobedo also let Gilbert Garcia, DeLuna's parole officer, interview the defendant in jail—an effort, possibly, to see if DeLuna would confess to the crime. He didn't.

The lead detective worked to get local and state forensic scientists to identify Wanda's blood or fingerprints on Carlos's clothes and on the money found in his pocket.

At Escobedo's direction, other officers retrieved the audiotape that recorded 911 calls and police radio traffic. They preserved the part of the tape beginning with Wanda's call saying there was a man in the store with a knife and ending when she screamed and her attacker hung up the phone.

Prosecutor Hunter prepared a criminal complaint against DeLuna, charging him with murder. Later in February, he presented the case to a grand jury, allowing him to do a dry run of the testimony of police witnesses who would later testify at the actual trial. The grand jury indicted DeLuna for capital murder.

Beginning in late February and continuing into March, Hunter identified the witness statements and evidence he would let De Peña see and invited him over for a look. Throughout March, Hunter collected documents from law-enforcement agencies on Carlos DeLuna's run-ins with the law, as well as the ambulance and hospital records on Wanda Lopez's injuries and the futile fight to save her life.

Hunter then began identifying and preparing the State's witnesses for the trial—Escobedo herself, the first officers at the scene (Fowler, Reserve Officer Bill McCoy, Mejia), the arresting officers (Mylett, Rivera, Schauer, Carolyn Vargas), the cops who organized the show-up identifications in the Sigmor Shamrock parking lot (R. W. Glorfield, Lieutenant J. Knox, Eddie McConley), officers who helped in the scene investigation (Infante) and interviewed witnesses (Gary Garrett, Sergeant M. Shedd), police dispatcher Escochea, fingerprint examiner Ernest Wilson, Medical Examiner Joseph Rupp, several emergency technicians and the doctor and nurse who treated Wanda Lopez on the night she died, Sigmor manager Pete Gonzalez, and witnesses Kevan Baker, George Aguirre, John and Julie Arsuaga, Theresa Barrera, and Armando Garcia.

In April and May, Detective Escobedo, Identification Technician Infante, and Assistant District Attorney Schiwetz took a momentary detour and worked the Carlos *Hernandez* angle that Detective Eddie Garza and his informants had identified. Infante took Hernandez's fingerprints, and Escobedo and Schiwetz reviewed Hernandez's rap sheet and those of six other men with the same name.

Fully expecting the jury to convict DeLuna at the first stage of trial, the prosecutors spent May and June identifying the witnesses and arrest, prison, and parole records they would use to try to convince the same jury, at the second stage of the trial, to sentence Carlos DeLuna to die.

*     *     *

In the three weeks that Lawrence and De Peña had to come up with a defense to the case that two dozen law-enforcement officers had spent four months assembling, they found nothing that was helpful to Carlos that they didn't already know about—no witness or other evidence. When Lawrence later submitted an invoice for the work of the investigator the judge had agreed to fund, he had to explain why the investigator went over budget when, in fact, "much of the information developed was not used or, as a matter of fact, was not usable."

During those weeks, DeLuna was still refusing to name the man he said he saw committing the crime, and Lawrence and De Peña didn't come up with a name themselves or any information that could help them find him. The only names DeLuna did offer were those of Linda and Mary Ann Perales, sisters who he claimed to have run into at the skating rink on the night of the killing.

Linda Perales did indeed know Carlos DeLuna, the little brother of her junior high sweetheart, Manuel DeLuna. When the out-of-town investigators visited her in 2004, Linda also recalled going to the skating rink at SPID and Kostoryz when she was younger. But she couldn't remember seeing Carlos DeLuna there on any particular day in 1983, twenty-one years earlier, and thought she had probably been too old by then to be at the rink. Linda was sure, however, that no one from either side of the case had approached her in 1983 to ask her about Carlos DeLuna's claim.

The court-appointed defense investigator did talk to Linda's sister Mary Ann, who told him she was certain she had *not* been at the skating rink on the evening of February 4. She was seven months pregnant then and had attended her own baby shower at her mother's house that very night. She said she had photos to prove it.

Even though Lawrence and De Peña realized that Mary Ann could only hurt their client's case, they subpoenaed her to appear in court at DeLuna's July 1983 trial, and they told the State's lawyers what Carlos had said about her. The prosecutors promptly sent officers to interview Mary Ann, who told them as well—after they assured her that DeLuna was a "liar"—that she was not at the skating rink that night. Mary Ann's denial of a detail in their client's story was the only hard information that Lawrence and De Peña came up with, and it helped the prosecutors' case.

It is unclear whether Lawrence or De Peña told *Carlos* that Mary Ann disputed his recollection, that the prosecutors knew that, and that it would be foolish for him to claim otherwise at the trial. There was no reason for DeLuna to testify about the Perales sisters, in any event. He only claimed to have seen them earlier in the evening, not later, when he saw a man attacking Wanda Lopez. So he wasn't claiming them as an alibi, and they weren't important to his story.

·     ·     ·

By telling the prosecutors about the Perales sisters, De Peña and Lawrence had gone out of their way to give the State information that they knew could damage their client's case. They expected law enforcement to reciprocate. Unlike the defendant, who has a right not to tell the State anything, prosecutors have a moral and legal duty to tell the defendant about any evidence they have that could help provide a defense. But this was another lesson De Peña would learn from the DeLuna case. Prosecutors and police aren't always diligent in finding evidence that helps the defense, or in disclosing it to the other side when they do find it.

An example of this lesson lay in psychiatrist Kutnick's report concluding that DeLuna's low IQ score was either a fluke or malingering. The doctor said he might change his mind if there was any information about "how far this defendant got in school, and whether there was a question of his being retarded." Kutnick asked prosecutors to look for the information in DeLuna's school records. But as he said in his report, he never "heard back from Mr. Schiwetz," so he assumed the information was "not obtainable." Judge Moore, as well as Lawrence and De Peña, read Kutnick's caveat and evidently joined the doctor in assuming that Schiwetz had followed up and found no relevant school records. DeLuna's lawyers didn't look for themselves.

All that happened in 1983. In 2004, the private investigators *did* look. Within hours, they were handed a sheaf of school records showing that, from the elementary grades on, teachers and psychologists alike had diagnosed Carlos DeLuna as a slow learner with a low IQ and learning problems that required special education classes and led him to drop out before finishing middle school. DeLuna's juvenile records show the same thing.

·   ·   ·

Another example of evidence that law enforcement didn't produce was the audiotape of the manhunt. Within a month of the crime, De Peña and prosecutor Hunter had discussed the police tapes in the case, and Hunter offered to let De Peña listen to the portion of the tape that recorded Wanda Lopez's 911 call to the police. The defense lawyers had asked in writing for much more, however, including records of "all incoming calls and outgoing broadcasts made concerning the reports and whereabouts of any suspect or suspicious persons reported via the Corpus Christi Police Department arising out of the" incident at the Sigmor Shamrock on February 4.

"[W]e originally tried to get those tapes," De Peña explained in 2005, but law-enforcement officials said everything had been erased, "the explanation being that the master tape was only kept for thirty days and then it was erased and reused." In the end, all De Peña and Lawrence received was a cassette of Wanda's ninety-second 911 call.

A police communications technician explained at trial that the February 4 master tape had been preserved for months after the point when it normally would have been reused, and that on June 29, 1983, he had spliced the ninety-second 911 call out of the master tape so the call could be played at trial. The technician testified that the only portion of the tape his law-enforcement superiors had asked him to preserve, even as of late June, was "the call made in reporting a man with a knife at 2602 SPID" up to "the point where that call ends" when the attacker hung up the phone.

In the meantime, police dispatcher Jesse Escochea had made his own copy of the master tape, which turned up in his possession in Los Angeles in 2004. His copy includes not only the 911 part of the call, but the forty-minute manhunt as well. When Schiwetz was asking Escochea questions during the trial, the dispatcher mentioned in passing that he and Schiwetz had gone over the manhunt part of the tape together in preparing for trial. But police and prosecutors never gave the manhunt part of the tape to De Peña or Lawrence, and the jury never learned about it. The police evidently destroyed the original of that part of the master tape recording a few days before the trial began.

The defense lawyers and jury in DeLuna's trial never heard the repeated police bulletins describing a suspect in a gray sweatshirt, red flannel jacket, and blue jeans sprinting north away from the Sigmor at around 8:11 P.M. They never heard Officer Mejia worrying out loud on the radio that the clean-shaven man in a white dress shirt and black slacks whom the Arsuagas saw jogging two blocks east of the gas station at around 8:05 P.M. was "another" person, different from the scruffy and mustachioed man whom Baker saw tangling with Wanda and fleeing north behind the station. And they never had a chance to compare any of the descriptions on the tape with DeLuna's white button-down shirt, black slacks, and recently shaved face at the time of his arrest.

The defense lawyers and jury didn't know that police tracked a suspect matching Baker's original description for twenty-five minutes running north on Dodd Street—the direction Baker saw the killer flee—and then along McArdle Street to the nursing home, Domino's Pizza, and a Circle K at Kostoryz, until Theresa Barrera spotted a man under her pickup truck and diverted the entire search party.

They also didn't know that Officer Fowler had questioned a man earlier that evening who was lurking around the Circle K and also matched the description that Baker gave of the fleeing killer. On the contrary, the only information provided to DeLuna's lawyers and the jury about the possibility of another suspect was the following question (by prosecutor Steven Schiwetz) and answer (by arresting officer Mark Schauer):

SCHIWETZ: Was there any other suspect seen at any other area, so far as you know?
SCHAUER: Not to my knowledge.
SCHIWETZ: Did the dispatcher disseminate any information regarding other suspects in other areas other than the one on Franklin?
SCHAUER: No.

Before evaluating Baker's and Aguirre's identification of DeLuna as the man they had seen, the defense lawyers and jury never heard the radio broadcasts reverberating around Baker and Aguirre at the Sigmor, broadcasts which made clear that police were sure the man they found under a truck was the killer, who they were bringing "back" to the Sigmor.

Left in the dark, Lawrence asked the judge to keep the jury from hearing about the Arsuagas' selection of DeLuna from a group of photos, and when the judge refused, Lawrence worked hard to discredit the Arsuagas in the eyes of the jury. Lawrence didn't ask the judge to keep the jury from hearing about Baker's and Aguirre's show-up identification.

Because he didn't hear the manhunt tape, Lawrence had no way of knowing that, far from *hurting* DeLuna, the Arsuagas actually gave his client an alibi. Describing the well-dressed DeLuna to a T, the Arsuagas placed him two blocks *east* of the Sigmor Shamrock on the SPID frontage road just seconds after Baker watched the killer run *west* behind the gas station to Dodd Street, and just as police officers were tracking a man matching Baker's description north on Dodd.

Speaking to a television reporter about the case years later, Lawrence was agitated about the tape the police withheld from the defense and the man it described running up Dodd Street. "What did I have to counteract anything—*anything*?" he asked, reflecting on the State's case. "Had we had that other tape, good gosh, I got something! Because then you could have said, 'Was that the Carlos Hernandez we've been looking for? Yes!'"

•   •   •

When he spoke to the private investigators in 2004, Hector De Peña was also annoyed that he went to trial without ever hearing the manhunt part of the tape that came after the 911 call the jury heard. He was truly angry, however, that law enforcement had never told him about what was recorded *before* the call the prosecutors had played at trial. The first he heard about the earlier recording was from newspaper coverage of the Vargas family's lawsuit against the Diamond Shamrock Company, owner of the Sigmor station, a few years after DeLuna's capital murder trial.

Rene Rodriguez was the Vargases' lawyer when they sued Shamrock on behalf of Wanda's young daughter. When it came to getting the evidence needed to prove his clients' right to money damages for Shamrock's failure to protect Wanda, Rodriguez wasn't going to rely on the good will of the police the way DeLuna's lawyers had. Instead, he got a formal court order telling the police department to give him everything it had about the killing of Wanda Lopez.

Rodriguez remembered well the reaction of De Peña and Lawrence when they came to his office to look at the evidence they had heard about from press coverage of the Vargas lawsuit. The evidence included photos of the crime scene never shown to the DeLuna jury, including pictures with the killer's bloody shoeprints inside the store and possibly on the sidewalk outside, a clump of the victim's hair, full panoramas of the blood stains and spatter behind the counter, and the lead detective standing on top of evidence. Rodriguez also had Shamrock records showing that employees were forbidden to keep more than $75 in the cash drawer at any one time.

"We didn't get any of this shit," De Peña told Rodriguez.

De Peña repeated the same complaint to the private investigators fifteen years later. "It was a result of the newspaper reporting what was transpiring in the courtroom and what the testimony was" in the Vargas suit that he found out what the police never told him—and what the jury never heard in 1983 at DeLuna's trial.

•   •   •

Rene Rodriguez was bothered by the police department's behavior, too. From his investigation, his heartbroken clients learned that they wouldn't have lost a mother, daughter, and sister if the police had done their job right.

Rodriguez had taken the Diamond Shamrock case personally. He turned the city upside down looking for evidence about what had happened to Wanda and who was to blame. He found police records, for instance, showing that the neighborhood around the Sigmor on SPID was teeming with crime during those years, and that the store there was no place to let a woman wait for even a second when she called 911 for help.

But that, Rodriguez discovered, is exactly what the cops did to Wanda that night. *Twice.*

Contrary to the impression left by the tape the prosecutors played for the jurors at DeLuna's trial—the only tape the police gave to defense lawyers and television stations—Rodriguez's evidence at the Diamond Shamrock trial showed that Wanda called 911 not once, but twice.

Although police never made the first call public, its existence was well known inside the police department. Olivia Escobedo, who had left Corpus Christi before the trial in the Diamond Shamrock case, readily remembered the two calls when she recounted the events of Wanda's death to an investigator years later.

"I remember listening to Ms. Lopez screaming on the tape," Escobedo said. "She had called once to say that there was a man outside with a knife, then I remember when she called back, trying to talk in a low voice" so the man wouldn't know that she was calling the police. On the second call, "you could hear her all of a sudden saying she would give him what he wanted" and "screaming as he attacked her."

There were other clues, too. When the private investigators looked at the D.A.'s file on the DeLuna case in 2004, they found the Corpus Christi Police Department "call card" reporting Wanda's 911 call to Escochea at 8:09 P.M., when she is heard screaming and struggling with someone. The record is on a "Supplementary" form, one used for follow-up situations after some earlier action initiated police contact.

And there was George Aguirre's statement to police and testimony at the DeLuna trial. He said he warned Wanda about a scary-looking guy outside with an open buck knife in his pocket and left only after hearing Wanda on the phone with the 911 operator, while the man with the knife was still *outside*. Aguirre saw Wanda making a different call from the one given to the defense lawyers on a tape cassette and played for the jury. The call the jury heard began with Wanda telling Escochea that she was calling because the man she believed had a knife was already *inside* the store.

Although no recording of the first conversation survived, both Rodriguez and television reporter Karen Boudrie, who covered both the DeLuna and Vargas trials, helped the private investigators reconstruct it later on:

"Is he in the store?" the female 911 operator asked Wanda.

"No, he's outside."

"He's not doing anything to hurt you?"

"No."

"Call back if he does anything, if he comes inside."

Wanda hung up and waited. Customers came and went. Only then did a man she suspected of having a knife come in.

She called back. The 911 operator was on another call and let the phone ring. Finally, Escochea, the dispatcher, picked it up.

To Escochea, the call seemed "routine" until Wanda started screaming and he realized that "something had gone wrong." At first, he was put off by what he thought was Wanda's "attitude." Not realizing that she had called before and been disregarded, Escochea didn't understand why she was so impatient when he began peppering her with his own set of questions.

Years later, when Rene Rodriguez described what he'd learned to the outside investigators, he was still angry:

> When she called, telling them she was at the Shamrock, the dispatcher, the police, everybody knew where she was, because of Wolfy's next door and that two-story naked lady there all lit up next to the freeway. Everyone that used the freeway saw it every day. They knew it was a high crime area. They knew all that! But they tell her, call us back if it looks serious.
>
> Some little minimum wage girl calling, concerned about something happening next to a topless place at night. She's trapped behind the counter, no place to run. No big deal to them. Then when she called back, they ask crazy questions instead of [doing] something!

Rodriguez believed that most people would feel the same way he did and that the police knew it. When he started the trial against Shamrock, uniformed officers and detectives came in and watched, sometimes several at once. Rodriguez knew that was out of the ordinary—that some kind of message was being sent. Cops show up in court for civil trials only when they're being sued. That's how the cops knew Rodriguez. He'd made a good living until then defending cops in brutality cases.

The police were there, Rodriguez believed, to make sure he didn't use the trial to embarrass the department. "They were there," Rodriguez said, "to make sure I focused on the Shamrock and not too much on them." Rodriguez did what he had to do for the Vargases, and they got a good settlement before the trial ended—one of the first ever from a convenience store company for putting an employee in danger. The law protects police from paying damages in cases like this, so Rodriguez didn't sue them. Still, it galled him that they showed up in court to try to intimidate him. He didn't represent cops much after that.

. . .

Later, when Hector De Peña found out what really had happened to Wanda Lopez, he felt that the same desire to protect the police department from embarrassment had influenced the DeLuna investigation and its aftermath.

Any time a lawyer tries to convince a jury that her client is innocent, the most natural question the jurors will have is why in the world the police would go after someone who didn't commit the crime, especially when the district attorney is seeking the death penalty.

When De Peña asked himself why the police hid Wanda's earlier call, he thought he had the answer to the jury's question: "C.Y.A." Cover your ass. If you're law enforcement, you're supposed to protect hard-working people like Wanda Lopez from knife-wielding attackers. If instead you screw up and let her get killed, the first thing you'd want to do is nab someone and put the focus on him, as quickly and dramatically as possible.

"I think that when Carlos was arrested," De Peña reflected in retrospect, "basically, they were just, they were out to find their goat."

That was another lesson that De Peña learned too late to help Carlos DeLuna: a lawyer has to know when to trust law enforcement to help him make his case and when to prove it himself, the way Rene Rodriguez had done.

. . .

"The sooner the better" was one more lesson the case taught. One of the biggest mysteries the private investigators failed to solve in 2004 was what had happened to the physical evidence in the case over the preceding two decades.

Although DNA analysis didn't exist in 1983 when DeLuna was being prosecuted, the genetic material it tests can last for centuries. The bloody murder knife, beer cans, cigarette butt, and cash, among other things that Escobedo and Infante picked up at the Sigmor Shamrock store, could to this day have traces of blood and saliva on them, which modern forensic analysis could detect and link to a human being.

In 2004, when the investigators looked in the courthouse vault for the evidence, they found evidence boxes indexed to cases from long before 1983.

The boxes were chock full of guns, knives, clothing, and all other manner of evidence. But there was no box for the DeLuna case there.

They soon found a court document explaining why: Assistant District Attorney Kenneth Botary had checked out all the materials right after the trial in July 1983 and never returned them.

Three times the investigators asked the D.A.'s office for all its materials in the Carlos DeLuna–Wanda Lopez case, relying on Texas's broad Public Records Act. In response to the first request, Assistant District Attorney Lance Kutnick (son of psychiatrist Joel Kutnick) said the office had no records. A second request netted about thirty pages of police reports. A third request made in person by a respected local attorney prompted a phone call from the D.A.'s office saying that there were some "boxes" waiting for the investigators to review. They'd better come look at them soon, though, because the office was planning to discard them.

When the investigators arrived two hours later, they received many more pages of documents than they had received before—about 200, including a stack of rap sheets for men named Carlos Hernandez with Escobedo's notes indicating that she passed them on to the prosecutors in early May 1983. But they were given only a single file—not any "boxes" containing the physical evidence in the case. Those items were nowhere to be found.

Any DNA from the case remains at large.

•   •   •

One other thing that Lawrence and De Peña never received from the police before trial was the information that Eddie Garza had picked up from his sources on the street that a man named Carlos Hernandez was telling people he had killed Wanda Lopez and that Carlos DeLuna had taken the fall.

"Carlos Hernandez" was the name De Peña and Lawrence were looking for. If the defense lawyers had known about Garza's information, and that police had picked up a 5-foot, 7-inch, 160-pound, wavy-haired Hispanic man named Carlos Hernandez on the night of April 3 after he was caught lurking outside a 7-Eleven with a knife, that would have given their investigation just the direction it needed in the face of their client's fear and silence.

So would knowing that Infante, the I.D. technician on DeLuna's case, had shown a lot of interest in this particular Hernandez's fingerprints, when the man was arrested in April. And that, of the seven "Carlos Hernandez" rap sheets that Detective Escobedo passed on to Assistant District Attorney Schiwetz in May, only the one belonging to this Carlos Hernandez revealed a history of violence and convictions for convenience store robberies. And that this Hernandez was well known to Escobedo and Assistant District Attorney Botary as the prime suspect in the knifing and beating death of young Dahlia Saucedo three years before.

Learning any of those things, De Peña told the investigators, "I mean, that obviously would have been a quantum leap in the defense had we gotten this information." Each piece of information would have made a "great deal of difference," a "tremendous difference," if any of them had been shared before trial. But none was.

"Leaves a pretty bad taste in my mouth, even now," De Peña said, many years later.

.    .    .

In fact, Lawrence and De Peña did get the name Carlos Hernandez before the trial started. What they got, however, was very little and very late.

The lawyers spent July 5 to July 13 selecting a jury to decide DeLuna's case. The judge gave the jurors a day off before the trial started on Friday, July 15.

For months until then, Carlos DeLuna had urged first De Peña and then Lawrence to find the unnamed—and frighteningly unnamable—man whom he said he'd seen attacking Wanda Lopez. He begged them to ask the judge for more help and more time. He even asked the judge himself, in his awkwardly scribbled missives with their jumble of ill-fitting words. He hoped that any trouble proving a case against him would push the police themselves to look elsewhere.

On July 15, time ran out. Trial was going to start without anyone calling the name of the man he saw. "We're down to the closing moments of this thing before we went to trial," De Peña recalled, when Carlos finally gave his lawyers the name himself: Carlos Hernandez.

But those two very common proper names were the only thing he would give his lawyers.

"'I gave you the name,'" De Peña remembered DeLuna saying, "and that was as far as he was going to go." He was a "dead" man, he said, whether the jury condemned him or not, if Hernandez found out that DeLuna "put the bite on" him.

De Peña believed that Carlos Hernandez existed, but he also could tell that "Carlos DeLuna was not going to assist me in actually pinpointing who the real Carlos Hernandez was."

"We didn't have doodly," Lawrence confirmed, "no height, weight, date of birth."

If he had had just a date of birth, Lawrence lamented, "I could've found [him]. We never got that far because we just had a name." With their client again putting the burden on them to prove his defense, Lawrence and De Peña did what they had done before, with their lead about Mary Ann Perales: they immediately passed the name on to Escobedo, Botary, and Schiwetz, still relying on the police and prosecutors to prove the defendant's case and blow up their own.

The prosecutors had another lesson in store for Hector De Peña.

## 12

# No Defense

WHEN CARLOS DELUNA COUGHED UP the name Carlos Hernandez on July 15, the person assigned by the prosecution team to look for the man was not Senior Prosecutor Kenneth Botary, Chief Detective Olivia Escobedo, or Identification Technician Joel Infante. All three of them had more than a passing familiarity with *the* Carlos Hernandez from the Dahlia Sauceda case, Eddie Garza's informants in the weeks after the Wanda Lopez killing, and Hernandez's arrest in April 1983 at the 7-Eleven.

Nor did Assistant District Attorney Steven Schiwetz try himself to locate and question "Carlos Hernandez," even though the D.A.'s file in the Lopez case contained the rap sheet of a man by that name whose criminal history and physical traits matched the offense and the knife-wielding assailant described by witnesses Kevan Baker and George Aguirre moments after Wanda Lopez was stabbed. That, too, was *the* Carlos Hernandez.

Instead, Schiwetz assigned the task to Corpus Christi police sergeant Ernest Wilson. Wilson was not an investigator or a detective and performed only one job for the police department: matching fingerprints found in the field to those on file with the police. Judging from his testimony in the DeLuna case, he did it with care and professionalism.

Right off the bat, however, Wilson hit a snag. The fingerprints that Infante had collected from the Sigmor Shamrock crime scene were of such poor quality that they couldn't be used to make comparisons with the prints of the seven Carlos Hernandezes with rap sheets in the D.A.'s file.

"In effect," as Schiwetz later told the jury, "there are no fingerprints in this case." As a result, there were no matches to anyone named Carlos Hernandez—or to Carlos DeLuna, for that matter.

•     •     •

The prosecution team also issued a couple of subpoenas to a "Carlos Hernandez" who lived on David Street in Corpus Christi. But as Jon Kelly later
explained to the private investigators, getting a subpoena just meant that a
constable would leave a paper summons at an address. Unless you send out
a cop to wait at the address and bring the witness in, "[y]our subpoenas,
despite what is said, aren't worth the paper they're written on."

Whoever he was, the David Street Carlos Hernandez never appeared
in court.

•     •     •

That was the sum total of the efforts by law enforcement and defense lawyers to locate "Carlos Hernandez."

No one on the police force or in the prosecutor's office told the defense
lawyers about (or made independent efforts to locate) Eddie Garza's informants who overheard a Carlos Hernandez from the area around Staples
and Mary near Carrizo Street say that he was the one who had "hurt"
Wanda Lopez with a knife. No one disclosed Hernandez's arrest in April at
the 7-Eleven or his suspected role in stabbing and beating Dahlia Sauceda
to death. No one mentioned that Hernandez was notorious in the Mary
Street area for his violence against women and his fondness for lock-blade
buck knives.

"[T]he prosecutors didn't give me a whole lot of assistance," DeLuna's
lawyer Hector De Peña dryly commented later. "[T]he correct individual
was never found." Carlos DeLuna had no defense.

•     •     •

People who spent any time around the criminal courts in Corpus Christi
in the 1980s had no sympathy for the possibility that Botary, Escobedo, or
any other experienced prosecutor or homicide detective would have had
trouble identifying and quickly finding the Carlos Hernandez in question
at the time.

Jesse Garza's lawyer Albert Peña pointed out that Botary knew Carlos
Hernandez well from the Dahlia Sauceda murder three years earlier.

Unless you "[p]ut the blinders on," Peña said years later, "that's not a
fellow that you're going to likely forget." Peña himself had heard rumors

at the time "through police sources and through people at the courthouse, people in the know, that Carlos Hernandez was suspected of doing it"— the Wanda Lopez killing—"not this fellow [De]Luna."

No one had to ask *which* Carlos Hernandez.

Hernandez's lawyer Jon Kelly agreed that "if the question had arisen in law-enforcement circles in Corpus Christi, Texas, in 1983, is there a Carlos Hernandez in this town who was capable of using a knife to hurt a woman, or at least ha[d] a reputation in that direction," it would take "two minutes"—in all seriousness, no more than a "half a day"—for any experienced detective to bring him in.

"If someone said, 'knife' and 'Carlos Hernandez,' they'd know exactly what you were saying. If you were an active detective. If you were experienced in patrol in . . . the Mary Street area, you'd know who Carlos was. I mean, come on! They all knew."

Famed homicide detective Eddie Garza was also emphatic about the notoriety of *the* Carlos Hernandez. "If somebody got up and testified that there was no Carlos Hernandez," he said, his voice rising, "there sure was, and I can testify to that because I arrested him several times."

"Myself and my partners, we were well aware of Carlos Hernandez and what he was capable of doing," Garza said. "Most of the detectives in the criminal investigation division knew of Carlos Hernandez."

Hernandez's reputation extended beyond cops to prosecutors, Kelly explained. "People in the D.A.'s office at that time knew who Carlos Hernandez was. Period."

"I know those people personally. I consider them friends. But I can say that without much hesitation. Anybody with any period of time and service in the Nueces County District Attorney's Office in that period of time, they knew who Carlos Hernandez was. Period." At the time, Schiwetz was new to the office, but Botary had been there for years.

.     .     .

Carlos DeLuna's sister Rose had a theory about why the authorities didn't bring in Carlos Hernandez when her brother gave up the name. "They hated my brother," she said. "I know they hated him." He'd been a cocky nuisance—a thorn in their side—for years.

"This was their chance to get rid of my brother"—to hang him by the rope he handed law enforcement when he dove underneath that truck.

•     •     •

News reporters later asked prosecutor Steven Schiwetz why he didn't do more to help the defense find Carlos Hernandez. Schiwetz said he didn't know any Carlos Hernandez himself and was never told of one by Ken Botary or anyone else besides DeLuna. He believed that DeLuna made the name up.

Schiwetz gave the reporters another explanation as well. DeLuna had told his lawyers that he met Hernandez in jail, but records "showed that the men were never in jail at the same time," so the prosecutor "didn't pursue DeLuna's claim further." To this day, Schiwetz is convinced that DeLuna was a woman-hater, a predator, and a liar, and that he killed Wanda Lopez.

Neither James Lawrence nor Hector De Peña remembers DeLuna saying that he knew Hernandez from jail. And Schiwetz himself never used the point against DeLuna at his trial, even as the prosecutor worked hard to discredit the defendant in the eyes of the jury by bringing up every fib he could show that DeLuna had ever told.

In any event, Corpus Christi police and parole records show that Carlos DeLuna and Carlos Hernandez evidently *were* in police custody at the same time on at least three occasions—around January 15, 1979, and May 23, 1980, as well as April 3–5, 1983, after DeLuna was arrested for the Lopez murder and Hernandez was arrested behind a 7-Eleven with a knife.

Detective Eddie Garza, investigator Eddie Cruz, Hernandez's former girlfriend Margie Tapia, and others recall seeing the two Carloses together at the Casino Club and on the streets of Corpus Christi in the late 1970s. When DeLuna testified at trial, that's where and when he said he had met Hernandez.

•     •     •

Because of Botary's close association with Hernandez in the Dahlia Sauceda case, he had more to explain when news reporters asked him the same question.

The *Chicago Tribune* described Botary's predicament and his response:

Three years [before the Wanda Lopez killing], Botary had prosecuted another murder [Dahlia Sauceda's] case and lost after defense lawyers argued that Hernandez was the real killer. Botary interviewed Hernandez before that trial and cross-examined him on the witness stand. Botary was even called to testify about his interview of Hernandez.

Just before trial, Carlos De Luna's lawyers identified Hernandez as Lopez's real killer. From that point on, any information about Hernandez was critical to the defense. Botary knew that a prosecutor has a duty to disclose evidence favorable to the defense, and that failure to do so can be cause for an appeals court to set aside a conviction and order a new trial.

Schiwetz said Botary never told him about Hernandez. By remaining silent, Botary allowed Schiwetz to misinform De Luna's jury.

In a series of interviews, Botary offered changing explanations of how he handled the information about Hernandez.

"I got the name right off the bat," Botary said. "I knew Carlos Hernandez was a dangerous man."

But Botary, now a criminal defense lawyer in Corpus Christi, says he may not have associated the Hernandez mentioned by De Luna's lawyers with the man he had interviewed and cross-examined in the earlier murder case.

He acknowledged that had he been De Luna's lawyer at the time, he would have wanted to know the information. "I think I should have told Schiwetz," Botary said.

In Botary's defense, Schiwetz noted that at the time of De Luna's trial, prosecutors in Corpus Christi carried heavy caseloads, so his colleague simply may not have made the connection.

But, Schiwetz added, if Botary had told him, he would have alerted the defense.

## 13

# Trial

CARLOS DELUNA'S TRIAL BEGAN ON FRIDAY, July 15, 1983, just over five months after the slaying of Wanda Jean Lopez.

Karen Boudrie, a novice beat reporter in her early twenties, covered the case for KZTV, the CBS affiliate in Corpus Christi. DeLuna's was the first trial of any kind that Boudrie had covered as a journalist. A bit overwhelmed—"like a deer in the headlights"—Boudrie sat in the courtroom, listening intently to the evidence against DeLuna and reporting her observations to the Corpus Christi community through frequent segments on *Newswatch 10* (figure 13.1).

The young reporter was fascinated by the criminal trial process and spent the next six years investigating and reporting on police and courtroom events in Corpus Christi. Throughout those years, she made it her business to stay in touch with Carlos DeLuna. "I thought, maybe one day I'll be the person he reveals some deep, dark secret to," she admitted.

Becoming a specialist on police and prosecutors, Boudrie moved on to cover criminal and capital trials for larger-market television stations near Atlanta and New Orleans. But the DeLuna case stayed in her mind in a way that no other did. Part of it, she believed, was that "[e]very time I talked to Carlos, and in every letter, he talked about how his life had gone astray, but he always denied committing this crime."

Twenty years later, discussing the case with investigators at a hotel near the Dallas–Fort Worth International Airport, Boudrie recalled one of the biggest "things the prosecution had going for it" at DeLuna's trial: a sensational tape recording of "Wanda Lopez calling the 911 dispatcher. And you can hear her on the tape begging for her life, and screaming."

FIGURE 13.1   Karen Boudrie in 1987 reporting outside the Sigmor gas station (remodeled since the 1983 stabbing incident), with Wolfy's in the background.

When prosecutors played the tape, the apprentice reporter realized that they weren't messing around. They were "out for blood." "It was going to be a feather in someone's cap to be able to get the death penalty in this case."

· · ·

DeLuna's sister Rose spent those days shuttling back and forth between the courthouse and the hospital where her mother lay dying, hoping that the defense attorneys would prove what Carlos had told her and she believed— that he hadn't killed Wanda Lopez.

Wanda's parents and her brother Richard sought something different— an end to their ordeal, some sign that Wanda's attacker realized that he shouldn't have done this to her, that she didn't deserve it.

· · ·

Wanda's cousin Becky Nesmith had been working at a different Diamond Shamrock convenience store on the night of Wanda's murder. Although several years younger than her cousin, Becky later described Wanda to the private investigators as "like a sister" and sometimes a "savior," as the two struggled to adjust to lives as single mothers deserted by the fathers of their children. Like others, Becky described Wanda as a "happy spirit . . . very loving, very friendly, very outgoing." Becky had worried about her cousin working alone in a dangerous area across the street from a topless bar.

Becky recalled getting "a phone call from my mother at work letting me know that Wanda had died." She rushed to the hospital and then to Wanda's mother's house, down the street from the hospital. Becky was wearing her blue Shamrock smock, and she recalled her aunt clutching Wanda's smock. "She was just curled in the blue smock, crying and crying," Becky remembered sadly. "And she had this picture [of Wanda] next to her, in color. It was just an awful ordeal."

In summer school later that year, Becky's history teacher announced that students would be required to watch a murder trial at the courthouse downtown and write reflections. "When he said what trial it was," Becky realized "it was my cousin Wanda's." Becky wondered how she would react to the monster she expected this DeLuna to be and to evidence of how he brutalized her cousin.

Becky's reaction to at least one piece of evidence was the same as Karen Boudrie's.

"[T]he worst part of the trial," Becky said, "was when they aired the 911 call, where we heard her speaking and the operator speaking, and the questions that they had asked her. And at the end of the phone call, she's screaming, and then the phone hangs up."

"It was terrifying hearing her voice," she recalled tearfully—"the last time we were ever going to hear [Wanda]."

•    •    •

In his opening summary for the jury, Assistant District Attorney Steven Schiwetz laid out what seemed like an open-and-shut case. Just after Wanda screamed on the call, the police dispatched all available officers to a manhunt near the Shamrock. Forty minutes later and three blocks away, they found Carlos DeLuna cowering under a truck. Shortly after that, four witnesses identified him as the man they'd seen at or near the gas station.

Schiwetz said his "final witness" would be Wanda Lopez herself, on tape—"asking for help, telling about a man who was in the store with a knife." Pointing to Carlos DeLuna, he drew his remarks to a close. "You will hear her final words to this Defendant telling him, 'I'll give you what you want,' and then you will hear her screaming as he knifed her."

.    .    .

The State's first witness was Wanda's father, Luis Vargas. He told the jury a little bit about his daughter and her job at the Sigmor Shamrock and displayed a picture of Wanda with her own daughter in her lap. Then police dispatcher Jesse Escochea testified about the 911 call he answered. Schiwetz directed Escochea's attention to a call received at "8:09 P.M.," leaving no room for mention of any other call.

The twenty-two-year-old Escochea said he took a call regarding a man with a knife from an unnamed female at 2602 SPID. She asked for assistance, he testified, and he quickly dispatched officers to the scene.

Officers Steven Fowler and Bruno Mejia described their arrival at the scene, where they found a man kneeling over Wanda Lopez. Fowler testified that her labored breathing and glassy eyes revealed a "Kussmaul" state from loss of blood through a wound on her left side.

Spread throughout the prosecution's case was additional testimony—by an emergency medical technician, the nurse who was treating Wanda at the hospital when she died, and Medical Examiner Joseph Rupp—describing Wanda's wound and her awful suffering. In the same vein, Lieutenant Eddie McConley, the commanding officer at the scene who secured the store until Detective Olivia Escobedo could get inside, described the "large amount of blood" he saw inside and outside the store, and on Wanda Lopez as she lay blocking the door while medics tried to revive her.

Mejia told of gathering the witnesses near the ice machine, getting descriptions, and broadcasting BOLOs. He described the weather that night as "clear, mild, warm." He didn't recall rain.

Fowler noted that bystanders at the scene said they'd seen someone running from the area. Introducing a directional theme the prosecutors came back to throughout the trial, Fowler only mentioned witnesses talking about a suspect running "eastbound" along the service road toward the Phase III nightclub (see figure 2.3, route A–E). At one point, Fowler said "westbound," but Schiwetz encouraged him to correct himself and refer again to an easterly direction.

Defense lawyers James Lawrence and Hector De Peña didn't have the manhunt tape. They didn't know that Mejia's nine BOLOs and numerous sightings by cops chasing a man gave a different direction of flight: eastward just a few feet along the Sigmor sidewalk to the end of the building where the ice machine was, and then north "behind" the store and west half a block to Dodd Street. Further sightings tracked a man sprinting north on Dodd toward McArdle and right on McArdle toward Domino's and a Circle K at Kostoryz (see figure 2.3, route 1–6). Nor did they know about Fowler's own encounter earlier that evening with a mustachioed man wearing a sweatshirt and suspiciously lurking around the same Circle K.

The jury heard none of this.

•    •    •

Only Deputy Constable Ruben Rivera described the manhunt at all, and he focused on DeLuna's arrest. He and his partner, Carolyn Vargas, he said, had responded to Theresa Barrera's call notifying police of a man hiding under her pickup truck on Easter Street. Rivera and Vargas set off on foot. Within minutes, they saw a group of bystanders on Franklin Street beside a different pickup truck, yelling that someone was underneath.

When Rivera reached the truck, he knelt down, shone his flashlight, and saw what he thought were a man's feet. Drawing his gun, Rivera sternly ordered the man to come out from under the car with his hands up. The man didn't move.

Corpus Christi police officer Mark Schauer then described his own arrival at Nemec and Franklin Streets, around the corner from Barrera's house. He saw Constable Rivera and his partner standing next to a vehicle and calling for backup. Schauer noticed that there was a man under the truck and rushed over. Together, Schauer and Rivera pulled DeLuna out from underneath the truck—shoeless, shirtless, and smelling of beer. The only words that DeLuna could muster were "Don't shoot. Don't hurt me."

Responding to Assistant District Attorney Kenneth Botary's questions, the twenty-four-year-old Schauer described DeLuna as "real hyperactive, real tense, very—very talkative . . . he wouldn't shut up."

"He had a kind of a stare in his eyes," Schauer dramatically elaborated, "like a—it's hard to describe, but it was a stare like a glare in his eyes, like an animal might have." Accompanying the stare, he said, was a "constant[ ] . . . smile on his face, kind of a smirk." There were "long scratches" on the right side of DeLuna's torso, Schauer said.

During his cross-examination of Schauer, defense lawyer Lawrence asked the officer why none of the details in his testimony—the stare, the smirk, the scratches—were in the report he filed on the night of the killing and showed up only in a second report written days later. Schauer responded that Detective Escobedo "caught me in the hallway of central records and asked me to—to add everything I could remember, as much as possible to my—to my [second report]."

    •    •    •

Toward the end of the first day of trial, Officer Thomas Mylett linked De-Luna to the Casino Club where Mylett worked at night as the bouncer. Armando Garcia, whose backyard adjoined the house where DeLuna was arrested, testified that he found a white dress shirt and shoes in his yard. Prosecutors showed the jury a diagram indicating that Garcia's yard was on a straight line connecting Theresa Barrera's pickup truck on Easter Street to the truck on Franklin Street that DeLuna was under when he was arrested.

    •    •    •

The prosecutors whipped quickly through the testimony of the witnesses who collected and examined the physical evidence. They began at the end of the first day of trial with Joel Infante, the I.D. technician, and finished up in the middle of the second day with lead detective Olivia Escobedo, fingerprint expert Ernest Wilson, and blood expert Donald Thain.

Much of this testimony was about things that didn't happen.

Infante didn't get any fingerprints from most of the surfaces and other pieces of evidence at the gas station, including the lock-blade buck knife that was the murder weapon and the Winston cigarette pack placed on the counter by the killer.

Wilson didn't actually compare the few fingerprints Infante did retrieve with Carlos DeLuna's prints because their quality was too "poor."

Along with the knife found at the scene (dramatically described by Es-cobedo as laden with human flesh) and the cigarette pack, Escobedo and Officer Fowler showed the jury ten of the thirty-eight photographs that Infante had taken at the scene.

But Escobedo didn't show the photos with bloody shoe prints headed out from behind the clerk's counter, what appear to be partial bloody shoe prints on the storeroom floor and sidewalk outside the store, the cigarette fragment and wad of pink chewing gum someone had spat out on the floor, Escobedo herself trampling evidence, or the wide shots revealing the full extent of the blood coating the floor and spattered several inches high on the walls and cabinets behind the counter. The defense lawyers didn't mention the missing photos either, probably because they never saw them until they reviewed Rene Rodriguez's evidence in the Diamond Shamrock lawsuit four years later.

Finally, chemist Donald Thain testified that he didn't find any trace of blood on DeLuna's white dress shirt, black slacks, and shoes and on the cash bills found in his pocket. Schiwetz took Thain through the following explanation:

SCHIWETZ: I'm showing you now what's marked as Exhibit 16, being these pants. Presume for a moment that the person got some blood, some blood dripped off a person who had been stabbed and dripped onto these pants somewhere and presume that that person laid down in one gutter and that in that gutter there was water and when this person got up, their pants were soaking wet. Would that have any influence on whether you found blood on them?

THAIN: Yeah. As I say, if it was fresh blood, it would—when water gets on fresh blood, it would wash away pretty easily.

SCHIWETZ: Same regarding the shirt . . . , if it was being worn by a person who was lying in a gutter with some water on them, could the blood, if there was any wash out that way?

THAIN: It could.

SCHIWETZ: Would it be difficult or easy?

THAIN: It would—as the water gets on the, you know, blood, and its fresh, it would go out pretty good.

Schiwetz asked a similar question, and got a similar answer, regarding DeLuna's shoes.

Cross-examined by Lawrence, Thain testified that blood that had dried on the cloth shoes, shoe laces, shirt, and pants would not come out with water, and that small smears and spatters would likely dry quickly in those kinds of porous cloth.

He offered no explanation for the absence of blood on the bills found in DeLuna's pocket.

. . .

Early Monday morning, Schiwetz called his star witnesses—the ones whom Mejia had corralled near the ice machine where they shared descriptions and discussed whether to do the show-up identification at the scene.

George Aguirre testified first. There was no "doubt in his mind," he said, that the shirtless and handcuffed man police brought to the gas station in the back of a squad car was the same one he'd seen outside the Sigmor store carefully situating a large, open lock-blade knife in his pants pocket before asking Aguirre for a ride to the Casino Club.

Logically, the next step in the examination was to ask Aguirre to point to the man in the courtroom who he'd seen at the gas station with a knife. But at an earlier hearing where no jury was present, Aguirre had been unable to identify DeLuna, who was sitting at a table a few feet away with his lawyers. With a jury in the courtroom, Schiwetz didn't even ask Aguirre to try.

On the manhunt tape, the description from Aguirre indicated that the man he saw wore a white, long-sleeved T-shirt or thermal shirt and blue jeans. But by the time of trial, Aguirre's description tracked the one he'd discussed by the ice machine with the insistent Julie and John Arsuaga: white *button-down* shirt and "*dark* blue" *or* "*black*" pants. Lawrence didn't have the manhunt tape. He didn't cross-examine Aguirre on the point.

Lawrence did question Aguirre's claim that, after he left the gas station and got on the SPID freeway, he was able to look across six other lanes of highway traffic and down off the elevated SPID roadway into the recesses of the Sigmor Shamrock store and see Wanda struggling with the man he'd encountered outside the store—all while driving at expressway speeds.

John Arsuaga testified next. He identified DeLuna in the courtroom as the man he'd seen jogging east past the Phase III nightclub. He explained that, on the night of Wanda's attack, he went back to the police station and selected a photo of DeLuna from a group of six Hispanic males. John was "sure" the man in the photo was the same man he'd seen "running earlier that night." A little later, Julie Arsuaga also identified DeLuna. As usual, Julie gave the most detailed description of the well-dressed jogger's attire: white dress shirt, unbuttoned and "untucked," flapping in the wind, with "black or dark blue" slacks. John's description had been similar.

Again, however, Lawrence didn't have the manhunt tape and didn't hear Mejia's remark that the Arsuagas seemed to be describing "another man," different from the one whom Kevan Baker saw fleeing the store. The defense lawyer didn't realize that the Arsuagas' testimony helped his well-dressed client by placing him blocks away when Baker came face-to-face with the scruffy assailant in the Sigmor doorway. Instead, Lawrence spent much of the trial attacking John and Julie's photo identification of DeLuna.

When Schiwetz called Baker to the stand, the prosecutor noted that the car salesman was "a little nervous" and urged the reluctant witness to "slow down" so the jury could follow him. Calming himself, Baker identified DeLuna—the "gentleman that's sitting right here in front of me"—as the man he'd met at the gas station door after watching Wanda struggling to break free of his grasp. Baker said that when he identified the suspect in the gas station parking lot later that night, he was sure the man was Wanda's attacker.

It came out during Baker's testimony that he had originally told Mejia that the attacker wore a red flannel jacket, had the unkempt look of a "transient," sported a mustache, was in his mid-twenties, and fled "east" only a few steps before turning and going north "behind" the Sigmor. Baker volunteered that DeLuna's face had cuts and scratches on it at the show-up, unlike the face of the man he saw running out of the store.

Guided by Schiwetz's follow-up questions, however, Baker said he no longer remembered the "kind" of shirt the attacker wore or where he went after exiting the door and turning "east."

Without the manhunt tape, Lawrence couldn't refresh Baker's recollection with the descriptions Baker had given—and Mejia's BOLOs had repeated nines times over forty minutes—of a man in a gray sweatshirt and red flannel jacket running north.

•    •    •

As one witness after another identified him, the "twenty-year-old Carlos DeLuna sat calmly, taking notes on a legal pad," Boudrie reported to her *Newswatch 10* viewers.

Later Boudrie told the private investigators that the I.D. witnesses hadn't impressed her, either. Even though she "had a tendency" at the time "to be very much believing of the prosecution, not wanting to question it as much" as the defense, Boudrie remembered thinking that "all they had" was a bunch of witnesses saying " 'boy, he ran by,' and whoever ran by ran by really quickly."

Boudrie recalled being outside the Sigmor Shamrock store herself, filming a report and "visualizing where [the witnesses] supposedly were when they saw it." "How good a look of [the man] would they have gotten at night?" she remembered thinking.

Boudrie had just come to Corpus Christi. She had "never met that many Hispanic people. And I'm thinking, if I was there in the gas station and I see a Spanish guy running by, would I be able to I.D. him? I don't know."

There was "another thing" about the DeLuna trial, Boudrie said, that "always stood out in my mind—no fingerprints. I think that would have made it a lot easier, if there were fingerprints. But there wasn't that one bit of evidence that would have really said, okay, he was in there. . . . That always bothered me."

Overall, Boudrie thought, "that's some pretty flimsy evidence." It "was amazing, that that's all they had." DeLuna, she thought, had a shot at beating this thing with the jury. Even the defendant, who was portrayed as "this heinous person, this woman-hater, this violent person," in the end "seemed like an average, nice guy in some respects."

.     .     .

Becky Nesmith had a similar reaction as she watched the prosecutors put on their case against the man they said had murdered her cousin Wanda.

She, too, thought the clean-cut young defendant swiveling his chair and chewing gum didn't "look like the type of person that would kill or do something bad."

Based on the evidence she heard, she, too, "couldn't even figure out if this man was guilty."

She recalled a male voice on the 911 tape buying cigarettes. "Why wasn't his voice compared to Carlos DeLuna's?" "There must have been blood on DeLuna's clothes," she remembered thinking. "Why wasn't any found?"

.     .     .

For all her misgivings, news reporter Boudrie didn't realize that the descriptions the witnesses had originally given to police were so different from one another. It didn't register that Baker had told the police that the killer wore a gray sweatshirt and red flannel jacket, while the man the Arsuagas saw wore a white, button-down dress shirt.

Boudrie also didn't recall that Aguirre first described a man in blue jeans and a T-shirt, while the Arsuagas saw a man in black well-pressed slacks; that the man Baker came face-to-face with wore a mustache, and the man who ran by the Arsuagas was clean shaven; that the unkempt "derelict" who Baker saw "sprint" away didn't match the well-dressed man out for a lei-surely "jog" who struck the Arsuagas as comical; or that the escape route Baker described was north "behind" the gas station toward Dodd Street, while the man the Arsuagas saw at the Phase III was headed east along the SPID service road.

"That never came out," the reporter said. "None of us knew . . . that there were actually conflicting witness statements."

As a flack for Republican candidates in Louisiana, Boudrie told the in-vestigators in 2005, she didn't think of herself as a pushover or a bleeding heart. She "was all for capital punishment." By then, she had covered mur-der cases for years, including "more brutal and heinous cases than this one," and often had thought, "That person needs to be put to death." But Bou-drie was always troubled by the DeLuna case. "It absolutely bothers me," she said, "that the defense never had the opportunity to put a case on with that as the crux of it, to really be able to attack the witness identification."

•    •    •

Along with presenting witness identifications of DeLuna, the prosecu-tors worked to tie the defendant to money from the Sigmor store. Officer Schauer testified that immediately after Carlos DeLuna's arrest, he discov-ered $149 in the suspect's pocket.

Schauer's initial report had described "a wad of paper currency rolled up in [DeLuna's] right pants pocket," with the twenties together at the bot-tom. To the jury, he described it somewhat differently: "It was in like a wad. It wasn't rolled up into a neat little roll with a rubber band around it or anything like that." Schauer said he shuffled the bills before bringing them to the station, so he didn't know what order they originally were in.

Botary's questions emphasized that the $149 was in DeLuna's front pocket, not in a brown or black wallet found in his back pocket, which contained only two $1 bills. This linked up with testimony that Aguirre had given that the man he saw at the gas station displayed a black wallet with only a small number of cash bills in it.

Pete Gonzalez, the Sigmor Shamrock area manager, testified that an inventory of the store at 11:00 P.M. the night Wanda was killed revealed a shortage of $166.86. He said it was "customary" for an inventory to be off by $25 or $50. Gonzalez never explained, and defense counsel never pointed out, that Diamond Shamrock's accounting methods made it impossible to inventory cash alone, and that shortages were often due to shoplifting, gasoline drive-offs, and short deliveries, as well as pilfered or stolen cash.

Among the evidence that Rene Rodriguez dug up for the Shamrock lawsuit and showed to De Peña and Lawrence in 1987 was a display card with company rules forbidding employees to have more than $75 in currency in the cash drawer at any time. Lawrence himself had emphasized to the private investigators in 2005 that DeLuna had more money in his pocket than would have been in the gas station till at the time. But the defense lawyers apparently didn't know this in 1983, and the jury never heard it.

.        .        .

Two of the State's final witnesses had no connection to the attack on Wanda Lopez and the investigation that followed. Their testimony was brief but very much to the point.

Estella Gonzalez, the bookkeeper for the jail commissary, testified that she had reviewed the order slips from the commissary and that Carlos DeLuna had consistently ordered Winston cigarettes from among the five brands available at the jail. Ernesto Gonzalez, a corrections officer for the Nueces County Sheriff's Department, confirmed that DeLuna smoked Winstons.

.        .        .

The final element of the State's case-in-chief against Carlos DeLuna was the recording of Wanda Lopez's 911 call to Jesse Escochea saying that a man had come into the store who she believed had a knife and was up to no good.

A police department communications supervisor, Lieutenant Robert Klemp, introduced the tape to the jury. Klemp explained that he maintained a "master tape" with various channels recording "all" Corpus Christi Police Department "dispatch[es], all the radio broadcasts, incoming and outgoing, and all the telephone conversations, both emergency lines and in-station extensions."

Klemp described how, nineteen days earlier, on June 29, he had created the cassette of the tape he would play for the jury. He "separated" the portion of the tape he wanted from the master tape and used "a cassette recorder which reproduced it off the master."

In his questions, especially those italicized in the quotation from the transcript, Schiwetz was careful not to invite Klemp to refer to the other portions of the master tape that related to the Wanda Lopez killing—the first 911 call and the radio traffic during the manhunt. Switching to "leading" questions that signal to the witness what he's expected to say, Schiwetz mirrored the surgical precision that Klemp had used in extracting only a 90-second segment off the tape:

SCHIWETZ: Who prepared that tape?

KLEMP: I prepared this tape, this cassette tape.

SCHIWETZ: Is it exactly the same as the recording made on February 4th, 1983?

KLEMP: That's correct.

SCHIWETZ: Have any changes been made in it?

KLEMP: No.

SCHIWETZ: *Have there been any—well, let me qualify that. That tape is a recording, is it not, of the tape of the call made in reporting a man with a knife at 2602 SPID, is it not?*

KLEMP: That's correct.

SCHIWETZ: *It ends at the point where that call ends, does it not?*

KLEMP: Yes.

SCHIWETZ: Okay. Now, *within that context,* have any changes been made to that conversation?

KLEMP: No....

SCHIWETZ: Have any deletions been made?

KLEMP: No.

Klemp's answers were accurate and truthful as far as they went, and Schiwetz's leading questions made sure they never went far enough to divulge the existence of other parts of the tape.

*       *       *

Ending the State's case with Wanda's pleading voice sent a clear message to the jury. Someone had done something terribly, horribly wrong to Wanda Lopez, for no fathomable reason. Now someone needed to pay:

JESSE ESCOCHEA: Police Department.

WANDA LOPEZ: Yes, can you have a officer come to 2602 South Padre Island Drive? I have a suspect with a—a knife inside the store.

ESCOCHEA: What place is this?

LOPEZ: Sigmor.

ESCOCHEA: What's he—

LOPEZ: Well, he—

ESCOCHEA: What's he doing with the knife?

LOPEZ: I don't know, he was outside bumming a ride off of this guy and he just told me right now—he just came inside the store.

ESCOCHEA: Has he threatened you or anything?

LOPEZ: Not yet.

  Could I help somebody?

ESCOCHEA: What does he look like?

LOPEZ: Por que?

ESCOCHEA: What does he look like?

LOPEZ: He's a Mexican. He's standing right here at the counter.

ESCOCHEA: Huh?

LOPEZ: Can't talk.

  Thank you.

ESCOCHEA: Ma'am?

LOPEZ: What?

ESCOCHEA: Don't hang up, okay?

LOPEZ: Okay.

  This? Eighty-five.

ESCOCHEA: Where is he at right now?

LOPEZ: Right here.

ESCOCHEA: Is he a white male?

LOPEZ: No.

ESCOCHEA: Black?

LOPEZ: No.

ESCOCHEA: Hispanic?

LOPEZ: Yes.

ESCOCHEA: Tall, short?

LOPEZ: Uh-huh.

ESCOCHEA: Tall?

LOPEZ: Yeah.

   Thank you.

ESCOCHEA: Does he have the knife pulled out?

LOPEZ: Not yet.

ESCOCHEA: Is it in his pocket?

LOPEZ: Uh-huh.

ESCOCHEA: All right. We'll get you someone over there.

LOPEZ: You want it, I'll give—I'll give it to you. I'm not going to do nothing to you. Please.

ESCOCHEA: Hold it, get a unit on a 17 to the Shamrock, 2602 South Padre, you've got an armed robbery going down right now. God, she's [sic] beating the shit out of him [sic]. Okay, hold on.

SECOND MALE VOICE: 165—

SECOND FEMALE VOICE: Are you through with your call?

THIRD MALE VOICE: 151, police department.

FOURTH MALE VOICE: Hello.

(Unintelligible.)


   (At this time the playing of [State Exhibit]-2 was concluded.)


●    ●    ●


Karen Boudrie recalled watching as the recording "sent chills up and down the spines of everyone in the courtroom." Years later, she set the scene when the tape ended.

   "The courtroom is in absolute silence," she said. "[W]e're all in shock, in a state of unbelievability that—Why did someone have to kill this woman? She said, 'I'll give you everything, I'll give you everything.' She could see what was coming. It was just horrible."

   Hearing Wanda Lopez beg for her life and die was "one of the most compelling pieces of evidence" against a defendant that Boudrie had encountered in a career spanning many murder trials. And that was true "even though [Wanda] didn't say who did this to me."

   "They did a good job of working everybody up," Boudrie said, "playing the tape as many times as they could get away with. Saying somebody's got to pay, here's the guy, let's put him away, let's put him to death."

   "I think that's the attitude everybody had," she said. "Everybody was kind of on the bandwagon."

.     .     .

Right after the tape ended, the State rested its case, and the judge sent the jurors home for the evening. They had the whole night to think about Wanda's last sentient moments.

"I had nightmares about it for a long time," Shirley Bradley, a juror in the case, told *Chicago Tribune* reporters in 2005. "That tape had a shock-value on us. . . . It was a clear-cut case."

.     .     .

But even then, at the end of the State's case, Boudrie herself wasn't certain the prosecutors had sealed DeLuna's fate. She remembered thinking that she "wouldn't want to be on the jury to decide this. He was hiding nearby, and he was identified by one or two witnesses who saw him for a fraction, for one or two seconds. What they had was great, titillating, sensational evidence, but they didn't have a lot on Carlos."

.     .     .

Wayne Waychoff was the first witness for the defense. Waychoff owned a paving company that employed Carlos's stepfather Blas Avalos. At Avalos's request, Waychoff had hired Carlos as well when he made parole in mid-January 1983.

Waychoff's testimony put enough money in DeLuna's pocket during the week preceding the Shamrock killing to more than cover the $149 found there at the time of the young man's arrest. Between January 28 and February 4, the day Wanda Lopez was stabbed, Waychoff paid Carlos just over $206 in wages, including $135 on the day Wanda was murdered. Waychoff noted that there was a lag between paychecks and work performed, so as of February 4, he owed Carlos an additional $77 for work done earlier that week.

Waychoff's testimony kicked off a chronology of DeLuna's day on February 4. The eighth of an inch of rain that fell that day in Corpus had started just before 11:00 A.M., so Waychoff sent Carlos's concrete-laying crew home early. A co-worker, Daniel Fino, testified that he and Carlos had immediately cashed their paychecks and gone over to Avalos's house to drink some beer that Carlos had bought.

Blas Avalos himself then testified that Carlos was living and eating at home and hitched a ride with his stepfather to and from work, so the young man had no big expenses in his first month back from prison. Although Avalos didn't put it quite this way, he indirectly disclosed that he even kept the household well stocked with the one discretionary product in which DeLuna did indulge: beer.

Testifying through an interpreter, DeLuna's alcoholic stepfather explained to the jury that between dropping Carlos off at the skating rink at about 7:00 P.M. on February 4 and receiving a call from his stepson at 8:00 P.M. or a little later asking for a ride home, he had gotten too drunk to drive. His wife didn't like to drive at night, and they knew that Carlos had money in his pocket, so they told him to take a taxicab home.

Carlos had hoped to have his mother give this testimony and convey a mother's belief that a son asking his parents for a ride home, with more money in his pocket than he could expect to get from a convenience store robbery, was not likely to commit one ten minutes later. But Margarita was in the hospital where she would shortly die, and the job of testifying fell to Carlos's taciturn stepfather.

Apart from some discussion of Carlos's shoes and clothes on the night of the incident— Avalos didn't remember what Carlos wore—the State's cross-examination zeroed in on only two questions. The first was about his and Margarita's conversation with Carlos after the young man's arrest:

SCHIWETZ: What did [Carlos] know had happened?
AVALOS: Just that he was being accused of a thing that he had not done.

To answer the second question, Avalos drew on all fifteen years he'd known his stepson:

SCHIWETZ: Do you know if Carlos De Luna owned a knife?
AVALOS: Carlos has never carried a knife, sir.

•    •    •

With his mother in the hospital, no investigation of Carlos Hernandez by law enforcement or his own lawyers, and little besides Mary Ann Perales's contrary recollection to show for the meager investigation his lawyers did conduct, DeLuna had no defense apart from his own testimony.

James Lawrence guided his client with questions that were short and to the point. DeLuna answered most of Lawrence's questions the same way, not always with the right word or grammar but understandably enough.

. . .

Lawrence picked up the story with Carlos's return to Corpus Christi in January after leaving prison on parole. Right off, Lawrence had his client disclose his convictions in Dallas for attempted rape and car theft.

Carlos testified that Avalos helped him get a job laying concrete and that he rode to work every day in his stepfather's car. He followed that routine on the morning of February 4 until he was paid and sent home early. He and co-workers cashed their checks, bought beer, and ended up back at his mother's house that afternoon.

After a trip to the Whataburger with a neighbor, showering and changing into dress clothes, and accompanying Margarita and Blas to a Kroger's for some payday marketing, DeLuna got his parents to take him to the Gulf Skating Rink between 7:00 and 7:15 P.M. "I went inside to see if this girl was there I was waiting for but she wasn't there, so I stepped back outside."

Here DeLuna's story merged with the one he'd first told De Peña in March, about his passing encounter with Mary Ann and Linda Perales at the skating rink before moving on to Wolfy's a mile away. Evidently, De-Luna didn't get the message from his lawyers that Mary Ann Perales—who played only a peripheral role in his story in any event—had a good reason to think she was elsewhere that night, and that the prosecutors were sure to inform the jury of it.

. . .

Carlos testified that when he left the skating rink, he ran into the Perales sisters, who were sitting in a yellow Ford Pinto. He had known them years before when he was in junior high school.

Then, Carlos said, "another guy" approached him outside the rink. "His name was Carlos Hernandez."

DeLuna said he didn't recognize Hernandez at first but then realized that Hernandez "did knew [sic] me." Carlos had "met him with my brother" at a dancing spot in 1978 and 1979, before DeLuna had gone to Dallas and then to prison, and after that "we started meeting each other a little better."

"Do you recall what this Carlos Hernandez looks like?" Lawrence asked.

"I can give you a little bit what he looks like," Carlos DeLuna answered. Black hair "somewhere to here (indicating)," about five-eight, five-nine and

150 pounds. "I remember the blue jeans, that's all I remember," the defendant said.

DeLuna testified that he and Hernandez decided to go look for a guy they both knew named Ronnie Gonzalez, who lived nearby. They asked the Perales sisters for a ride, but the sisters instead dropped them off at a store a couple of blocks from the skating rink. Carlos DeLuna bought a soda and called his stepfather to come and pick him up. Avalos was too drunk to get him and told him to take a taxi home.

"Since I got to catch a taxi home," DeLuna said he told Hernandez, "I'll go stick around there with you for a while." The two set off on foot to Ronnie Gonzalez's house but didn't find him.

"Carlos," DeLuna said, referring to Carlos Hernandez, "told me if I wanted to go to Wolfy's" because "Ronnie would hang around there sometimes." As they approached the entrance to Wolfy's, Hernandez said that he was going to buy something across the street at the Sigmor Shamrock store. Hernandez said that he'd find DeLuna inside the club, and DeLuna went in by himself.

He "bought a beer and sat down for a while listening to the music." When Carlos Hernandez never showed up, DeLuna said, he went over to the Shamrock to look for him.

"I noticed Hernandez inside the Shamrock Service Station," DeLuna testified. Then he "noticed Hernandez going in somewhere in the counter and started wrestling with that woman."

DeLuna "started walking away." Asked why he left, DeLuna said, "I know I got a record and if Carlos Hernandez came back to where I was, I knew these people would say I was involved with this guy."

When he heard sirens converging from all directions, DeLuna testified, he began to run. "I just kept running because I was scared, you know"— through backyards, over fences, whatever it took. He lost his shirt when it caught on a fence he jumped over.

Finally DeLuna heard people yelling. "I didn't know what was going on and I got scared and I dove under the truck, a truck I think it was." Police arrested him there.

•    •    •

Coming to his last two questions, Lawrence asked DeLuna, "Did you ever tell the police that you knew who did it?" DeLuna replied that he had.

While riding over to the gas station in the squad car, "I . . . told Officer Schauer that I didn't do it, but I knew who did it."

"And then at one time," he continued, seeming to lose his composure, "I also told you about it, my attorneys, about this guy and that you brought me some pictures to see if I noticed him, but—and he turned out to be the guy and the State right here wouldn't do nothing to help me or nothing to look for this guy."

Lawrence's final question calmed DeLuna down. "Did you ever go into that Sigmor Shamrock on February the 4th, 1983?" "I never went in there," Carlos responded.

·       ·       ·

Trying to recall the evidence presented by the defense twenty years earlier, Karen Boudrie and Becky Nesmith remembered only two words: "Carlos Hernandez." Nesmith didn't remember the Perales sisters at all. Boudrie vaguely remembered Mary Ann as a "very reluctant" witness who said she was somewhere else that night, but who had left room for doubt about whether she had the right day.

Neither Boudrie nor Becky remembered anything else. Just "Carlos Hernandez." And that was the problem. They distinctly remember that there was *only* a name, nothing more. At that point, both said, the thinness of the prosecutors' case was overwhelmed by the utter void at the core of the defense that Carlos DeLuna offered.

Before she heard DeLuna testify, Becky remembered, she had "questioned, did he do it? Because they did say that there was another man, that he was the one that did it." But "[w]hen Carlos DeLuna said that he did not do it, that it was another Carlos, when I heard that at the trial I thought, that's just a lie."

"Where was that other guy?" she remembered thinking. "There was no other guy."

"What a coincidence," Becky went on. "It's not me, it was him. It was another Carlos. It just sounds typical that he would blame that on someone else."

Sitting with the other reporters and interviewing people around the courtroom, Boudrie had the same feeling. Who is this "mystery Carlos—does he really exist?" "Why can't they produce this guy? How difficult would it be?"

The kicker for Boudrie, though, was what she was hearing from the State.

"We tried," the prosecutors told her. "[W]e exhausted all avenues to find Carlos Hernandez." "We couldn't find him, he doesn't exist." And Boudrie remembered thinking, "I'm sure they did [try]. They want to find the right man."

After that, she recalled, "there were . . . jokes" in the press section "about Carlos Hernandez, this fictional Carlos Hernandez. He could have thought of a better alibi than that."

"[E]verybody got caught up in it," she said.

•   •   •

Carlos's testimony was no joke to his sisters. Convinced by what Carlos had told them from the start, that he hadn't knifed Wanda Lopez to death, they believed his testimony and hoped the jurors would, too. They had no idea what others in the courtroom were thinking.

•   •   •

For Wanda Lopez's brother, Richard Vargas, what amused some spectators only angered him. After hearing the voice of his sister played for everyone to hear in the courtroom and at home, all Richard knew was that justice had to be done.

DeLuna was the man whom the State had charged, and he was arrested in suspicious circumstances just blocks from the scene of his sister's murder. How dare he try to blame some other Carlos? If he really hadn't done it, why didn't he turn in the other guy right away?

•   •   •

Looking back on it years later, Steven Schiwetz also pointed to things that Carlos DeLuna did and didn't say in his own testimony—and not the evidence that Schiwetz and Botary themselves had presented—as the main reason to think they had the right guy.

By then a respected lawyer in private practice in Corpus Christi, Schiwetz no longer put much stock in the eyewitness identifications. Speaking to *Chicago Tribune* reporters, "Schiwetz acknowledged that the case relied heavily on eyewitness testimony," but he was ambivalent about its strength. "'Sometimes it's reliable. Sometimes it isn't reliable,' he said in an interview. 'And sometimes, in cases like this, you're not entirely sure how reliable it is.'"

Although Schiwetz argued to the jury that DeLuna might have stabbed and struggled with the profusely bleeding Lopez without getting blood on his shirt and pant legs, and that the blood on his shoes might have washed off as he ran through the yards, the former prosecutor certainly knew it was a problem for his case that the crime lab found no blood or other evidence on his clothes.*

And in hindsight, Schiwetz realized that there *was* a Carlos Hernandez who claimed he had killed Wanda Lopez, and that his partner Botary knew the man and should have helped investigate him. "Anytime somebody's going around saying they killed somebody, I think it's worth looking at," Schiwetz told the *Tribune*. "But," he added, "I've heard a lot of people make claims for stuff they did or didn't do that weren't true."

"As for Hernandez's history of knife crimes," the *Tribune* reported Schiwetz saying, "Every man in this town has carried a knife. And most of us still do. I carry a knife. I did not kill Wanda Lopez or anybody else."

But what convinced the former prosecutor that DeLuna was the killer were what he believed to be DeLuna's lies. DeLuna "lied when he claimed to have talked to two women at a skating rink on the night of the crime," Schiwetz said. "In addition, while De Luna said he lost his shirt while scaling a fence, he gave no explanation for how he lost his shoes."

Finally, Schiwetz told the *Chicago Tribune* reporters years after the trial, DeLuna "lied when he apparently said he first met Hernandez in jail." Schiwetz based this last claim on two recollections. Contrary to defense lawyer De Peña's own memory of what DeLuna had told him—confirmed by the independent observations of police detective Eddie Garza, private investigator Eddie Cruz, and Carlos Hernandez's Carrizo Street neighbors—that the two Carloses hung out together on the streets of Corpus Christi near the Casino Club and Staples and Mary, Schiwetz remembered the defense lawyers telling him that DeLuna had said he met Hernandez in jail.

Schiwetz also recollected that, before trial, Olivia Escobedo had compared the jail records of DeLuna and Hernandez and found no overlap. But if this is true, it is inconsistent with Schiwetz's claim at trial that the

---

*On the day of the murder, it rained only one-eighth of an inch in Corpus Christi, starting in the morning. At the time of the killing, the rain had passed and there was only minor moisture on the ground. The amount of moisture present was unlikely to have washed away all, even microscopic, traces of blood that the assailant likely had on the bottoms, sides, and laces of his shoes, his pants cuffs, and elsewhere on his pants, shirt, hands, and body and on any money he took from the store.

State had no idea which Carlos Hernandez, if any, was the "right" one to compare with DeLuna.

Regardless, any comparison made was incomplete because Hernandez and DeLuna appear to have been in police custody on the same dates twice, in January 1979 and May 1980—as well as in April 1983.

"De Luna had lost all credibility," Schiwetz concluded. "He's lying about the most important story he's ever going to tell in his entire life."

•   •   •

After Lawrence sat down, Schiwetz approached Carlos DeLuna on the witness stand.

Schiwetz was an imposing figure, tall and stout. He made an impression on Boudrie. Although she was new to Corpus Christi and to criminal trials, she remembers being immediately struck by how good he was with the jury. Years later, she could barely remember the other lawyers on the case. "Steve Schiwetz just really stands out," she recalled. And "not just because of his stature." "I remember feeling that this guy was good. He's going to win his case, he's got everybody believing this." He was "captivating, he told a good story. He made you want to believe him."

•   •   •

Schiwetz began by asking DeLuna whether he'd ever told anyone anything different from what he told the jury. He then showed that DeLuna had done just that by telling James Plaisted and Joel Kutnick that he couldn't remember what had happened on the night of Wanda Lopez's murder.

When Schiwetz asked Carlos whether he knew a man named Gilbert Garcia, Carlos said he did not. Moments later, DeLuna recalled telephoning his parole officer, Gilbert Garcia, soon after he was arrested.

Next Schiwetz asked permission to leave the courtroom, returning moments later with Mary Ann Perales. Answering Schiwetz's questions, Carlos identified her as the Mary Ann he had spent fifteen or twenty minutes with on the night of the incident. Before that, Carlos said, he had last seen Mary Ann "[b]ack in '78, '79, I would say."

The charismatic prosecutor then made a show of asking Carlos to compare his recollection of Mary Ann years earlier in 1979 with what she looked like in the courtroom that day. "Has she changed much?" he asked. No, Carlos answered, she was "[j]ust the same." Schiwetz never asked Carlos about Mary Ann's appearance on the *night of the incident* or asked him to compare her appearance that night either with how she looked in 1979 or with how she looked in the courtroom.

The prosecutor pressed DeLuna about where he met Carlos Hernandez ("with my brother at a dance and we started meeting each other a little better"), where Hernandez lived ("at one time . . . over by the city Bakery on 19th Street"—a location not far from Carlos Hernandez's known residences), if he was aware of all the efforts "made by the State of Texas to locate Carlos Hernandez" (only what his lawyer had told him), whether he told his lawyers everything he knew about Carlos Hernandez so they could locate him ("I did"—perhaps his biggest fib), and whether Hernandez had ever been arrested in Corpus ("I thought he had but I'm not too sure").

DeLuna told Schiwetz that he had no bank account and always kept cash in his front pocket, where officer Schauer had found the $149. Carlos said he had $35 left over from his prior paycheck when he cashed his $135 paycheck on February 4—minus what he spent on a twelve-pack of beer on his way home from work, a Whataburger later that day, and a beer at Wolfy's.

De Luna testified that he was a regular at the Casino Club in the late 1970s before going to prison, and he repeated his criminal record for the prosecutor and jury. Schiwetz concluded by asking DeLuna if he had killed Wanda Lopez. "I didn't kill that girl," DeLuna answered.

He said he "couldn't kill nobody" or "hurt nobody" unless they tried to hurt him first.

*     *     *

Mary Ann Perales was the first person called by the State in its "rebuttal" (figure 13.2). The lawyers repeatedly had to tell her to speak up and give her answers over again, a result, perhaps, of the reluctance to testify that Karen Boudrie recalled.

Mary Ann said she'd known Carlos DeLuna through his brother in about 1978 but hadn't seen him at the skating rink on February 4. "I was attending a baby shower," she said, her voice so quiet that she had to repeat her answer twice.

The baby shower was for her. She produced a picture of herself at the event, visibly pregnant. When questioned on the point by Lawrence, Mary Ann admitted that the photo was not dated and gave the jury "no way of

FIGURE 13.2  Courtroom sketches during the DeLuna trial of (*counter-clockwise from top right*) the jury, visiting Judge Wallace C. Moore, and Carlos DeLuna, and (*bottom right*) television news shot of Mary Ann Perales waiting to testify.

knowing" where she was on February 4. Mary Ann said her sister Linda Perales was not at the baby shower with her.

Then Schiwetz asked Mary Ann to make the comparison he had not asked DeLuna to make, between her appearance on February 4, 1983 ("fat . . . I was seven months pregnant") and in '78 and '79 (thinner). The prosecutor never repeated the question he had asked DeLuna: how her appearance *in court that day* compared to her appearance in the late 1970s.

•     •     •

Next Ernest Wilson testified that he was not "able to make any kind of comparison" between the poor-quality fingerprints Infante had taken from the crime scene and the prints on file from seven Carlos Hernandezes with criminal records.

That concluded the evidence for both sides.

• • •

On the morning of the third day of trial, the lawyers got their chance to argue directly to the jury. The State of Texas went first.

In his powerful closing argument, Schiwetz pulled together all the pieces of his and Botary's case into a coherent picture. "There shouldn't be any doubt in this case whatsoever about who committed this murder or about why he did it," he assured the jury.

The prosecutor began with the witnesses at the gas station and Phase III, arguing that each got a close look at the man whom he or she identified as DeLuna and that each fingered DeLuna shortly afterward.

In the absence of the manhunt tape—in which each of the BOLOs gave Baker's and Aguirre's original descriptions to the police (gray sweatshirt, red flannel jacket, blue jeans)—Schiwetz emphasized the details from the Arsuagas' descriptions and the conforming parts of Aguirre's testimony. He brushed aside Baker's contrary descriptions, saying Baker now remembered only the face.

Everything else, Schiwetz said, pointed to DeLuna as well: the $166 inventory shortage at the Sigmor, mirroring the $149 in DeLuna's pocket; DeLuna's preference for Winston cigarettes; his criminal record; his flight from police and capture cowering under a pickup truck soon after the crime.

Then, expressing concern that "[y]'all got to hear it rather hurriedly [only] the other day," Schiwetz played the 911 tape again.

This time, though, he stopped the recording several times to linger over details. Now the killer is inside the store; now other customers are gone, and she's alone with him; now she's terrified for her life, and he's pulled the knife out. And then the climactic moment, again: "[T]he person didn't give her a chance. He walked right up, you can hear . . . the sound of a struggle, and then she starts screaming. She lets out that one horrible scream, and I submit to you that's when he pushed that knife into her."

"Why would he do that," Schiwetz continued, "just walk up there and kill a woman who's willing to give him what he wants?" He answered his own question. "She's talking on the telephone, giving the police a description of this guy, calling for help. . . . He knows she knows what's up so he killed her."

Turning philosophical, Schiwetz reflected that "[w]e use the term cold-blooded murder real loosely sometimes." But the jurors, he said, "ought to take a long look at the face of Carlos DeLuna, the face that George Aguirre saw, the face that Kevan Baker saw, the face that Julie Arsuaga saw, the face that John Arsuaga saw, because that's about the best look you're ever going to get at a cold-blooded murderer."

. . .

This time, however, Schiwetz didn't end with the tape recording. Instead, he played what he thought was an even better trump card.

The best evidence that Carlos was guilty, he said, was that he was a liar. Exhibit A was Mary Ann Perales, whom DeLuna said he ran into that night, though she in fact was at her own baby shower.

Then, engaging in some sleight-of-hand himself, Schiwetz turned testimony by DeLuna that Mary Ann did not contradict—that she looked the same *in court* as four years earlier—into another lie, which DeLuna in fact never told. DeLuna had not been asked and had not said that Mary Ann looked the same *on February 4*, when she was pregnant, as she looked in court months after her baby was born, or had looked four years before. But Schiwetz attributed that lie to DeLuna.

"I ran [Mary Ann] out [into the courtroom]," Schiwetz said, and "I asked him a few questions about her."

"'She looks the same now as she did that night?'" the prosecutor said, claiming to repeat a question he never actually asked DeLuna.

"'Yes,'" he then said, mimicking an answer DeLuna never gave.

"'She looked the same that night as she did several years ago when you saw her?'"

"'Yes.'"

But Mary Ann was only a sideshow for Schiwetz as he came to his dramatic conclusion. The lie for which Carlos DeLuna should truly be convicted, he said, his voice rising, was his pathetic fabrication of "*this phantom Carlos Hernandez.*" Based on that invention, Schiwetz argued, looking straight at DeLuna, "this man lied under oath."

"Anyone who would go out and fabricate events like this man did can't be believed in any fashion whatsoever. He's a convicted car thief, he's a convicted attempted rapist, and he murdered Wanda Lopez for no good reason whatsoever."

"When you go back out there in that jury room and open up the jury forms," he concluded, making a final suggestion to the jury, "it shouldn't take you a whole long time to . . . say[ ] that, 'We, the Jury, find the Defendant, Carlos De Luna, guilty of the offense of capital murder as alleged in the indictment.' "

•    •    •

Splitting the defense argument between them, Lawrence and De Peña did their best to defuse the drama generated by Schiwetz, whom Lawrence immediately likened to a "frustrated Hollywood would-be actor[ ]."

Lawrence's own flourishes tended in the direction of personal attacks. He attacked Schiwetz for his theatrics, particularly for using the 911 tape solely for "dramatic effect." He also attacked Mary Ann Perales, suggesting that she had some unexplained vendetta against Carlos DeLuna.

In the end, however, Lawrence conceded that he couldn't "explain whether" what Carlos said about Mary Ann was "true or not true." He didn't acknowledge his own role in failing to dissuade his client from bringing up Mary Ann at all.

Lawrence was more effective when he attacked the reliability of witness identifications made in moments of "high stress," especially when there's "only one person" to look at.

But the defense lawyer didn't have the manhunt tape showing that the Arsuagas placed DeLuna, whom they quite accurately described, two blocks *east* of the location where Baker saw a man wrestling with Wanda Lopez and fleeing *north*. So Lawrence was reduced to arguing that "we don't know which way that person ran" and to personally attacking John Arsuaga, his client's best alibi, as not credible, a man relying on intuitions suited only to the "female gender," someone "out of a soap opera."

As if to heighten the contrast between himself and the bellicose Schiwetz and sarcastic Lawrence, Hector De Peña rose and spoke in a barely audible voice with a bit of a stammer. "I'm sorry, Hector, I can't hear you," the court reporter admonished.

In almost apologetic tones, the inexperienced lawyer pointed out gaps in the State's case, such as Aguirre's failure to identify DeLuna in the courtroom, the absence of DeLuna's fingerprints at the scene, and the lack of blood on DeLuna's clothing.

"I'm—I'm pointing these out just as small points," he said meekly, as the judge hounded him for taking too much time.

•   •   •

But no matter what the defense lawyers might have argued, the die was already cast. DeLuna had no defense without "Carlos Hernandez" in flesh and blood.

Any Carlos Hernandez would have made a difference, but especially a Winston-smoking, cheap-beer-drinking, Casino Club–frequenting 5-foot, 7-inch, 160-pound Carlos Hernandez who resembled his *tocayo* Carlos De-Luna and had an explosive temper, a history of armed robberies of convenience stores and deadly violence against Hispanic women, the sartorial style of a "hobo"—a "winter uniform" of blue jeans, sweatshirt, and red flannel shirt-jacket—and the constant companionship of a lock-blade buck knife.

The best Lawrence could come up with to meet Schiwetz's climactic attack on DeLuna's invention of "the phantom Carlos Hernandez" was to blame the prosecutors for the "fact that we can't get ahold of Carlos Hernandez."

"Evidently, from what you have heard," Lawrence said, emphasizing the very worst point for his client, "you can deduce that they haven't been able to find Carlos Hernandez."

•   •   •

Judge Wallace C. Moore turned the case over to the jury around lunchtime on the third day of trial. After going out to a restaurant to eat, the members of the jury began discussing what they had heard. When the judge brought the jurors into the courtroom to explain arrangements for dinner that evening, the foreman told him not to bother. They would have a verdict shortly, which they did at around 5:30 P.M.

While the jury was discussing the case, Schiwetz went to DeLuna and his lawyers and offered the same deal he'd proposed earlier. If Carlos would plead guilty to murder, Schiwetz would withdraw his request for a death sentence. DeLuna refused. He was innocent, he said, so it made no sense for him to negotiate about a sentence.

The jury's swift verdict was the one that Schiwetz had urged: "the Defendant, Carlos DeLuna, [is] guilty of the offense of capital murder as alleged in the indictment."

.     •     •

Linda Carrico, a reporter for the *Corpus Christi Caller-Times*, described the scene in a front-page article the next morning.

"After deliberating 4½ hours yesterday afternoon, a Nueces County jury found DeLuna guilty," she wrote.

"Only after the seven-man, five-woman jury was dismissed for the night did DeLuna display any emotion over the jury's decision. Tears welled in his eyes after several sobbing family members ran to him—embracing him and comforting him."

Carrico then described the highlights of the day in court and the reason the State had given the jury to reject DeLuna's defense: "The prosecutor attacked the existence of what he called 'the phantom' Carlos Hernandez, who DeLuna claimed killed Ms. Lopez."

# 14

# Sentence

THE SECOND STAGE OF CARLOS DELUNA'S capital murder trial decided whether his sentence would be life in prison or death. It began the next morning, Thursday, July 21, 1983, in front of the same jury.

The fact that a unanimous jury had found the defendant guilty of cold-blooded murder just the day before was a bad sign for anyone facing the death penalty, but it was especially bad for DeLuna.

In most capital trials, the defendant offers an excuse—a mental defect or disease, for example—that may be strong enough to avoid a conviction for capital murder by justifying a verdict of not guilty by reason of insanity or guilty of only a lesser crime such as manslaughter. If that fails, the same defense may still lay the groundwork for a sentence less severe than death. Even if the impairment is not great enough to excuse the defendant entirely, it still may be "mitigating" enough to convince the jury to spare the defendant's life.

But DeLuna and his lawyers offered no reason to doubt that he was fully responsible for his actions and instead argued for acquittal at the first stage of trial by claiming that someone else committed the crime. When the jury promptly decided "beyond a reasonable doubt" that he did commit the offense—a very bad one at that—only a single, dubious option remained open to DeLuna at the sentencing stage.

Lawyers have a name for this defense to the death penalty, which reveals just how desperate the ploy is. "Whimsical doubt," they call it. The hope is that, even after all twelve jurors have found the defendant guilty of a very bad crime beyond any "reasonable" doubt, at least one juror will still have a tiny inkling left over that someone else may have committed the crime and will vote against a death sentence because of it.

Reducing even this slim chance of escaping a death verdict was another strike against DeLuna: the sentencing jurors almost certainly believed that he lied to them at an earlier stage of the trial. That made three strikes. The jurors had found him guilty beyond a reasonable doubt. They believed that he disrespected them by trying to deceive them. And they probably thought that he was convinced of his own guilt, because only a guilty person or a fool would tell a lie under oath, especially a lie that's easy to expose or so obviously false that no reasonable person would believe it.

The day before, Assistant District Attorney Steven Schiwetz had ended his dramatic argument in favor of guilt on "lies" of both sorts—the easily exposed Mary Ann Perales detail in DeLuna's testimony, and the defendant's seemingly ridiculous claim that "some other dude named Carlos did it." By emphasizing those "lies," Schiwetz had cleverly set the stage for a death verdict even before the sentencing trial began.

Carlos's lawyers did their part to seal his fate. They didn't impress upon their client the idiocy of bringing up Mary Ann Perales when they knew that she would dispute his claim and that the prosecutors would find her because the defense lawyers had alerted law enforcement to talk to her. Far worse, they gave no bodily reality to "the phantom Carlos Hernandez."

The sentencing stage went forward in about the same way as the guilt stage had gone. Schiwetz and Kenneth Botary did their job capably. The defense lawyers did little—even less at this stage than at the prior one. And by declining Schiwetz's second offer of a plea bargain while the jury was still deliberating on his guilt, Carlos DeLuna burned the best remaining bridge he had to a sentence of life rather than death. Now he had nothing to offer the prosecutors in return for a deal. They already had their murder conviction and a life sentence at least.

·     ·     ·

The second stage of a capital trial starts with the State presenting evidence of "aggravating factors," or reasons why the jury should impose a death sentence. Schiwetz began this process with three so-called character witnesses. Following a formula that courts have used for centuries to enable juries to decide whether a criminal defendant is a good or bad person by relying on what amounts to gossip, Schiwetz elicited how each witness knew DeLuna and asked each a single question about DeLuna's reputation. The witness could answer the question with only one of two words: "good" or "bad."

Schiwetz first called a Corpus Christi police officer to the stand, then a retired sheriff's department deputy constable, and finally Detective Eddie Garza and asked each to describe Carlos DeLuna's "reputation in the community." Each witness answered that it was "bad." Garza's network of informants made him a particularly reliable expert on the reputations of young Hispanic men in the city. Defense counsel let the testimony pass without asking a single question on cross-examination.

•    •    •

With these formalities behind them, the prosecutors got down to business.

They called several witnesses to testify about a family party on May 14, 1982, to welcome home Marcos Garcia from the state penitentiary. Frail, sick, and looking much older than her fifty-four years, Marcos's mother, Juanita Garcia, testified that Marcos had invited Carlos DeLuna, a friend from the penitentiary, to join them. Only days before, DeLuna himself had made parole—for the first time—from his convictions in Dallas. He arrived at the party dressed in black slacks and a button-down dress shirt with the sleeves rolled up.

Garcia testified that, after everyone had left and she went to sleep, she awoke to find Carlos DeLuna lying on top of her. Threatening to kill her if she screamed, Carlos pulled his pants down, removed Garcia's underwear, and kissed her. When she protested, he hit her, breaking three ribs. Although DeLuna never attempted to have intercourse, he stayed on top of Garcia for twenty minutes.

Garcia's description of DeLuna's acts did not speak to whether he was guilty of killing Wanda Lopez, but that was no longer the issue. The issue was whether DeLuna deserved to live or die, and the effect of the invalid's account was devastating.

It was Juanita Garcia's unexpected testimony that led Hector De Peña, seated next to DeLuna at the defense table, to whisper "Oh shit" loudly enough for the court reporter to hear it. "In my opinion," news reporter Karen Boudrie explained later, "when they put on, in the death penalty phase, the 5[4]-year-old woman that Carlos supposedly tried to rape . . . that sealed his fate. That one person's testimony sealed his fate as far as whether he would get life or death. She was the most pathetic-looking woman you would ever want to see."

.     .     .

Before trial, the prosecutors had disclosed to the defense that they intended to call Juanita Garcia and other members of her family to testify in favor of a death sentence for Carlos DeLuna. When the prosecutors did so, they also gave James Lawrence and De Peña a court record indicating that De-Luna had been convicted of misdemeanor assault in the incident, a minor offense.

Although the incident caused DeLuna's parole to be revoked and sent him back to prison for several months, and although their client's life was at stake, Lawrence and De Peña decided that it wasn't worth interviewing Garcia and her daughters before trial.* Unlike the prosecutors, who sent detectives to talk to Mary Ann Perales the minute they got her name from De Peña and Lawrence, the defense lawyers decided to fly blind when it came to Garcia. They had no idea what was coming when she took the stand.

Lawrence and De Peña also failed to look for the case file on the incident, which explains why it was treated as a minor misdemeanor, not a serious crime. One of Botary's and Schiwetz's colleagues in the D.A.'s office had investigated the complaint, talked to Garcia, and "determined that there was no rape or attempted rape that was prosecutable in this case." The explanation at least would have prevented the prosecutors at DeLuna's trial from referring to the incident—as Schiwetz repeatedly did—as an attempted rape.

Lawrence and De Peña, however, never saw that record until after Garcia testified, when the prosecutors showed them the file in the case. At that point, the only thing the defense lawyers could think to do was object to all the records, which the jury never saw.

De Peña later chalked up the incident to more prosecutorial sharp practice. Gentlemen, he believed, would have shared the entire Juanita Garcia

---

*In his 2005 interview, Hector De Peña acknowledged that he and James Lawrence were "surprised" by the testimony of Juanita Garcia and her daughters because the two lawyers had relied entirely on the single document provided to them by the prosecutors before trial, which indicated that the offense was a misdemeanor. The two lawyers conducted no independent investigation into the matter.

file with the defense before trial, tipping them off to what was coming. Instead, the prosecutors gave them only one page in the file, which indicated that the incident was minor.

•    •    •

After showing the jury other court records, which described DeLuna's convictions in Dallas for attempted rape and car theft, the State rested its case for the death penalty.

Now it was the time for the defense lawyers to present their client's evidence of mitigating factors—everything about Carlos DeLuna's life, background, age, poverty, mental problems, family relationships, and good deeds that might, singly or together, give at least one juror a reason to grant mercy. Because death verdicts have to be unanimous, one juror's vote for mercy would spare DeLuna's life.

Incredibly, in a step that today would be an almost automatic reason for an appeals court to throw out a death sentence, Lawrence and De Peña immediately rested DeLuna's case as well. They didn't call a single witness or put on any mitigating evidence.

The jury heard nothing about Carlos's limited intelligence, "specific learning disabilities," and inability to handle the mental rigors of the seventh grade. His lawyers presented no testimony from his former teachers, the school psychologist who discovered his reading and memory problems, or a family member who had watched him struggle with his schoolwork. They didn't even offer a school or juvenile court record.

Although Carlos's sisters were in the courtroom, his lawyers called none of them to testify to his sweetness as a child or that one of them had to raise him when she was still a girl because his father had abandoned the family and his mother was too exhausted to bring him up. His younger sister, Rose, never got a chance to describe his suggestibility and manipulation by their older brother, or Carlos's generosity with his paltry Whataburger wages so Rose didn't have to stand in the paupers' line in the school cafeteria.

His lawyers didn't chase down records showing that Carlos had stayed out of trouble while in prison on the Dallas convictions and had provided information to prison officials and testimony leading to the conviction of four inmates for killing a fifth.

They called no one to say that she believed in Carlos's basic goodness and redeemability and to beg for the twenty-one-year-old's life.

Summarizing DeLuna's defense to the death penalty, the local newspaper reported the next morning that "[d]efense attorneys neither called witnesses nor presented evidence in yesterday's punishment phase of the trial."

·     ·     ·

Schiwetz's closing argument in favor of a sentence of death was shorter and less dramatic than his argument that DeLuna was guilty.

He began by reminding the jurors that they all had "promised" the judge that they were willing to impose death. People with a problem imposing a death sentence are excluded from juries in capital murder cases.

Schiwetz then explained that, to impose a death sentence in Texas, the jury had to find that the killing was deliberate and that the defendant would be a danger to other people if he wasn't executed.

To help the jurors decide whether the murder of Wanda Lopez was deliberate, Schiwetz invited them to take the buck knife used to kill Wanda into the jury room with them "and look at it, open it up and try to imagine what effect that would have sticking it in the lungs or the heart and . . . decide whether that was all done deliberately."

"Listen to the tape again," Schiwetz recommended. "Listen to her begging for mercy. Listen to that scream."

On "future dangerousness," Schiwetz referred the jurors to DeLuna's criminal record. Carlos had "become mentally a convict," Schiwetz said, coining a phrase the newspapers quoted the next day. The prosecutor noted that within days of being paroled in 1982, DeLuna "went over and tried, I submit to you, tried to rape his best friend's mother. That says about everything you need to say about Carlos DeLuna."

Rejecting the idea that life in prison was punishment enough, Schiwetz claimed that DeLuna "doesn't mind the penitentiary. He kind of likes it, he . . . would just as soon kill to get back in there."

The prosecutor ended by reminding the jury of Wanda Lopez's six-year-old daughter, who was gaily seated in her smiling mother's lap in the photograph that Wanda's father had shown the jury on the first day of the trial.

·     ·     ·

Lawrence and De Peña again split the defense argument, but they didn't coordinate their statements to the jury. De Peña had no idea what his co-counsel would say until he listened to Lawrence along with the jury.

De Peña, for his part, argued that the killing was not deliberate and that DeLuna would not be a danger in the future if he was imprisoned instead of executed. The jury, he reminded them, had to find both things to be true in order to come back with a death sentence.

Bizarrely, and perhaps disastrously for Carlos DeLuna, Lawrence argued the exact opposite. He said that the way Texas law was written, *everyone* found guilty of murder at the first stage of a capital trial (which required a finding that the killing was "intentional") also was guilty of "deliberate" killing. He then argued that only someone who was entirely without sin could avoid a "yes" answer to the second question, whether he might be a danger in the future. Lawrence criticized both legal rules as silly and unfair. The first, he said, was "ridiculous"; the second was "impossible."

Having in this way told the jurors that, if they followed the law, they had to impose death on his client, Lawrence then indulged his fondness for personal attacks by insulting the jurors. As Schiwetz had already reminded them, all the jurors had promised the judge that they *would* follow the law and consider the death penalty. Lawrence now argued that they would be "absurd" and "selfish" "destroyers of life" who put themselves "above God" if they imposed the penalty.

Even in arguing that enough doubt about DeLuna's guilt existed to justify a life sentence, Lawrence put the matter in personal terms, telling the jury that, as was his right, he disagreed with them about DeLuna's guilt.

The barbs that Lawrence directed at the jury left De Peña "aghast." A lawyer friend sitting in the audience with De Peña's wife caught De Peña's eye and mimed someone hammering a nail. Both spectating lawyers could see that Lawrence was putting the last nail in DeLuna's coffin.

De Peña finished up for the defense. He closed by saying, "If any of us, myself, cocounsel, Mr. Schiwetz, if we have said anything to offend you personally, I ask that you overlook that, [and] don't hold it against Carlos De Luna."

•     •     •

Even with all the strikes against him, including the ones pitched by his own lawyers, Carlos DeLuna came close to avoiding a death sentence. After hours of discussion, the jury twice came back with a "yes" answer to the question whether the killing was deliberate but said they could not agree on whether DeLuna would "constitute a continuing threat to society" if he was not executed.

Judge Moore asked the foreman, juror Morales, if he thought the jury could come to a decision on the second question after more discussion. Morales said the jury could try, but "it would be rather difficult to go back in there and try and make a decision."

The judge then asked each of the other jurors whether they all might be able to reach agreement after further discussion. All but one responded that agreement might be "possible." Judge Moore directed the bailiff to take the jurors to dinner and then to return them to the courthouse to deliberate further, adding that he would stay as long as they wanted to work that night.

Later that evening, the jury returned with a verdict of death.

"I know what you have been through," the judge told the jurors. "I'm glad that you had the courage of your convictions, and you may be excused with my thanks."

· · ·

In the *Corpus Christi Caller-Times* the next day, reporter Linda Carrico described Carlos DeLuna's reaction to the verdict: "At first undisturbed by the jury's decision, DeLuna became agitated when Nueces County sheriff's deputies attempted to escort him back to jail before he could say good-bye to his sister."

" 'Let me hold my sister, man!' a sobbing DeLuna screamed."

# PART IV

# The Passion of Carlos DeLuna

# 15

# Appeals

THE NEXT DAY, FRIDAY, July 22, 1983, Assistant District Attorney Kenneth Botary acted as though he'd seen a ghost.

That day, Botary asked a judge for permission to remove all the physical evidence from the court file and take it to the district attorney's office: the lock-blade buck knife used to stab Wanda Lopez, the Winston pack the killer had left on the counter, the beer cans that George Aguirre saw him drinking from, the partly smoked cigarette fragment that probably broke off during the struggle. The court granted the request (figure 15.1).

Botary's written motion listed all the items he took from the court, including Carlos DeLuna's pay stub and paycheck from the day Wanda Lopez was killed. But Carlos DeLuna was not the name that Botary wrote on his list. Instead, he twice identified the man the jury had convicted and sentenced to die as "Carlos *Hernandez*"—whom, just days before, his fellow prosecutor Steven Schiwetz had dismissed as a "phantom."

· · ·

Botary's request, with the judge's signature granting it, is the last remaining trace of the physical evidence in the Wanda Lopez murder case. In 2004, the private investigators asked the court for the material, hoping to perform DNA tests. Court officials produced the order authorizing Botary to take the evidence to the D.A.'s office. When the investigators looked for it there, they found boxes of evidence from cases older than DeLuna's in the storage area, but no one in the office could account for the missing DeLuna evidence.

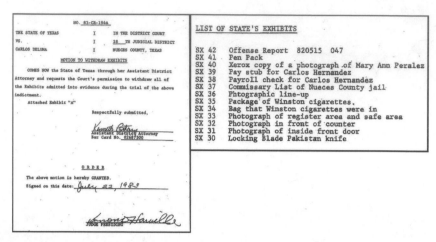

FIGURE 15.1  *(Left)* Prosecutor Kenneth Botary's motion of July 22, 1983, to withdraw the physical evidence in the DeLuna case from the court file, and order granting the motion. *(Right)* Part of the list of exhibits that Botary asked to withdraw, in which he inadvertently attributed to "Carlos Hernandez" items that relate entirely to Carlos DeLuna.

This was not the first time that evidence in Kenneth Botary's charge had disappeared. Twenty years earlier, Carlos Hernandez escaped prosecution for killing Dahlia Sauceda because Botary had misplaced a tape recording and transcript of his own conversation with Hernandez earlier in the Sauceda case.

*       *       *

The next Tuesday, six days after hearing the jury condemn his client to death, defense lawyer James Lawrence collected his $5,000 payment from the county for representing DeLuna. A month later Hector De Peña collected his $4,500.

*       *       *

That same Tuesday, Carlos DeLuna arrived on death row.

His new home was the Ellis Unit near Huntsville, Texas, where people sentenced to die wait out the years it takes for state and then federal appeals courts to decide whether their convictions and sentences are legally sound enough to permit them to be executed. On average across the United States, the appeals process takes thirteen years.

The day after arriving, Carlos wrote his half-sister Vicky Gutierrez the first of fifteen letters from death row. "I Finally made it to Death Roll," Carlos wrote. "Don't worry About me I am Fine. But If you could come visit me some time let me know when. Bring our brothers + sisters I got there name on the List to all of you'll can come."

Carlos's second letter, written two weeks later, was a similar mix of bravado, anxious requests for visitors, and bad spelling:

> send my Regards to Every body. Tell Manuel I as still Alive they haven't killed me yet? Ha Ha. tell Him to write Atleast until I am still Alive its going to be to Late once I am DeaD. Well Vicky I will be expecting you to come whenever you can. Don't you"ll worry About me What Ever happen. . . . Rember I told you one I am not scare to go. I Don't want to Die but IF I have to Die will that's All I can say is bye Right.

And then a month later, mistaking an order setting a *hearing* on his lawyer's routine motion for a new trial for the *granting* of a new trial, Carlos wrote:

> I want to know why you didn't tEll me mom DieD? Also IF you would have SAID something I could have gone to the Funeral. Say hello to All your Family For me. . . .
>
> I went to Corpus to go to Court. I got a New trial. But They haven't set A Date yet ok. I will let you know as Soon As they Do.
>
> P.S. I hope you can come visit me Real soon. Because I really have to tell your something Important. I am REALLY SeRious About this Matter Vicky.

.     .     .

Not long after Carlos reached death row, *Corpus Christi Caller-Times* reporter Linda Carrico interviewed him, eager to give her readers news of the notorious killer whose trial she had covered. "He told me it was strictly a case of mistaken identity," she later told the out-of-town investigators.

Around the time of his trial, she said, Carlos had put on a lot of weight. "Looked like a mess," she recalled. "I was surprised on death row, when this Adonis appeared for the interview. It was the same face, but there was a big transformation."

Speaking to DeLuna face to face also gave Carrico a different impression of the intellect of the man she had only observed in court. "I remember Carlos DeLuna—he was very simpl[e], you know. He didn't really understand he was on death row and that they were trying to execute him."

In his early days at the Ellis Unit, DeLuna also received a letter from news reporter Karen Boudrie asking if he would let her interview him on camera for her television station. DeLuna agreed. When Boudrie came and DeLuna took his place on the opposite side of the glass partition, she, too, noticed differences between the cocky young man she'd watched in the courtroom in Corpus Christi and the young man she spoke to face to face on death row.

"He had found God," Boudrie told the private investigators years later, rolling her eyes. "Oh, yeah, I believe that," she remembered thinking. "But he really was so much more subdued, so much calmer in his demeanor."

DeLuna "didn't seem terribly anxious," Boudrie recalled. He was confident his appeals were going to work for him.

After Boudrie's interview, DeLuna sent her a card, the first of many that he would send the journalist. She read a portion of the note to the investigators in which Carlos looked back on when he "first came to prison, then when I ended up on Death Roll."

"He didn't even know he was on Death Row," she said, shaking her head. "He was on Death Roll, R-O-L-L, to him. . . . He winds up here, and he doesn't even know where he is."

That first letter caused Boudrie to consider DeLuna in a slightly different light. "I started thinking, someone like him, he never had a chance. . . . I really tried to put myself in his shoes and think a little bit more about what it was like to be Carlos DeLuna and what he had to face."

The big question facing DeLuna at that point was whether any lawyer responsible for his case would make a similar effort to look at things from his perspective—and whether any appeals court would do the same.

•   •   •

When Hector De Peña's wife attended DeLuna's trial, she was annoyed that, after suffering prosecutor Schiwetz's jibes in court for presenting a "Carlos Hernandez" defense based on "a figment of Carlos DeLuna's imagination," her husband would go have a cup of coffee with his adversary during a break.

Even after the trial ended, however, De Peña continued to take an oc-casional coffee break with Schiwetz. It was during one such interlude, well after DeLuna's trial, when the name Carlos Hernandez came up again.

Years later, De Peña wasn't sure of the exact date of the conversation. It may have been triggered by the appearance of Carlos Hernandez's pic-ture in the *Caller-Times*. In the photograph, Detectives Eddie Garza and Paul Rivera are escorting the mustachioed Hernandez, in a white T-shirt and jeans, to jail for murdering Dahlia Sauceda. Hernandez committed the crime in 1979, the police claimed, and had recently confessed to Diana Gomez.

The photo illustrated two stories in the newspaper on Hernandez's ar-rest, which was front-page news. The date was July 25, 1986, three years al-most to the day after DeLuna's trial ended.

By then, De Peña had fought through his financial woes and was about to be elected judge, like his father. He had long since stopped representing Carlos DeLuna. Right after the trial, DeLuna had again asked Judge Wal-lace Moore to kick De Peña off the case. James Lawrence handled the first round of appeals himself. After that, other lawyers took over.

Schiwetz had left the D.A.'s office by then and joined a private law firm. The two grabbed a cup of coffee at the courthouse.

Schiwetz "recollected" the "name Carlos Hernandez," De Peña told in-vestigators in late 2004. It was in connection with the killing of a woman in a van with her baby close by.

De Peña recalled the former prosecutor suggesting that Carlos Hernan-dez "might have been involved in the killing of [that] young mother that happened some years prior to the Shamrock killing . . . and the fact that it might have been the same Carlos Hernandez who had been involved in the Shamrock incident."

Schiwetz's comment stuck in De Peña's mind. Evidently, even for Schi-wetz, Carlos Hernandez wasn't a ghost any more.

•     •     •

It wouldn't be surprising if Carlos DeLuna was also on the lawyers' minds that day in July 1986 when Carlos Hernandez's picture appeared in the *Caller-Times*. Just the day before, Linda Carrico had reported in the same newspaper that a Texas appeals court had approved DeLuna's conviction and death sentence. Retired Judge Moore, still being paid by the local court to manage the case, had set a date for DeLuna's execution in October of that year.

"DeLuna, now 24, still maintains his innocence," Carrico wrote, "despite a jury finding him guilty of Ms. Lopez's death and two appeals courts upholding that conviction and death sentence."

DeLuna, she reminded her readers, claimed that "a man named Carlos Hernandez killed Ms. Lopez. However, repeated attempts by both prosecutors and defense attorneys to locate Mr. Hernandez were unsuccessful."

Reading a day later about the arrest of Carlos Hernandez for beating a young Hispanic woman and carving an *X* on her back, De Peña and Schiwetz may not have been the only ones in Corpus Christi to see a possible connection between the *Caller-Times* reports about the Carlos Hernandez whom DeLuna had named and the recently arrested Carlos Hernandez—and wonder whether there was about to be a break in DeLuna's case.

One thing is certain, however. Neither De Peña nor Schiwetz went to District Attorney Grant Jones, Schiwetz's former boss, or to Judge Moore or any other judge to ask that the case be reopened. Neither requested that the climactic "phantom" argument that Schiwetz used to send the jury off to deliberate on DeLuna's fate be reconsidered or stricken. Neither asked that another jury be assembled to rethink the case with the new facts in front of it.

•       •       •

In 1986, Carlos's sister Rose Rhoton paid for a new attorney to take over her brother's case. Up to that point, she had stood by helplessly as her brother's defense failed at trial and in his first appeal. She felt that even his own lawyers, paid for by the court, had taken it for granted that he was guilty.

Rose no longer trusted attorneys assigned by judges. Attorneys like that seemed to work for the State, not her brother. The motion for a new trial that James Lawrence had filed with Judge Moore in September 1983 was typical. It claimed that Carlos wasn't able to put up a proper defense to the death penalty because his mother—his main character witness—was too ill to testify. That was true enough, Rose thought, but the lawyers hadn't called *any* character witnesses, even ones like herself who were right there in the courtroom. Judge Moore had quickly denied Lawrence's request for a new trial.

Carlos, too, thought that his lawyers were not helping him. For a second time, in September 1983, he handwrote a motion—incomprehensibly

stringing together quotations from published court decisions—asking the
court to dismiss his lawyer and let him represent himself. Two months later,
however, De Luna wrote another letter to the judge asking to keep Lawrence and add a second attorney to replace De Peña.

The court assigned Lawrence to handle DeLuna's first appeal by himself.

•      •      •

In January 1984, while waiting for his appeal to be filed, Carlos wrote Vicky
a letter with some good news:

> Oh, vicky I almost forgot to tell you. I bet you can't guess what. well I got
> put into population. That's Right I am no longer in Death ROW. Well what
> I mean I am still sentence to Die. But I am no longer Lock up All the time.
> I now have a Job in I can Also have visits on Saturdays In Sunday. So now
> There's no Excuse you'll can't Come. But I have to be good to say out here.
> I hope that I don't get in trouble. Because I Don't want to go back to Death
> Row. I hope you'll come soon to visit me. . . . Telll [their sister] Mary I said
> that I am no longer in DEAth Row. I am very happy I got moved Away From
> There.

Carlos was still on death row. For his good behavior and lack of infractions
or gang ties, the prison assigned him to a "death row work program" and
to a cell block in the Ellis Unit with a slightly lower security classification.
Even after being caught sniffing glue and paint thinner in a pipe chase with
another inmate and going to "solitary" for two weeks, Carlos retained his
eligibility to work.

In a letter after the glue incident, Carlos fessed up to Vicky and her husband, Fred: "[A]s for me I am ok I guess got into a little trouble I try to Stay
out of trouble But am only human. Well how is fred doing tell him I Sent
my Regards. in Tell him not to get mad am trying to Stay out of Trouble. . . .
well why haven't you written to me I wrote once But you never answer. So
what happen?"

•      •      •

In James Lawrence's brief to the Texas Court of Criminal Appeals in March
1984, his main complaint was that Judge Moore had allowed the trial to
go forward after one of the jurors had herself been the victim of a convenience store robbery while the case was going on. Lawrence also argued

that Moore should have imposed a life sentence when the jury twice told him it was deadlocked on the "future dangerousness" question.

Two years later, in June 1986, the Court of Criminal Appeals rejected all of Lawrence's complaints. The juror who'd been robbed, the court noted, later told Judge Moore that the incident didn't prejudice her against De-Luna. Moore had likewise made a reasonable decision to push the jurors to agree after all but one of them had said they thought they might be able to reach consensus after more discussion.

· · ·

Because the highest court in Texas had approved DeLuna's sentence, Judge Moore wrote an order on July 23, 1986, directing the State of Texas to ex-ecute him in the early-morning hours of October 15, 1986.

In the stilted language judges use to say such things, Moore wrote:

> CARLOS DE LUNA . . . shall before the hour of sunrise on Wednesday, the 15th day of October A.D., 1986 at the state penitentiary at Huntsville, Texas, be caused to die by intravenous injection of a substance or substances in a lethal quantity sufficient to cause death into the body of the said CARLOS DE LUNA.

It was this order that the *Caller-Times* had described the day before it gave front-page coverage to Carlos Hernandez's arrest for the murder of Dahlia Sauceda. It was this order to which Steven Schiwetz and Hector De Peña raised no formal objection even after the newspaper printed a picture of Car-los Hernandez in the flesh and in the grasp of Detectives Garza and Rivera.

· · ·

With an execution date looming and a record of failure by lawyers assigned by the courts, Rose hired a new lawyer to represent her brother. At that time, there were only a few lawyers in Dallas, where Rose was then living, who specialized in capital appeals. Rose chose Richard Anderson, believing that he was Carlos's last and best shot at proving his innocence.

Anderson didn't want to represent Carlos DeLuna, especially on an in-nocence claim. Living hundreds of miles from Corpus Christi, he saw no reason to believe there was a Carlos Hernandez or that Carlos DeLuna was innocent. He didn't think that there was anything he could do, and he told Rose so. Desperate for a lawyer to do something for her brother, Rose pressed Anderson to take the case, and he eventually agreed.

In October 1986, when Anderson informed the judges and district attorney's office in Corpus Christi that he now was representing DeLuna, no one in Carlos's hometown said anything to Anderson to alter his opinion that DeLuna's claim of innocence was baseless.

At the time, Carlos Hernandez was still in jail in Corpus Christi, being prosecuted by the same district attorney's office for killing Dahlia Sauceda. Kenneth Botary was particularly aware of Hernandez's case because Judge Jack Blackmun, who was handling it, was pressing Botary to produce the transcript of his conversation with Hernandez in January 1980, just before the first trial for the Sauceda murder.

As he had mentioned to Hector De Peña over coffee, even former assistant district attorney Steven Schiwetz was aware of Hernandez around this time. Yet, aside from Carlos DeLuna and his sister Rose, no one said anything to Anderson about Hernandez's existence.

.    .    .

Looking back, Rose was bitter about the legal help that Carlos received throughout the entire case, even after she began paying for a lawyer to represent him. Her mother had made her promise to take care of Carlos, and she blamed herself for not doing it.

"I asked him, 'Carlos, did you do this?'" she said in 2004 through tears. "I asked him when he was in Death Row. I asked him, 'Did you do this?'"

"He said, 'No, I didn't do it. If you would just go to Corpus, this is where this guy lives. His name is Carlos Hernandez.' He committed the crime."

Rose found out that even her older brother Manuel knew Carlos Hernandez. They'd hung out at the Casino Club.

"I kept saying that over and over to the attorney[s]," Rose said, starting with De Peña and Lawrence at trial and with Anderson later.

But, just as Schiwetz had told the jury, Carlos's lawyers told Rose that it "was a lie, there was no Carlos Hernandez, that they hired private investigators [to look for him]. There was no Carlos Hernandez, it was a made-up name, there's no such thing."

"Nothing, nothing, nothing."

"I feel horrible," she lamented, "that I could not help him in any way. I did not understand any of the laws. I did not understand anything they were saying in the trial. And every person that I spoke to said he committed this crime, would not give him a chance."

Even when she hired attorneys to help Carlos, "*They* even said he did this crime. They never gave him a chance."

•    •    •

On October 7, 1986, Anderson filed an "Application for Writ of Habeas Corpus" for Carlos DeLuna in the local court in Corpus Christi. Anderson also asked that court and the Texas Court of Criminal Appeals to delay the execution set to occur eight days later. *Habeas corpus* is a Latin phrase meaning "bring the body." It is an ancient method of petitioning a court to require officials holding a person in custody to produce him in court and prove that his imprisonment is legal.

Anderson offered two main reasons why Carlos's imprisonment and sentence were not legal.

First, Anderson accused Corpus Christi prosecutors of unlawfully deciding when to seek the death penalty based on the race and ethnicity of murder victims. Those prosecutors, he claimed, believed that crimes against whites were more serious than ones against blacks and Hispanics, so if you were charged with murdering a non-Hispanic white person, you were more likely to face the death penalty than someone charged with killing a black or Hispanic victim. That, Anderson urged, was illegal discrimination.

In fact, Anderson had no information about the kinds of murder cases in which Corpus Christi prosecutors did and did not seek the death penalty. Instead, he relied on statistics for Texas as a whole.

"Recent studies of the death penalty practice by Texas prosecutors," he wrote, "show[ ] that of the 389 capital murder cases filed in the State of Texas where the victim was black or Mexican-American, only 2.3% resulted in a death sentence, whereas in 1501 capital cases filed in which the victim is [Caucasian], 10.7% resulted in the death penalty."

Anderson claimed that this practice harmed DeLuna because he "is an hispanic male," and "[t]he victim of the offense as listed by autopsy records is a white female."

Legal claims like this were being made by death row inmates all over the country at the time. But there was a problem with raising the point in DeLuna's case. Like DeLuna himself, his alleged victim, Wanda Lopez, was not Anglo. She was Mexican American.

At the time, it was common in official documents in Texas to distinguish between race (based mainly on skin color) and ethnicity (referring to the person's or the family's country or region of origin)—sometimes reporting one or the other and sometimes reporting both. The autopsy that Anderson referred to reported Wanda's *race* or skin color as white but didn't report her ethnicity. As Wanda's common Spanish surnames (both maiden and married) and her lapse into Spanish on the 911 recording indicated, she was ethnically Mexican American and Hispanic—as well as racially white—just as Carlos DeLuna was. The prosecutors' decision to seek a death sentence for the murder of Wanda Vargas Lopez—a Mexican American victim—actually seemed to *disprove* Anderson's claim.

Anderson evidently didn't consult anyone in Corpus Christi about Wanda's Mexican American heritage. He probably was making the same claim in his other cases at the time and may have decided *not* to investigate and risk losing the slender hook the word "white" in the autopsy gave him to fish the claim into DeLuna's case.

* * *

As Jon Kelly had predicted years before, when Judge Blackmun surprised everyone and appointed the inexperienced Hector De Peña to a capital murder case, Anderson's second argument was that Carlos's trial lawyers were incompetent.

De Peña and Lawrence, Anderson contended, didn't speak to Carlos for months at a time; improperly advised him not to cooperate with the court-appointed psychiatric experts; failed to present available mitigating evidence, including his history of substance abuse; and left important arguments out of his first appeal.

In the middle of making this claim, Anderson added a sentence that was as far as he would go in arguing DeLuna's innocence and Carlos Hernandez's guilt: "Counsel at trial failed to thoroughly investigate an alternative hypothesis concerning an assailant other than [DeLuna] even when provided with a name and location of the assailant and information concerning similarities between [DeLuna's] appearance and the alternative assailant." Anderson wasn't even willing to name this "alternative hypothesis . . . assailant."

Anderson apparently conducted no investigation of his own to look for Carlos Hernandez in Corpus Christi. He didn't realize that a convicted convenience store armed robber by that name—with the same height, weight, wavy black hair, and appearance as his client—was then in Corpus Christi police custody awaiting trial for beating, strangling, and knifing a young Hispanic woman to death, or that this Hernandez was familiar to locals from the *Caller-Times* coverage of his arrest.

As the lawyer told Rose, he doubted his client's claim that some other man named Carlos did it. So he decided that the Carlos Hernandez who had remained unseen at DeLuna's trial would go unnamed in DeLuna's habeas petition.

Two days later, a Corpus Christi judge rejected DeLuna's petition and his request to delay the execution. It was Thursday, October 9, 1986. Only six days remained before DeLuna's scheduled execution.

Anderson immediately filed papers making the same arguments to the Texas Court of Criminal Appeals.

The following Monday, with two days left to go before Texas was required to euthanize Carlos DeLuna, its highest appeals court rejected all of Anderson's requests.

In most states and most cases, it takes lawyers and state courts three to six years to resolve claims of the sort Anderson made in his state habeas corpus petition. In Carlos DeLuna's case, it took six days, including a weekend.

The courts' adverse decisions made the news. United Press International reported that DeLuna continued to "den[y] that he killed the woman, saying another man wielded the knife. But investigators have been unable to find the man DeLuna says was responsible."

"I'm at peace with myself and whatever happens," DeLuna is quoted as saying. "I do hope I get a stay, though."

•   •   •

Carlos's last resort was a habeas corpus petition filed in a federal court—the United States District Court for the Southern District of Texas in Corpus Christi. He couldn't ask the federal court to hear the case before then because of a legal rule that federal courts may not step in until after a prisoner "exhausts" all avenues in state court.

Anderson's federal papers made the same two arguments as his state papers had—discriminatory use of the death penalty against defendants charged with murdering non-Hispanic white victims and incompetent representation by De Peña and Lawrence. Anderson's brief criticized an earlier appeal that Lawrence had filed as "wholly inadequate" because it "consisted of [only] seventeen pages." Anderson's own appeal was thirteen pages long. Again, Anderson failed to give a name to or substantiate his client's "alternative hypothesis concerning an assailant other than Petitioner."

•    •    •

With DeLuna a day away from execution, Steven Schiwetz broke his silence. But it wasn't to provide DeLuna's Dallas attorney with clues to the whereabouts of a Carlos Hernandez or to draw anyone's attention to Hernandez's recent arrest for the killing of Dahlia Sauceda. Rather, Schiwetz responded to statements made by DeLuna for Linda Carrico's eve-of-execution article in the *Caller-Times* that day.

DeLuna, Carrico wrote,

> contends he will die for a crime he did not commit if he is executed for the 1983 fatal stabbing of a Corpus Christi service station clerk. But the prosecutor who successfully sought and won the death penalty for DeLuna said his claims that another man was responsible for the clerk's death are outright lies. "Everything he passed onto us was checked out. The bottom line is he lied to us," said former Assistant District Attorney Steve Schiwetz, now in private practice.
>
> In a *Caller* interview, DeLuna said he was arrested because he was in the area and authorities needed a suspect. DeLuna claimed he was across the street and saw the killing, but walked away without reporting what he saw.
>
> "I knew since I had been convicted before in Dallas County they would pin this one on me," DeLuna said. . . . DeLuna claims he is a victim of mistaken identity. He said a friend, Carlos Hernandez, killed the clerk but authorities refuse to believe him.
>
> "That's a lie," Schiwetz said. "He lied throughout the trial, and he's lying now." It was on the first day of the trial, Schiwetz said, that DeLuna told his court-appointed attorney, Jim Lawrence, about Hernandez, whom he said he met while both were in the Nueces County Jail.
>
> "Further checks showed that DeLuna had never been in jail the same time as a Carlos Hernandez," the former prosecutor added.
>
> DeLuna was arrested a block away from the murder scene after he was found hiding under a car. In his pants pocket was a wad of money—the

same amount that had been taken from the service station's cash register, Schiwetz said.

*     *     *

The same day—with only twelve hours to go before DeLuna's scheduled execution—Schiwetz's former boss, District Attorney Grant Jones, agreed to a delay. Federal Judge Hayden W. Head, Jr., immediately granted it.

"Death row inmate Carlos DeLuna missed his appointment with death yesterday," Carrico wrote in her front-page article the next day. She quoted Schiwetz as saying that he was not surprised. "'I expected it. . . . You just have to be patient,' he said."

But Mary Vargas, Wanda Lopez's mother, told Carrico that she was out of patience.

"[DeLuna's execution is] the only way I feel that justice will be done because [Wanda] didn't deserve to die," she said, visibly upset. "I want him to pay for what he did to her. She offered him everything, yet he still killed her. . . . I have asked over and over again, 'Why her?'"

Press reports said Carlos spent the day quietly with his sister Rose and several of his half-sisters and -brothers.

"Thank goodness!" he reportedly said when given news of the delay.

*     *     *

A month later, on November 10, District Attorney Jones and lawyers from the Texas attorney general's office in Austin asked Judge Head to "summarily" deny DeLuna's habeas petition. A "summary" denial would keep the judge from holding a hearing at which DeLuna could subpoena Carlos Hernandez to appear and testify.

In their brief, the State's lawyers immediately tripped up Anderson on his claim that DeLuna was a victim of a policy to reserve the death penalty for people accused of killing white Anglos. As was obvious just from her name, the State's lawyers said, Wanda Lopez was Hispanic, not Anglo. Even if such a policy existed—which Anderson hadn't proved—DeLuna couldn't complain about it because it didn't affect him.

The State's lawyers also exploited an obvious weakness in Anderson's claim of incompetent legal representation: he had no evidence from an investigation of his own to back up the claim. The lawyers pointed out that DeLuna's claim of incompetent counsel required more than proof that the former lawyers did a bad job. DeLuna also had to prove that the result at trial or on appeal probably would have *changed* if his lawyers had done a better job. Anderson, the State noted, offered no evidence to show that.

The State ridiculed Anderson's claim that DeLuna's trial attorneys failed to explore an "alternative hypothesis concerning an assailant other than Petitioner," using a word invented by lawyers to mean something merely asserted but never proved. Anderson's claim, the State's lawyers wrote, was "conclusory," "without factual support."

"DeLuna," the State told Judge Head, offering a less colorful version of Schiwetz's "phantom" argument, "does not identify who the alleged other assailant might have been, nor does he indicate what evidence existed that might have implicated someone else. The contention is simply speculation."

.     .     .

As Carlos DeLuna faced these new difficulties in federal court, things were looking up for Carlos Hernandez, in jail in Corpus Christi.

Two days after the district attorney's office filed its brief in Carlos De-Luna's case, it got word that Judge Blackmun had appointed a new lawyer—the more formidable Jon Kelly—to represent Carlos Hernandez against the D.A.'s charges that he'd murdered Dahlia Sauceda.

Kelly set to work filing motions to dismiss the charges against Hernandez unless Kenneth Botary produced the tape or transcript of his January 1980 conversation with Hernandez. It was after that conversation that Botary had decided to let Hernandez off the hook for killing Sauceda and to pursue Jesse Garza instead.

On New Year's Eve, Judge Blackmun ordered Hernandez released because the D.A.'s office had procrastinated and never produced the missing evidence.

On New Year's Day, Carlos Hernandez was back on the front page of the *Caller-Times*. "Judge Frees Man Charged in Murder," the two-column headline read. The article described the crime and the evidence against Carlos Hernandez, including his fingerprints and underwear in the back of Sauceda's van next to her "severely beaten blood-stained body" and his confession to a witness who had recently come forward.

Again, however, no one told Anderson or the federal court that the "phantom" Carlos Hernandez was again on the front page of the Corpus Christi newspaper.

·    ·    ·

By late January 1987, when Richard Anderson replied to the State's reasons for throwing DeLuna out of court, the lawyer had been on the case for four months, had been taken to task by the State's lawyers for not coming up with any evidence to support his arguments, had been directed by Judge Head to provide more details, and had requested and received two extensions of time to file his response. Even with the additional time, Anderson's seventeen-page response reported only a couple of tidbits of new information that he had uncovered after filing his initial petition.

Anderson admitted to having no statistics showing a pattern of unfair treatment of Corpus Christi murder defendants whose victims were white Anglos, as opposed to black or Hispanic, and requested more time to come up with some. He also acknowledged that the autopsy referred only to Wanda's race as "white" and had no "separate category" for her ethnicity. Then he proceeded to demolish his own claim entirely by appending Wanda's death certificate, which confirmed that Wanda's race was white, but listed her ethnicity as "Spanish origin . . . Mexican." The new piece of evidence flatly disproved his claim that his client was a victim of a policy of reserving the death penalty only for people charged with killing *non*-Hispanic whites.

Anderson provided a few new details to support his argument that De Peña and Lawrence did less for Carlos than they should or could have. He pointed out how infrequently each spoke with DeLuna before trial (De Peña twice, Lawrence four times) and listed people that the trial lawyers could have called as witnesses at the sentencing stage of the trial (five relatives, a former girlfriend, and a schoolteacher).

Even the new details mentioned by Anderson, however, were ones that Carlos and Rose could have supplied from the start, not the kind that an on-the-ground investigation of witnesses in Corpus Christi would have produced. Yet it took the latter type of facts to prove Anderson's case.

As the State lawyers had hammered home in their "Motion for Summary Judgment," a successful claim of incompetent counsel required Anderson to prove that extra effort by De Peña and Lawrence—for example, more conversations with Carlos or calling mitigation witnesses to testify—

would have generated information strong enough to cause a jury to change its mind.

Anderson had almost no evidence like that.

•   •   •

Anderson did offer one new piece of information to support his claim about an "alternative hypothesis . . . assailant," whom the lawyer finally gave a name: Carlos Hernandez. But out of haste or negligence—the same deficiencies he blamed De Peña and Lawrence for exhibiting—Anderson presented the fact as if it were *not* new but was known to DeLuna's two trial lawyers when they represented him.

Anderson blew the punch line. He robbed the new evidence of all of its potential power.

"Carlos Hernandez," Anderson wrote in his brief, "came up as an individual who had a prior criminal background and who had the same physical characteristics as Petitioner. On July 25, *1983, shortly after Petitioner was convicted of this offense*, Carlos Hernandez was arrested on another charge."

Anderson's support for this claim was a clipping of the *Caller-Times*'s front-page article reporting Carlos Hernandez's rearrest in July *1986* for the murder of Dahlia Sauceda. Although Anderson put the news article in an appendix to his brief, its first page, clipped from the bottom of page 1A of the newspaper, was undated.

If Anderson had informed himself and Judge Head of the actual date of the article, it would have provided good evidence of what was true: Carlos Hernandez existed and lived in Corpus Christi in 1983, the middle of the 1979 to 1986 period covered by the article. The failure of DeLuna's lawyers and the prosecutors to find him and check him out revealed a shoddy investigation, or the absence of even that.

Along with incorrectly dating the clipping, however, Anderson said something different, something that was false and much less powerful: that Lawrence and De Peña *had* come across this Carlos Hernandez in *1983*, right after DeLuna's trial but before they filed their request for a new trial.

If Lawrence and De Peña knew about this Carlos Hernandez in July 1983, one of two things had to be true about DeLuna's trial lawyers. Either, improbably, they saw this "Carlos Hernandez" in the newspaper and ignored him altogether—though they said they'd been frantically looking for a dangerous criminal by that name—or, more likely, they did check out this Carlos Hernandez and found he was of no interest to the DeLuna case and was just a man with a common Hispanic name.

•   •   •

The value of the 1986 article, of course, was as a clue. It revealed that there was a man named Carlos Hernandez in Corpus Christi who police believed had used a knife in the murder of a young Hispanic woman in November 1979. The article also showed where to locate Hernandez (in jail) and how to find his criminal record to see if he matched what was known about the man who had used a knife to kill Wanda Lopez in February 1983.

Once Anderson had attached the name to an actual person with a known date of birth and other identifying traits—something Lawrence and De Peña had never been able to do when they represented DeLuna—it was his job to show Judge Head that this was the "real" Carlos Hernandez, and that if the jurors had known what there was to know about him, they might have reached a different verdict.

A simple search of public records at the courthouse in Corpus Christi would have revealed Carlos Hernandez's age—twenty-eight, closer to eye-witness Kevan Baker's mid- to late twenties estimate of the culprit's age than DeLuna's twenty years—his 5-foot, 7-inch height and 160-pound weight, almost identical to DeLuna's; his history of armed robberies of convenience stores; his frequent use of a lock-blade buck knife in his crimes and his daily life; his arrest lurking outside a 7-Eleven with a knife two months after the Wanda Lopez killing; a raft of mug shots showing a resemblance to Carlos DeLuna; and his habit of wearing shabby T-shirts and blue jeans like those Kevan Baker and George Aguirre saw on the man with the knife at the Sigmor Shamrock gas station who sprinted away to the north.

If Anderson had interviewed any of the victims of the crimes that Hernandez's courthouse records revealed—or individuals named in the De-Luna trial transcript—he would have come across people like Linda Perales and her stepdaughter Pricilla Hernandez. Both women knew of Carlos Hernandez's admissions that it was he who had killed Wanda Lopez while his "*tocayo* Carlos DeLuna" took the blame. That, in fact, is exactly how the private investigators later discovered that this Carlos Hernandez existed.

Anderson did none of these things. All he produced was the July 1986 *Caller-Times* clipping, to which he attributed the wrong date—July *1983*.

That mistake, in turn, invited a logical, but false and devastating, interpretation: Lawrence and De Peña must have seen the front-page article supposedly published right after DeLuna's trial in July 1983 and must have looked into this particular Hernandez as they prepared their new-trial request. They then must have discovered he was just a Hispanic "John Smith" and found themselves back where they started, with the "phantom Carlos Hernandez" who haunted only their client's imagination.

*          *          *

After nothing happened in Carlos DeLuna's habeas corpus case for over a year, District Attorney Jones filed a "Motion to Expedite," requesting a ruling from Judge Head so the State of Texas could get on with DeLuna's execution.

Because Anderson had suggested in papers submitted to the judge that, with more time, he could find proof of racial and ethnic discrimination and that he was working on a new petition "flesh[ing] out" the claims of poor legal representation at DeLuna's trial, the State worried that Judge Head might be waiting for Anderson to file something more. If so, the State argued, the year that had passed was enough time for Anderson to have investigated further and provided additional information. His failure to file anything proved there was nothing to find.

*          *          *

In the meantime, Carlos Hernandez, now free of the Sauceda murder charges, was arrested several times for public intoxication. Each time he was carrying a knife, or "several" of them. He was also arrested—for a second time since Wanda Lopez was stabbed to death at the Sigmor Shamrock—on an outstanding traffic warrant after being found behind a store at night with a knife.

At some point in 1988, Hernandez ended up in the hospital for several months after falling out of the back of Freddy Schilling's pickup truck, sustaining head injuries.

*          *          *

On death row, anxiously awaiting Judge Head's decision, Carlos De-Luna wrote Vicky a letter on May 27, 1988, his first letter to her in four years:

Hello my sister. I hope every one is well and fine do give every body my love and Regards. I don't know why you don't write anymore I hope you haven't forgotten about me or your mad at me in any way But what ever the case is I would like to get a letter at least one the last time you wrote to me was 1984 I think just one letter Vicky. I know you ain't got nothing to say but at-least, right in say hi I would be very happy with that.

I got a degree in college. I graduated from a Business course 2½ years of college. I hope I get to use all my knowledge I pick up her one day soon . . .

well you take care and I hope to at least get a hi letter from you. . . . Hey If not I will understand and that's ok. I well always love all of you'll no matter what ever happens to me. I still haven't heard any thing from the federal court in corpus Christi. . . . I heard Blas [Avalos] is sick. I hope he gets well soon. I feel sorry my heart goes out to him. I rember he did a whole lot for Manuel, me and Rose. I just never'ed pay much attention when I was around cause I was very stupid. . . . Bye now. Love Brother Carlos.

•    •    •

On June 13, 1988, Judge Head rejected both arguments made by Anderson on Carlos DeLuna's behalf and lifted his earlier order that had temporarily delayed the execution.

DeLuna lost, the judge said, because he had no evidence to support his arguments. He had come up with no proof that Wanda Lopez was Anglo, not Hispanic. Or that Corpus prosecutors discriminated against defendants charged with murdering Anglo whites (even assuming Wanda was Anglo). Or that better lawyering by Lawrence and De Peña would have improved DeLuna's chances at the trial.

As for the claim about an assailant other than DeLuna, Judge Head repeated Anderson's mistake. He identified the *Caller-Times* article of July *1986* as instead having appeared in July *1983*, just after DeLuna's trial while his attorneys were working on a request for a new trial.

Assuming, then, that Lawrence and De Peña knew this Carlos Hernandez existed, Judge Head put the burden on Anderson to prove both that the two lawyers "made no investigation of the arrested suspect to determine if there could be grounds for a new trial" and that a proper investigation would have revealed persuasive evidence of a connection between this Hernandez and the murder of Wanda Lopez.

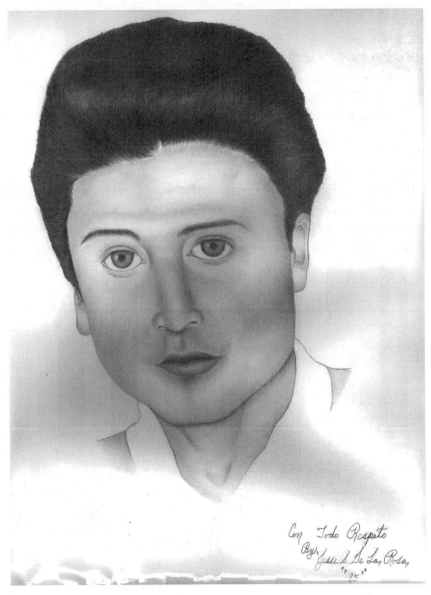

FIGURE 15.2 Portrait of Carlos DeLuna, with inscription "Con Todo Respeto [With All Respect] By, Jesse S. De La Rosa, '85." Texas executed De La Rosa on May 14, 1985.

Anderson, however, had come up with nothing that "undermine[d]" Judge Head's "confidence in the outcome of the trial."

"Significant time has been allowed for Petitioner to substantiate his claims, and no substantiation has been forthcoming," the judge wrote. After reading everything Anderson had provided him, Judge Head said, he had "substantial doubt that Carlos Hernandez even existed."

Hernandez was officially a phantom once again.

·          ·          ·

After hearing about Judge Head's decision, Carlos again wrote to Vicky. Although she rarely wrote back to Carlos, Vicky saved every letter he wrote and dug them out for the investigators in 2004. She had Carlos's GED and correspondence course certificates, as well as a jewelry box and a model church he had made for her while on death row. She also had a sketch of Carlos drawn by another young Hispanic inmate, Jesse De La Rosa, who was executed soon after finishing the portrait (figure 15.2).

Vicky cried when she read some of her brother's letters to investigators, including his June 1988 letter about Judge Head's ruling. In it, Carlos was nostalgic, even reflective—another sign of how much death row had changed the cocky young man. Carlos fondly recalled the pork chops that Vicky had made for him as a kid and his fishing trips with her husband, "big Fred." Fred "would always give me some advice," Vicky read. "If only I would have taken it. How stupid I was."

Carlos remembered his mother telling him, "'Son, one day you're going to find yourself in a hole and you won't be able to get out. . . .' And I used to tell her, 'Who, me? A hole? No way.' But how right she was." For the first time since his arrest, Carlos seemed to realize just how big a hole he was in.

"I am sure you heard the federal court in Corpus Christi ruled against me on my appeal," Carlos wrote. Soon he would go back to Corpus, "so they can set another date of execution."

> I have a good chance of being put to death this time around. [I]t's getting to a point where the courts just don't want to hear our appeals any more on Death Row. . . .
>
>     I sometimes sit here at night and I cry to myself, and I wonder, how could I have ever let some stupid thing like this happen because of a friend who did it, and I kept my mouth shut about it all.

But I don't blame anyone but myself and I accept that. That is why I will accept it if the state of Texas decides to execute me.

.    .    .

Fourteen years later, listening to investigators describe what they had learned about Carlos Hernandez, Wanda Lopez's brother, Richard Vargas, took a moment to reconsider his hatred of Carlos DeLuna. Vargas's unforgiving conclusion was remarkably similar to Carlos DeLuna's own moment of reflection in his June 1983 letter to Vicky.

"[I]t's a harsh way of putting it," Richard said, also stumbling over his words a little. But "[i]f you play with fire and you want to cover up for your friend and you want to look good and not get your friend in trouble and you know who did it and you take it, you take it to your death."

.    .    .

In an act of desperation, Richard Anderson filed a new flurry of papers with Judge Head in late June and early July 1988 with names like "First Amended Application for Writ of Habeas Corpus" and "Motion to Attach Affidavits and Evidentiary Matters to Previously Filed Pleadings." Anderson's papers brazenly sought permission to do now, in July 1988, what the rules required him to have done, but he did not do, in October 1986—investigate, organize the facts, and present them in court.

For the first time, Anderson submitted sworn statements from several of Carlos's friends and relatives saying that Lawrence and De Peña didn't contact them before DeLuna's trial, but if they had been contacted, they would have testified about Carlos's many acts of kindness and generosity. Anderson also came up with twenty-odd pages of reports on Carlos's arrests for sniffing paint in the late 1970s—behavior, Anderson claimed, that might have caused brain damage and mental illness, though he offered no doctor's opinion that it had done so.

As Judge Head could see from Anderson's papers, everything he accused Lawrence and De Peña of doing was true of Anderson himself. The lawyer could have asked all the people who signed statements in July 1988 to do so months earlier and likewise could have retrieved DeLuna's criminal records before the final buzzer had sounded.

But Judge Head didn't know the half of it. The same police and court-house file cabinets with the DeLuna arrest records that Anderson belatedly produced had a much thicker dossier on the Carlos Hernandez described in the *Caller-Times* article that Anderson had attached to his earlier brief. Yet Anderson never asked to look at that file, before or after the final buzzer. Instead, he focused his late filings entirely on the claim that DeLuna did not get a fair shake at the sentencing stage of his trial. Anderson conceded his client's guilt and asked the judge to reconsider only the legality of the young man's death sentence.

·  ·  ·

It was just after Anderson filed his untimely papers that Carlos complained to Vicky about courts not "want[ing] to hear our appeals any more on Death Row." Carlos was right. In the 1980s, there was a monumental shift in how courts handled capital cases—a backlash against death row inmates, who the courts thought were deliberately holding back information un-til the last minute to delay the inevitable. In response, the courts replaced the centuries-old rule that judges in capital cases should act *"in favorem vitae"*—in favor of life, by giving every benefit of the doubt to the prisoner to be sure that he or she got a fair trial and appeal before being executed—with an unspoken rule of *"in favorem mortis"*—in favor of death.

Judges began assuming that mix-ups and missteps by lawyers for even poor and uneducated death row inmates were not accidental and instead were deliberate efforts to delay executions and make a mockery of courts and the death penalty itself.

To fight back, judges started applying procedural rules more harshly in cases where life was at stake than, for example, when the matter at hand was a failure to pay a $2 debt. One such rule was that relevant evidence must be presented at the first available opportunity.

·  ·  ·

Judge Head denied all of Carlos DeLuna's requests on July 19, 1988. He wouldn't let Anderson slip new information into the case long after the deadline for doing so had passed.

Only one additional court was obliged to review DeLuna's case before the State of Texas would be free to execute him: the United States Court of Appeals for the Fifth Circuit in New Orleans. That court gave Anderson three months to file a brief.

* * *

For many death row prisoners, the climactic event in their appeals is their lawyer's briefing and argument to one of the nation's eleven federal courts of appeals. Those regional courts sometimes have a dozen or more judges overall, but a panel of only three decides most federal habeas corpus appeals.

Those three judges have a panorama of the trial and all the prior appeals in the case. An error at any of those earlier stages might provide a reason for the judges to order a new capital murder trial, or at least a new hearing to determine whether the death penalty should be imposed.

The three judges know that their decision will probably be the last word on the legality of the prisoner's conviction and sentence. The other judges on the regional court can vote to put aside the decision of the panel of three and "rehear the case *en banc*," meaning in front of all the judges on the court, but that rarely happens. Also rare is review by the United States Supreme Court. Rarer still is a favorable ruling by any court on a successful "successive federal habeas corpus petition"—an effort to go through the entire federal habeas corpus process a second time, starting back in the district court.

If there is a time for lawyers representing clients on death row to put their best foot forward, therefore, it is in the federal court of appeals.

* * *

Carlos DeLuna's appeal to the Fifth Circuit Court of Appeals was all anticlimax, however—a whimper, not a clarion call for either truth or justice.

Anderson's brief was twenty-five pages—half the usual length in a capital case. Eight of those pages went to preliminaries and five more to an argument not made in any of the earlier appeals, which meant the judges weren't even allowed to consider it.

The Dallas lawyer did not attack the jury's verdict that Carlos DeLuna had killed Wanda Lopez. He devoted his eleven-page argument to the claim that James Lawrence and Hector De Peña provided substandard legal representation at the sentencing stage by presenting no mitigating evidence.

Anderson was forced to spend much of that argument explaining his own deficiencies—why he failed to provide any sworn statements or paper records between October 1986 and June 1988 to support his client's claim and did so only after Judge Head had already ruled against his client and time had run out.

Anderson's brief never mentioned Carlos Hernandez or even an "alternative hypothesis . . . assailant." The three judges decided the case without knowing that the capital prisoner whose fate they had in their hands had insisted from the moment of his arrest that police had collared the wrong man.

·    ·    ·

While waiting for the Fifth Circuit's decision, Carlos wrote a letter to Vicky's teenage son Noel, the last letter Vicky saved:

> all we have to do is believe in god and everything well be alright you well see what I'm saying Ok? I hope you are getting passing grades and I hope you do well in school rember school is Very important, so always try to do your best ok? . . . Hey when ever y you ant to write and I well write Back to you. Do take care and you be carefull, and pay attention to your mom & Dad the usually are always right ok?

·    ·    ·

The judges began their short, almost offhand, decision rejecting Carlos De-Luna's appeal with a simple declarative sentence: "Appellant, Carlos De-Luna, was convicted of capital murder of a gasoline station clerk during the course of committing a robbery."

Then, a little further on: "The claims asserted on appeal all revolve around the issue of the adequacy of representation by counsel at the *punishment* stage of the trial."

In other words, the judges had no doubt that the jury had arrived at the truth about who committed the gasoline station murder. The only question was whether he deserved to die for that crime.

The decision next noted that Judge Head had indulged "appellant's counsel Anderson" by allowing "various pleadings and delays," and that, even so, Anderson had presented his client's claim that his trial lawyers performed poorly "without details and affidavits." It was only after Judge Head had ruled against DeLuna, the court noted, that Anderson "undertook to name the names of family members and friends who would testify and to supply affidavits from them as to appellant's personal conduct with them."

Under those circumstances, the court ruled, there was "no abuse of discretion" when Judge Head declined to look at the materials that Anderson had belatedly produced. All that remained were Anderson's bare allegations, which made "no showing that appellant's counsel fell below accepted standards of competence and conduct."

"CONSOLIDATED APPEALS AFFIRMED," the opinion concluded. Across the panorama of the trial and all the appeals that had come before, nothing had gone wrong.

The date was April 26, 1989, not yet six years since the jury had sentenced Carlos to die.

*        *        *

Anderson tried to get the full set of judges on the court of appeals to "rehear the case en banc," and he asked the United States Supreme Court to step in. By October 10, 1989, both courts had refused.

*        *        *

After losing all these rounds, DeLuna's only remaining option was one of the longest shots the legal system knows—something called a "successive habeas corpus petition." Courts wouldn't even consider that kind of petition unless something had gone horribly wrong the first time around. Realizing that it might have been his own representation that went wrong, Anderson decided that he had to get another lawyer on the case to make that call.

Anderson turned to Kristen Weaver, another of the rare Dallas lawyers willing to take capital appeals for a fee. Weaver was a former assistant district attorney who had recently switched to defense work and specialized in capital appeals.

As Weaver told the private investigators years later in his Dallas home, he was reluctant to take on the case. He knew that the chances of getting a capital sentence reversed in a successive writ in Texas "were, quite literally, statistically, less than winning the lottery."

"It just didn't happen," Weaver answered when asked how often successive petitions had succeeded in Texas before then. "This is the state where the [Texas] court of criminal appeals concluded that there was nothing ineffective when a lawyer slept through a capital trial."

Although Weaver told Carlos's sister Rose and her husband that the chance of getting Carlos's sentence overturned was "absolutely zero," the Rhotons "felt, for the family's sake, that they needed to do everything that was possible." Weaver agreed to take the case.

Rose tried to convince Weaver that her brother was innocent and that another man named Carlos had committed the crime. Weaver told her that the police had her brother cold. All he could do was try to save Carlos DeLuna from being executed for the crime. Weaver told Carlos the same thing the one time they met.

•     •     •

On November 2, 1989, Eric Brown, a Corpus Christi judge new to DeLuna's case, set Pearl Harbor Day, December 7, 1989, as the date for Carlos's execution. With just a month to go before that date, Weaver immediately presented Judge Brown with a "successive" application for habeas corpus relief and a request for a delay of the execution.

Anticipating rapid orders denying DeLuna's requests, Weaver had prepared nearly identical sets of papers to file in the Texas Court of Criminal Appeals in Austin, then the federal district court in Corpus Christi, the federal court of appeals in New Orleans, and finally the United States Supreme Court in Washington, D.C.

•     •     •

Funny thing was, the papers Weaver filed for Carlos—which the lawyer knew had almost no chance of helping his client, no matter how convincing they might be—were the best filed on the young man's behalf at any stage of his case. Weaver's arguments were clear and backed up by legal citations and evidence. Unlike arguments made earlier in the case, Weaver's conveyed a real sense of injustice crying out for a cure, and they didn't defeat themselves.

Several months earlier, in a case called *Penry* after Johnny Paul Penry, a mentally impaired death row inmate in Texas, the U.S. Supreme Court had called into question the entire Texas capital-punishment statute. Ironically, the reasons the Court gave were almost exactly those that Lawrence had pressed upon a bewildered jury at the sentencing stage of DeLuna's trial.

For years, the Supreme Court had been saying that capital juries had to be able to consider everything that was mitigating about information the defendant presented at the capital-sentencing stage. The Texas statute required jurors to impose death, however, if the answer to two questions was "yes"—that the killing was deliberate and that the defendant posed a danger to society in the future.

The problem with that, Justice Sandra Day O'Connor wrote in the Supreme Court's *Penry* opinion, was that the Texas law could turn "mitigating" factors about the defendant—such as mental defects—into "aggravating" factors.

A jury, Justice O'Connor pointed out, might find a mentally disabled person less responsible for his actions than other people, which counts as a mitigating factor. Yet, if the defendant deliberately killed the victim for reasons that would appeal to only a slow thinker, and if his mental problems made it likely that he couldn't learn from his mistakes and end his bad behavior, the Texas statute required the jury to sentence the man to die. Even if the jurors felt that the man was less at fault or more sympathetic because he was slow-witted from birth, they couldn't use that as a reason to spare his life.

If that happened—if the two Texas questions kept the jury from making what Justice O'Connor called a "reasoned moral response" to the mitigating evidence—then the death verdict had to be thrown out.

This was the same argument that Lawrence had made at the sentencing stage of DeLuna's trial, when he tried to convince the jury that the Texas statute was "ridiculous" and "impossible." The only problem with Lawrence's argument was that he had made it to the wrong audience. The jurors he was lambasting weren't to blame for the law and couldn't do anything to change it. On the contrary, they were duty bound to follow it.

Sadly, though, Lawrence didn't make the same argument when he had the chance to do it in front of the right audience. Lawrence didn't object to the legal instructions that Judge Moore gave to the jury at the guilt stage of DeLuna's trial, and he didn't make the argument during DeLuna's first appeal.

.     .     .

Now, for the first time in DeLuna's case, Kristen Weaver was trying to make the argument to the right audience—judges who were themselves duty bound to follow Justice O'Connor's lead and who might find that the same mistake was made at DeLuna's trial as at Penry's.

Because the Supreme Court's *Penry* decision had been announced so recently, Weaver argued that the state and federal courts couldn't evaluate how it affected DeLuna's case in the short time remaining before the date set for his execution. Only by delaying the impending execution could they reach a reasoned decision.

Weaver had two problems, though. First, Lawrence and De Peña hadn't told the jury that DeLuna was slow-witted or that he may have been brain-damaged from sniffing paint—or even that he had been sweet and generous as a child. The State's lawyers were sure to argue that the Texas statute could not have misled the jury about how to use the mitigating evidence in DeLuna's case because there wasn't any.

Second, although lawyers for capital prisoners like Penry had been making the same argument for years in hopes of getting the Supreme Court to pay attention to it one day, no lawyer for DeLuna had made the claim until it was too late. De Peña and Lawrence never made this legal objection at the trial, and Lawrence didn't raise it in DeLuna's first appeal. Anderson did mention the argument in passing, but only in the papers that Judge Head and the court of appeals ruled were filed too late. Weaver couldn't make a claim in a successive habeas petition unless he had a good reason why the claim wasn't made in DeLuna's earlier petitions. But if Penry's lawyers had enough gumption to raise the claim in state and federal courts before the Supreme Court agreed to take a look, there was no good reason why De Peña, Lawrence, and Anderson had failed to make the argument when they had the chance.

Weaver answered the first argument by giving Lawrence and De Peña more benefit of the doubt than they perhaps deserved. The trial lawyers didn't put on any mitigating evidence, Weaver supposed, because they figured the jury wouldn't consider it anyway. Texas's two sentencing questions would keep the jurors from seeing the mitigating value. To show that mitigating information about DeLuna did exist, Weaver attached the sworn statements from Carlos's family and friends, the police reports on his paint sniffing, and Dr. Kutnick's and Dr. Plaisted's reports showing DeLuna's low IQ scores.

Weaver answered the second argument by begging the courts not to hold against DeLuna that De Peña, Lawrence, and Anderson hadn't had as much foresight as Penry's lawyers and hadn't realized that the argument existed until Justice O'Connor accepted it in her recent opinion in Penry's case.

.     .     .

Weaver made his argument in the county court in Corpus Christi, the Texas Court of Criminal Appeals in Austin, the federal district court in Corpus Christi, and the federal court of appeals in New Orleans. At each level, the State lawyers responded with the two arguments Weaver had predicted. The *Penry* claim didn't apply to DeLuna because De Peña and Lawrence presented no mitigating evidence on his behalf. In any event, it was too late to raise the claim now because De Peña, Lawrence, and Anderson had failed to make it at all or on time before.

Each court agreed with the State: DeLuna's prior lawyers had presented too little mitigating information and had objected too late.

.     .     .

Each step of Weaver's way was steeply uphill, and he had to take it at breakneck speed.

Weaver knew that the least likely source of any good news for Carlos DeLuna was Judge Brown in the local court in Corpus Christi.

Brown knew that whatever he did would immediately be appealed by the losing side to the Texas Court of Criminal Appeals. Because that court was notoriously hostile to requests from capital prisoners, especially successive requests, Brown had little reason to take a risk and grant the request.

Despite this foregone conclusion, wrangling in Brown's court ate up more than three of the five weeks that Weaver had before his client was due to be strapped to a gurney and executed. Most of that time was gobbled up by the State's lawyers. Eleven days after Weaver filed his papers, District Attorney Grant Jones finally filed a short response. To emphasize how important the matter was to him, Jones took the unusual step of signing the papers himself rather than having a subordinate sign them.

Two days later, Jones adopted a maneuver commonly used by State's attorneys in capital cases. Taking advantage of judges' natural human desire to avoid work when they can, and removing any risk that Judge Brown might stray from the exact decision Jones wanted, the D.A. submitted something called "Proposed Findings of Fact, Conclusions of Law and Order."

The document was written as if it were the opinion of Judge Brown. All Brown had to do was sign and date it, and Jones would have his preferred decision.

Two days after the district attorney submitted the "Proposed Findings," Weaver filed objections to it.

Five days after that, on November 22, 1989, Judge Brown issued his "Findings of Fact and Order." He did more work than the district attorney had hoped, but only a little more—scissoring out nine and a half of Jones's twenty-three numbered "Findings of Fact" and issuing an order with thirteen and a half "findings" taken verbatim from the D.A.

•       •       •

On November 24, 1989, with less than two weeks left before the date set for Carlos's execution, Weaver filed objections with Judge Brown and also immediately asked the Texas Court of Criminal Appeals to overturn Brown's order. Although he knew that both courts would reject his petitions, Weaver still had to "exhaust" the remaining state court avenues before he could take his arguments to a federal court.

The Texas Court of Criminal Appeals ate up five more days before rejecting DeLuna's petition. Carlos could now go to federal court, where his chances were slightly better—"vanishingly slim," rather than "none."

Weaver had lost four of DeLuna's five weeks in two state courts that he knew would never help his client. He had only a week left to convince one of three federal courts—in Corpus Christi, New Orleans, and Washington, D.C.—that Carlos should not be executed. In case all that failed, Weaver had to save enough time to try to convince Governor William P. Clements, Jr., to commute DeLuna's death sentence to life imprisonment.

•       •       •

The next day, November 30, reporter Kathy Fair published an article in the *Houston Chronicle* under the headline EACH TICK OF CLOCK INCREASES TERROR OF CONDEMNED KILLER.

"I'll be honest," DeLuna told Fair. "I'm really scared that I'm going to have to go through this . . . but if it does happen, I have peace within myself."

•       •       •

The same day, Weaver filed papers in Judge Head's federal district court in Corpus Christi. Judge Head did not want to give Weaver a chance to argue the case to him, but he relented near the end of the day on Saturday, December 2.

Weaver had undergone jaw surgery the day before in Dallas and asked Judge Head to postpone the hearing—and the execution—for a few days while he recuperated. Judge Head refused, accommodating Weaver only by holding the Saturday evening hearing by telephone so the lawyer didn't have to fly from Dallas to the Gulf Coast.

Later that night, Judge Head denied Carlos's habeas corpus petition and request to postpone the execution. It took the judge two days, however, to issue an order allowing Weaver to take the case up the ladder another rung.

Only two days remained for a plea to the federal court of appeals, a long-shot request to the Supreme Court, and clemency discussions with the governor.

.    .    .

The moment Judge Head finalized the appeal on December 4, Weaver had his papers asking for a delay in the execution in front of the Fifth Circuit Court of Appeals in New Orleans and the United States Supreme Court in Washington, D.C.

The court of appeals denied DeLuna's appeal the next day, December 5, 1989.

Adopting Judge Head's conclusions and adding some of its own, the court left DeLuna in the same place he had been at the end of his trial six years before.

As for what happened on the night of February 4, 1983, the court said simply "that during a robbery of a Shamrock gas station on South Padre Island Drive in Corpus Christi, DeLuna fatally stabbed the clerk, Wanda Lopez."

"He was seen and identified by witnesses before, during, and after the offense," the order continued. "Police apprehended DeLuna after they conducted a search of a nearby neighborhood and found DeLuna hiding underneath a parked truck."

The only other facts the court mentioned were that DeLuna "presented no evidence during the punishment phase of the trial" and failed at every stage of the proceedings to object to how Texas law dealt with mitigation.

"APPLICATION FOR HABEAS CORPUS DENIED," the court's decision concluded. "STAY OF EXECUTION DENIED."

.     .     .

People in the execution business have a name for how death row inmates spend their last day. They call it "death watch." Carlos would spend the next day, December 6, with a pastor provided by the prison and four of his brothers and sisters, watching for death to come.

Apart from divine intervention—or perhaps as a sign of it—the only thing that could keep death away was a rare order from the U.S. Supreme Court staying the executioner's hand or an even rarer decision by the Texas governor to commute the death sentence to life in prison.

.     .     .

Talking to the private investigators in his Dallas living room fifteen years later, Weaver was still bitter. He pointed out that the legal issues he'd raised in DeLuna's case "were later acknowledged" by the federal court of appeals and the Supreme Court, "and other people got off [death row] on them." Carlos DeLuna, he said, just had the misfortune of making the argument at the wrong time.

.     .     .

Weaver noticed something else about Carlos's appeals. They shot through the courts quickly—in a little more than six years, less than half the national average.

"Unbelievably swift," Karen Boudrie agreed, comparing DeLuna's capital case with many others she covered during a career as a television journalist in three southern states that frequently carry out executions.

She remembered asking her Corpus Christi sources in law enforcement and the courts why DeLuna's appeals went so fast. "I never got a really good explanation from anybody," she said.

"It just was unimaginable to me. There were people on Death Row that had been there ten years, fifteen years longer than Carlos, who were still there" when they executed him. "[H]e was just rushed through. It was unheard-of."

.     .     .

Boudrie had maintained a professional interest in DeLuna ever since he'd agreed to let her interview him on camera after he arrived on death row. When he began writing her letters, Boudrie had put aside her misgivings about being a convicted killer's pen pal and cultivated him, hoping, she admitted later, that he might someday confess to her, giving her a scoop that could propel a young reporter's career.

Three times, Boudrie aired exclusive on-camera interviews with DeLuna on death row, as he spoke to her through a small metal grate in a thick glass partition laced with chicken wire. Each time, he talked about what happened on the night of the incident that put him there.

The first time DeLuna talked about "standing there when somebody else did what they did, you know. But I won't name no names. I already named names, and the court—and the case is due to appear, and I won't name names."

The next time, he said more. "[T]hey're not trying to find this person," he said. "They say they've tried but they have not tried, no."

"When I had my turn in court," he revealed for the first time, "I offered to take a lie-detector test or any kind of test the district attorney wanted. Mr. Steve Schiwetz, the district attorney . . . told me he did not want me to take a lie-detector test."

Boudrie's report then cut to a shot of former prosecutor Steven Schiwetz, on camera in a coat and tie.

"But as far as the state was concerned," Boudrie pointed out in a voice-over, "this particular Carlos Hernandez didn't exist."

In Boudrie's interview with Schiwetz that followed, the former prosecutor disputed DeLuna's claim that he didn't look for Hernandez. We "tried," he said, but "[i]t was all dead ends." Instead, Schiwetz continued, he was "able to disprove conclusively" that the Perales sisters "could have been with him that night" as DeLuna had claimed.

Schiwetz, however, did not dispute that he'd turned down DeLuna's offer to take a lie-detector test.

Boudrie gave DeLuna the last word. "Maybe one day the truth will come out," the young man, dressed in a white prison uniform, said. "I'm hoping it will. If I end up getting executed for this, I don't think it's right."

Boudrie's third report was on Rene Rodriguez's lawsuit against Diamond Shamrock on behalf of the Vargas family, but Boudrie found a place in it for DeLuna (figure 15.3). After noting that Rodriguez was waiting for a response from Diamond Shamrock, Boudrie cut to a shot of Carlos DeLuna behind the glass partition.

"Carlos DeLuna is also waiting, on Death Row," she said, "hoping he'll get good news about his appeal. He says he feels bad about what happened

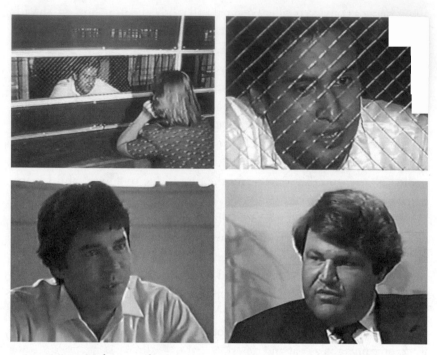

FIGURE 15.3   Mid-1980s television news reports by Karen Boudrie in which she interviewed Carlos DeLuna on death row (*top*); Rene Rodriguez, lawyer for the Vargas family in their suit against Diamond Shamrock (*bottom left*); and former prosecutor Steven Schiwetz (*bottom right*).

to Wanda Lopez, and also somewhat responsible because he was there. But he doesn't feel he should die for something he didn't do."

"I just wish people would . . . look for that person," DeLuna pleaded, concluding the broadcast interview.

"He continued to profess his innocence," Boudrie later said, summing up all her talks with DeLuna. He was confident in his appeals.

•   •   •

Boudrie recalled that when the end of DeLuna's appeals approached, her professional interest in the case had begun to change. She couldn't say precisely why. It may have been getting to know DeLuna better, the changes in him she'd observed during his years on death row, how freely he admitted the many bad things he'd done, or the earnestness of his denials that he had killed Wanda Lopez.

Whatever the cause, Boudrie had started thinking that there might be more to DeLuna's "Carlos Hernandez" story than her neighbor and friend Steven Schiwetz thought. "Did we dot all the *i*'s and cross all the *t*'s in this case?" she wondered.

She knew that Carlos DeLuna was right in one respect: "Nobody was really trying to find Carlos Hernandez for him." Someday, she thought, she would take on the search for Hernandez. While DeLuna was appealing his case, she "kept thinking there's more time, there's more time" to track this Hernandez down. She never dreamed that DeLuna's appeals would end as quickly as they did.

.     .     .

Whatever concerns Boudrie was having privately, she and the other members of the press covering the story gave the case for DeLuna's execution ample space and air time in the first week of December 1989. "DeLuna has continued to maintain his innocence, claiming that the murder was committed by a friend named Carlos Hernandez," an article in the *Corpus Christi Caller-Times* reported.

"But," the article continued, "those whose lives were touched by the crime doubt the story. 'He'll be lying until he dies,' said Mary Vargas, Lopez's mother. 'He'll lie like he's been lying. Now he has to pay for what he did to my daughter.'"

.     .     .

The *Houston Chronicle*'s Kathy Fair began her second-to-last article on Carlos DeLuna by noting that the twenty-seven-year-old death row inmate "who started a life of crime stealing cars and sniffing paint as a juvenile was awaiting his execution late Wednesday night."

Her article alternated between paragraphs devoted to Schiwetz's descriptions of DeLuna's criminal record—"'His was more of a surreptitious violence,'" the former prosecutor told Fair—and other passages in which Wanda Lopez's mother described her anguish.

"'I want him to pay for what he did to my daughter,'" Fair quoted Mary Vargas.

"But [Vargas] said DeLuna's death would not erase all of the pain she has felt in the six years since her daughter was stabbed to death while she frantically called police."

"'You feel an emptiness, in yourself,'" Vargas said. "'Something is missing. It's not the same.'"

In memorializing DeLuna's case for posterity, however, Fair made things a little too easy. Sandwiched between paragraphs quoting Schiwetz's description of DeLuna and the evidence the former prosecutor had presented was Fair's summary of the evidence at trial.

"One witness at his trial identified him as the knife-wielding man seen outside the store, and another witness saw him struggling with the victim inside the store," Fair wrote. "DeLuna was found hiding beneath a parked vehicle about a quarter mile from the store, barefoot and without a shirt."

"His bloody shirt and shoes were found in a yard the next day."

# 16

# Execution

ABOUT THE TIME CARLOS DELUNA arrived on death row, Rosie Esquivel was working in a warehouse in Garland, Texas, with Mary Conejo, the wife of Carlos's half-brother Danny. Mary asked Rosie if she'd be willing to write to Carlos sometimes to help keep his spirits up. Although Rosie had never met Carlos, she was about his age and, in her succinct and straightforward way, said she didn't have a problem with that. Over the next six years, she wrote to Carlos and received "hundreds" of letters back from him. She saved them in a big box for a long time but threw them out a couple of years before the private investigators found her in Garland in 2004.

Rosie also visited Carlos on death row a few times and was struck by how handsome and well mannered he was, a lot more so than the guys who paid her any attention on the outside (figure 16.1). Even so, it was hard to invest that much time in someone on death row without asking the obvious question, and, in her straightforward way, Rosie asked it: Did he kill the girl?

"Carlos never liked talking about what happened. He would rather look to the future," Rosie remembered. But when she asked Carlos, he answered. "[H]e did not kill the woman ... it was another Carlos, I think Hernandez."

Rosie believed him. "I know you hear that [they are] all nice guys. They are really not nice," Rosie said, emphasizing the "not." She'd had her share of bad experiences with cons and ex-cons, including Carlos's brother Manuel some years later, and felt confident in the comparison based on experience: "Carlos, he was [a nice guy]. He was a gentleman. I don't think he could have done it."

FIGURE 16.1  Carlos DeLuna on October 27, 1989, when he was brought back to Corpus Christi for the hearing at which his execution was set for December 7, 1989.

Rosie tried to follow Carlos's appeals—his lawyers, his chances—but it was confusing. "Carlos fought all the way to the end," she knew. "He maintained his innocence all the way to the end." He told her that his lawyers were doing something called "habeas corpus." She didn't know what that was, but she knew that it wasn't about his innocence. Carlos told her that he'd talked to his lawyers many times about Carlos Hernandez. "I tell them this. I give them all the information," she remembered him saying. "They just don't want to listen."

"He fought the way he could fight," Rosie said finally. "Sometimes he just wanted to give up. They just would not listen to him when he told them it was someone else."

Rosie knew that Carlos's last appeal hadn't worked out for him, but she was surprised when she got a call on a Wednesday in early December 1989 from Carlos's sister Rose. "She told me that Carlos was up for execution that night. They were hoping for a stay of his execution." Carlos "was afraid," his sister had said. Rosie prayed for him.

•    •    •

Ever since Judge Hayden Head had ruled against him on his first habeas petition in federal court in June 1988, Carlos had done his best to prepare himself and his sisters for what might be next. He said he was prepared to die, and that if he should be executed, "it's okay, don't worry, I'm okay."

Most of the time the best explanation he could come up with for what was happening was simple fatalism. Someone else laid the cards on the table, and he just played along—that's how Karen Boudrie described his thinking. "Whatever happens, happens," he told his sister Rose. "But I did not commit this crime," he continued. "I want you to know that."

Other times, he tried to find some justice in his situation and found it in the bad things he'd done—putting his mother and sisters through all their trips to bail him out of jail, not calling out Carlos Hernandez right from the start, dragging his family to death row to see him. "I don't blame any one but my self," he wrote. "[T]hat is why I well accept If the state of Texas decides to execute me."

"[I]n his heart," his sister Rose said, Carlos "accepted that he was going to be executed. That it was going to be okay, because of all the hurt that he caused, all the hurt that he did—not on this crime that he was convicted for—but all the other things that he did, [that] would even things out." Rose believed that Carlos had found some peace. "He knew that he was forgiven," she said, by her and by God. There was one letter in particular that Carlos had written, late in the ordeal, which had made her feel that way. She lost the letter and other things from Carlos when a garage flooded out, but she continued to find solace in the forgiveness he said he felt.

During the first week in December, Carlos went back and forth between the fear he'd admitted to *Houston Chronicle* reporter Kathy Fair and the peace his sister Rose described. In a letter he wrote to Karen Boudrie late on Tuesday night, December 5, he said he'd felt scared all day Monday. But Monday night, for the first time ever on the row, he'd slept soundly and straight through his alarm clock going off. "I woke everybody else up in the same tank with me," he wrote to Boudrie. "I can't believe I am sleeping too good with all this happening."

Boudrie read the letter to the investigators in a videotaped interview years later, smoothing out Carlos's spelling and punctuation. "'But you know what, Karen?'" she read, "'I am not scared like I was yesterday. I feel like this peace came from somewhere and entered my body, and I feel very peacefully about everything.'"

.    .    .

The Reverend Carroll Pickett would soon dig more deeply and expertly into what Carlos DeLuna was thinking, and how well equipped the young man was to understand what was going on.

Between 1982, when Texas ended an eighteen-year hiatus in executions, and 1995, the Reverend Pickett quite literally ushered ninety-five men to their death by lethal injection. He also ministered to dozens of death row inmates who began the day thinking they would die at midnight but ended it alive, with a stay of execution. If Texas went through with DeLuna's execution, it would be Pickett's thirty-third (figure 16.2).

A bit of a historian and chronicler of Texas's modern executions, Carroll Pickett was aware, even before meeting DeLuna, that the date scheduled for his execution was the sixth anniversary of the first-ever court-sanctioned execution by lethal injection in the world, on December 7, 1982.

Pickett had stood beside Charles Brooks, Jr., the man executed that day. The minister had been handpicked for the job by the prison warden, a member of Pickett's former Presbyterian congregation in Huntsville, where the Death House was located. Not long before, Pickett had given up the large congregation, believing that his mission there was complete. The warden asked him to become chaplain at the Walls Unit of the Texas Department of Corrections—"the Walls," everyone called it—and to move his family into a home on the prison grounds.

FIGURE 16.2  The Reverend Carroll Pickett.

Pickett was impatient with the many people who mistook him for a death row chaplain. Death row chaplains ministered to "the living," Pickett explained. He ministered to the soon-to-be dead. He had never in his life visited death row, at the Ellis Unit sixteen miles outside of Huntsville. State law required Texas to execute people "at Huntsville," and so the Death House—the small building where executions occurred—was located at the Walls Unit inside that city's limits. Pickett was the "death chaplain"—or a "Death Angel," as he preferred to be called. His ministry was to be with each man for a single day, the day he was to die.

·      ·      ·

Executions have been around for millennia, ever since there has been something resembling a "state" to execute its people. Still, Texas's lethal injection of Charles Brooks was an experiment, the first legal killing ever carried out in that manner. "There was no book to go by, no manual to go by," Pickett explained later. "Nobody ever executed a person this way. So nobody, including the doctors, could tell us what to expect." For the fifteen years he was part of the lethal injection process, Pickett said, it was "a fearful situation, all the time, because we never knew" what might happen.

The warden wanted everything to go smoothly: to get the inmate quietly onto the gurney so the executioners could strap the prisoner down and insert drips for three lethal drugs into veins in both arms. That's a big part of why the warden hired Pickett and provided him with a place to live only fifty feet from the Death House.

"My responsibility, according to the warden, was to be there in the Death House . . . when [the condemned prisoner] walked in. I was to be the face that he saw outside of the guards. That was important," the preacher explained in his slow, soothing cadence. "Because every inmate distrusts guards. They have to. They're taught that. They're abused by them" sometimes, Pickett said. "[The warden's] charge to me was, and these are his words, 'to seduce their emotions so they won't fight getting out of the cell or getting up on the table.'

"I could be a pastor to them, I could be a minister to them, I could work with them whatever their religious presence was. But he told every one of them, the first warden did, and all the other ones that followed him . . . 'I suggest you talk to him because he's a good counselor. If you don't want to talk about religion, that's fine. But whatever you do, just talk to him.'

"And all but one of those ninety-five talked to me," Pickett recalled, quietly proud of how well he had carried out his second calling as a pastor. "Of course there were fifty or sixty more that came in and got stays [of execution]. But as far as going to the table, I did that ninety-five times."

Every bit of Pickett's time, from early in the morning to after midnight, on every "execution day was set aside just for that." Most of the day was spent talking to the prisoner, going over the steps that would lead to his execution that night, advising him about his burial and the disposition of his things that required a lot of paperwork, and mentally preparing him for his last moments. There also "were reports to give the warden, reports to give to the executioners, and there was a time when I would go visit with the [inmate's] family" to help them decide whether to watch the execution or not. And there were confessions to hear, a lot of them.

Pickett was serious about his work and attentive to each detail that could pacify or rile up a condemned inmate in his charge. The holding area of the Death House, for example—a small, "dungeonlike" room with a cell for the inmate and some space outside of it where Pickett and the attending guards stayed—had only a single small window to let in a little outside light and air.

The chaplain noticed that an inmate's mood would often darken when he glanced at the window. He realized that the men were using the tiny patch of natural light to gauge the progress of their last day's journey into night and the execution that awaited. "I sought and was granted permission to have the panes of the window painted black," he disclosed in his book on his last ministry, *Within These Walls: Memoirs of a Death House Chaplain.*

"That it took so long to determine the cause" of the inmates' darkening moods "angered me," the Death Angel wrote. "My job—'seduce the prisoner's emotions, calm him, help him in whatever way you can'—had been undermined by my own inability to recognize an elementary problem."

.  .  .

A description of that darkened window introduces chapter 13 of Pickett's book, to illustrate the importance he placed on "reading" the personality of each man on death watch and "avoid[ing] any attitude or mannerism that might set [the inmate] off." "It was those prisoners who were mentally retarded," Pickett wrote, "who were the most difficult to read."

Pickett then discusses two Death House inmates. The first is Johnny Paul Penry, who, Pickett wrote, "came to the Death House in 1989 with crayons and a coloring book and comics he couldn't read." Penry was never executed, however. The Supreme Court gave him a last-minute reprieve and overturned his death sentence.

It was in Penry's case that the Supreme Court had criticized Texas for making it difficult for jurors to consider "mitigating" evidence. Kristen Weaver spent the day scheduled for DeLuna's execution trying to convince the Court to apply its *Penry* decision to Carlos DeLuna, as a reason to grant him a last-minute reprieve.

Pickett wrote in chapter 13 that, after hours "trying in vain to make [Penry] understand what would happen to him once we entered the death chambers," and just before the Supreme Court intervened, the minister noticed his latest congregant "idly thumbing through a comic book . . . lost in a world of make-believe [and] occasionally laugh[ing] quietly to himself." Penry's "innocent, childlike sounds chilled me," Pickett recalled.

.  .  .

"Carlos DeLuna shared a troubling kinship with Penry," Pickett wrote, introducing the other inmate whose Death House day Pickett chronicles in chapter 13. "Though he was twenty-seven when I met him, he seemed much younger. That he'd managed to pass through the first nine years of public school was a sad commentary on our education system," the minister wrote. "As we talked, I found myself trying to imagine my own children—teenagers at the time—attempting to grasp the concept of their own death."

Much of what Pickett did during the hours he spent with an inmate was to answer questions about how the killing process would unfold. Chapter 13 categorizes inmates by the amount and quality of their curiosity about their impending death. Inmates of average and above-average intelligence had "an endless series of questions" about the different steps of the process. Those of lower intelligence "seemed disoriented." Some couldn't latch onto any thought at all. That was Johnny Paul Penry.

Pickett placed Carlos DeLuna on the same end of the scale: "[H]e demonstrated the characteristics that, since Penry, I'd so often prayed never to see again. . . . [H]e had no real understanding of why he was there." "[A]ll DeLuna was concerned with was what pain he might feel when the needles were inserted into his arms."

Pickett replayed his conversation with Carlos:

> "It'll be like getting a shot in the doctor's office," I tried to explain.
> "You promise it won't hurt?"
> "I promise."
> "Will you hold my hand?"
> That, I told him, would not be possible.
> "Why?"
> Because, I explained, his hands would be taped down to the gurney. . . .
> [W]hen the warden removed his glasses, it would be the signal for the injections to begin, and I assured him that once they started it would be no more than seven to twelve seconds before he was unconscious. Several times before the time came for him to leave the cell, we counted the numbers off together: one . . . two . . . three. . . .

•     •     •

During a decade and a half as the death chaplain, Carroll Picket sought psychological help only twice. Both times were a result of Carlos DeLuna's trip to the Death House. "I'll never forget Carlos DeLuna," Pickett told the private investigators in 2004.

Carlos arrived at the Death House early on the morning of December 6. As Pickett did with all the condemned prisoners, one of the first things he

did when he met Carlos was to mentally sort him by type. Some prisoners were "inmates," the pastor said. They had "adjust[ed] to the fact that
they [were] in prison, for right or wrong, for innocent or for evil," and were
"honest and . . . supportive" most of the time, not "troublemakers." A "convict," however, was "a troublemaker," who had "committed multiple felony
crimes," resisted the rules, and didn't "care how he act[ed]" or how often he
was punished.

"We had people who were sent in to be executed who were convicts, and
we had some who were inmates," Pickett said. Right away, he could see that
Carlos was an inmate. Carlos was cooperative throughout the day, Pickett
recalled. He "came in [that morning] quiet, very, very scared. Because he
was so young. He was basically a child." All day long, Pickett commented,
"I was with a boy. He was a man by age but he was a boy." He was "simple.
He began to hang on me . . . he didn't want me to leave. He wouldn't let me
leave."

The only thing that Pickett knew about the twenty-seven-year-old was
what he'd read in an article that Kathy Fair published in the *Houston Chronicle* on November 30 under the headline EACH TICK OF CLOCK INCREASES
TERROR OF CONDEMNED KILLER. DeLuna, he'd read, was accused of stabbing Wanda Jean Lopez in a convenience store robbery while she was on
the phone with 911 begging for help. "Shortly afterward, police found him
hiding beneath a truck parked only a few blocks away." Yet DeLuna claimed
he was innocent and that another man had committed the crime.

Pickett told the investigators that before he'd even met DeLuna, "I had
questions . . . about Carlos's guilt or innocence." His instincts about criminals, honed by years of listening to them confess what they'd done and why,
told him that a detail in Fair's story didn't make sense. "The average convict
will not stop a block away and hide underneath a truck. If they're going to
run, you keep running and running and running. You get as far away from
the scene as possible," Pickett explained.

Pickett spoke to Carlos about the *Chronicle* article several times during
the day. It was his way of introducing the question of what happened at the
time of the killing, in case Carlos had anything he wanted to get off of his
chest. Bringing condemned inmates to a point where they trusted the pastor well enough to confess their sins after only a day together was a big part
of Pickett's peculiar ministry. But it would be a while before DeLuna would
be ready for that.

In the morning, to gain the inmate's trust, Pickett talked about other things, beginning with the family members who were expected at the prison that day and how much time the inmate wanted to spend with each. Early in this discussion, Carlos revealed that he'd never met his father and never felt good about his stepfather. Pickett knew that he was making progress when at some point during the morning, Carlos "wanted to know if he could call me 'daddy,' if it would hurt my feelings. Because he had never had anybody stick by him who was in a fatherly position."

Pickett told Carlos that would be fine, but "it sort of shook me," Pickett admitted to the investigators. "I've got four children and three step-children and fourteen grandchildren, and I know what 'daddy' means." After that, Pickett could see, Carlos "was willing to discuss anything" with him.

Carlos had a lot of family members to attend to, Pickett recalled. Several were at the prison that day, including his sister Rose; his half-siblings Vicky, Mary, and Danny; and their spouses. Later Carlos made phone calls to his half-sister Toni Peña in Corpus Christi and his brother Manuel, who was in a prison unit south of Houston. Carlos also contacted Karen Boudrie. In the middle of a move from Corpus Christi to a job with a television station in Georgia, Boudrie wasn't covering Carlos's story any more. He reached her by phone in Cincinnati, where she was visiting her parents.

"[T]hey were good people," Pickett remembered. "A lot of inmates who died have good people." Whatever the inmate had done wrong, "their families were innocent," and Pickett made it his business to treat them with dignity.

Family visits with inmates about to be executed occurred in a building near the Death House incongruously called the "hospitality house." Carlos wanted to see his people separately, not all at once. According to Pickett's notes, Carlos saw his sister Rose and her husband Brad from 10:00 A.M. to noon, Danny and his wife for the two hours after that, half-sisters Mary and Vicky from 2:00 to 3:00 P.M., and Rose and Brad a second time after that.

The first time Carlos faced an execution date, in October 1986, officials hadn't yet moved him to the Walls when he got his reprieve from Judge Head. As Rose drove over to the prison that morning in 1989, she remembered that day three years earlier as a "happy moment." But she knew that "when you go to the Walls, that's it. The chances of you getting out of there are thin."

Still, Rose, a deeply religious woman, was filled with hope. Recently she had hired a new lawyer, Kristen Weaver, to get a reprieve for her brother, and he had asked the United States Supreme Court to grant a stay of execution. If that failed, Weaver would ask Governor William Clements for clemency.

It was "very painful," Rose said, seeing Carlos at the hospitality house that morning. He was as thin as she'd ever seen him, "maybe 125 pounds." She could see that her brother was nervous, but he was also "very quiet, very peaceful, more peaceful than the ones there that were not in that situation"—including Rose herself. She and Brad spent their time with Carlos in the morning talking about the Supreme Court and the governor. "I thought, for sure, for sure, he was going to get out of it. Deep in my heart, I believed God's going to get him out of this. And I told him that," Rose recalled.

That afternoon, they heard that the Supreme Court had rejected Carlos's petition.

*     *     *

Kristen Weaver remembers the days leading up to December 6 as "a flurry of [court] filings and denials, then more filings and denials," which he orchestrated from his office in Dallas, 175 miles north of the Walls. "And finally, when we'd run out of everything else," he placed a phone call to the governor's general counsel and chief of staff, Rider Scott, "trying to explain all of the different reasons I thought [Carlos] shouldn't be executed, and then waiting for Rider to call back. That was basically the process."

In deciding whether to spare a man's life, most governors look for evidence of what lawyers like to call "actual innocence"—not legal reasons why the verdict wasn't fully reliable, but facts to show that the condemned man didn't commit the crime. The courts have already decided the legal reasons repeatedly. For a governor considering whether to stick his own neck way out and give a convicted killer a break, there's no percentage in second-guessing the judges. For the governor, it comes down to a simpler question of justice and truth: Did the man do it?

Weaver didn't have any good answers for the governor on that question. He hadn't done his own investigation, and the records from DeLuna's trial and appeals gave him nothing to go on. Sure, Carlos *said* he was innocent, and Rose had pleaded with Weaver about that. But the only thing they had was a dubious name, Carlos Hernandez, which everyone from the prosecutor and jury to Federal District Judge Head had rejected as De-Luna's shameless invention. Weaver felt he had to concede, as he told the governor's counsel right off the bat, that DeLuna's was a "case where guilt was clear and obvious."

With no other leg to stand on, Weaver urged the governor to do exactly what the governor had said he would not do: second-guess the courts. Fresh off losses in five successive courts, Weaver argued the *Penry* issue again, urging Scott to advise the governor that all the courts were wrong. The Texas statute had kept the jurors in DeLuna's case from giving proper weight to "mitigation." Fresh off five victories, the State's attorney, William Zapalac, made his same arguments as well. DeLuna didn't have a *Penry* issue because his lawyers didn't present any mitigating evidence that a jury could have been confused about. Johnny Paul Penry's lawyers, Zapalac reminded the governor's aide, had presented substantial evidence that he was mentally defective. Carlos DeLuna's lawyers had presented none.

After listening to both sides, Scott said that he had already gone over the case with the governor earlier that evening and had taken the phone call from Weaver armed with the governor's decision: because "we find that there are no new issues of fact or law that have not had an opportunity to be resolved in the appellate courts or the trial courts," Scott announced, "the Governor has indicated that he will not substitute his opinion for that of the appellate courts of this country. . . . I have been empowered by the Governor to tell you that he would deny the reprieve."

Weaver phoned Carlos to give him the news, which he remembers Carlos accepting calmly with a "thank you." Before and afterward, Weaver always found a way to save his death row clients. Carlos, the one exception, just "fell through the crack," he said.

When Weaver heard from the investigators a decade and a half later that Carlos had twice been given a chance to plead guilty to avoid a death sentence and had twice turned down the offer, citing his innocence, the lawyer was surprised. He had never heard about that before. "It just breaks your heart," he said.

·     ·     ·

Rose was shocked when she heard that the Supreme Court and Governor Clements had rejected Carlos's pleas. "We thought for sure he would get out of this because [of] our faith," she told the investigators tearfully. "I'm not angry with God anymore," she continued, now fifteen years later, but for a long time it had shaken her faith.

After getting the bad news, Rose asked to see Carlos a second time, late in the afternoon. Earlier she had decided to view the execution if it came to that, but now she realized that she wouldn't be able to watch Carlos die. She wanted to see Carlos one last time and make her real goodbyes.

 •        •        •

With all his visits, Carlos had no time for lunch that day, but just after 6:00 P.M., after seeing Rose for the last time, he had his dinner—the fabled last meal.

Pickett was critical of records kept by the Texas Department of Corrections listing what each inmate ate for his last meal and said for his last words. It wasn't the use of antiseptic routines to paper over the deliberate killing of people that bothered Pickett. Rather, it was the prison system's failure to get the details right. Pickett understood from experience, however, why mistakes always happened. No matter how good your routines are, he explained, when it *is* the deliberate killing of someone that you're part of, you're going to be "in shock," "your emotions are going to be involved," and "you're not going to hear or report exactly what [happened]."

Carlos DeLuna's last meal was a case in point, Pickett explained. At first Carlos had said that he didn't want any dinner. That was typical. Despite all the hoopla about the steak and lobster that condemned killers devour on the last night of their existence, most of them don't want anything or just pick at their food. In Pickett's experience, it was only the "mentally challenged" who displayed much of an appetite. In any event, the Texas prison didn't serve steak and lobster, the chaplain pointed out. What the corrections department records said about that just "wasn't true."

"About six o'clock," Pickett recalled, he asked Carlos if he was sure he didn't want anything. Carlos asked if Pickett could still get him something. "Just tell me what you want," the warden said. Carlos's answer was "[s]trawberries and ice cream and a shake."

"Now the book," Pickett said during his interview with the investigators in 2004, reaching over for the volume—"the classic book" by the Department of Corrections "about what happens on Texas death row, what they eat and the last meal"—says that DeLuna "ate nothing. I sat right there by him, and he ate strawberries and ice cream and drank the shake, and we talked."

•       •       •

Around 8:00 P.M., the guards let Carlos use the telephone to call relatives. His conversation with his oldest half-sister, Toni Peña, was short and unadorned, and years later Toni spoke about it to an investigator in that same way. The investigator's notes record the moment: "Toni told me about the phone call from Carlos the night of his execution. . . . Carlos told Toni he loved her. At this point [in the interview], tears welled up in her eyes and rolled down her cheeks. It was a very painful and sad moment."

Carlos also called his brother Manuel at a prison farm in South Texas. It was while Manuel was there that another inmate, Miguel Ortiz, had called him out to the rec yard and recounted Carlos Hernandez's chilling confession to three killings, including one at a gas station for which "Carlos De-Luna" had taken Hernandez's "rap."

"[D]on't blame God, if I am killed and I am innocent," Carlos told Manuel, having heard their sister Rose blaming God earlier in the day. Manuel wanted to hear it straight and clear from his brother, however, so at the end of the conversation he asked Carlos directly: "Did you kill the lady at the gas station?" Carlos said he didn't. Carlos Hernandez was the killer. Manuel believed his brother. He said he could always tell when his little brother was lying, and Carlos wasn't lying.

•       •       •

The Reverend Pickett had the same question for Carlos as had Manuel, but the prison chaplain had a lot more experience helping his charges get things off their chest.

When Carlos finished his family phone calls, it was almost 10:00 P.M. The time set for the execution was a little over two hours away. It was at this point that Pickett explained to the inmate exactly what would happen as they strapped him into the gurney and prepared his veins to receive the injections. "Now, I want you to follow me in there," Pickett would tell them. "And don't fight. Because I'll have some guys with me. You'll be two feet behind me and just follow me."

It was in those final two hours, Pickett said, that the inmates often became eager to confess their crimes to him, even crimes for which they had never been convicted. Curious to know whether inmates were embroidering their records for his sake, Pickett said he checked out some of the things he heard with friends in law enforcement. "They were true," he said. "There was a lot of confession. At ten o'clock to midnight is a very traumatic situation."

Pickett didn't leave anything up to chance, however. He spent the whole day preparing each inmate for this moment, gaining the inmate's trust, promising that he himself would tell the truth about anything the inmate asked, no matter what. He did this repeatedly with Carlos. Then he would calmly and in detail explain the procedures the executioners would use to inject three drugs into his veins to kill him, and the violence the guards would have to use if he resisted. Again, he would invite as many questions as the inmate had, promising to answer each honestly and in detail, which he would do.

Finally, the reverend would ask the guards to leave, to give him complete privacy with the inmate, and he would invite the prisoner to do just what he had been talking about doing, and doing himself, all day: tell the truth. "It was our program, our philosophy," Pickett explained, "that I will ask questions and guide [the inmate] and talk to him. Whatever he wanted to confess to or talk about, that was fine."

As a final step in the program, Pickett would ask a set of questions he carefully tailored to each inmate. In Carlos DeLuna's case, Pickett had repeatedly talked to Carlos about Kathy Fair's November 30 article in the *Houston Chronicle* and the account it gave of the killing of Wanda Lopez and Carlos's arrest. Using that account, Pickett worked out two simple questions to ask DeLuna: one about a detail of the crime that only the killer would know, and one about circumstances of the arrest that Carlos would surely recollect.

"So, I explained all this to Carlos," Pickett told the investigators, at the point in his narrative where he had just taken DeLuna through the steps that would be used to execute him. Then the chaplain put the question directly to Carlos: Did he want to tell the truth? "I did them all that way," Pickett explained.

Carlos said he did.

"Go ahead," Pickett said. "I want to know the whole story."

Carlos told him first what was at the front of his mind and had been all day. He was scared. He was "not so afraid of dying," Pickett said, but of "how, and what's going to happen after that." Mainly Carlos wanted to know what it would feel like. Would it hurt?

Pickett explained the process to Carlos again, letting him ask questions and answering as honestly as he could. "[It]'s going to take . . . nine to twelve seconds for that first medication to go to work. And you'll be totally asleep, you won't feel another thing." He promised Carlos that, apart from two pinpricks when they put the needles in each of his arm, the process would be painless. Carlos asked him, "Will you be with me, daddy?" Pickett assured him, "I'll be right with you."

With the guards now out of the room, Carlos said he "wanted to talk about" the crime. The reverend was ready himself with "those two issues"— the questions he'd formulated for Carlos using the *Houston Chronicle* article.

"Why did you let her talk on the phone[, and] why did you stay [under] the truck" rather than run far away?

"I didn't do it," Carlos said.

That was "clear as a bell to me," Pickett told the investigators. "And I believed him."

Pickett ministered to hundreds of terminal patients in the prison hospital—"heart attacks, C.O.P.D., AIDS, cancer, you name it," he said—and he watched ninety-five prisoners die in the execution chamber. "I went through this for sixteen years, listening to them on their last days and nights. I spent way too many hours, I suppose, listening to their last confession. But some of them I believed. And some of them I checked out." "I fully believe Carlos DeLuna was an innocent man," he continued, "and I will always believe that."

Pickett helped Carlos practice his last words. The pastor felt that he understood exactly what Carlos wanted to say, and why.

•     •     •

The chaplain had gotten Carlos permission to make one last phone call, at 11:00 P.M., to Karen Boudrie in Cincinnati. She was the last person De-Luna called.

The television journalist had thought about this moment for a long time and expected a confession, especially, she said, after Carlos "chose me to be the last person to talk with." In the past, he had admitted many other wrongs to her and had curbed what he said about the killing of Wanda Lopez only because of his appeals. Those were over now. "He had nothing to lose at this point," she told the investigators. There was no reason left why he wouldn't tell her the truth.

Boudrie wasn't sure how to start a conversation with a man an hour away from death, to whom she had no relation, and who had chosen her to receive his last call. So, "ever the journalist," she said with a laugh, she just "gave him the opportunity . . . to say anything he wanted to say, to get it off his chest."

"Do you have something you want to confess to me? Do you have something you want to tell me, Carlos?"

"No," he said quietly. "[T]hey're putting to death an innocent man."

For the first time, Boudrie said later, recalling what Carlos said, "it really hit me that maybe they were."

Boudrie was "devastated." She hung up the phone and grabbed her mother, "just crying and crying." She didn't think that it was going to happen so soon and felt guilty that she had never done the investigation she planned. "There's any number of things I could have done," she told the investigators, but it "wasn't until that last phone call that I really, truly believed him." By then, it was "too late."

•       •       •

As midnight approached, Carlos asked the Reverend Pickett to pray with him. Carlos had a little card in his pocket with a prayer printed on it. He said to Pickett, "I want to pray this prayer, but I can't read very well." Again, the chaplain was overcome by his impression of the young man. Even much later, as he thought about it again, he could barely keep his composure. This was not a hardened murderer. This was an immature, poorly educated, helpless boy on the verge of execution.

Carlos asked if he could hold Pickett's hand. "We were not permitted to touch an inmate," Pickett explained, "but . . . he wanted me to hold his hands. I'd been warned by the warden . . . never put your hands through the gate, through the bars. Because they can either pull you forward— And we had on death row out here, not long ago, a chaplain put his hands through, and the guy had a knife, and he slit his arm open wide. But that didn't bother me about Carlos."

Pickett put his hands through the bars. Carlos grasped them and held tightly. As Carlos gripped his hands, Pickett began to pray. He soon felt the downward tug of Carlos sinking to his knees. "By the time I finished the prayer—and it was probably four minutes, five minutes long—he was on his knees, crying," Pickett remembered.

Carlos got up from his knees and asked Pickett to recite the twenty-third psalm again and explain what it meant. Pickett read the psalm and said to him, "We're in the valley of the shadow of death, Carlos." The guards entered the room and saw Pickett holding Carlos's hands, but they didn't say anything. "The warden knew what I was doing," Pickett explained.

•    •    •

Carlos stood up and said he was ready to go. The guards walked him into the execution chamber and strapped him down (figure 16.3). As he had promised, Pickett held Carlos's left hand, at the same time checking to make sure Carlos's veins were suitable for injection—another of Pickett's execution-day responsibilities.

When the two executioners came in, they wanted to start on Carlos's left side, so Pickett switched hands. The executioners firmly taped down Carlos's left arm and went for a large vein in the middle. Pickett had promised Carlos that the first prick of the needle would be the only pain he would feel. Watching it pierce DeLuna's skin—the thirty-third time he'd seen it happen—still made Pickett wince.

Carlos asked again: Would Pickett keep holding his hand? Pickett told Carlos that he could do so only until they strapped down the other arm.

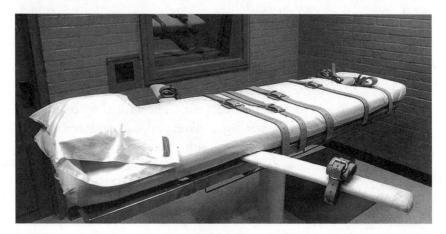

FIGURE 16.3  The Texas execution "table."

"Would you hold my leg?" Carlos asked. The executioners switched arms and inserted a second needle into Carlos's right arm. Pickett let go.

After strapping Carlos down with needles in both arms, the executioners left his side and entered a little room next door where they would release the chemicals. The warden left the execution chamber, shutting the heavy metal door behind him. "He gave me about forty-five seconds. I had about forty-five seconds, just me and the inmate. And that is the forty-five seconds that is never recorded anywhere," Pickett explained.

In their last seconds together, Carlos told Pickett, "I just want to thank you, daddy, for being my daddy for one day." He asked Pickett again to hold his leg when it started, and Pickett put his hand on Carlos's knee.

Just then, the witnesses took their places. None of Carlos's people were there, nor anyone from Wanda Lopez's family, though they'd been invited. The known witnesses, besides the Reverend Pickett and the prison officials and guards, were Michael Graczyk, an Associated Press reporter, and Jim Mattox, the elected attorney general of Texas. Mattox would occasionally slip over from the capital in Austin to watch an execution. Mattox came, Pickett noticed, when he felt a need for a last-minute confession or new details on a crime.

"Carlos looked over at [the witnesses]," Pickett recalled, "and then he looked back. He kept his eyes on me, and he said he was going to [keep his eyes there]. He said, 'Will you be where I can see you?' I said, 'Yes, I'll stand right here. I won't move.'"

The warden asked Carlos if he had any last words. Carlos gave his final statement. With that, everything was ready. Pickett kept his hand on Carlos's knee.

.    .    .

According to Pickett, Carlos's last words were not accurately recorded in the press or in the prison record—they almost never were, he said. By all accounts, Carlos did not confess to the crime and offered no pleas for forgiveness or understanding.

Carlos's first concern was his family. The press accounts confirmed this, and so did the Reverend Pickett. Although she wasn't there, Rose DeLuna Rhoton confirmed it as well. Several days after the execution, Rose received a letter from Carlos that Pickett had mailed later that morning. Although the letter, along with all of Carlos's last possessions, was lost in a flood in

Garland, Texas, Rose would never forget Carlos's final gesture to her. "He knew that I would be hurting for him," Rose recalled, and he said "he was so sorry for all the pain he had caused" over the years "to his family members and to . . . our mother."

Carlos's other concern was the friends he was leaving behind on death row. To them, his last words—which Pickett knew were "very, very important" to him—were "Don't give up." That was Carlos's message, Pickett said, to others "striving to prove their innocence."

*     *     *

Carlos's time was up.

After he said his final words, Pickett recalled, "he looked up at me, and he had these big old brown eyes. I'll never forget those brown eyes. I can dream about those brown eyes." Pickett motioned to the warden that it was time.

The warden took off his glasses—his signal to the executioners to start the process of dripping the three chemicals into Carlos's veins—and then he focused his eyes on his watch.

The first drug, Pentothol, was supposed to put Carlos to sleep in seven to twelve seconds. The second, Pavulon, would start to flow after twenty-four seconds and would paralyze him, so that he couldn't breathe. The third, potassium chloride, would stop his heart.

Pickett had promised Carlos that he would be asleep within twelve seconds. But after the twelve-second mark passed, Carlos raised his head and fixed his brown eyes on Pickett again. That scared Pickett. "I knew the time had passed. The other guys had gone to sleep. They'd given their cough or whatever it was. And I wonder, to this day, what was he thinking," Pickett said, and what he was feeling.

If the first drug failed—and Pickett was sure it did, at least at first—then Carlos would be awake when the second drug started suffocating him. He also would feel a torturous burning when the third drug—a poison with no therapeutic use—entered his veins. But the paralysis from the second drug would prevent him from showing any distress. Carlos would be tortured to death, but only he would know it.

Ten seconds later, over twenty seconds into the execution, Carlos raised his head again. Pickett was frantic, though he kept himself stock-still so that none of the observers would be alarmed. "Nobody had ever done this,"

Pickett explained, "Those big, brown eyes were wide open. Here I am, five inches from his knee, five feet from his face, and he's looking straight at me. . . . And I don't know what the question was in his brain. I don't know what he was thinking. If I wanted to be paranoid, I could say he was thinking, 'You lied to me.'"

After the twenty-four second mark, the paralytic drug flowed into the tubes. Carlos closed his eyes and didn't raise his head again. The whole process was supposed to take six minutes. Carlos was not pronounced dead until ten minutes had passed (figure 16.4). The extra minutes were excruciating for Pickett. No one will ever know what they were like for Carlos DeLuna.

                        •        •        •

DeLuna's execution haunted Pickett. He was unable to sleep for the next five nights running. For the first and last time, he had to seek counseling. "That's when I started thinking," he told the private investigators, "we are killing innocent people. We are killing children. We are killing [the] mentally retarded."

FIGURE 16.4  Carlos DeLuna's grave site in Corpus Christi, where his family brought him back to be buried. The inscription reads, "I'm with God."

●    ●    ●

The day after the execution, the Associated Press summarized the intersecting tragedies of Wanda Jean Lopez and Carlos DeLuna in two sentences early in its short article: "The lethal injection began at 12:14 A.M. [Carlos DeLuna] had insisted all along that he was not responsible for the death of Wanda Jean Lopez, 24, whose final words of terror on Feb. 4, 1983 were captured on a police emergency dispatcher's tape recording."

# PART V

# The Scars of Dina Ybañez

# 17

# Recidivism

ANYONE WHO SPENT TIME AROUND Carlos Hernandez after 1978, when he made parole on his armed robbery convictions, almost surely saw him being arrested for one thing or another. It happened dozens of times. But Hernandez's arrests were an especially important part of Dina Ybañez's four-year friendship with him. Dina met him *because* he was being arrested—in mid-April 1985, his thirteenth trip to jail since 1978. Four years later, in mid-April 1989, Hernandez used a lock-blade buck knife to rip a 4-inch incision in Ybañez's abdomen, prompting his twentieth arrest.

April was a bad month to be around Hernandez, whatever the year. That was the month he held up three gas station attendants at gunpoint in 1972 and when he was arrested behind a 7-Eleven with a knife in 1983 and promptly fingerprinted in connection with the Wanda Lopez killing. April also saw arrests for drunk and disorderly in 1985 and drug possession in 1990, as well as the knife attack on Dina Ybañez in 1989.

When Corpus Christi police took Carlos Hernandez into custody on the occasion of his first encounter with Dina, Carlos DeLuna was on death row waiting for the Texas Court of Criminal Appeals to decide his first appeal. When Hernandez's knife attack on Dina triggered Hernandez's arrest in April 1989, DeLuna was seven and a half months away from being executed.

Still, although Carlos Hernandez was far from an apparition to Dina Ybañez and the officers and prosecutors who repeatedly arrested and tried him in the mid- and late 1980s, he remained one to the lawyers and judges who decided Carlos DeLuna's fate. None of Hernandez's nine arrests while

Carlos DeLuna was on death row—not even the arrests for killing one and for nearly killing another young Hispanic women with a knife—triggered action by the Corpus Christi police or the district attorney's office to alert the lawyers or judges responsible for DeLuna's appeals that a Corpus Christi criminal named Carlos Hernandez had been found.

•   •   •

Carlos Hernandez's association with Dina began innocently enough around 8:30 P.M. on April 17, 1985, when the police picked up Hernandez for public intoxication while erratically riding a bicycle past Dina's house on Buford Street. She lived around the corner from the Hancock Street residence that Hernandez was then sharing with Diana Gomez. Gomez would soon walk out on Hernandez, after he told her how he had killed Dahlia Sauceda. Soon after that, Gomez would report Hernandez to Eddie Garza and Paul Rivera, who would then arrest him for murder.

But in mid-April 1985, the arrest of a mustachioed man in a white T-shirt and jeans for drunk driving while on a bicycle probably occasioned some amusement on Buford Street and attracted Dina Ybañez outside her house to watch. Never one to miss a chance to flirt with an attractive young woman, even while in the clutches of police officers, Hernandez asked Dina to look after his bicycle.

When Hernandez was finally able to pay the $63 fine several days later, he returned to Dina's house for his bike. Although both his intoxication and his criminal offense violated his parole conditions, the police didn't bother to report either to the parole board.

Fifteen years later, Dina talked at length with private investigators about her ill-starred friendship with Hernandez. After the bicycle incident, she got to know Carlos better and became friendly with his long-suffering girlfriend Cindy Maxwell (figure 17.1). Carlos disappeared for a time in 1986 after Detectives Garza and Rivera arrested him, but he was back in the neighborhood after New Year's, when his lawyer Jon Kelly got rid of the Sauceda charges for good.

After that, Carlos and Cindy were often at Dina's place and even lived in Dina's garage for several months in 1989. Dina trusted Carlos enough to have him and Cindy babysit her ten- and twelve-year-old sons while she was at work—not realizing that Carlos was buying her sons beer and teaching them how to sharpen and flip open the buck knife he always carried.

FIGURE 17.1  Carlos Hernandez following his arrest in April 1985 for public intoxication on a bicycle (*left*) and with Cindy Maxwell in the 1990s (*right*), when he was suffering from cirrhosis and diabetes.

But like all of Carlos's women friends, Dina soon saw his other side. "He was a nice person, if he was your friend," she explained. "But every time he would argue with somebody, he would try to stab him with a knife." He "was always threatening people with knifes," she said. "He would say, I'll put the knife on their life if they mess with me. And that's the first thing he would think about, the knife." Increasingly frightened by Carlos, especially when he drank, Dina's boys begged her to stop hanging out with Carlos and Cindy.

A tough woman who didn't take orders from anyone, Dina didn't listen to her sons and freely confronted Carlos about his mistreatment of Cindy. Cindy was mentally slow, and Carlos was quick to manipulate and abuse her, taking her disability checks, threatening and hitting her, even bringing women home to have sex with him while Cindy was there. When Dina stuck up for Cindy and later took Cindy into her home, Carlos got angry. Dina eventually learned that Carlos had sexually molested his own niece Pricilla, and she twice herself stopped him from molesting Cindy's five-year-old niece.

Sometimes Carlos "would bring out this thick like notebook of legal work" and brag about his legal case, Dina's oldest son Johnny recalled. "It made him feel big." Dina and Cindy looked through the papers one time and discovered that Carlos had been accused of murdering a woman in a van. "[T]hat's when I started wondering if I should let him around my kids," Dina said. "Made me wonder."

Later, sitting in his living room, Carlos admitted to Dina and Cindy that he had killed Dahlia Sauceda in her van in front of her little girl, and he told them about another woman he had stabbed at a Sigmor Shamrock gas station. In both cases, he said, the cops blamed someone else—"Jesse" something for Dahlia and Hernandez's *tocayo* Carlos" for the Shamrock lady. Hernandez laughed about what had happened to both young men.

Poor and uneducated with four kids to raise on her own, Dina balanced what she thought was right and what was necessary in her own pragmatic way. When Carlos's evils were in plain sight, she would take him to task for them. Otherwise, she took a quiet pride in her equal footing with a man whom others feared and took advantage of his free babysitting to help her hold down a day and a night job. The balance broke down when Carlos wanted her to have sex with him or no one else and she refused. One night, after she had insisted on seeing a man named Gilbert Limon and resisted Carlos's advances, he went after her with his knife.

.        .        .

While talking to the investigators, Dina almost choked on the name Carlos Hernandez and struggled to express herself in her self-taught second language. But midway through the conversation, struggling without success to keep from crying, she pulled together the story of her changing relationship with Carlos Hernandez and her altered view of the man himself. "Tell me about Carlos Hernandez," an investigator asked. "What was your relationship with him? Tell me about who he was."

"At first I thought he was a good person," Dina said, "because he was good to the kids. And then after I met Carlos's girlfriend, who was Cindy, it was different. He was bad. He was real abusive with Cindy."

But Dina really started to see Hernandez differently when she heard him laughing about the two women he'd killed—how he'd carved an $X$ on the back of one of them and thought about killing her baby daughter, too. And how he "put the knife" on the other woman at the Shamrock and let his stupid *tocayo* take the fall.

"[A]fter I met him for a while," Dina continued, "he stabbed me too. I never thought it would happen to me. You know, I never—[*Pause.*] I don't want to start crying. He did it to me, I was just lucky. My little boy saved me." Through tears she could no longer hold back, Dina explained:

INVESTIGATOR: What did Carlos Hernandez do to you?

YBAÑEZ: He stabbed me in my stomach.

INVESTIGATOR: Do you still carry those scars with you today?

YBAÑEZ: They're here. [*Lifts up shirt to reveal scar.*] And my fingers. I don't have no feelings on this one and this one. If it wasn't for my little boys I would have been dead too. He already had me on my back. . . .

INVESTIGATOR: What was [he] going to do to you when he had you on your back?

YBAÑEZ: [He said] he was going to put an *X* on my back like the way he did Dahlia.

INVESTIGATOR: Did he tell you other things that he was going to do to you?

YBAÑEZ: That he was going to rape me. Said that if I wasn't going to be his, that I wasn't going to be for nobody else. That he always gets what he wants. That's why he did the other girls.

During the remainder of the interview, Dina elaborated as best she could on Carlos Hernandez's confession to the gas station killing, and on her own violent encounter with her former friend. Although Hernandez spoke more frequently about Dahlia and her baby's fortunate near miss, he told Dina enough about the woman at the Sigmor Shamrock and about his *tocayo* who got the blame to reveal what had happened. Hernandez made sure in other ways that Dina would never forget what he did to the gas station lady—and what more he had intended to do to Dina herself.

As for the Shamrock woman, Hernandez told Dina that "he went up to her and put the knife on her." He "[p]ut the knife on her life," he explained, because she didn't do something that Carlos Hernandez wanted. Dina didn't know if Carlos had demanded that "something" right there at the Shamrock station, or if it was something—as in Dahlia's and her own case—that happened before and became a justification, in Carlos's twisted mind, to beat and stab and try to rape the object of his ire.

As for Hernandez's *tocayo*—meaning someone, Dina translated, with the "same name, different last name"—Hernandez said he was "stupid for not running fast and for getting under cars."

Hernandez himself "ran away, the other way." He was always "making fun of Carlos DeLuna," always "talking about how he," Hernandez, had "stabbed her and then he started running and they caught that other guy.

Laughing, because his *tocayo* was going to pay for something like that, even though he didn't do it. Just because they look the same."

"He ran, they got that other guy."

•   •   •

As for herself, Dina described being dropped off at home by a friend late on April 14, 1989, after finishing her night job waitressing at Rosita's Kitchen. Cindy Maxwell was babysitting the kids and told her that Carlos was drunk and had left with Dina's car. Carlos returned around 12:30 A.M., and Dina went outside to demand the keys from him. He refused.

Then Carlos came at Dina, pushing her up against a tree next to the driveway. He "went into his pocket and came out with a knife . . . [a] buck knife" and held it against her neck. Dina had known before then that he was jealous because she was dating Gilbert Limon, even though Carlos himself was with Cindy. Carlos asked her in Spanish, "How come you can give him some and not me?" Then he stabbed her in the stomach. Dina said the knife was so sharp that she didn't even feel Hernandez make the 4-inch slit. She saw the knife and reached out to push it away, badly slicing two fingers on her right hand (figure 17.2). Interviewed in prison, Dina's son Johnny later said that he had to live with the knowledge that "the knife [Carlos] stabbed my mother with, I had sharpened for him."

After stabbing Dina while they were in the front of the house, Carlos dragged her into the backyard to rape her. That was Carlos, she told the investigators. Stab a woman, and try to rape her while she bled. She recalled an ugly look on his face—the same look he'd get in his eyes when he drank and talked about the other women he'd hurt. "He looked evil," Dina recalled. "He wasn't Carlos, he was a different person. He looked . . . real bad, like he wasn't all there."

Soon Dina was on the ground. Carlos turned her over and was on top of her. He said that he "was going to put an *X* on my back like the way he did Dahlia." It was then that he said he was going to rape her, that "if I wasn't going to be his, I wasn't going to be for nobody else. That he always gets what he wants."

When Carlos first put his knife on her neck, Dina kept still, hoping that he wouldn't hurt her. Now, however, she screamed. Before he could cut her again or rape her, Dina's twelve-year-old son, Andy, came out of the house and hit Hernandez over the head with a large stick. Cindy had awakened

Dina's fourteen-year-old son, Johnny, and he came after Carlos with a kitchen knife. Carlos took off running.

Andy went inside and called the police. After receiving the 911 call, the police put out a BOLO for a thirty-four-year-old Hispanic male with a mustache, wearing a T-shirt. The police soon picked up Carlos in a convenience store parking lot at Third Street and Buford. His blue jeans were bloodstained, and he had a large lock-blade buck knife in his right back pocket. The police took the knife and jeans as evidence.

When the police arrived at Dina's house, she was sitting on the steps holding her stomach with a cloth. Her insides were showing from the wound. Johnny and Andy had wanted to call an ambulance right away, but Cindy had stopped them. She didn't want Carlos to get in trouble. "So, I was just there bleeding," Dina recalled. "I lost a lot of blood . . . until I was [passed] out." Before losing consciousness and being taken to the emergency room, Dina provided a description of Carlos Hernandez that matched the person the police had arrested.

At first, Carlos told the police that he didn't remember anything. "He had a blackout." Later he admitted to stabbing Dina but said it was an

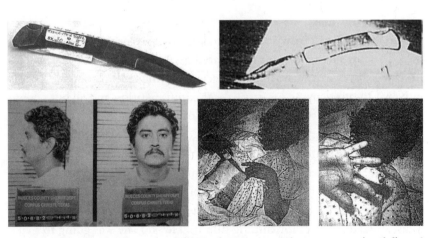

FIGURE 17.2 The knifes used to kill Wanda Lopez on February 4, 1983 (*top left*), and to assault Dina Ybañez on April 15, 1989 (*top right*), with a note that the latter is 7 inches long. (*Bottom left*) Booking photographs of Carlos Hernandez following his arrest for the assault on Ybañez. (*Bottom right*) Police photographs showing bandages on the stomach and hand wounds suffered by Ybañez in the attack. (The photographs of the knife used to stab Ybañez and of her wounds are available only in poor-quality photocopies.)

accident. In a written statement, he said he'd been in a fight with another man who had threatened him. He claimed that Dina had tried to break it up and got in the way of his knife. Carlos didn't know the man, he said, and didn't see his face in the dark. The only other witness the police interviewed was Dina's son Andy. He backed up Dina's version of the story.

Robert Mayorga was the Corpus Christi police officer who arrested Carlos Hernandez and took Dina's statement. Mayorga was the cop who had dated Wanda Lopez in the months before she was killed at the Sigmor Shamrock and arranged a set of hand signals with her so he'd know she was okay when he drove past in his cruiser without having time to stop.

Well aware of the fate of Dahlia Sauceda and the clerk at the Shamrock, and of the plan Carlos Hernandez had for her, Dina knew that she was fortunate to survive. If her sons hadn't been there, she would certainly have joined the other two. Even with her sons' aid, she was left with a scar ripped from navel to sternum. For months following emergency surgery, Dina had trouble eating and using the bathroom, and effects remain. "Everything makes me sick," she told the investigators, "and I get a lot of cramps and pains to my stomach. To this day. So, I'll never forget it." "[E]very time I see my stomach, I see his face," she said.

. . .

Six days after Dina Ybañez was stabbed, District Attorney Grant Jones indicted Carlos Hernandez for aggravated assault. At the time, Carlos De-Luna was just five days away from a decision by the federal court of appeals in New Orleans denying his first habeas corpus petition and all but sealing his fate in the courts. No one in Jones's office informed the court or De-Luna's Dallas lawyer that this Carlos Hernandez had struck again with a lock-blade buck knife and was again in police custody.

Instead, a day after the indictment—and before Dina Ybañez had even been released from the hospital—Jon Kelly got Carlos Hernandez out on bail. In the months that followed, Hernandez repeatedly appeared at Dina's house, threatening her for turning him in. He said "he was going to make sure I died," Dina recalled with a shudder, so "I wasn't going to be alive to testify against him." Both she and Johnny told the private investigators about a time Hernandez came around with a knife and tried to break down the front door. Johnny again attacked him with a kitchen knife, stabbing him repeatedly in the back. Carlos left only after Dina made a show of calling the police.

Abandoning any claim that Dina's stabbing was accidental, Carlos pled guilty once Kelly reached a deal for a reduced sentence. Signing off on the deal for District Attorney Grant Jones was a young prosecutor named Mark Skurka, who was elected district attorney himself in 2010. If anyone had asked her, Dina Ybañez would have opposed the deal with Hernandez, both for her own sake and for the sake of the other young Hispanic women whom Carlos had attacked. On the day set for Carlos's hearing, she recounted, "I went upstairs and I asked, where do they have Carlos Hernandez up here, because he stabbed me, and . . . I wanted to be there . . . to see what they do to him, because I was the one that got hurt." A clerk told her the case had settled without a trial. Why? she asked. "[Hernandez] hurt me, he hurt other people, you're still [not] going to bother with him?" They told her it was over.

Although Dina didn't understand what she was doing at the time, a statement she had previously signed may have helped Hernandez get the deal. She remembers Kelly handing her a paper that said the attack was "heat of passion"—lawyer talk for the claim that a man's rage in the midst of a lover's spat should partly excuse him from attacking her. Dina said she signed the paper because Kelly promised to keep Hernandez from going to her house and to make sure her son Johnny wasn't prosecuted for stabbing Carlos with a kitchen knife. On October 9, 1989, Judge Vernon D. Harville sentenced Carlos Hernandez to ten years in prison, with the understanding that he would be eligible for parole in a year if he stayed out of trouble.

The day after Judge Harville sentenced Hernandez, the United States Supreme Court refused to review Carlos DeLuna's first federal habeas corpus petition. That triggered a request by District Attorney Jones, whose office had just accommodated Carlos Hernandez with a favorable plea bargain, to have the local court set December 7, 1989, as the day when the State of Texas would execute Carlos DeLuna.

Again it crossed no one's mind to rethink former assistant district attorney Steven Schiwetz's confident declaration to the jury, which promptly convicted Carlos DeLuna and sentenced him to die, that Carlos Hernandez was a "phantom" and that DeLuna's testimony about him was a lie. And no one questioned federal Judge Hayden Head's conclusion, which signaled the end of DeLuna's claim of innocence on appeal, that there was "substantial doubt that Carlos Hernandez even existed."

By May 1991, 19 months into his 120-month sentence, a year and a half after Carlos DeLuna's execution, Carlos Hernandez was back out on parole haunting the streets of Corpus Christi. First among those he frightened were Dina Ybañez and her children. Even after she moved to another house to avoid Hernandez, he tracked her down and threatened to kill her. "Every time he would see me," Dina recounted, "he would say that 'I didn't get rid of you the last time, but the next time I'm going to make sure you die.' I still get nightmares." The attacks stopped only after she moved with her children to San Antonio.

.    .    .

Harassing Dina wasn't Hernandez's only offense in the years after he was paroled. It was during this period that he and his friend Mary Ellis were caught with twenty-four grams of heroin, bagged for sale at a cheap motel along the waterfront. Somehow invisible again, Carlos was not even charged, and his parole on the Ybañez assault remained intact.

Finally, in September 1996, after being assigned a female parole officer with less patience than her male predecessors had shown for Hernandez's brand of violence, his parole was revoked for one last time. His final offense was threatening several neighbors with a 9-inch knife.

By now in the terminal stages of cirrhosis of the liver, with complications from years of excessive drinking and smoking, Carlos Hernandez spent the rest of his life in prison. He died on May 6, 1999, just shy of his forty-fifth birthday. Because Hernandez's ten-year sentence for nearly eviscerating Dina Ybañez ended on October 1, 1999, if Hernandez had survived another five months, he would have been returned to the streets of Corpus Christi free of any prison or parole supervision for the first time since 1972. In keeping with the wishes of his mother, Fidela, who refused to use a life insurance payout on her son to transport his body back to Corpus Christi, Carlos Hernandez was buried in a pauper's grave on prison grounds.

.    .    .

"When you think of Carlos Hernandez today," the investigator asked Dina Ybañez at the end of her interview, "what do you think?"

Dina answered without pausing. "I don't feel sorry for him. I'm glad he's dead. He won't hurt nobody else no more. That's what I think of him." Then she said, "If you had asked me this years ago maybe I could have saved Carlos DeLuna, because he was innocent."

# Epilogue

I want to say I hold no grudges. I hate no one. I love my family. Tell everyone on death row to keep the faith and don't give up.
—Last words of Carlos DeLuna, December 7, 1989,
as recorded by the Texas Department of Criminal Justice

"I DIDN'T DO IT, BUT I KNOW WHO DID." From the moment Mark Schauer and other officers pulled Carlos DeLuna out from under the truck on Franklin Street—wet, agitated, and smelling of beer—to the moment of his execution, DeLuna's claim remained the same. He didn't do it, but he knew who did. "I'll help you," he told Officer Schauer, "if you help me."

Contrary to the prosecution's assertion at trial, Carlos DeLuna's claim was no eleventh-hour creation. Although it took him five months to overcome his well-founded fears and utter the name Carlos Hernandez, DeLuna never wavered about his own innocence or his knowledge of who had killed Wanda Lopez: "I didn't do it, but I know who did." Carlos said the same thing to his family, friends, lawyers, prosecutors (whom he asked to give him a lie-detector test), and any member of the media who would listen. He was innocent, and he knew who the real murderer was.

After his conviction, Carlos DeLuna continued to insist that he was innocent and that Carlos Hernandez was the killer. In correspondence and a series of death row interviews with Karen Boudrie and other news reporters, DeLuna repeatedly declared his innocence and identified Hernandez as the culprit. An hour before his execution, DeLuna called Boudrie in Cincinnati, his final conversation with anyone outside the death chamber.

With nothing left to lose, he said it once more: Texas was about to execute an innocent man.

As the Reverend Carroll Pickett had done for thirty-two death row inmates before Carlos DeLuna and would do for sixty-two more after him, the Death House chaplain organized the last day of DeLuna's life around a central objective: unburdening the condemned prisoner of the truth about his awful crimes as he prepared to meet his Maker. Even before Carlos arrived, Pickett believed that he had a simple soul on his hands, with an instinct to hide under cars—and, previously, under a bed and bushes—rather than to run away from the police. When the prison-hardened minister, who'd seen it all before, encountered a twenty-seven-year-old with the demeanor and thought processes of a boy—who called Pickett "daddy," feared needles, and wanted his hand to be held through the execution—the Death Angel was confident that he could elicit a soul-baring confession in response to two questions he'd carefully prepared: Why did Carlos let the store clerk call the police, and why did he hide under a pickup truck? Carlos confessed other misdeeds, but his answer to Pickett's questions was simple and direct: "I didn't do it."

Strapped to the gurney, with the Reverend Pickett's hand on his knee and only seconds to go before his death, Carlos still maintained his innocence. His final words forgave those who had accused him and urged other innocent men on death row to keep fighting. Carlos DeLuna never wavered. He did not kill Wanda Lopez, but he knew who did.

*     *     *

There was another player in the case who was equally adamant and consistent on the same point: Carlos Hernandez himself. Although his namesake Carlos DeLuna took the blame for the crime, Hernandez confessed again and again that it was he, and not DeLuna, who had killed Wanda Lopez.

Hernandez proudly admitted this to his family and neighbors on Carrizo Street in the days following the killing. He broadcast his admission so widely that Detective Eddie Garza learned of it from informants within weeks of the killing. And in April 1983, well before DeLuna produced the name in July, the police officers and prosecutors handling the murder case became sufficiently interested in Carlos Gonzalez Hernandez that they brought him in on what looks like a pretext to check out his "major case" fingerprints and rap sheet. They had caught up with Hernandez after an officer spotted him lurking behind a 7-Eleven at night with a knife in his pocket.

Hernandez's newly shorn mustache at the time of that arrest—the only time he was without it during his entire adult life—suggests how little interest he had just then in letting police compare his usual appearance with Kevan Baker's description of the mustachioed killer. His precipitous relocation from his last known address soon after Wanda Lopez was killed suggests the same about his desire to be located by the police and subpoena servers. Although there is no way of knowing how much of an opportunity Hernandez had to send DeLuna a message while both were in jail in Corpus Christi in early April 1983, one wonders whether a message did reach the younger man. If it did, and if it was anything like the message that Hernandez's henchmen conveyed with their fists to Pedro Olivarez in the Casino Club parking lot in 1979—when DeLuna himself was in Hernandez's orbit—the message just might have kept DeLuna quiet until the eve of trial.

As Carlos DeLuna did for the rest of his short life, Carlos Hernandez told the same story until he died in 1999 at age forty-five: he, not DeLuna, "put the knife on Wanda's life." He confessed it to Miguel Ortiz in Armada Park in the mid-1980s and to Dina Ybañez in her Buford Street living room in the late 1980s, and he intimated the same thing to Lina Zapata in the early 1990s.

Given the chatter that former detective Eddie Garza picked up on the streets around Staples and Mary, the information that Linda Perales got from multiple directions, what friends told Hernandez's girlfriend Cindy Maxwell and what she herself confided to her sister, and the courthouse scuttlebutt that lawyer Albert Peña overheard, it is no overstatement to call it "common knowledge" in Corpus Christi in the 1980s and 1990s that Carlos Gonzalez Hernandez had committed the crime for which Carlos DeLuna paid with his life.

There are others still living who probably know more. Cindy Maxwell almost certainly knows the truth. So may Rosa Anzaldua, Carlos Hernandez's wife at the time of the Sigmor Shamrock killing, who refused to be interviewed and relive those "very painful" memories. Rosa's car, which Hernandez had taken from her at the time, may have provided a getaway once Hernandez reached the Circle K at McArdle and Kostoryz Roads, where Sergeant Steven Fowler had likely seen him earlier on the evening of the killing, and where dozens of officers abandoned their search for the killer when Theresa Barrera spotted the hapless DeLuna under her truck a mile west of the Circle K.

And so may Carlos Hernandez's lawyer Jon Kelly, who admitted to being distressed by the crimes Hernandez confessed to having committed but would not violate his deceased client's confidences by repeating what was said. Perhaps most intriguing, but least certain at this point, is what former assistant district attorney Kenneth Botary knows about Hernandez. Answers may lie in the tape recording and transcript from the Dahlia Sauceda case, which mysteriously disappeared while in Botary's care, and the physical evidence in the Wanda Lopez case, the trail of which also disappears at Botary's desk.

Whatever else may be said, Carlos Hernandez was not a phantom. He was a frighteningly violent, strangely charismatic figure, who apart from his suspiciously rare trips to prison almost never left a two-square-mile area in the Corpus Christi barrio during the 1980s and 1990s—not even to go to a mall to buy presentable clothes. Within that limited place and time, even as he was drinking himself to death, Carlos Hernandez exercised a horrifying degree of capricious power over the lives of the people around him. That he was allowed to do so for so many years at such a great cost to so many is no less a marker of the abject failure of the Texas criminal justice system during the period than is the wrongful execution of Carlos DeLuna.

In both these senses, it is not Carlos Hernandez but justice and truth that are the phantoms of the story told here. It is not the ghost of Chipita Rodriguez, wrongly executed in 1863, but the specter that the criminal justice system of Texas has mistaken the innocent for the guilty and the guilty for the innocent that stalks the river bottoms whenever the state punishes the "guilty" with the infinite finality of death.

·        ·        ·

For those close to Carlos DeLuna, the pain of his execution is still fresh. Carlos's sister Rose moved away from Corpus Christi and now lives in suburban Houston, where she works as an accountant for a software company. She has two grown children, a son and a daughter. Her son served with the U.S. Marines in the second Iraq War, including six months in Fallujah during the worst of the fighting there. He is a doctoral student in psychology at the University of Texas. Rose avoids Corpus Christi, where the memories are too painful. She is an outspoken opponent of the death penalty.

Wanda Lopez's family remains equally burdened by the tragedy. Her parents raised her daughter, who is now grown and has children of her own. Wanda's brother, Richard Vargas, still lives in Corpus Christi. He keeps a scrapbook on his sister and visits her grave from time to time. His anger toward Carlos DeLuna remains—for reasons that equally tormented DeLuna as his execution approached: he had it within his power to expose Carlos Hernandez immediately after Wanda Lopez died, and he didn't do it. In June 2006, however, Richard issued a signed statement acknowledging the tragedy that befell the DeLuna family as well as his own. "After carefully reviewing the information recently uncovered and printed by Steve Mills and Maurice Possley in the *Chicago Tribune*," Richard said, "I am convinced that Mr. DeLuna did not kill my sister and that Carlos Hernandez was the real murderer. . . . My heart goes out to Mr. Hernandez's other victims and also to the DeLuna family, whose loss I share."

Eddie Garza continued to work as a private investigator in Corpus Christi until his death in 2007 at the age of seventy-one. Upon his death, the Texas Senate passed a resolution honoring him and recognizing his contributions to the Corpus Christi community.

Carlos Hernandez's brother-in-law, Freddy Schilling, died in Corpus Christi the same year. He is survived by four children, three with Paula Hernandez, who died in 1994 of cervical cancer, and by his stepdaughter Pricilla. Pricilla still bears the horrific psychological scars of her uncle Carlos's sexually charged violence while both lived at Fidela Hernandez's house on Carrizo Street. Neither Pricilla nor most other members of the family have anything to do with Fidela. The matriarch perhaps consoles herself with the knowledge that she correctly predicted the premature, often violent, deaths of four of her six children, and with the proceeds from the life insurance policies in which that prediction led her to invest.

Both Kenneth Botary and Steven Schiwetz have left the district attorney's office, and each has his own private practice in Corpus Christi.

Around the time of Carlos's execution, Karen Boudrie left Corpus Christi to work as a television anchor and reporter in Georgia, and then in New Orleans. She now runs a public-relations and advertising company in Kenner, Louisiana, and is working on her own memoir about the Carlos DeLuna case.

DeLuna's execution also had a profound effect on the life of the Reverend Carroll Pickett. Then and after, he stood at the front lines of the death penalty and saw it for what it was. He looked into the eyes of men on the verge of death at the hands of the state for crimes he believed that some did not commit. Prompted in part by Carlos DeLuna's unjust and probably tortuous execution, he came to believe this was not right. While working as the Death House chaplain, Pickett publicly maintained neutrality on the issue of the death penalty. Since leaving his position at the Walls Unit in Huntsville, he has become a staunch anti-death-penalty activist. He has offered powerful stories from his personal experience to audiences around the country, as well as in his book, *Within These Walls: Memoirs of a Death House Chaplain*. Pickett was also the subject of an IFC documentary, *At the Death House Door*, which told his story in part through that of Carlos DeLuna.

•  •  •

Our immersion in this case has, of course, affected us as well. Although we have worked hard until now to keep the focus on the facts and away from our own conclusions, we have reached conclusions nonetheless, in much the same way as we have invited readers to do: by putting the facts together as best we are able, using common sense as the glue. Based on our study of the facts, we are convinced that Carlos Hernandez murdered Wanda Lopez, and Texas executed Carlos DeLuna for Hernandez's crime—a classic case of mistaken identity. Our criminal justice system is supposed to punish people for what they demonstrably did, not for who they are, even people like Carlos DeLuna whose lives have certainly not been without sin. But along with DeLuna's final lawyer, Kristen Weaver, we believe that Carlos DeLuna slipped through disturbing cracks in our justice system. He was arrested because he fit the bill, and he was convicted and condemned because no one cared enough to use the many tools at hand to discover what really had occurred. So, too, did Wanda Lopez slip through the cracks of a law-enforcement process supposed to protect law-abiding people like her. In neither case did the responsible players ensure that justice was served or that the equal protection of the laws was afforded. No one cared enough about these two poor and obscure Hispanic residents of Corpus Christi, Texas, to pursue the truth. With the investigation of this case and the publication of this book, we attempt to right a tiny fragment of those wrongs by exposing the truth as best we have been able to discover it using the tools still at hand thirty years later.

The facts of Carlos DeLuna's case first came to the attention of senior author James Liebman in late 2003. Liebman, a professor at Columbia Law School, and Douglas Jaffe, then a Columbia law student and now a technologically savvy public-education reformer, were looking for Texas executions predicated on what many observers believe is the most alluring yet least reliable of evidence: eyewitness testimony. The case came to light because DeLuna's conviction rested mainly on an identification—quite shaky, it turns out—by a single person: Kevan Baker. Although George Aguirre and Julie and John Arsuaga also identified DeLuna, none of them actually saw the killing take place. Worse, Aguirre was unable to identify DeLuna in court, and it is very likely that the Arsuagas' sighting of DeLuna two blocks from the Sigmor Shamrock station provided him with an alibi—not corroboration of his guilt—given that it occurred at the same moment as Baker saw the killer fleeing the gas station in the opposite direction.

Liebman and Jaffe's search was an outgrowth of Liebman's *Broken System* studies, which documented exceptionally high rates of serious error in capital cases reviewed by state and federal courts between 1973 and 1995. Nearly all of that error, it turned out, was the kind that undermines the factual reliability of the determination that the defendant committed the crime or that he or she deserved to die for it. Liebman was looking for a case study to address a question left open by the *Broken System* study: whether the courts' discovery of so much reliability-impugning error proved that the system worked to winnow mistakes out of the system before executions occurred or, instead, revealed so much smoke that there had to be fire somewhere—one or more terrible errors that the courts failed to catch.

A posthumous inquiry into Carlos DeLuna's case did not originally look promising. As a law professor colleague said at the time, DeLuna's "some other dude named Carlos" defense looked absurd on its face. Nevertheless, Peso Chavez, an investigator from Santa Fe, New Mexico, was on his way to Corpus Christi on another case, and the Columbia team figured it couldn't hurt to have him spend an extra day looking into DeLuna's claim that a killer named Carlos Hernandez had escaped responsibility for stabbing Wanda Lopez to death. As it turned out, there was much to be found.

Chavez began by contacting people mentioned in the trial transcript who may have come across Hernandez. He first went to Mary Ann and Linda Perales. The Perales sisters had played a supporting role in Carlos DeLuna's trial because he had testified that they were present when he first saw Hernandez on the night of the attack on Wanda Lopez. Chavez was able to locate both sisters, but Mary Ann's husband told the investigator that she was not interested in talking. Linda, however, agreed to talk briefly to Chavez.

This case is full of tragic fortuities that sealed the fate of Wanda Lopez and Carlos DeLuna. An example is the failure of the operator who took Lopez's first 911 call to pick up her second call several minutes later, before the untrained Jesse Escochea answered it. Another is the coincidence of Theresa Barrera's distracting phone call to the 911 operator at the very moment police officers were closing in on the man they had chased from the Shamrock station north along Dodd Street and east along McArdle Road to the Domino's Pizza and Circle K at Kostoryz. A third fortuity is Judge Jack Blackmun's decision to appoint an inexperienced general practitioner, Hector De Peña, to represent Carlos DeLuna in 1983, rather than an ambitious, full-time criminal defense lawyer such as Albert Peña, who brilliantly saved Jesse Garza from conviction for Carlos Hernandez's killing of Dahlia Sauceda in 1980, or Jon Kelly, who adeptly turned Kenneth Botary's inability to keep track of important evidence into a "get-out-of-jail-free" card for Carlos Hernandez following his subsequent arrest for the same murder. Peso Chavez's choice of Linda Perales as the recipient of his second phone call, and her willingness to talk to him, are fortuitous circumstances of a lower order of magnitude. But in the scheme of this investigation, they were no less consequential and are fitting testaments to Chavez's instincts and skills as an investigator.

Carlos DeLuna's family lived for years in the La Armada housing project in central Corpus Christi and later moved to a small house in the western part of the city. Carlos Hernandez's family was rooted in the bayside barrio farther north and east. Although Carlos DeLuna found his way to the latter area when he briefly joined Carlos Hernandez's circle in 1977 and 1978—evidently making the connection through the Casino Club and the nomadic Aida Sosa—only one of the many dozens of people identified in our investigation had strong connections to both families. That person was Linda Perales (now Ayala), who had dated and briefly was married to Carlos DeLuna's brother Manuel and was the stepmother of Carlos Hernandez's tragically abused niece Pricilla. No other person in our entire investigation could have provided the link that Linda Perales did. Our investigation almost certainly would not have gotten off the ground if Chavez had not found Linda Perales in the one day allotted for his needle-in-a-haystack search for the "right" Carlos Hernandez.

Linda Perales provided Peso Chavez with a great deal of useful information, including that a man named Carlos Hernandez did exist and had said things to Perales's stepdaughter and Hernandez's niece Pricilla suggesting that he, not the other Carlos, had killed Wanda Lopez. The interview with Pricilla then broke open the investigation. With information from her— Carlos Hernandez's confession to killing Wanda Lopez, and his Bastille Day birth date—the team had enough information to identify the relevant Carlos Gonzalez Hernandez and to document his outsized criminal record using publicly available files at the Nueces County Courthouse in Corpus Christi. Hernandez's criminal record led to Dina Ybañez, another of his knife-assault victims, who also repeatedly heard Carlos Hernandez confess to murdering Wanda Lopez, as well as Dahlia Sauceda.

No less important to the subsequent investigation was Rene Rodriguez's civil suit against Diamond Shamrock. Typically, defense lawyers representing a capital defendant get their only clear shot at police files in the case before trial. After that, the files are enshrouded in a veil of secrecy, guarded by law-enforcement officials jealous to preserve their conviction and death sentence and to keep themselves beyond reproach. But in the late 1980s, Rodriguez used the subpoena power of a parallel civil suit against a private party to uncover a treasure trove of information in the case. That material is a testament to the ingenuity and persistence of Rene Rodriguez. Consider, again, a fortuity just mentioned. Had Rodriguez been Carlos DeLuna's lawyer, instead of the inexperienced and passive Hector De Peña and the overworked James Lawrence, there almost certainly would have been no need for our later investigation.

Dumb luck—or an odd sort of hubris—also played a role in our investigation in 2004 and 2005. Despite steps the Corpus Christi Police Department and prosecutors took to keep the tape recordings before and after Wanda Lopez's death from coming to light at the trial, it turned out that Jesse Escochea, the police dispatcher on the night of Wanda's murder, had pirated a copy of the dispatch tape as a personal memento. That tape proved invaluable in re-creating the events surrounding Wanda's murder and the subsequent manhunt.

In this way, bit by bit, witness by witness, document by document, lucky break by lucky break, the team of investigators pieced together the evidence in 2004 and early 2005 until they arrived at their own conclusion about events that would have been so much easier to establish more than twenty years earlier: Carlos Hernandez murdered Wanda Lopez. Carlos DeLuna was put to death for Hernandez's crime.

. . .

Following up on his team's investigation, Liebman looked for independent investigative professionals to test the conclusion that things had gone badly wrong in the search for Wanda Lopez's killer and the prosecution and execution of Carlos DeLuna. The *Chicago Tribune* was a natural place to go. The *Tribune*'s Pulitzer Prize nominee Steve Mills and Pulitzer Prize winner Maurice Possley had made careers by exposing deep flaws in America's administration of criminal justice and the death penalty. When Illinois governor George Ryan declared a moratorium on the state's use of the death penalty in January 2000 out of fear that the state risked executing the innocent, he relied on a five-part series by Mills and fellow *Tribune* journalist Ken Armstrong called "The Failure of the Death Penalty in Illinois." When Ryan closed out his term in January 2003 by commuting all the state's death sentences to life in prison without parole, he again cited the *Tribune* series as influencing his loss of faith in the state's capital system. These events led directly to Illinois's subsequent repeal of capital punishment in 2011.

Liebman approached Mills and Possley in November 2005. He gave them the evidence and information that he had discovered and carte blanche to reinvestigate and publish whatever they found. Mills and Possley launched their own inquiry, spending weeks in Texas digging into the evidence. Among the many people they interviewed who knew one or both of the Carloses were several key players who had not been part of the earlier investigation, including the two trial prosecutors and Miguel Ortiz, another person to whom Carlos Hernandez had confessed that he, not Carlos DeLuna, had killed Wanda Lopez.

In June 2006, the *Tribune* published a three-part series on the case. Based on "interviews with dozens of people and a review of thousands of pages of court records," Mills and Possley reported that "16 years after De Luna died by lethal injection, the *Tribune* has uncovered evidence strongly suggesting that [an] acquaintance he named, Carlos Hernandez, was the one who killed Lopez in 1983." Relying on accounts by "Hernandez's relatives and friends [of] how the violent felon repeatedly bragged that De Luna went to

Death Row for a murder Hernandez committed," the "eer[ie] echo" of the "circumstances of Lopez's murder" in "the details of Hernandez's lengthy rap sheet," evidence documenting a "shaky eyewitness identification, sloppy police work and a failure to thoroughly pursue Hernandez as a possible suspect," and an "analysis of financial records from the Sigmor gas station . . . suggest[ing that] no money was taken at all" from the store, the *Tribune* concluded that the "case represents one of the most compelling examples yet of the discovery of possible innocence after a prisoner's execution."

For their work on the case, Mills and Possley were again recognized as finalists for a Pulitzer Prize in National Reporting. They were featured, along with Carroll Pickett, in Peter Gilbert and Steve James's documentary *At the Death House Door*, which is itself a moving and artful telling of part of Carlos DeLuna's story.

·    ·    ·

Although we are not the first to bring this tragic story into public view, we are the first to do so with the depth and detail that a book permits. We live in a popular culture that expects criminal cases to be decided with scientific precision by a single forensic test, be it DNA or a composite of surveillance videos pristinely recording what went down. In that sense, this book is a throwback to an earlier age, marked by names such as Nick Charles, *Perry Mason*, and *Columbo*, not *CSI* and *NCIS*. In this story, answers emerge not upon the climactic analysis of a single piece of deductively decisive proof, but through the aggregation of many small, inferential facts, including neighborhood milieu, family context, and individual motivation. Unlike even a three-part newspaper series or a documentary touching on the De-Luna story, a book allows a deeper exploration of all the relevant facts, big and small.

We intend our fuller treatment to help readers—lay and professional—evaluate the story of Carlos DeLuna and Carlos Hernandez informed by the dozens of snapshots (literal and otherwise) of what each Carlos said, wore, drank, smoked, and carried in the way of a weapon at the time of their encounters with police, family, neighbors, and friends over decades. We hope that by elucidating the two Carloses' dispositions, habits, and character, we have shed light on their actual behaviors at moments crucial to the lives and deaths of Wanda Lopez and the *tocayos* Carlos themselves. We hope, as well, that we have provided sufficient context for evaluating our witnesses and what they independently told our investigators about Carlos Hernandez's confessions to murdering Wanda Lopez and about his many other crimes.

More generally, a book permits an anatomy of not only a single obscure murder, but also the ensuing criminal investigation, trial preparation, two-part capital trial, multilayered appeals, and botched execution in a case whose very obscurity makes it a far better representation of what usually goes on in criminal cases than do the facts and proceedings in more notorious and idiosyncratic cases, such as those of Nicola Sacco and Bartolomeo Vanzetti, Julius and Ethel Rosenberg, O. J. Simpson, William Kennedy Smith, and George Zimmerman's self-defense acquittal after killing Trayvon Martin. Finally, this medium has allowed us to delve at least tangentially into the many ironies of American capital punishment. One that stands out for us is how death row reformed the cocky Carlos DeLuna, for crimes not charged and by way of a rehabilitative process that the death penalty denies. Given the tight security and single cells in which capital inmates are typically housed, death row is sometimes the safest and calmest place its inhabitants have ever known, allowing it to do a better job of straightening out people the state executes than prisons normally do for those the state returns to the street.

Finally, combining a book with a Web site (thewrongcarlos.net) containing all the primary materials in the case has enabled us to pursue the competing goals of broad accessibility to a lay audience and comprehensive references and reference checking. The Web site links the text to extensive reference notes that are substantially longer than the text itself and support each important factual statement in the narrative, often with liberal quotations of the supporting primary materials. Student editors of the *Columbia Human Rights Law Review*—which published an earlier version of this work—checked each reference and the text the reference supports for accuracy and for the reasonableness of inferences drawn. On the Web site, each primary source cited in the notes, including audio- and videotapes, is hyperlinked, allowing note readers, with a single click, to view or listen to the complete cited source and check our references themselves. Readers interested in taking their own self-guided tour through the police, sheriff, district attorney, state police, prison, social services, television, newspaper, criminal and civil court, trial and appellate court, state and federal court, and other records, photographs, and audio- and videotapes pertaining to the Dahlia Sauceda and Wanda Lopez murders, Rene Rodriguez's lawsuit against Diamond Shamrock, and Carlos Hernandez's near-fatal assault on Dina Ybañez, as well as our own investigators' notes of interviews with approximately 100 witnesses and videotaped interviews with two dozen witnesses, can click on the index of these materials on the Web site (thewrongcarlos.net/primarysources) and establish their own itinerary.

•    •    •

Although more thoroughly investigated and documented than other cases, DeLuna's is not the only one that poses urgent questions about whether our capital system can reliably separate the guilty from the innocent. There is a growing list of executed individuals whose guilt has been called into serious question after significant postexecution investigations. They include Ruben Cantu, Larry Griffin, Claude Jones, David Spence, and Cameron Todd Willingham. Together with these other cases, our conclusion—that Carlos Hernandez stabbed Wanda Lopez to death and stood by while his *tocayo* Carlos DeLuna took the fall—invites questions that should trouble our sleep, just as the blood on Hernandez's hands seems, in the end, to have troubled his. Most crucially, how much doubt about a prisoner's guilt can we tolerate as a society while we continue to put human beings to death? And if there is too much doubt, what are its principal causes, and what can be done to allay the concerns? Regrettably, the answers to these questions that our investigation suggests are not encouraging.

One obvious place to start is where we began our search for a capital case to reinvestigate: with the perils of eyewitness testimony. Corpus Christi prosecutors rested their case-in-chief primarily on Kevan Baker's identification of Carlos DeLuna as the man he saw wrestling Wanda Lopez to the ground and fleeing. It is well known, however, that eyewitnesses often make mistakes when identifying strangers as individuals they observed committing crimes. Mistakes are especially likely in cases such as this one, in which

- The identification occurred in a hasty and chaotic, nighttime, face-to-face show-up between the witness and a recently arrested suspect, rather than in a carefully organized and scientific lineup at the station house.
- The witness was under stress when he viewed the perpetrator because at the very moment the killer left the store and came into Baker's view, he threatened to shoot Baker and then immediately sprinted away.

- Rather than allowing the witness's stress to subside before commencing identification procedures, police compounded it by giving Baker a misplaced sense of responsibility to protect the public from a serious threat—imploring him to engage in a procedure that he said he was too scared to take part in, surrounding him with a phalanx of officers to shield him from a presumptive killer, and conducting the identification under the expectant eyes of an anxious crowd of onlookers while officers trained flashlights on the handcuffed suspect.
- Before the identification, police telegraphed to the witness that they were sure they had their man.
- The identification took place across ethnic lines.

The best-known solution to these problems—adopted, to date, by a handful of criminal-justice agencies across the country—is to conduct identifications under close-to-laboratory conditions: through one-way mirrors; in a safe, calm, and well-lit environment; and using sequential and double-blind techniques. Sequential lineups require witnesses to view one by one what they know will be a succession of potential suspects. This procedure is better than a face-to-face show-up with a single suspect because it forces witnesses to compare their recollections with multiple individuals, not just with the single individual they have reason to believe is the likely suspect. The procedure also is better than traditional *simultaneous* lineups, in which witnesses view all the potential suspects at once. Witnesses often perceive simultaneous lineups as posing a dangerously misleading question, which often leads to misidentification: Which one of the subjects being viewed all at once looks *most* like the perpetrator? By contrast, sequential lineups are more likely to be perceived as posing the real question: Is this subject, among the others you expect to see, the actual person you saw committing the crime? In turn, double-blind procedures ensure that no police prompting can consciously or unconsciously sway the witness because neither the officers present nor the witness knows which of the lineup subjects is the likely suspect.

·    ·    ·

As useful as these steps are, they cannot prevent all mistaken identifications, nor, as is revealed by research we undertook in the wake of the De-Luna investigation, can they dispel a set of cognitive biases that magnify the effect of such mistakes. These biases are systematic tricks that the mind plays, which prompt people (in this case, police officers and jurors) to give too much weight not only to the identification itself but to other evidence that appears to be consistent with the identification—for example, evidence that DeLuna was arrested cowering under a truck and that he lied at trial. Worse, these biases lead law-enforcement officials and jurors to give too little weight to evidence that clearly contradicts the identification. Examples of this latter sort of evidence from the DeLuna case include the fact that DeLuna's dress clothes, recently shaved face, and arrest east of the gas station did not match Baker's description moments earlier of a slovenly, mustachioed killer running west and north away from the station; that there wasn't a drop of blood on DeLuna or his shoes and clothes despite the blood-drenched crime scene and Baker's description of the assailant manhandling the profusely bleeding victim; or that George Aguirre was unable to identify DeLuna in court as the man he saw lurking around the gas station with an open buck knife shortly before the killer entered the store. Because police officers and jurors succumb to heuristic fallacies and ignore these important clues to the truth, they tend to place blind faith in eyewitness testimony; "adhere to their beliefs [though] the original evidential basis of the beliefs is shown to be flimsy, false, or nonexistent"; and fail to search for alternative theories to explain obviously contradictory evidence. The unconscious confusions that eyewitness identifications unleash are especially troubling, given that identifications are wrong as much as 30 percent of the time, and even improved procedures cannot bring the error rate close to zero.

•     •     •

Our research shows that the process through which cognitive biases lead police and jurors astray is even more general than we have suggested thus far, extending beyond eyewitness testimony to all so-called direct evidence of guilt. Along with eyewitness evidence, a defendant's confession and certain kinds of informant testimony may be thought of as classic, or "big," evidence of identity—evidence likely to impress police officers and jurors as identifying a unique feature of the perpetrator that matches only the defendant. In more recent times, police and jurors have come to think of fingerprint and DNA matches in the same way, as a unique feature of the perpetrator that, if shared by the suspect, conclusively proves that the two are the same person. In reaching conclusions about the identity of unknown perpetrators of crimes, human decision makers instinctively contrast such big or unique-seeming matches to "small" clues found at a crime scene that clearly are not unique because they could have been left by more than one individual and thus can only inferentially or probabilistically link a defendant who has that feature to the crime, or weaken the case against a defendant who does not have the feature.

As is noted earlier in regard to eyewitness testimony, recent research has documented the danger of giving too much weight to most seemingly big or unique *matches* between the perpetrator and a suspect, as well as to other evidence that appears to corroborate the big evidence. The DeLuna case reveals, however, that an equally serious danger that has received far less attention is the tendency of law-enforcement officers and jurors to give too little weight to *nonmatches* between the suspect and small or nonunique clues found at the crime scene. Examples of such clues in the DeLuna case include a wad of pink chewing gum, a partially smoked cigarette, and a maroon button found at the crime scene that may or may not have been left by the perpetrator, and the presence there of the victim's blood and hair that may or may not have transferred to the perpetrator's clothing or person. Because any such nonmatch can be explained away on grounds unrelated to the defendant's guilt or innocence—for example, that someone unconnected to the crime left the trace, or that the culprit somehow escaped contact with trace materials present at the crime scene or rain later washed them off his clothes—police and juries are predisposed to ignore the nonmatch *entirely*. Ignoring these small indications of innocence, however, systematically excludes from consideration evidence of innocence that in the *aggregate* may deserve as much weight as, or even more weight than, police and jurors typically give big evidence of guilt.

That is the real lesson of DNA evidence, which is powerful evidence of guilt *not* because it is a unique "genetic fingerprint" but because it is an aggregate of many—typically thirteen or more—genetic features that the criminal and a suspect share. A match of only a single genetic feature is weak evidence of guilt because it is present in many millions of people in the general population, so only an aggregation of many matches generates a high probability (but never total certainty) that the perpetrator and the defendant are the same person. The same is true of fingerprint evidence, which is the product of many matches between lines, twirls, and intersections in prints left by oils in the perpetrator's and the suspect's skin; by it-self, any single match is not decisive or even very powerful. Properly un-derstood, confessions and eyewitness testimony also acquire evidentiary weight as a result of large aggregations of *nonunique* matches. A confession is stronger or weaker depending on the number of unprompted details of the crime known to only the perpetrator (as well as to law enforcement) that the confessing suspect volunteers. Because a nonperpetrator might ac-curately guess one or another such detail, it is only an inexplicably large aggregation of matches between details of the crime and what the defen-dant knows that makes a confession strong evidence of guilt. Likewise, an eyewitness identification is stronger or weaker depending on how many or few features of the perpetrator the witness was able to recall and describe to police soon after a crime that match a suspect arrested later. Any single remembered feature of the perpetrator that the suspect happens to share is unlikely, by itself, to be convincing evidence of guilt. It is fair to conclude, therefore, that there is no such thing as big or unique evidence; there are only greater and lesser aggregations of small, nonunique evidence. Because of the tendency of human decision makers to give nearly decisive weight to clues erroneously perceived as big or unique evidence of guilt, and to give virtually no weight to evidence perceived as small or nonunique indi-cations of innocence—even though all such evidence should be evaluated based on how many small indications of guilt or innocence are aggregated in each case—the danger of overvaluing evidence of guilt and undervaluing evidence of innocence, and convicting the innocent because of it, is ever present in any case characterized by seemingly big evidence.

．　　　．　　　．

In a separate, technical article prompted by the DeLuna case, we demon-strate the importance of small matches, using Carlos DeLuna's case as an example. There we identify twenty-nine bits of small evidence in the case—thirty, if George Aguirre's observation of a man outside the store with a knife is included. Among those thirty clues, three match neither Carlos De-Luna nor Carlos Hernandez. Seven more were never tested as to either man owing to police neglect—including Detective Olivia Escobedo's failure to test large amounts of blood found at the crime scene in order to determine if any of it belonged to someone other than Wanda Lopez and her failure to spot, much less test, key evidence visible in the crime photographs, such as bloody shoe prints and a wad of chewing gum spat onto the floor. Only seven of the thirty traces match Carlos DeLuna, and all seven of those also match Carlos Hernandez: height, weight, ethnicity, sex, hair color, hair style, and cigarette brand. Two of the thirteen remaining *nonmatches* as to DeLuna were never tested as to Hernandez, including the fact that there was not a scintilla of blood on DeLuna or his shoes, clothing, or possessions, though it is hard to imagine how Wanda Lopez's killer could have escaped the grisly crime scene without a speck of blood on his hands, hair, fingernails, shirt, pants, shoes, and cash bills found in his possession. We will never know what bodily fluids were on Hernandez's clothes, shoes, or shoelaces; on any cash in his pocket; or staining the automobile in which he may well have escaped on the evening of February 4, 1983, because police never properly followed up after hearing soon after the Lopez killing that Hernandez had confessed to it.

That leaves eleven clues that did not match Carlos DeLuna and can be compared with Carlos Hernandez. Our investigation twenty years after the fact revealed that *all eleven match Hernandez*, including age, clothing, mustache, and weapon of choice. Although the jury convicted DeLuna based on a faulty eyewitness identification and seven matches that appeared to corroborate it, the jurors never had a chance to consider Hernandez, much less the eighteen or more small traits that matched him. Nor did the jurors learn that Hernandez repeatedly linked *himself* to the crime via the big evidence of a confession—in fact, *repeated* confessions that were unusually reliable because they were volunteered, not obtained through potentially coercive interrogation.

Our technical article ends by describing a number of ways that police, prosecutors, courts, and legislators could substantially neutralize these cognitive biases by adopting more thoroughly scientific approaches to the collection, documentation, and mathematical evaluation of the aggregate value of small pieces of evidence. Thus far, however, none of these institutions has shown any inclination to move in the necessary direction, much less to go far enough to allay the clear and present danger, illustrated by Carlos DeLuna's case, of executing the innocent. So even if more immediate and rudimentary solutions, such as sequential double-blind identification procedures, are more widely adopted in the near term, they are unlikely to provide a sufficient solution to the problem of unreliable eyewitness identifications and other big evidence in criminal and especially capital cases.

.     .     .

Making matters worse, there are strong motivational pressures on prosecutors, jurors, and judges in the small minority of American counties that use the death penalty to impose it frequently while skimping on the resources and procedures needed to ensure its accuracy. Our own and other studies show that these "death-prone" communities are dominated by political and cultural sentiments that make them simultaneously (1) susceptible to an often-inflated fear of crime committed by offenders from outside the community or whose offenses cross economic and racial boundaries, yet (2) mistrustful of government and reluctant to spend public funds to fight crime or prosecute suspects professionally and scientifically. Together, these motivations dispose death-prone communities to use "quick and dirty" applications of the death penalty in many, often marginal, homicide cases as an expressive but ineffective substitute for scientific law enforcement, prosecution, and punishment of the full range of serious crimes, including those that most often terrorize people, such as rape, armed robbery, kidnapping, burglary, and carjacking. Two well-documented results of the stingy, unscientific approach to law enforcement that prevails in these counties are well below average "criminal clearance rates" for serious crimes—the proportion of those crimes that end in arrest, conviction, and incarceration—and well above average rates of serious error in the capital verdicts they impose.

Because of the notorious transience of criminals, these communities' low clearance rates have the effect of exporting crime to other communities. Likewise, because statewide and federal, not local, courts are responsible for curing error in capital cases, death-prone communities are able to shift the cost of remedying the high rates of capital error that their corner-cutting prosecutorial and adjudicative practices generate to the majority of jurisdictions that do not use the death penalty. As a result, the majority of the public who reside in counties that rarely or never use the death penalty—including the majority of citizens who reside in non-death-prone counties in most states that permit the death penalty—end up subsidizing death-prone counties' risky policies by paying to capture and prosecute criminals whom the former counties failed to apprehend, and by funding the disproportionate amounts of time that state and federal judges spend fixing faulty capital verdicts.

Largely because of these subsidies, the small minority of death-prone counties vastly overproduce death verdicts, generating something like six times more death sentences than the courts actually will validate for execution after overturning the most obviously—if not always the most seriously—erroneous ones. Additional factors exacerbate this distortion, beginning with the incentives of police and prosecutors. Sheriffs and district attorneys elected to office in death-prone counties can amass substantial political capital by imposing death sentences on suspects who appear to be the vilest of killers, and often suffer politically if they fail to obtain capital verdicts. These incentives aggravate the cognitive biases discussed earlier, leading law enforcement to work hard to obtain the big evidence of guilt that is most likely to impress jurors, even if it means cutting corners—for example, by using unreliable show-up procedures in lieu of more scientific lineups or by informing witnesses whom they have asked to consider identifying a suspect that they have good reason to believe the suspect is guilty. Thereafter, for the reasons just discussed, law enforcement is likely to (1) overvalue identifications that are made, (2) do little to recover and test small evidence that might undermine identifications, (3) undervalue even substantial aggregations of small nonmatches that turn up, and (4) discount fears that cutting corners will lead to dangerous error by assuming that lengthy appeals paid for by others will catch any problems that arise, and will take so long—about thirteen years on average—that political blowback from overturned verdicts will be minimal.

Typically, of course, we rely on our adversarial system to mitigate imbalances like these. But the well-documented failure of death-prone communities to appoint and support the competent and specialized lawyers required in capital cases largely negates this solution. Nor can the nation's small number of expert anti-death-penalty lawyers and big-firm lawyers who handle capital cases *pro bono publico* fill the breach because they target their limited resources on the much smaller number of cases that are in the end stages of appeals, with executions looming. While understandable, this allocation of resources increases the majority-to-minority subsidy. It allows death-prone communities to impose flawed death sentences with only minimal resistance from underpaid, ill-prepared, and overmatched local lawyers and to leave state and federal taxpayers to foot the bill for the elaborate appeals needed to cure errors under the vigilant eyes of the expert defense lawyers who intervene at those latter stages.

Nor, finally, can we expect local judges to resist prosecutors or steer public resources to high-quality defense lawyers. Like local prosecutors, local
judges are elected, and in death-prone communities often run for office
based in part on the number of death sentences imposed in their courts. If
their opponents can characterize them as lenient on criminal defendants,
they risk losing their seat. Outside judges who are paid to handle overflow
cases face similar pressure: if they are perceived as going out of their way
to help capital defendants, they are unlikely to be invited back to handle
future cases. Death-prone communities exacerbate these tendencies by
systematically underfunding their courts compared with courts in other
communities.

·     ·     ·

All these cognitive and motivational factors came into play in Carlos De-
Luna's case. After the police arrested DeLuna and obtained a dicey identification from a reluctant Kevan Baker, Detective Escobedo considered
the identification so decisive that she almost immediately shut down the
crime-scene investigation and returned control of the store to the gas station manager. She spent less than two hours going over the scene and never
viewed it in the light of day. By 6:00 A.M. the following day, the station
manager had washed it down and reopened, wiping away forever evidence
that could have exonerated DeLuna and implicated Hernandez. Armed
with the identification, Escobedo didn't bother to use appropriate steps to
lift fingerprints off the murder weapon, to ensure that the few prints lifted
from the scene were of high enough quality to allow analysis (none were),
or to test most of the other evidence she found to see if any of it matched—
or possibly excluded—DeLuna, including the blood dousing the crime
scene and saliva on a cigarette fragment, beer cans, and a wad of chewing
gum. Nor did she or the prosecutors study the crime scene or photographs
for other evidence that, in fact, was there but went unnoticed and untested,
including bloody shoe prints, a bloody handprint, and a clump of hair. Police and prosecutors also ignored the many mismatches between Carlos
DeLuna and the evidence they had collected—for example, that the Arsuagas saw DeLuna two blocks east of the gas station just as Baker watched
the assailant run west and north away from the station; that DeLuna's dress
clothes and recently shaved face did not match Baker's and Aguirre's description of a man dressed like a derelict and wearing a mustache, a reddish

flannel jacket, and blue jeans, and likewise failed to match a maroon button found at the crime scene; that Aguirre was unable to identify DeLuna in court; and that the nature of the crime and weapon were out of character for DeLuna.

Given Corpus Christi police officers' eagerness to find Wanda Lopez's killer—which almost certainly was exacerbated by their motivation to avoid blame for not coming quickly enough to Lopez's rescue—and given their palpable sense of vindication when Baker identified DeLuna as the culprit, it is hardly surprising that law enforcement would ignore a bunch of small clues that at best could have modestly improved their chosen theory of guilt and at worst could have badly muddied it. No more surprising is the State's later construction of its case at trial around the big eyewitness identification, and for the jury to fall into the same dismissive trap when presented with the few small nonmatches that emerged at trial.

Worse, Carlos DeLuna had the bad luck to be arrested, tried, convicted, and sentenced in Nueces County, Texas—a classic example of a death-prone criminal jurisdiction. Liebman's 2000 and 2002 *Broken System* study of thousands of capital verdicts imposed nationwide between 1973 and 1995 found that rates of serious error in capital cases are strongly associated with how often the relevant county uses the death penalty—in other words, how death-prone the county has shown itself to be. The greater the proportion of a county's homicides that end in a death sentence, the higher the probability that serious error will infect any particular capital conviction and sentence imposed there. On one measure of red-flag counties where the probability of error in capital verdicts is high, Nueces County ranks in the top *one-half of 1 percent* nationally—fifteenth out of the nation's 3,141 counties in the number of executions carried out since the United States Supreme Court allowed executions to begin again in 1976 after a ten-year legal hiatus. Given Nueces County's relatively small population, when the measure used instead is the number of executions *per capita*—not just the raw number of state killings—Nueces County jumps to *sixth* place nationally out of 3,141 counties in its propensity to execute. No wonder, then, that the ghost of the wrongfully executed Chipita Rodriguez haunts the bottoms along the Nueces River near Corpus Christi whenever the state of Texas—the top executing *state* in the nation—executes someone.

True to form for a death-prone county, DeLuna's alleged crime was charged capitally, even though it was not a good candidate for the death penalty. Lopez was the single victim. Her murder was terrible, but it lacked aggravating factors, such as intentional physical torture, that typically characterize capital cases. Also true to form for counties ill-disposed to spend the resources necessary to make sure they have the right man, neither police nor prosecutors searched diligently for Carlos Hernandez after Detective Eddie Garza reported hearing from informants that Hernandez was saying that he, not DeLuna, had "put the knife on" Wanda Lopez, and even after DeLuna himself identified Hernandez as the man he had seen attacking Lopez. Worse, prosecutors told the jury that DeLuna fabricated Carlos Hernandez, even though one of them knew Hernandez well and could see that the mustachioed Hernandez matched the eyewitness descriptions better than DeLuna did and, unlike DeLuna, always carried a buck knife and had a history of knife violence and armed robberies of gas stations.

Local officials likewise cut corners in selecting counsel whose job it was to protect Carlos DeLuna from the results of a shoddy investigation. Hector De Peña was a small-time general practitioner with no experience in criminal felony trials, much less a death penalty trial. Although more experienced, James Lawrence made a living by handling as many poorly compensated court-appointed cases as he was able, including a major trial that consumed most of the scant number of weeks between his belated appointment as co-counsel and the date set for DeLuna's trial. Neither launched an investigation into DeLuna's main line of defense—that another man, initially not identified, had committed the crime—and when DeLuna did finally disclose Carlos Hernandez's name, his lawyers trusted the prosecution to find Hernandez, undertaking little or no independent investigation of their own. Then at trial, the defense lawyers failed to exploit important weaknesses in the prosecution's evidence. DeLuna's appellate lawyers likewise failed to take seriously their obligation to look into their client's claim of innocence and, until the very end when it was too late, did not effectively illuminate the flaws that led to his conviction and death sentence.

The courts, in turn, did little to provide a fail-safe against a miscarriage of justice. Wallace Moore, a retired judge from Houston who presided over DeLuna's trial on a precarious sinecure, contributed to inadequate representation by providing a pittance for a defense investigator and too little time for a real investigation. The Texas Court of Criminal Appeals tolerated poor representation on appeal, ruling against DeLuna in two successive rounds of court challenge based on abbreviated and uninformative briefs. The Texas courts as a whole devoted only a few days to state habeas corpus proceedings that in most states would have merited several years. And the federal habeas court in Corpus Christi failed to provide the last line of defense, misstating the date of a *Corpus Christi Caller-Times* article and photograph documenting Carlos Hernandez's recent arrest for the murder of Dahlia Sauceda and, as a result, rejecting DeLuna's claim of innocence on the ground that "Carlos Hernandez probably never existed."

As all these analyses indicate, Corpus Christi in Nueces County, like the other minority of jurisdictions that most use the death penalty, was the least likely to embrace the scientific reforms that are needed to restore confidence in eyewitness identifications and other big evidence and provide reasonable certainty that death verdicts based on such evidence will be imposed on only the guilty. There is little chance that this situation will change, moreover, as long as the majority of citizens living in counties that rarely or never use the death penalty continue subsidizing death-prone counties' leaky law-enforcement and risky capital-sentencing practices. Short of repealing the death penalty—as majorities in Connecticut, Illinois, New Jersey, New Mexico, and New York have done recently and voters in California came close to doing in 2012—there is little assurance that the tragedy that befell Carlos DeLuna will not occur again.

•   •   •

The worst problem with executions is that the truth about them can so easily die with the executed prisoner. Sadly, the certainty that DNA and other forensic testing now makes possible has not changed this situation. This is because once executions occur, the same officials whose deadly mistakes might be exposed by DNA testing control the crucial physical evidence in the case and consistently bar forensic testing of—or, as in Carlos DeLuna's case, lose or perhaps destroy—the evidence. The public has no recourse to freedom of information laws or the courts to obtain forensic testing. Instead, legislators, judges, and prosecutors steadfastly refuse to allow forensic testing that could provide unassailable proof of the accuracy, or not, of executions. Their refusal to allow DNA testing powerfully discredits their own repeated assurances that the men and women whose executions they have sanctioned were undoubtedly guilty.

Put bluntly, we have no idea how many Carlos DeLunas there are among the well over 1,300 men and women executed since the reinstatement of the death penalty in the 1970s, and officials who control the evidence that could help answer that question refuse to make it available. Indeed, absent the many fortuities we have cataloged, the story of Carlos DeLuna would never have come to light. Had things gone only a little differently, DeLuna would have remained in the obscurity that deprived him during his life of any chance of proving his innocence—just 1 of more than 500 people put to death in Texas since its reinstatement of the death penalty in 1982. Central to DeLuna's obscurity from the moment of his arrest to the end of his evidently botched execution and even afterward was the same failure of the professionals in the case with the ability to do so—police, prosecutors, judges, defense lawyers, and even members of the media—to have the curiosity and gumption to look for the truth just an inch or two below the surface.

Obscurity, in fact, lies at the root of this tragedy and affected all its victims. It contributed as much to Wanda Lopez's premature and undeserved death as to Carlos DeLuna's. As lawyer Rene Rodriguez expressed so eloquently through his groundbreaking lawsuit against Diamond Shamrock and in his interviews for this case, if anyone had cared just a little about Wanda Lopez's safety, she likely would be alive today. Her employer didn't do so. Neither did the Corpus Christi Police Department, which easily could have saved her if it had responded to her initial 911 call rather than trying, after the fact, to obscure evidence that the earlier call had taken place. Indeed, the police probably could have saved Wanda Lopez if they had responded immediately to her *second* 911 call, rather than a minute and a half later after grilling her as if she were the guilty party.

It is accepted anti-death-penalty lore that the worst injustices occur in cases involving the worst imbalances of status and power—the prosecution, say, of a poor, friendless, and uneducated Latino or African American outsider for the death of a pillar of the local white community. Our work in this case leads us to a different conclusion. Wanda Lopez's worthy and unimpeachable life was dishonored not only by the inattention to her plight on the night of February 4, 1983, by everyone in a position to help her, but also by the nonchalance with which everyone in a position to find her killer carried out that responsibility. Her obscurity in life, which forced her, through no fault of her own, into a position of defenselessness in the face of the likes of Carlos Hernandez, should not have been repaid by the indifference of police, for example, to crucial items of evidence that her killer left at the crime scene but no one found.

It thus is the case of the obscure accused of murdering the obscure that is the most ripe for miscarriage, particularly when the case becomes embroiled in the cauldron of state killing. As the Reverend Pickett pointed out in his interviews for this project, the capital context is so fraught and abnormal that functionaries and news reporters cannot even keep straight the last meals and last words of the condemned. How, then, can we expect police, prosecutors, defense lawyers, and judges to exercise the meticulous, scientific care that supremely complicated capital investigations, trials, and appeals require if they are to end in a reliable verdict? And how especially can we expect that care in cases to which little real attention is paid because of the low status of both principals in the case? When the obscurity of the victim and the accused coincide, the chances of a proper capital outcome are unbearably low.

•    •    •

By a different path, we arrive at the same conclusion as was expressed recently by Grant Jones, district attorney of Nueces County from 1983 to 1991, whose office secured Carlos DeLuna's conviction and execution. In a 2012 *Houston Chronicle* op-ed, Jones and another former Texas district attorney wrote: "As district attorneys in the 1980s, we believed that the death penalty was the best punishment for certain crimes. We no longer believe that today. We haven't gone soft. We have come face to face with some hard truths. Both of us have been involved in the execution of men who may well have been innocent."*

In reaching this conclusion, Jones referred to our investigation and the possibility that Kevan Baker "might have mistaken Carlos DeLuna, who was executed for murder in 1989, for another man also named Carlos. The

---

*Grant Jones's coauthor, Samuel Milsap, was the district attorney of Bexar County (San Antonio) whose office secured the conviction and execution of Ruben Cantu, mentioned earlier in the epilogue.

two men bore such a strong resemblance that even family members mistook photographs of one man for the other."

Noting that "only 22 of 254 Texas counties have imposed death sentences over the last five years," which "means the significant financial burden of the death penalty is generated by a small minority, but paid for by all taxpayers," the two former district attorneys concluded: "The professionals who administer our justice system cannot guarantee that they will never be without fault. Once we accept that fact, we have to ask ourselves, as a civilized society, whether we can live with a system that promises nothing more than to get it right most of the time in death penalty cases. We submit that we cannot."

* * *

We end this epilogue where we began our preface, with Supreme Court Justice Antonin Scalia's assertion in 2006 that there has not been "a single case—not one—in which it is clear that a person was executed for a crime he did not commit. If such an event had occurred in recent years, we would not have to hunt for it; the innocent's name would be shouted from the rooftops." Let it be said now, as loudly as we can proclaim it, from as high a vantage point as we can reach, that this is such a case. Beyond a reasonable doubt, the professionals who administered our criminal justice system in this case were not without fault, and Carlos DeLuna, an innocent man, was executed because of it.

Carlos DeLuna's execution is a story of a system that failed from top to bottom—of professionals who failed to do their job well from start to finish. Our investigation did nothing more than the people responsible for Carlos DeLuna's case could and should have done between 1983 and 1989, when much more of the evidence remained at hand. The most tragic fortuity of all for Carlos DeLuna—as also for Wanda Lopez's right to justice—was the failure of even one police officer, prosecutor, defense lawyer, or judge handling the case between 1983 and 1989 to insist on a more conscientious search for Wanda Lopez's killer, or to give serious consideration to Carlos DeLuna's consistent claim—which he did his meager best to shout from the rooftops—that he didn't do it, but he knew who did.

# People

Janie Adrian, neighbor of Carlos Hernandez

George Aguirre, witness to events outside Sigmor Shamrock gas station

Richard Anderson, posttrial lawyer for Carlos DeLuna

Rosa Anzaldua, wife of Carlos Hernandez

Mary Conejo Arredando, half-sister of Carlos DeLuna

John Arsuaga, witness to man running near Sigmor Shamrock gas station

Johnny Arsuaga, cousin of Carlos Hernandez

Julie Arsuaga, witness to man running near Sigmor Shamrock gas station

Blas Avalos, stepfather of Carlos DeLuna

Linda Perales Vela Ayala, stepmother of Pricilla Hernandez Jaramillo and
    former wife of Manuel DeLuna

Kevan Baker, eyewitness to attack on Wanda Lopez

Theresa Barrera, resident of neighborhood where manhunt occurred

Mary Ann Perales Benavides, witness against Carlos DeLuna

Floyd Bieniek, retired police officer and character witness against Carlos DeLuna

Jack Blackmun, judge who appointed counsel for Carlos DeLuna and ordered
    Carlos Hernandez's release in Dahlia Sauceda case

Kenneth Botary, prosecutor at trials of Jesse Garza and Carlos DeLuna

Karen Boudrie, Corpus Christi television reporter

Shirley Bradley, member of jury that convicted Carlos DeLuna and sentenced
    him to die

Eric Brown, judge who set final execution date for Carlos DeLuna
Marcella Brown, friend of Carlos Hernandéz

Connie Campos, sentencing witness against Carlos DeLuna
Linda Carrico, *Corpus Christi Caller-Times* reporter
Beatriz Castro, friend of Fidela Hernandez
William P. Clements, Jr., governor of Texas who denied clemency to Carlos
    DeLuna
Daniel Conejo, half-brother of Carlos DeLuna
Mary Conejo (later Arredando), half-sister of Carlos DeLuna
Mary Conejo, sister-in-law of Carlos DeLuna
Rebecca Conejo, half-sister of Carlos DeLuna
Vicky Conejo (later Gutierrez), half-sister of Carlos DeLuna
Vincent Conejo, half-brother of Carlos DeLuna
Elmer Cox, Nueces County sheriff's deputy
Eddie Cruz, private investigator for Jesse Garza in Dahlia Sauceda case
Shirley Currie, friend of Carlos Hernandez

Jesse De La Rosa, Texas death row inmate who drew Carlos DeLuna's
    portrait
Carlos DeLuna, defendant in killing of Wanda Lopez
Joe DeLuna, father of Carlos DeLuna
Manuel DeLuna, brother of Carlos DeLuna
Rose DeLuna (later Rhoton), sister of Carlos DeLuna
Hector De Peña, Jr., trial lawyer for Carlos DeLuna
Hector De Peña, Sr., Corpus Christi judge and father of Hector De Peña, Jr.

Mary Ellis, friend of Carlos Hernandez
Olivia Escobedo, Corpus Christi police detective
Jesse Escochea, Corpus Christi police dispatcher
Rosie Esquivel, girlfriend of Carlos DeLuna while he was on death row

Kathy Fair, *Houston Chronicle* reporter
Daniel Fino, co-worker of Carlos DeLuna
Steven Fowler, Corpus Christi police sergeant
Roger Fuentes, stepbrother of Jesse Garza

Armando Garcia, resident of neighborhood where manhunt occurred

Enrique (Rick) Garcia, Corpus Christi police sergeant

Gilbert Garcia, parole officer for Carlos DeLuna

Juanita Garcia, sentencing witness against Carlos DeLuna

Lucinda Garcia, sentencing witness against Carlos DeLuna

Marcos Garcia, friend of Carlos DeLuna

Richard Garcia, brother-in-law of Margie Tapia

Gary Garrett, Corpus Christi police officer

Eddie Garza, Corpus Christi police detective

Jesse Garza, initial defendant in Dahlia Sauceda killing

Michelle Garza, neighbor of Carlos Hernandez

R. W. Glorfield, Corpus Christi police captain

Diana Gomez, girlfriend of Carlos Hernandez

Dorothy Gomez, Memorial Medical Center nurse

Ernesto Gonzalez, Nueces County Sheriff's Department Jail correction officer

Estella Gonzalez, Nueces County Sheriff's Department Jail commissary bookkeeper

Pedro (Pete) Gonzalez, area supervisor of Sigmor Shamrock gas station

Ronnie Gonzalez, acquaintance of Carlos DeLuna and Carlos Hernandez

Michael Graczyk, Associated Press reporter who witnessed numerous Texas executions

Vicky Conejo Gutierrez, half-sister of Carlos DeLuna


George Hamilton, judge in Jesse Garza trial

Hayden W. Head, Jr., United States district judge in Carlos DeLuna's habeas corpus proceeding

Carlos Gonzalez Hernandez, Jr. (referred to here as Carlos Hernandez), suspect in Dahlia Sauceda and other killings

Carlos Hernandez, Sr., father of Carlos Hernandez

Efrain (Frankie) Hernandez, brother of Carlos Hernandez

Fidela Hernandez, mother of Carlos Hernandez

Gerardo (Jerry) Hernandez, brother of Carlos Hernandez

Javier Hernandez, brother of Carlos Hernandez

Jesus Hernandez, son of Carlos Hernandez

Paula Hernandez (later Schilling), sister of Carlos Hernandez

Pricilla Hernandez (later Jaramillo), niece of Carlos Hernandez

Rita Hull, friend of the Hernandez family

Jack Hunter, prosecutor in pretrial phase of Carlos DeLuna's case

Joel Infante, Corpus Christi police identification technician

Mary Jackson, mother of Cindy Maxwell

Pricilla Hernandez Jaramillo, niece of Carlos Hernandez

Grant Jones, Nueces County district attorney

Jon Kelly, lawyer for Carlos Hernandez

Robert Klemp, Corpus Christi police lieutenant

J. Knox, Corpus Christi police lieutenant

Joel Kutnick, psychiatrist who examined Carlos DeLuna for the court

Lance Kutnick, Nueces County assistant district attorney

James Lawrence, trial and appellate lawyer for Carlos DeLuna

Gloria Licea (later Sanchez), girlfriend of Carlos Hernandez

Gilbert Limon, acquaintance of Carlos Hernandez

Wanda Jean Vargas Lopez, victim of killing at Sigmor Shamrock gas station

Maria Margarita Martinez, mother of Carlos DeLuna

Jim Mattox, attorney general of Texas

Cindy Maxwell, girlfriend of Carlos DeLuna

Robert Mayorga, Corpus Christi police officer who dated Wanda Lopez

Eddie McConley, Corpus Christi police lieutenant

Bill McCoy, Corpus Christi reserve police officer

Bruno Mejia, Corpus Christi police officer

Wallace "Pete" Moore, judge in Carlos DeLuna's trial

[First name unknown] Morales, foreman of jury that convicted Carlos
    DeLuna and sentenced him to die

Thomas Mylett, Corpus Christi police officer

Becky Nesmith, cousin of Wanda Lopez

Pedro Olivarez, witness against Jesse Garza in Dahlia Sauceda case

Horacio Ortiz, trial investigator for Carlos DeLuna

Miguel Ortiz, acquaintance of Carlos Hernandez

Yolanda Ortiz, owner of Casino Club

Albert Peña, lawyer for Jesse Garza in Dahlia Sauceda case

Toni Peña, half-sister of Carlos DeLuna

Johnny Paul Penry, Texas death row inmate

Linda Perales (later Vela Ayala), stepmother of Pricilla Hernandez Jaramillo
and former wife of Manuel DeLuna

Mary Ann Perales (later Benavides), witness against Carlos DeLuna

David Petrusaitis, former Nueces County sheriff's deputy

Carroll Pickett, Texas Death House chaplain

James Plaisted, psychologist who examined Carlos DeLuna for the court


Santiago Ramos, first husband of Fidela Hernandez

Al Reyna, Juvenile Department investigator

Rose DeLuna Rhoton, sister of Carlos DeLuna

Paul Rivera, Corpus Christi police detective

Ruben Rivera, Nueces County deputy constable

Rene Rodriguez, lawyer for Wanda Lopez's family in suit against Diamond
Shamrock

Glenda Ruggles, Corpus Christi Police Department 911 operator

Joseph Rupp, Nueces County medical examiner


Gloria Licea Sanchez, girlfriend of Carlos Hernandez

Dahlia Sauceda, girlfriend of Carlos Hernandez and Freddy Schilling who was
raped and murdered

Mark Schauer, Corpus Christi police officer

Eddie Schilling, nephew of Carlos Hernandez

Freddy Schilling, brother-in-law of Carlos Hernandez

John Michael Schilling, nephew of Carlos Hernandez

Paula Hernandez Schilling, sister of Carlos Hernandez

Steven Schiwetz, prosecutor at Carlos DeLuna's trial

Rider Scott, general counsel and chief of staff to Governor William P.
Clements, Jr.

L. Serna, Corpus Christi police officer

M. Shedd, Corpus Christi police sergeant

Louis Sissamis, fiancé of Paula Hernandez who was killed in Carlos Hernandez's car accident

Mark Skurka, prosecutor in Carlos Hernandez's plea deal for stabbing Dina
Ybañez; later Nueces County district attorney

Sidney Smith, Corpus Christi police sergeant who interrogated Pedro Olivarez

Romeo Solis, uncle of Carlos Hernandez
Aida Sosa, girlfriend of Carlos DeLuna while he was an adolescent
Robert Stange, manager of Sigmor Shamrock gas station

Beatrice Tapia, neighbor of Carlos Hernandez
Mary Jane Tapia, sister of Margie Tapia
Mary Margaret (Margie) Tapia, girlfriend of Carlos Hernandez
Donald Thain, Texas Department of Public Safety blood analyst

James J. Vanecek, Fire Department emergency medical technician
Carolyn Vargas, Nueces County deputy constable
Luis Vargas, father of Wanda Lopez
Mary Vargas, mother of Wanda Lopez
Richard Louis Vargas, brother of Wanda Lopez
Beto Vela, father of Pricilla Hernandez
Robert Veregara, Corpus Christi police officer

Mark Wagner, City of Corpus Christi paramedic
Wayne Waychoff, employer of Carlos DeLuna
Kristen Weaver, posttrial lawyer for Carlos DeLuna
Ernest Dave Wilson, Corpus Christi police fingerprint examiner

Andy Ybañez, neighbor of Carlos Hernandez
Dina Ybañez, neighbor of Carlos Hernandez who was assaulted by him with a
    lock-blade buck knife
Johnny Ybañez, neighbor of Carlos Hernandez

William Zapalac, assistant attorney general
Lina Zapata, friend of Carlos Hernandez

## BY CATEGORY

### Carlos DeLuna Associates

#### FAMILY

Blas Avalos, stepfather of Carlos DeLuna
Daniel Conejo, half-brother of Carlos DeLuna
Mary Conejo (later Arredando), half-sister of Carlos DeLuna
Mary Conejo, sister-in-law of Carlos DeLuna

Rebecca Conejo, half-sister of Carlos DeLuna

Vicky Conejo (later Gutierrez), half-sister of Carlos DeLuna

Vincent Conejo, half-brother of Carlos DeLuna

Joe DeLuna, father of Carlos DeLuna

Manuel DeLuna, brother of Carlos DeLuna

Rose DeLuna (later Rhoton), sister of Carlos DeLuna

Maria Margarita Martinez, mother of Carlos DeLuna

Toni Peña, half-sister of Carlos DeLuna

### GIRLFRIENDS

Rosie Esquivel, girlfriend of Carlos DeLuna while he was on death row

Aida Sosa, girlfriend of Carlos DeLuna while he was an adolescent

### OTHER ASSOCIATES

Jesse De La Rosa, Texas death row inmate who drew Carlos DeLuna's portrait

Daniel Fino, co-worker of Carlos DeLuna

Marcos Garcia, friend of Carlos DeLuna

Ronnie Gonzalez, acquaintance of Carlos DeLuna

Yolanda Ortiz, owner of Casino Club

Johnny Paul Penry, Texas death row inmate

Linda Perales (later Vela Ayala), stepmother of Pricilla Hernandez Jaramillo
    and former wife of Manuel DeLuna

Carroll Pickett, Texas Death House chaplain

Wayne Waychoff, employer of Carlos DeLuna

### *Carlos Hernandez Associates*

### FAMILY

John Arsuaga, witness to man running near Sigmor Shamrock gas station; also
    cousin of Carlos Hernandez's cousin

Johnny Arsuaga, cousin of Carlos Hernandez

Carlos Hernandez, Sr., father of Carlos Hernandez

Efrain (Frankie) Hernandez, brother of Carlos Hernandez

Fidela Hernandez, mother of Carlos Hernandez

Gerardo (Jerry) Hernandez, brother of Carlos Hernandez

Javier Hernandez, brother of Carlos Hernandez

Jesus Hernandez, son of Carlos Hernandez

Paula Hernandez (later Schilling), sister of Carlos Hernandez

Pricilla Hernandez (later Jaramillo), niece of Carlos Hernandez
Santiago Ramos, first husband of Fidela Hernandez
Eddie Schilling, nephew of Carlos Hernandez
Freddy Schilling, brother-in-law of Carlos Hernandez
John Michael Schilling, nephew of Carlos Hernandez
Romeo Solis, uncle of Carlos Hernandez

### WIFE AND GIRLFRIENDS

Rosa Anzaldua, wife of Carlos Hernandez
Diana Gomez, girlfriend of Carlos Hernandez
Gloria Licea (later Sanchez), girlfriend of Carlos Hernandez
Cindy Maxwell, girlfriend of Carlos Hernandez
Dahlia Sauceda, girlfriend of Carlos Hernandez and Freddy Schilling who was
    raped and murdered
Mary Margaret (Margie) Tapia, girlfriend of Carlos Hernandez

### CARRIZO STREET NEIGHBORS

Janie Adrian, neighbor of Carlos Hernandez
Beatriz Castro, friend of Fidela Hernandez
Beatrice Tapia, neighbor of Carlos Hernandez
Mary Jane Tapia, sister of Margie Tapia
Lina Zapata, friend of Carlos Hernandez

### OTHER ASSOCIATES

Marcella Brown, friend of Carlos Hernandez
Shirley Currie, friend of Carlos Hernandez
Mary Ellis, friend of Carlos Hernandez
Richard Garcia, brother-in-law of Margie Tapia
Michelle Garza, neighbor of Carlos Hernandez
Ronnie Gonzalez, acquaintance of Carlos Hernandez
Rita Hull, friend of the Hernandez Family
Mary Jackson, mother of Cindy Maxwell
Jon Kelly, lawyer for Carlos Hernandez
Gilbert Limon, acquaintance of Carlos Hernandez
Miguel Ortiz, acquaintance of Carlos Hernandez
Yolanda Ortiz, owner of Casino Club
Linda Perales (later Vela Ayala), stepmother of Pricilla Hernandez Jaramillo
    and former wife of Manuel DeLuna

Louis Sissamis, fiancé of Paula Hernandez who was killed in Carlos Hernandez's car accident

Beto Vela, father of Pricilla Hernandez

Andy Ybañez, neighbor of Carlos Hernandez

Dina Ybañez, neighbor of Carlos Hernandez who was assaulted by him with a lock-blade buck knife

Johnny Ybañez, neighbor of Carlos Hernandez

## *Wanda Lopez Associates*

### FAMILY

Becky Nesmith, cousin of Wanda Lopez

Luis Vargas, father of Wanda Lopez

Mary Vargas, mother of Wanda Lopez

Richard Louis Vargas, brother of Wanda Lopez

### OTHER ASSOCIATES OF WANDA LOPEZ OR HER FAMILY

Robert Mayorga, Corpus Christi police officer who dated Wanda Lopez

Rene Rodriguez, lawyer for Wanda Lopez's family in suit against Diamond Shamrock

Robert Stange, station manager of Sigmor Shamrock gas station

## *Participants in Prosecution of Carlos DeLuna for Murder of Wanda Lopez*

### DEFENDANT

Carlos DeLuna

### EYEWITNESSES

George Aguirre, witness to events outside Sigmor Shamrock gas station

John Arsuaga, witness to man running near Sigmor Shamrock gas station

Julie Arsuaga, witness to man running near Sigmor Shamrock gas station

Kevan Baker, eyewitness to attack on Wanda Lopez

### OTHER WITNESSES

Theresa Barrera, resident of neighborhood where manhunt occurred

Floyd Bieniek, retired police officer and character witness against Carlos DeLuna

Connie Campos, sentencing witness against Carlos DeLuna

Olivia Escobedo, Corpus Christi police detective

Jesse Escochea, Corpus Christi police dispatcher

Steven Fowler, Corpus Christi police sergeant

Armando Garcia, resident of neighborhood where manhunt occurred

Gilbert Garcia, parole officer for Carlos DeLuna

Juanita Garcia, sentencing witness against Carlos DeLuna

Lucinda Garcia, sentencing witness against Carlos DeLuna

Eddie Garza, Corpus Christi police detective

Dorothy Gomez, Memorial Medical Center nurse

Ernesto Gonzalez, Nueces County Sheriff's Department Jail correction officer

Estella Gonzalez, Nueces County Sheriff's Department Jail Commissary
   bookkeeper

Pedro (Pete) Gonzalez, area supervisor of Sigmor Shamrock gas station

Joel Infante, Corpus Christi police identification technician

Robert Klemp, Corpus Christi police lieutenant

Joel Kutnick, psychiatrist who examined Carlos DeLuna for the court (did not
   testify)

Eddie McConley, Corpus Christi police lieutenant

Bruno Mejia, Corpus Christi police officer

Thomas Mylett, Corpus Christi police officer

Mary Ann Perales (later Benavides), witness against Carlos DeLuna

James Plaisted, psychologist who examined Carlos DeLuna for the court (did
   not testify)

Ruben Rivera, Nueces County deputy constable

Joseph Rupp, Nueces County medical examiner

Mark Schauer, Corpus Christi police officer

Donald Thain, Texas Department of Public Safety blood analyst

James J. Vanecek, Fire Department emergency medical technician

Mark Wagner, City of Corpus Christi paramedic

Ernest Dave Wilson, Corpus Christi police fingerprint examiner

### LAW-ENFORCEMENT, JAIL, AND PRISON PERSONNEL

Elmer Cox, Nueces County sheriff's deputy

Olivia Escobedo, Corpus Christi police detective

Jesse Escochea, Corpus Christi police dispatcher

Steven Fowler, Corpus Christi police sergeant

Enrique (Rick) Garcia, Corpus Christi police sergeant

Gary Garrett, Corpus Christi police officer

Eddie Garza, Corpus Christi police detective

R. W. Glorfield, Corpus Christi police captain

Ernesto Gonzalez, Nueces County Sheriff's Department Jail correction officer

Estella Gonzalez, Nueces County Sheriff's Department Jail Commissary
bookkeeper

Joel Infante, Corpus Christi police identification technician

Robert Klemp, Corpus Christi police lieutenant

J. Knox, Corpus Christi police lieutenant

Eddie McConley, Corpus Christi police lieutenant

Bill McCoy, Corpus Christi reserve police officer

Bruno Mejia, Corpus Christi police officer

Thomas Mylett, Corpus Christi police officer

David Petrusaitis, former Corpus Christi sheriff's deputy

Carroll Pickett, Texas Death House chaplain

Al Reyna, Juvenile Department investigator

Ruben Rivera, Nueces County deputy constable

Glenda Ruggles, Corpus Christi Police Department 911 operator

Mark Schauer, Corpus Christi police officer

L. Serna, Corpus Christi police officer

Carolyn Vargas, Nueces County deputy constable

Robert Veregara, Corpus Christi police officer

Ernest Dave Wilson, Corpus Christi police fingerprint examiner

### PROSECUTORS AND OTHER STATE OFFICIALS

Kenneth Botary, prosecutor at trials of Jesse Garza and Carlos DeLuna

William P. Clements, Jr., governor of Texas who denied clemency to Carlos
DeLuna

Jack Hunter, prosecutor in pretrial phase of Carlos DeLuna's case

Grant Jones, Nueces County district attorney

Lance Kutnick, Nueces County assistant district attorney

Jim Mattox, attorney general of Texas

Steven Schiwetz, prosecutor at Carlos DeLuna's trial

Rider Scott, general counsel and chief of staff to Governor William P.
Clements, Jr.

Mark Skurka, assistant district attorney in Carlos Hernandez's plea deal for
stabbing Dina Ybañez; later Nueces County district attorney

William Zapalac, assistant attorney general

### JUDGES AND JURORS

Jack Blackmun, judge who appointed counsel for Carlos DeLuna and ordered Carlos Hernandez's release in Dahlia Sauceda case

Shirley Bradley, member of jury that convicted Carlos DeLuna and sentenced him to die

Eric Brown, judge who set final execution date for Carlos DeLuna

Hector De Peña, Sr., Corpus Christi judge and father of Hector De Peña, Jr.

Hayden W. Head, Jr., United States district judge in Carlos DeLuna's habeas corpus proceeding

Wallace "Pete" Moore, judge in Carlos DeLuna's trial

[First name unknown] Morales, foreman of jury that convicted Carlos De-Luna and sentenced him to die

### DEFENSE LAWYERS AND INVESTIGATOR

Richard Anderson, posttrial lawyer for Carlos DeLuna

Hector De Peña, Jr., trial lawyer for Carlos DeLuna

James Lawrence, trial and appellate lawyer for Carlos DeLuna

Horacio Ortiz, trial investigator for Carlos DeLuna

Kristen Weaver, posttrial lawyer for Carlos DeLuna

*Participants in Prosecution of Jesse Garza and Carlos Hernandez for Murder of Dahlia Sauceda*

### DEFENDANTS

Jesse Garza, initial defendant in Dahlia Sauceda killing

Carlos Hernandez, suspect in Dahlia Sauceda and other killings

### LAW ENFORCEMENT

Olivia Escobedo, Corpus Christi police detective

Eddie Garza, Corpus Christi police detective

Paul Rivera, Corpus Christi police detective

Sidney Smith, Corpus Christi police sergeant who interrogated Pedro Olivarez

### PROSECUTOR

Kenneth Botary, prosecutor at trials of Carlos DeLuna and Jesse Garza

### JUDGES

Jack Blackmun, judge who ordered Carlos Hernandez's release in Dahlia
Sauceda case

George Hamilton, judge in Jesse Garza trial

### DEFENSE LAWYERS AND INVESTIGATOR

Eddie Cruz, private investigator for Jesse Garza in Dahlia Sauceda case

Jon Kelly, lawyer for Carlos Hernandez in Dahlia Sauceda case

Albert Peña, lawyer for Jesse Garza in Dahlia Sauceda case

### WITNESSES AT TRIAL

Olivia Escobedo, Corpus Christi police detective

Roger Fuentes, stepbrother of Jesse Garza

Carlos Hernandez, suspect in Dahlia Sauceda and other killings and witness at
Jesse Garza trial

Fidela Hernandez, mother of Carlos Hernandez

Gloria Licea (later Sanchez), girlfriend of Carlos Hernandez (did not testify)

Pedro Olivarez, witness against Jesse Garza in trial for murdering Dahlia
Sauceda

Joseph Rupp, Nueces County medical examiner

Freddy Schilling, brother-in-law of Carlos Hernandez

### *News Reporters*

Karen Boudrie, Corpus Christi television

Linda Carrico, *Corpus Christi Caller-Times*

Kathy Fair, *Houston Chronicle*

Michael Graczyk, Associated Press reporter who witnessed numerous Texas
executions

## BIBLIOGRAPHY

The bracketed number or numbers following each entry refer to the chapter or chapters for which these sources were used.

### COURT DECISIONS AND RULES

Abdnor v. State, 808 S.W.2d 476 (Tex. Crim. App. 1991). [13]

Abdnor v. State, 871 S.W.2d 726 (Tex. Crim. App. 1994). [13]

Adams v. Texas, 448 U.S. 38 (1980). [14]

Barefoot v. Estelle, 463 U.S. 880 (1983). [15]

Baze v. Rees, 553 U.S. 35 (2008). [16]

Brady v. Maryland, 373 U.S. 83 (1963). [11]

Clark v. State, 717 S.W.2d 910 (Tex. Crim. App. 1986). [15]

Coleman v. Balkcom, 451 U.S. 949 (1981). [15]

Cordova v. State, 733 S.W.2d 175 (Tex. Crim. App. 1987). [15]

Deleon v. State, 126 S.W.3d 210 (Tex. App. 2003). [13]

DeLuna v. Lynaugh, 873 F.2d 757 (5th Cir. 1988).[15]

DeLuna v. Lynaugh, 890 F.2d 720 (5th Cir. 1989). [15]

DeLuna v. Lynaugh, 493 U.S. 999 (1989). [15]

DeLuna v. McCotter, Order Dismissing Petition for Writ of Habeas Corpus; Order Vacating Stay of Execution, No. 86-cv–234 (S.D. Tex. June 13, 1988). [15]

DeLuna v. State, 711 S.W.2d 44 (Tex. Crim. App. 1986). [P, 14, 15]

Eddings v. Oklahoma, 455 U.S 104 (1982). [14]

Ex Parte DeLuna, No. 83-CR–194-A (Nueces Cty., 28th Dist. Tex. Nov. 22, 1989). [15]

Francis v. Franklin, 471 U.S. 307 (1985). [11]

Franklin v. Lynaugh, 487 U.S. 164 (1988). [15]

Gregg v. Georgia, 428 U.S. 153 (1976). [11]

Haynes v. State, 663 S.W.2d 118 (Tex. App. 1983). [13]

Jurek v. Texas, 428 U.S. 262 (1976). [11, 15]

Kansas v. Marsh, 548 U.S. 163 (2006). [P, E]

Kyles v. Whitley, 514 U.S. 419 (1995). [11]

Lockett v. Ohio, 438 U.S. 586 (1978). [11, 14, 15]

Lockhart v. McCree, 476 U.S. 162 (1986). [14]

McCleskey v. Kemp, 481 U.S. 279 (1987). [15]

Penry v. Lynaugh, 492 U.S. 302 (1989). [14, 15]

Penry v. Johnson, 532 U.S. 782 (2001). [14]

Penry v. Lynaugh, 832 F.2d 915 (5th Cir. 1987), aff'd in part and rev'd in part, 492 U.S. 302 1989). [15]

Rompilla v. Beard, 545 U.S. 374 (2005). [14]

Sandstrom v. Montana, 442 U.S. 510 (1979). [11]

Schlup v. Delo, 513 U.S. 298 (1995). [16]

Smith v. Murray, 477 U.S. 527 (1986). [15]

Stephens v. Kemp, 464 U.S. 1027 (1983). [15]

Swindler & Berlin v. Hamilton, 524 U.S. 399 (1998). [E]

Tex. Evid. R. 503(a)(3). [E]

Wiggins v. Smith, 539 U.S. 510 (2003). [14]

Wilkerson v. State, 736 S.W.2d 656 (Tex. Crim. App. 1987). [13]

Williams v. Taylor, 529 U.S. 362 (1999). [14]

Zant v. Stephens, 462 U.S. 862 (1983). [11]

### TESTIMONY IN COURT AND DEPOSITIONS

George Aguirre, Witness to Events Outside Shamrock Gas Station, Pretrial Testimony, Texas v. DeLuna, No. 83-CR–194-A (Nueces Cty., 28th Dist. Tex. June 20, 1983). [2, 3, 10, 11, 13]

George Aguirre, Witness to Events Outside Shamrock Gas Station, Trial Testimony, Texas v. DeLuna, No. 83-CR–194-A (Nueces Cty., 28th Dist. Tex. July 18, 1983). [2, 3, 4, 5, 10, 11, 13]

Argument of Counsel on Pretrial Motion for Continuance, Texas v. DeLuna, No. 83-CR–194-A (Nueces Cty., 28th Dist. Tex. June 10, 1983). [12]

John Arsuaga, Witness to Man Running Near Shamrock Gas Station, Pretrial Testimony, Texas v. DeLuna, No. 83-CR–194-A (Nueces Cty., 28th Dist. Tex. June 20, 1983). [2, 3, 11, 13]

John Arsuaga, Witness to Man Running Near Shamrock Gas Station, Trial Testimony, Texas v. DeLuna, No. 83-CR–194-A (Nueces Cty., 28th Dist. Tex. July 18, 1983). [2, 3, 11, 13]

Julie Arsuaga, Witness to Man Running Near Shamrock Gas Station, Pretrial Testimony, Texas v. DeLuna, No. 83-CR–194-A (Nueces Cty., 28th Dist. Tex. June 20, 1983). [2, 3, 13]

Julie Arsuaga, Witness to Man Running Near Shamrock Gas Station, Trial Testimony, Texas v. DeLuna, No. 83-CR–194-A (Nueces Cty., 28th Dist. Tex. July 18, 1983). [2, 3, 11, 13]

Blas Garcia Avalos, Stepfather of Carlos DeLuna, Trial Testimony, Texas v. DeLuna, No. 83-CR–194-A (Nueces Cty., 28th Dist. Tex. July 18, 1983). [5, 11, 13]

Kevan Baker, Eyewitness to Attack on Wanda Lopez, Pretrial Testimony, Texas v. DeLuna, No. 83-CR–194-A (Nueces Cty., 28th Dist. Tex. June 20, 1983). [1, 2, 3, 10, 13]

Kevan Baker, Eyewitness to Attack on Wanda Lopez, Trial Testimony, Texas v. DeLuna, No. 83-CR–194-A (Nueces Cty., 28th Dist. Tex., July 18, 1983). [2, 3, 4, 10, 13]

Theresa Barrera, Resident of Neighborhood Where Manhunt Occurred, Trial Testimony, Texas v. DeLuna, No. 83-CR–194-A (Nueces Cty., 28th Dist. Tex. July 18, 1983). [2, 13]

Floyd Bieniek, Retired Police Officer and Character Witness Against Carlos DeLuna, Sentencing Testimony, Texas v. DeLuna, No. 83-CR–194-A (Nueces Cty., 28th Dist. Tex. July 21, 1983). [14]

Kenneth Botary, Prosecutor at Trial of Jesse Garza and Trial of Carlos DeLuna, Trial Testimony, Texas v. Jesse Garza, No. 79-CR–881-C (Nueces Cty., 94th Dist. Tex. Jan. 31, 1980). [7]

Deposition of Harry Caldwell, Former Houston Police Chief and Witness in Civil Suit Against Shamrock, Vargas v. Diamond Shamrock, No. 84–4951-D, 86–5900-D (Nueces Cty., 105th Dist. Tex. Oct. 8, 1987). [4]

Sarah Cooks, Corpus Christi Police Department Identification Technician, Trial Testimony, Texas v. Jesse Garza, No. 79-CR–881-C (Nueces Cty., 94th Dist. Tex. Jan. 31, 1980). [6]

Connie Campos, Sentencing Witness Against Carlos DeLuna, Sentencing Testimony, Texas v. DeLuna, No. 83-CR–194-A (Nueces Cty., 28th Dist. Tex. July 21, 1983). [5, 14]

Carlos DeLuna, Defendant in Killing of Wanda Lopez, Trial Testimony, Texas v. DeLuna, No. 83-CR–194-A (Nueces Cty., 28th Dist. Tex. July 18, 1983). [5, 11, 12, 13]

Hector De Peña, Jr., Trial Lawyer for Carlos DeLuna, Closing Statement, Texas v. DeLuna, No. 83-CR–194-A (Nueces Cty., 28th Dist. Tex. July 20, 1983). [13]

Hector De Peña, Jr., Trial Lawyer for Carlos DeLuna, Closing Statement on Sentence, Texas v. DeLuna, No. 83-CR–194-A (Nueces Cty., 28th Dist. Tex. July 21, 1983). [14]

Joe Louis Duran, Witness Who Discovered Dahlia Sauceda's Body, Trial Testimony, Texas v. Jesse Garza, No. 79-CR–881-C (Nueces Cty., 94th Dist. Tex. Jan. 31, 1980). [6]

Olivia Escobedo, Corpus Christi Police Detective in Wanda Lopez and Dahlia Sauceda Cases, Pretrial Testimony, Texas v. DeLuna, No. 83-CR–194-A (Nueces Cty., 28th Dist. Tex. June 20, 1983). [3]

Olivia Escobedo, Corpus Christi Police Detective in Wanda Lopez and Dahlia Sauceda Cases, Trial Testimony, Texas v. DeLuna, No. 83-CR–194-A (Nueces Cty., 28th Dist. Tex. July 18, 1983). [2, 4, 5, 9, 10, 11, 13]

Olivia Escobedo, Corpus Christi Police Detective in Wanda Lopez and Dahlia Sauceda Cases, Trial Testimony, Texas v. Jesse Garza, No. 79-CR–881-C (Nueces Cty., 94th Dist. Tex. Jan. 31, 1980). [6, 7]

Jesus (Jesse) Escochea, Corpus Christi Police Dispatcher, Trial Testimony, Texas v. DeLuna, No. 83-CR–194-A (Nueces Cty., 28th Dist. Tex. July 15, 1983). [2, 13]

Daniel Fino, Carlos DeLuna's Co-worker, Trial Testimony, Texas v. DeLuna, No. 83-CR–194-A (Nueces Cty., 28th Dist. Tex. July 19, 1983). [13]

Steve Fowler, Corpus Christi Police Sergeant, Trial Testimony, Texas v. DeLuna, No. 83-CR–194-A (Nueces Cty., 28th Dist. Tex. July 15, 1983). [2, 13, 15]

Roger Fuentes, Stepbrother of Jesse Garza, Trial Testimony, Texas v. Jesse Garza, No. 79-CR–881-C (Nueces Cty., 94th Dist. Tex. Jan. 31, 1980). [7]

Armando Garcia, Resident of Neighborhood Where Manhunt Occurred, Trial Testimony, Texas v. DeLuna, No. 83-CR–194-A (Nueces Cty., 28th Dist. Tex. July 15, 1983). [2, 13]

Gilbert Garcia, Parole Officer for Carlos DeLuna, Sentencing Testimony, Texas v. DeLuna, No. 83-CR–194-A (Nueces Cty., 28th Dist. Tex. July 21, 1983). [5, 14]

Juanita Garcia, Sentencing Witness Against Carlos DeLuna, Sentencing Testimony, Texas v. DeLuna, No. 83-CR–194-A (Nueces Cty., 28th Dist. Tex. July 21, 1983). [5, 14]

Lucinda Garcia, Sentencing Witness Against Carlos DeLuna, Sentencing Testimony, Texas v. DeLuna, No. 83-CR–194-A (Nueces Cty., 28th Dist. Tex. July 21, 1983). [5, 14]

Gary Garrett, Corpus Christi Police Officer, Sentencing Testimony, Texas v. DeLuna, No. 83-CR–194-A (Nueces Cty., 28th Dist. Tex. July 21, 1983). [14]

Eddie Garza, Corpus Christi Police Detective, Sentencing Testimony, Texas v. DeLuna, No. 83-CR–194-A (Nueces Cty., 28th Dist. Tex. July 21, 1983). [5, 10, 14]

Irma Gaytan, Witness at Jesse Garza's Trial for Killing Dahlia Sauceda, Trial Testimony, Texas v. Jesse Garza, No. 79-CR–881-C (Nueces Cty., 94th Dist. Tex. Jan. 31, 1980). [7]

Dorothy Gomez, Memorial Medical Center Nurse, Trial Testimony, Texas v. DeLuna, No. 83-CR–194-A (Nueces Cty., 28th Dist. Tex. July 15, 1983). [3, 13]

Ernesto Gonzalez, Nueces County Jail Correction Officer, Trial Testimony, Texas v. DeLuna, No. 84-CR–194-A (Nueces Cty., 28th Dist. Tex. July 18, 1983). [13]

Estella Gonzalez, Nueces County Sheriff's Department Jail Commissary Bookkeeper, Trial Testimony, Texas v. DeLuna, No. 84-CR–194-A (Nueces Cty., 28th Dist. Tex. July 18, 1983). [13]

Pete Gonzalez, Shamrock Gas Station Area Supervisor, Trial Testimony, Texas v. DeLuna, No. 83-CR–194-A (Nueces Cty., 28th Dist. Tex., July 15, 1983). [3, 4, 13]

Carlos Hernandez, Trial Testimony, Texas v. Jesse Garza, No. 79-CR–881-C (Nueces Cty., 94th Dist. Tex. Jan. 31, 1980). [6, 7, 9]

Fidela Hernandez, Mother of Carlos Hernandez, Trial Testimony, Texas v. Jesse Garza, No. 79-CR–881-C (Nueces Cty., 94th Dist. Tex. Jan. 31, 1980). [6, 7, 9]

Joel Infante, Corpus Christi Police Identification Technician, Trial Testimony, Texas v. DeLuna, No. 83-CR–194-A (Nueces Cty., 28th Dist. Tex. July 18, 1983). [4, 9, 10, 13]

Robert Klemp, Corpus Christi Police Lieutenant, Trial Testimony, Texas v. DeLuna, No. 83-CR–194-A (Nueces Cty., 28th Dist. Tex. July 18, 1983). [2, 11, 13]

James Lawrence, Trial and Appellate Lawyer for Carlos DeLuna, Pretrial Testimony, Texas v. DeLuna, No. 83-CR–194-A (Nueces Cty., 28th Dist. Tex. June 10, 1983). [11]

James Lawrence, Trial and Appellate Lawyer for Carlos DeLuna, Closing Statement, Texas v. DeLuna, No. 83-CR–194-A (Nueces Cty., 28th Dist. Tex. July 18, 1983). [11, 13]

James Lawrence, Trial and Appellate Lawyer for Carlos DeLuna, Closing Statement on Sentencing, Texas v. DeLuna, No. 83-CR–194-A (Nueces Cty., 28th Dist. Tex. July 21, 1983). [11, 14]

Johnny Longoria, Witness at Jesse Garza's Trial for Killing Dahlia Sauceda, Trial Testimony, Texas v. Jesse Garza, No. 79-CR–881-C (Nueces Cty., 94th Dist. Tex. Jan. 31, 1980). [7]

Eddie McConley, Corpus Christi Police Lieutenant, Pretrial Testimony, Texas v. DeLuna, No. 83-CR–194-A (Nueces Cty., 28th Dist. Tex. June 20, 1983). [2, 3]

Eddie McConley, Corpus Christi Police Lieutenant, Trial Testimony, Texas v. DeLuna, No. 83-CR–194-A (Nueces Cty., 28th Dist. Tex. July 15, 1983). [3, 10, 13]

Bruno Mejia, Corpus Christi Police Officer, Trial Testimony, Texas v. DeLuna, No. 83-CR–194-A (Nueces Cty., 28th Dist. Tex. July 15, 1983). [2, 3, 10, 13]

Thomas Mylett, Corpus Christi Police Officer, Trial Testimony, Texas v. DeLuna, No. 83-CR–194-A (Nueces Cty., 28th Dist. Tex. July 15, 1983). [2, 13]

Margie Naranjo, Witness at Jesse Garza's Trial for Killing Dahlia Sauceda, Trial Testimony, Texas v. Jesse Garza, No. 79-CR–881-C (Nueces Cty., 94th Dist. Tex. Jan. 31, 1980). [7]

Pedro Olivarez, Witness Against Jesse Garza in Trial for Killing Dahlia Sauceda, Trial Testimony, Texas v. Jesse Garza, No. 79-CR–881-C (Nueces Cty., 94th Dist. Tex. Jan. 31, 1980). [7]

Charles Parker, Corpus Christi Police Fingerprint Analyst, Trial Testimony, Texas v. Jesse Garza, No. 79-CR–881-C (Nueces Cty., 94th Dist. Tex. Jan. 31, 1980). [7]

Mary Ann Perales, Witness Against Carlos DeLuna, Trial Testimony, Texas v. DeLuna, No. 83-CR–194-A (Nueces Cty., 28th Dist. Tex. July 18, 1983). [11, 13]

Paul Rivera, Corpus Christi Police Detective, Trial Testimony, Texas v. Jesse Garza, No. 79-CR–881-C (Nueces Cty., 94th Dist. Tex. Jan. 31, 1980). [7]

Ruben Rivera, Nueces County Deputy Constable, Trial Testimony, Texas v. De-Luna, No. 83-CR–194-A (Nueces Cty., 28th Dist. Tex. July 15, 1983). [2, 10, 13]

Joseph Rupp, Nueces County Medical Examiner, Trial Testimony, Texas v. De-Luna, No. 83-CR–194-A (Nueces Cty., 28th Dist. Tex. July 15, 1983). [11, 13]

Joseph Rupp, Nueces County Medical Examiner, Trial Testimony, Texas v. De-Luna, No. 83-CR–194-A (Nueces Cty., 28th Dist. Tex. July 21, 1983). [10]

Joseph Rupp, Nueces County Medical Examiner, Trial Testimony, Texas v. Jesse Garza, No. 79-CR–881-C (Nueces Cty., 94th Dist. Tex. Jan. 31, 1980). [6, 7, 10]

Mark Schauer, Corpus Christi Police Officer, Pretrial Testimony, Texas v. DeLuna, No. 83-CR–194-A (Nueces Cty., 28th Dist. Tex. June 20, 1983). [2, 3, 10, 11, 13]

Mark Schauer, Corpus Christi Police Officer, Trial Testimony, Texas v. DeLuna, No. 83-CR–194-A (Nueces Cty., 28th Dist. Tex. July 18, 1983). [2, 3, 10, 11, 13]

Freddy Schilling, Brother-in-Law of Carlos Hernandez, Trial Testimony, Texas v. Jesse Garza, No. 79-CR–881-C (Nueces Cty., 94th Dist. Tex. Jan. 31, 1980). [6, 7, 9]

Sentencing Transcript, Texas v. DeLuna, No. 83-CR–194-A (Nueces Cty., 28th Dist. Tex. July 21, 1983). [14]

Steven Schiwetz, Prosecutor at Trial of Carlos DeLuna, Closing Statement, Texas v. DeLuna, No. 83-CR–194-A (Nueces Cty., 28th Dist. Tex. July 18, 1983). [2, 3, 11, 13]

Steven Schiwetz, Prosecutor at Trial of Carlos DeLuna, Closing Statement on Sentence, Texas v. DeLuna, No. 84-CR–194-A (Nueces Cty., 28th Dist. Tex. July 21, 1983). [14]

Steven Schiwetz, Prosecutor at Trial of Carlos DeLuna, Opening Statement, Texas v. DeLuna, No. 83-CR–194-A (Nueces Cty., 28th Dist. Tex. July 15, 1983). [2, 3, 10, 12, 13]

Steven Schiwetz, Prosecutor at Trial of Carlos DeLuna, Oral Argument on Pretrial Motion for a Continuance, Texas v. DeLuna, No. 83-CR–194-A (Nueces Cty., 28th Dist. Tex. June 10, 1983). [10]

Steven Schiwetz, Prosecutor at Trial of Carlos DeLuna, Rebuttal, Texas v. DeLuna, No. 83-CR–194-A (Nueces Cty., 28th Dist. Tex. July 19, 1983). [13]

Statement of Steven Schiwetz, Prosecutor at Trial of Carlos DeLuna, Texas v. De-Luna, No. 83-CR–194-A (Nueces Cty., 28th Dist. Tex. July 18, 1983). [10]

Sidney L. Smith, Corpus Christi Police Detective in Dahlia Sauceda Case, Trial Testimony, Texas v. Jesse Garza, No. 79-CR–881-C (Nueces Cty., 94th Dist. Tex. Jan. 31, 1980). [7]

Statement of Facts, Trial Transcript, Texas v. DeLuna, No. 83-CR–194-A (Nueces Cty., 28th Dist. Tex. July 15, 1983). [13]

Stipulation of the Parties, Texas v. DeLuna, No. 83-CR–194-A (Nueces Cty., 28th Dist. Tex. July 15, 1983). [13]

Donald Thain, Texas Department of Public Safety Blood Analyst, Trial Testimony, Texas v. DeLuna, No. 83-CR–194-A (Nueces Cty., 28th Dist. Tex. July 18, 1983). [2, 10, 13]

Transcript of Pretrial Hearing, Texas v. DeLuna, No. 83-CR–194-A (Nueces Cty., 28th Dist. Tex. June 20, 1983). [11]

Trial Transcript—Alphabetical List of Witnesses, Texas v. DeLuna, No. 83-CR–194-A (Nueces Cty., 28th Dist. Tex. July 15, 1983). [11]

Trial Transcript, Texas v. DeLuna, No. 83-CR–194-A (Nueces Cty., 28th Dist. Tex. July 17, 1983). [9, 13]

Trial Transcript of 911 Call, Texas v. DeLuna, No. 84-CR–194-A (Nueces Cty., 28th Dist. Tex. July 18, 1983). [1, 2, 13]

Deposition of Mary Vargas, Mother of Wanda Lopez, Vargas v. Diamond Sham-rock, No. 84–4951-D, 86–5900-D (filed Apr. 20, 1988). [1]

Luis Vargas, Father of Wanda Lopez, Trial Testimony, Texas v. DeLuna, No. 83-CR–194-A (Nueces Cty., 28th Dist. Tex. July 15, 1983). [13]

Mark Wagner, Paramedic, Trial Testimony, Texas v. DeLuna, No. 83-CR–194-A (Nueces Cty., 28th Dist. Tex. July 15, 1983). [2, 10, 13]

Wayne Waychoff, Employer of Carlos DeLuna, Trial Testimony, Texas v. DeLuna, No. 83-CR–194-A (Nueces Cty., 28th Dist. Tex. July 19, 1983). [9, 13]

Ernest Dave Wilson, Corpus Christi Police Fingerprint Examiner, Trial Testimony, Texas v. DeLuna, No. 83-CR–194-A (Nueces Cty., 28th Dist. Tex. July 15, 1983). [10, 12, 13]

Ernest Dave Wilson, Corpus Christi Police Fingerprint Examiner, Trial Testimony, Texas v. DeLuna, No. 83-CR–194-A (Nueces Cty., 28th Dist. Tex. July 18, 1983). [9, 10, 11, 12, 13]

## OTHER PRIMARY RECORDS

Accident Report No. 70–7905, Corpus Christi Police Department (Dec. 30, 1970). [6]

Acknowledgment of Guilty Plea, Texas v. Carlos Hernandez, No. 89-CR–957-H (Nueces Cty., 105th Dist. Ct. Tex. Oct. 9, 1989). [17]

Additional Information [on Carlos DeLuna], Texas Department of Corrections (Mar. 13, 1986). [14]

Admission Summary [for Carlos Hernandez], Texas Department of Corrections (Nov. 6, 1972). [6]

Aerial Photograph of Shamrock Gas Station, Vargas v. Diamond Shamrock, No. 84–4951-D, 86–5900-D (Nueces Cty., 105th Dist. Tex. 1983). [2, 3]

George Aguirre, Witness to Events Outside Shamrock Gas Station, Statement to Corpus Christi Police Department (Feb. 4, 1983). [2, 3, 9, 10, 11, 13]

Marta Aguirre, Untitled Witness Report, Dallas Police Department. [5]

Pedro Aguirre, Statement of Witness, Untitled Witness Reports, Dallas Police Department. [5]

Ambulance Service Dispatch Report No. 00980, Corpus Christi Police Department, M. L. Williams (Feb. 4, 1983). [10]

Ambulance Patient Record for Wanda Lopez (Feb. 4, 1983). [2]

Appellant's Objections to State's Proposed Findings of Fact and Conclusions of Law, Ex Parte DeLuna, No. 83-CR–194-A (Nueces Cty., 28th Dist. Tex. Nov. 17, 1989). [15]

Appendix M: Carlos Hernandez Addresses; Employment History, in James S. Liebman, Outline of the DeLuna Investigation (Nov. 5, 2005). [13]

Application and Brief in Support of Stay of Execution, DeLuna v. McCotter, 86-cv–234 (5th Cir. Oct. 13, 1986). [15]

Application by Court Appointed Defense Counsel for Compensation, Texas v. Garza, No. 79-CR–881-C (Nueces Cty., 94th Dist. Tex. Jan. 31, 1980). [7]

Application for a Stay of Mandate, Texas v. DeLuna, No. 83-CR–194-A (Nueces Cty., 28th Dist. Tex. Oct. 7, 1986). [15]

Application for Protective Order, In re Fidela Gonzalez Hernandez and Javier Hernandez, No. 87–6919-H (Nueces Cty., 347th Dist. Tex. Dec. 22, 1987). [7]

Application for Stay of Execution and Application for Stay of Mandate of the United States Court of Appeals for the Fifth Circuit Pending Certiorari, DeLuna v. Lynaugh, No. 89–336 (5th Cir. Dec. 4, 1989). [15]

Application for Stay of Execution, DeLuna v. Lynaugh, No. 83-CR–194-A (S.D. Tex. Nov. 30, 1989). [15]

Application for Stay of Execution, Ex Parte DeLuna, No. 83-CR–194-A (Nueces Cty., 28th Dist. Tex. Nov. 2, 1989). [15]

Application for Stay of Execution, Texas v. DeLuna, No. 83-CR–194-A (Nueces Cty., 28th Dist. Tex. Oct. 7, 1986). [15]

Application for Subpoena Duces Tecum to Dr. Arringdale, Texas v. DeLuna, No. 83-CR–194-A (Nueces Cty., 28th Dist. Tex. Feb. 28, 1983). [11]

Application for Subpoena, Texas v. DeLuna, No. 83-CR–194-A (Nueces Cty., 28th Dist. Tex. Mar. 8, 1983). [11]

Application for Subpoena, Texas v. DeLuna, No. 83-CR–194-A (Nueces Cty., 28th Dist. Tex. Mar. 10, 1983) . [11]

Application for Subpoena, Texas v. DeLuna, No. 83-CR–194-A (Nueces Cty., 28th Dist. Tex. May 26, 1983). [11]

Application for Subpoena, Texas v. DeLuna, No. 83-CR–194-A (Nueces Cty., 28th Dist. Tex. June 1, 1983). [11]

Application for Subpoena, Texas v. DeLuna, No. 83-CR–194-A (Nueces Cty., 28th Dist. Tex. June 9, 1983). [11]

Application for Subpoena, Texas v. DeLuna, No. 83-CR–194-A (Nueces Cty., 28th Dist. Tex. June 16, 1983) . [11]

Application for Subpoena, Texas v. DeLuna, No. 83-CR–194-A (Nueces Cty., 28th Dist. Tex. July 6, 1983). [12]

Application for Subpoena, Texas v. DeLuna, No. 83-CR–194-A (Nueces Cty., 28th Dist. Tex. July 19, 1983). [11]

Application for Subpoena of Estella Flores Jimenez, Texas v. DeLuna, No. 83-CR–194-A (Nueces Cty., 28th Dist. Tex. Sept. 9, 1983). [15]

Application for Writ of Habeas Corpus, DeLuna v. Lynaugh, No. 83-CR–194-A (S.D. Tex. Nov. 30, 1989). [15]

Application for Writ of Habeas Corpus, DeLuna v. Lynaugh, No. 89–6262 (5th Cir. Nov. 30, 1989). [15]

Application for Writ of Habeas Corpus, Ex Parte DeLuna, No. 83-CR–194-A (Nueces Cty., 28th Dist. Tex. Nov. 2, 1989). [15]

Application for Writ of Habeas Corpus and Brief, Application for a Stay of Mandate, Texas v. DeLuna, No, 83-CR–194-A (Nueces Cty., 28th Dist. Tex. Oct. 7, 1986). [15]

Argument on Pretrial Continuance Motion, Texas v. DeLuna, No. 83-CR–194-A (Nueces Cty., 28th Dist. Tex. June 10, 1983). [11]

Arrest No. B22380, Corpus Christi Police Department, Offense No. N–2722 (Mar. 21, 1971). [6]

Arrest No. 08176, Nueces Cty. Sheriff's Department (Oct. 19, 1978). [6]

Arrest Report for Carlos Hernandez, Corpus Christi Police Department (Jan. 22, 1971). [6]

Arrest Report for Carlos Hernandez, Corpus Christi Police Department (July 29, 1978). [6, 9]

Arrest Report for Carlos Hernandez, Corpus Christi Police Department (Aug. 19, 1978). [6, 9]

Arrest Report for Carlos Hernandez, Corpus Christi Police Department (Jan. 10, 1980). [6, 9]

Arrest Report for Carlos Hernandez, Corpus Christi Police Department (May 4, 1980). [9]

Arrest Report for Carlos Hernandez, Corpus Christi Police Department (Oct. 26, 1981). [6, 9]

Arrest Report for Carlos Hernandez, Corpus Christi Police Department (Oct. 10, 1982). [9]

Arrest Report for Carlos Hernandez, Corpus Christi Police Department (Apr. 3, 1983). [6, 9]

Arrest Report for Carlos Hernandez, Corpus Christi Police Department (May 9, 1985). [9]

Arrest Report for Carlos Hernandez, Corpus Christi Police Department (Mar. 27, 1986). [9]

Arrest Report for Carlos Hernandez, Corpus Christi Police Department (Jan. 21, 1987). [9]

Arrest Report for Carlos Hernandez, Corpus Christi Police Department (May 5, 1987). [9]

Arrest Report for Carlos Hernandez, Corpus Christi Police Department (July 16, 1987). [9]

Arrest Report for Carlos Hernandez, Corpus Christi Police Department (Apr. 15, 1989). [9]

Arrest Report for Carlos Hernandez, Corpus Christi Police Department (May 25, 1996). [9]

Arrest Sheet No. C08973 for Carlos DeLuna, Corpus Christi Police Department (May 31, 1978). [5]

Arrest Sheet No. 11515 for Carlos Hernandez, Corpus Christi Police Department (Aug. 19, 1978). [6]

Arrest Sheet No. C16196 for Carlos DeLuna, Corpus Christi Police Department (Jan. 12, 1979). [5, 9]

Arrest Sheet No. C28914 for Carlos DeLuna, Corpus Christi Police Department (Nov. 30, 1979). [5]

Arrest Sheet No. C29910 for Carlos DeLuna, Corpus Christi Police Department (Dec. 22, 1979). [5]

Arrest Sheet No. 30803 for Carlos Hernandez, Corpus Christi Police Department (Jan. 10, 1980). [6]

Arrest Sheet No. C31988 for Carlos DeLuna, Corpus Christi Police Department (Feb. 6, 1980). [5]

Arrest Sheet No. 32053 for Carlos DeLuna, Corpus Christi Police Department (Feb. 7, 1980). [5]

Arrest Sheet No. C33299 for Carlos DeLuna, Corpus Christi Police Department (Mar. 5, 1980). [5]

Arrest Sheet No. C34425 for Carlos DeLuna, Corpus Christi Police Department (Mar. 28, 1980). [5]

Arrest Sheet No. C37221 for Carlos DeLuna, Corpus Christi Police Department (May 23, 1980). [5]

Arrest Sheet No. 59662 for Carlos Hernandez, Corpus Christi Police Department (Oct. 26, 1981). [6, 9]

Arrest Sheet No. 80508 for Carlos DeLuna, Corpus Christi Police Department (Jan. 21, 1983). [2, 5]

Arrest Sheet No. C81177 for Carlos DeLuna, Corpus Christi Police Department (Feb. 4, 1983). [2]

Arrest Sheet No. 83758 for Carlos Hernandez, Corpus Christi Police Department (Apr. 3, 1983). [6]

Arrest Sheet No. D12834 for Carlos Hernandez, Corpus Christi Police Department (Apr. 17, 1985). [6, 17]

Arrest Sheet No. 13747 for Carlos Hernandez, Corpus Christi Police Department (May 9, 1985). [6]

Arrest Sheet No. 26265 for Carlos Hernandez, Corpus Christi Police Department (Mar. 27, 1986). [6]

Arrest Sheet No. 31365 for Carlos Hernandez, Corpus Christi Police Department (July 24, 1986). [6]

Arrest Sheet No. 38884 for Carlos Hernandez, Corpus Christi Police Department (Jan. 21, 1987). [6, 15]

Arrest Sheet No. 43426 for Carlos Hernandez, Corpus Christi Police Department (May 5, 1987). [6, 15]

Arrest Sheet No. 10920 for Carlos Hernandez, Corpus Christi Police Department (July 29, 1987). [6, 15, 17]

Arrest Sheet No. 46352 for Carlos Hernandez, Corpus Christi Police Department (July 16, 1987). [6]

Arrest Sheet No. 68362 for Carlos Hernandez, Corpus Christi Police Department (Apr. 15, 1989). [6]

Arrest Sheet No. 48855 for Carlos Hernandez, Corpus Christi Police Department (Sept. 14, 1994). [6, 17]

Arrest Sheet No. C21250 for Juan Velasquez, Robstown Police Department (May 25, 1979). [6]

Arrest Warrant for Carlos Hernandez, Nueces Cty. (Feb. 8, 1984) [9]

John Arsuaga, Witness to Man Running Near Gas Station, Statement to Corpus Christi Police Department (Feb. 4, 1983). [2, 13]

Julie Arsuaga, Affidavit (Feb. 13, 2005). [3]

Autopsy Findings for Wanda Lopez, Joseph C. Rupp, Nueces County Medical Examiner (Feb. 5, 1983). [1, 10, 15]

Kevan Baker, Eyewitness to Attack on Wanda Lopez, Statement to Corpus Christi Police Department (Feb. 4, 1983). [2, 3, 9, 10, 11]

Theresa Barrera, Resident of Neighborhood Where Manhunt Occurred, Statement to Corpus Christi Police Department (Mar. 14, 1983). [2]

Allan Bayle, Draft Statement on Handling of Shamrock Gas Station Crime Scene (Nov. 8, 2004). [4]

Allan Bayle—Training and Experience, Independent Fingerprint Expert Web Site, http://onin.com/ukridges/#Training (last visited May 12, 2012). [4]

William Belford, Summary of Criminal Record of Juan Velasquez (Aug. 2, 2005). [6]

William Belford, Summary of Efrain Hernandez Death Record at Nueces County Clerk's Office (July 7, 2005). [6]

Sergeant Bible, Corpus Christi Police Officer, Offense Report (June 19, 1978). [5]

Floyd Bieniek, Retired Police Officer and Character Witness Against Carlos DeLuna, Corpus Christi Police Department Motor Vehicle Report (Dec. 30, 1978). [5]

Floyd Bieniek, Retired Police Officer and Character Witness Against Carlos DeLuna, Corpus Christi Police Department Motor Vehicle Report (Jan. 2, 1979). [5]

Ben Blake and Annie Slemrod, Information Regarding Matches for Carlos Ortiz (Aug. 15, 2004). [8]

D. M. Blank, Corpus Christi Police Officer, CCPD Arrest Report (Oct. 10, 1982). [9]

Board of Pardons and Paroles Minutes, Texas Department of Corrections (Aug. 28, 1978). [6]

Board of Pardons and Paroles Minutes, Texas Department of Corrections (Sept. 20, 1978). [6]

Officer R. M. Boos, Corpus Christi Police Officer, Crime Against Person Report (Nov. 20, 1979). [6]

Kenneth G. Botary Law Offices, Yellow Pages Goes Green, http://www.yellow pagesgoesgreen.org/Corpus+Christi-TX/Law+Offices+Of+Kenneth+G+ Botary/2004596 (last visited Mar. 30, 2012). [E]

Boudrie Communications LLC, PowerProfiles.com, http://www.powerprofiles .com/profile/00005151172146/BOUDRIE+COMMUNICATIONS+LLC -KENNER-LA (last visited Nov. 23, 2011). [E]

Judy Braselton, Educational Diagnostician, Corpus Christi Ind. Sch. Dist., Psychological Report on Carlos DeLuna (Apr. 9, 1974). [5]

Brief of Appellant Carlos DeLuna, DeLuna v. Texas, No. 69,245 (Tex. Crim. App. Mar. 2, 1984). [15]

Brief of Petitioner-Appellant, DeLuna v. Lynaugh, 873 F.2d 757 (5th Cir. 1989). [15]

Call Sheet, Juvenile Case No. 9699, Corpus Christi Police Department (Mar. 21, 1971). [6]

Carlos DeLuna and Carlos Hernandez Height and Weight Comparison. [6, 9]

S. Carrizo St, Corpus Christi, TX 78401 Map, Google Maps, http://goo.gl/fzkJf (last visited May 12, 2012). [8]

Case History for Carlos Hernandez, Clark J. Miller, Corpus Christi Juvenile Case Officer (Feb. 11, 1971). [6]

Certificate of Parole for Carlos Hernandez, Texas Board of Pardons and Parole (Dec. 7, 1997). [6]

J. Cervantes, Corpus Christi Police Sergeant, CCPD Supplementary/Narrative
 Report (Mar. 15, 1994. [9]

J. Cervantes, Corpus Christi Police Sergeant, Field Arrest Report (Mar. 15, 1994).
 [9, 17]

Timoteo Clark's Stipulation and Judicial Confession, Texas v. Clark, Jr., No. 14–
 986 (Nueces Cty., 105th Dist. Tex. Aug. 30, 1974). [6]

Command to Summon Capt. Jones, Corpus Christi Police Department,
 Texas v. De Luna, No. 83-CR–194-A (Nueces Cty., 28th Dist. Tex. July 7,
 1983). [2]

Complaint, Texas v. DeLuna, No. 83-CR–194-A (Nueces Cty., 28th Dist. Tex. Feb.
 7, 1983) (Nueces Cty. Ct. records compendium at 18). [11]

Complaint, Texas v. Hernandez, No. 85806–2 (Nueces Cty. Ct. No. 2 Nov. 8,
 1983). [6, 9]

Corpus Christi Ind. Sch. Dist., Medical Assessment Record for Carlos DeLuna
 (Feb. 26, 1976). [5]

Corpus Christi Police Department, Ambulance Service Dispatch Report
 No. 00980 (Feb. 4, 1983). [2, 3]

Corpus Christi Police Department, Interrogation Report on Jesus Zaragosa Garza,
 Jr. (Nov. 28, 1979). [7]

Corpus Christi Police Department, Interrogation Report on Pedro Olivarez,
 Jr. (Nov. 29, 1979). [7]

Corpus Christi Police Department, Supplementary Call Card No. 1 (Feb. 4,
 1983). [2]

Corpus Christi Police Department, Supplementary Call Card No. 2 (Feb. 4, 1983).
 (D.A. records set B-1 at 4). [2]

Corpus Christi Police Department, Supplementary Call Card No. 4 (Feb. 4, 1983)
 (D.A. records set B-1 at 7). [3]

Crime Scene Diagram, Corpus Christi Police Department (Feb. 4, 1983). [3, 4]

Crime Scene Photograph 25500001, Corpus Christi Police Department (Feb. 4,
 1983). [4, 10, 15]

Crime Scene Photograph 25500002, Corpus Christi Police Department (Feb. 4,
 1983). [4, 10, 15]

Crime Scene Photograph 25500003, Corpus Christi Police Department (Feb. 4,
 1983). [4, 10, 15]

Crime Scene Photograph 25500004, Corpus Christi Police Department (Feb. 4,
 1983). [4, 10, 13]

Crime Scene Photograph 25500005, Corpus Christi Police Department (Feb. 4,
 1983). [2, 4, 10]

Crime Scene Photograph 25500006, Corpus Christi Police Department (Feb. 4, 1983). [2, 4, 10, 13]

Crime Scene Photograph 25500007, Corpus Christi Police Department (Feb. 4, 1983). [2, 4, 10, 11, 13]

Crime Scene Photograph 25500008, Corpus Christi Police Department (Feb. 4, 1983). [4, 10, 11, 13]

Crime Scene Photograph 25500009, Corpus Christi Police Department (Feb. 4, 1983). [4, 10]

Crime Scene Photograph 25500010, Corpus Christi Police Department (Feb. 4, 1983). [3, 4, 10, 13]

Crime Scene Photograph 25500011, Corpus Christi Police Department (Feb. 4, 1983). [4, 10]

Crime Scene Photograph 25500012, Corpus Christi Police Department (Feb. 4, 1983). [4, 10]

Crime Scene Photograph 25500013, Corpus Christi Police Department (Feb. 4, 1983). [2, 4, 10, 13]

Crime Scene Photograph 25500014, Corpus Christi Police Department (Feb. 4, 1983). [4, 10]

Crime Scene Photograph 25500015, Corpus Christi Police Department (Feb. 4, 1983). [4, 10, 13, 15]

Crime Scene Photograph 25500016, Corpus Christi Police Department (Feb. 4, 1983). [4, 10, 15]

Crime Scene Photograph 25500017, Corpus Christi Police Department (Feb. 4, 1983). [4, 10, 15]

Crime Scene Photograph 25500018, Corpus Christi Police Department (Feb. 4, 1983). [4, 6, 10, 15]

Crime Scene Photograph 25500019, Corpus Christi Police Department (Feb. 4, 1983). [3, 4, 10, 11, 13, 15]

Crime Scene Photograph 25500020, Corpus Christi Police Department (Feb. 4, 1983). [2, 4, 10]

Crime Scene Photograph 25500021, Corpus Christi Police Department (Feb. 4, 1983). [4, 10, 13]

Crime Scene Photograph 25500022, Corpus Christi Police Department (Feb. 4, 1983). [3, 4, 10, 13]

Crime Scene Photograph 25500023, Corpus Christi Police Department (Feb. 4, 1983). [2, 3, 10]

Crime Scene Photograph 25500024, Corpus Christi Police Department (Feb. 4, 1983). [1, 2, 3, 4, 10]

Crime Scene Photograph 25500025, Corpus Christi Police Department (Feb. 4, 1983). [2, 3, 10, 15]

Crime Scene Photograph 25500026, Corpus Christi Police Department (Feb. 4, 1983). [2, 3, 4, 10, 13, 15]

Crime Scene Photograph 25500027, Corpus Christi Police Department (Feb. 4, 1983). [4, 10, 15]

Crime Scene Photograph 25500028, Corpus Christi Police Department (Feb. 4, 1983). [4, 10, 11, 13, 15]

Crime Scene Photograph 25500029, Corpus Christi Police Department (Feb. 4, 1983). [1, 3, 4, 10]

Crime Scene Photograph 25500030, Corpus Christi Police Department (Feb. 4, 1983). [4, 10, 11, 13, 15]

Crime Scene Photograph 25500031, Corpus Christi Police Department (Feb. 4, 1983). [2, 4, 10, 11, 13]

Crime Scene Photograph 25500032, Corpus Christi Police Department (Feb. 4, 1983). [2, 3, 10, 13]

Crime Scene Photograph 25500033, Corpus Christi Police Department (Feb. 4, 1983). [2, 3, 4, 10, 11, 13]

Crime Scene Photograph 25500034, Corpus Christi Police Department (Feb. 4, 1983). [1, 3, 4, 10, 13]

Crime Scene Photograph 25500035, Corpus Christi Police Department (Feb. 4, 1983). [1, 3, 4, 10]

Crime Scene Photograph 25500036, Corpus Christi Police Department (Feb. 4, 1983). [4, 10]

Crime Scene Photograph 25500037, Corpus Christi Police Department (Feb. 4, 1983). [4, 10, 11, 13]

Crime Scene Photograph 25500038, Corpus Christi Police Department (Feb. 4, 1983). [4, 10]

Crime Scene Photograph P10100001, Corpus Christi Police Department (Nov. 20, 1979). [7]

Crime Scene Photograph P10100004, Corpus Christi Police Department (Nov. 20, 1979). [7]

Crime Scene Photograph P10100007, Corpus Christi Police Department (Nov. 20, 1979). [6]

Crime Scene Photograph P10100008, Corpus Christi Police Department (Nov. 20, 1979). [6]

Crime Scene Photograph P10100011, Corpus Christi Police Department (Nov. 20, 1979). [6]

Criminal Case Report for Michael Ortiz, Nueces County District Clerk. [8]

Criminal Docket, Texas v. DeLuna, No. 83-CR–194-A (Nueces Cty., 28th Dist. Tex., Feb. 17, 1983). [5]

Criminal History for Carlos DeLuna, Texas Department of Public Safety (May 25, 1983). [5]

Criminal History Records for Carlos Hernandezes in District Attorney's file (May 2, 1983). [6, 9]

Criminal Offense Report, Texas Department of Public Safety (Nov. 21, 1979). [7]

Cuate—Definition, Reverso Collins Spanish-English Dictionary, Http:// dictionary.reverso.net/spanish-english/cuate (last visited Jan. 30, 2012). [8]

Death Sentence After Mandate, State v. DeLuna, No. 83-CR–194-A (Nueces Cty., 28th Dist. Tex. Nov. 2, 1989). [15]

Defendant Diamond Shamrock's Answers to Plaintiffs' Second Set of Interrogatories, Vargas v. Diamond Shamrock, No. 84–4951-D, 86–5900-D (Nueces Cty., 105th Dist. Tex. Feb. 12, 1987). [4]

Defendant's Ex. 1, Vargas v. Diamond Shamrock, No. 84–4951-D, 85–5900-D (Nueces Cty., 105th Dist. Tex. June 3, 1988). [1, 2, 3]

Defendant's First Amended Motion for New Trial, Texas v. DeLuna, No. 83-CR–194-A (Nueces Cty., 28th Dist. Tex. Sept. 7, 1983). [14, 15]

Defendant's First Mot. for Continuance, Texas v. DeLuna, No. 83-CR–194-A (Nueces Cty., 28th Dist. Tex. June 10, 1983). [11]

Defendant's Motion for a Continuance (handwritten), Texas v. DeLuna, No. 83-CR–194-A (Nueces Cty., 28th Dist. Tex. June 17, 1983). [11]

Defendant's Motion for Change of Counsel, Texas v. Hernandez, No. 86-CR–1032-B (Nueces Cty., 117th Dist. Tex. 1986). [7]

Defendant's Motion for Continuance, Texas v. Hernandez, No. 86-CR–1032-B (Nueces Cty., 117th Dist. Tex. 1986). [7]

Defendant's Motion for Court Appointed Co-Counsel, Texas v. DeLuna, No. 83-CR–194-A (Nueces Cty., 28th Dist. Tex. Apr. 5, 1983). [11]

Defendant's Motion for Court Appointed Psychiatrist, Texas v. DeLuna, No. 83-CR–194-A (Nueces Cty., 28th Dist. Tex. Apr. 6, 1983). [11]

Defendant's Motion for Discovery, Texas v. Hernandez, No. 86-CR–1032-B (Nueces Cty., 117th Dist. Tex. Dec. 2, 1986). [7]

Defendant's Motion for Investigative and Expert Assistance in Indigent Case, Texas v. DeLuna, No. 84-CR–194-A (Nueces Cty., 28th Dist. Tex. Undated). [11]

Defendant's Motion to Dismiss, Texas v. Hernandez, No. 86-CR–1032-B (Nueces Cty., 117th Dist. Tex. Dec. 30, 1986). [7]

Defendant's Motion to Quash Indictment, Texas v. DeLuna, No. 83-CR–194-A (Nueces Cty., 28th Dist. Tex. June 1, 1983). [11]

Defendant's Request That the State Elect, Texas v. DeLuna, No. 83-CR–194-A (Nueces Cty., 28th Dist. Tex. June 1, 1983). [11]

Defendant's Statement on Ineffective Counsel, Texas v. DeLuna, No. 83-CR–193-A (Nueces Cty., 28th Dist. Tex. June 17, 1983). [11]

M. DeLeon, Corpus Christi Police Officer, CCPD Arrest Report (Apr. 15, 1989). [9]

M. DeLeon, Corpus Christi Police Officer, Supplementary Report (Apr. 15, 1989). [17]

Carlos DeLuna Feb. 4, 1983 Paycheck, Issued by Triarch Corporation (Feb. 4, 1983). [9]

Carlos DeLuna Mirror Mug Shot, Corpus Christi Police Department (Jan. 21, 1983). [9]

DeLuna—New Document Analysis—Carlos Ortiz Chart 8-15-04. [8]

DeLuna—New Document Analysis—Players Data Base 6-05, entry for Karen Boudrie Evers (Aug. 9, 2005). [13]

DeLuna—New Document Analysis—Players Data Base 6-05, entry for Carlos G. Hernandez (Aug. 9, 2005). [13]

DeLuna—New Document Analysis—Players Data Base 6-05, entry for Fidela Hernandez (Aug. 9, 2005). [13]

DeLuna—New Document Analysis—Players Data Base 6-05, entry for Mary Lou Jackson (Aug. 9, 2005). [8]

DeLuna—New Document Analysis—Players Data Base 6-05, entry for Cindy Maxwell (Aug. 9, 2005). [8, 13]

DeLuna—New Document Analysis—Players Data Base 6-05, entry for Bernadina Ybañez (Aug. 9, 2005). [13]

DeLuna v. McCotter, Order Dismissing Petition for Writ of Habeas Corpus; Order Vacating Stay of Execution, No. 86-cv–234 (S.D. Tex. June 13, 1988). [15]

Demand for Individual Voir Dire, Texas v. DeLuna, No. 83-CR–194-A (Nueces Cty., 28th Dist. Tex. June 1, 1983). [11]

Department of Health, Bureau of Vital Statistics, Certificate of Death for Carlos Hernandez (May 28, 1999). [P]

Edwin DeSha, Jr., Polygraph Report on Carlos Hernandez, Texas Department of Public Safety (Dec. 11, 1979). [7]

Edwin DeSha, Jr., Polygraph Report on Freddy Schilling, Texas Department of Public Safety (Nov. 20, 1979). [7]

Hector De Peña, Application for Payment of Statutory Fee and Order Granting Application, Texas v. DeLuna, No. 83-CR–194-A (Nueces Cty., 28th Dist. Tex. Aug. 24, 1983). [11]

Diamond Shamrock Station Sigmor No. 47, Consolidated Operating Report (Feb. 4–5, 1983). [4]

Disciplinary Hearing Record on Carlos DeLuna, Texas Department of Corrections (May 16, 1984). [15]

Disciplinary Report on Carlos DeLuna, Texas Department of Corrections (May 11, 1984). [15]

Disciplinary Report on Carlos Hernandez, Texas Department of Corrections (Apr. 15, 1990). [17]

E-mail from Allan Bayle to James S. Liebman (July 3, 2004). [9, 10]

E-mail from James S. Liebman to William Belford (July 12, 2005, 10:14 A.M.). [9]

Emergency Services Record for Wanda Lopez, Memorial Medical Center, Corpus Christi, Texas (Feb. 4, 1983). [1]

Olivia Escobedo, Corpus Christi Police Detective in Wanda Lopez and Dahlia Sauceda Cases, Memorandum on Elimination Prints from Wanda Vargas Lopez (Feb. 8, 1983). [10, 11]

Olivia Escobedo, Corpus Christi Police Detective in Wanda Lopez and Dahlia Sauceda Cases, Supplementary Report (Feb. 5, 1983) [2, 3, 4, 6, 10, 11, 15]

Olivia Escobedo, Corpus Christi Police Detective in Wanda Lopez and Dahlia Sauceda Cases, Supplementary Report (Feb. 10, 1983). [2, 3, 10, 11, 13]

Olivia Escobedo, Corpus Christi Police Detective in Wanda Lopez and Dahlia Sauceda Cases, Supplementary Report (Feb. 12, 1983). [9, 11]

Olivia Escobedo, Corpus Christi Police Detective in Wanda Lopez and Dahlia Sauceda Cases, Supplementary Report in Homicide of Dahlia Sauceda (Nov. 20, 1979). [6, 7]

Olivia Escobedo, Corpus Christi Police Detective in Wanda Lopez and Dahlia Sauceda Cases, Texas Department of Public Safety Laboratory Physical Evidence Submission Form (Feb. 9, 1983). [10]

Felony Bail Bond Before Indictment, Texas v. Carlos Hernandez, No. 89-CR–957-H (Nueces Cty., 105th Dist. Tex. Apr. 21, 1989). [17]

Felony Theft of a Car, Case No. 14948, 105th Judicial District of Nueces County (Jan. 31, 1972). [6]

J. R. Fernandez, Corpus Christi Police Officer, Supplementary Report Form for Carlos DeLuna, Corpus Christi Police Department (July 19, 1978). [5]

Finding Carlos Ortiz (undated internal memo). [8]

Findings of Fact and Order, Ex Parte DeLuna, No. 83-CR–194-A (Nueces Cty., 28th Dist. Tex. Nov. 22, 1989). [15]

Fingerprint Record No. 55682 of Carlos Hernandez, Corpus Christi Police Department (Feb. 4, 1972). [9]

Fingerprint Record No. 74204, Major Case Fingerprints of Carlos Hernandez, Corpus Christi Police Department (Oct. 26, 1981, with additional notations made Apr. 4, 1983). [9]

First Amended Application for Writ for Habeas Corpus and Brief, DeLuna v. McCotter, No. C–86–234 (S.D. Tex. June 29, 1988). [15]

Steven Fowler, Corpus Christi Police Sergeant, Supplementary Report (Feb. 4, 1983). [2, 3, 4, 10, 11]

O. N. Fulton, Field Arrest Report, Nueces County Sheriff's Department (filed Jan. 12, 1996). [17]

O. N. Fulton, Corpus Christi Police Officer, Corpus Christi Police Department Offense Report (Jan. 11, 1996). [8]

R. N. Garcia, Corpus Christi Police Sergeant, CCPD Arrest Report (Mar. 27, 1986). [9]

Diana Gomez, Girlfriend of Carlos Hernandez, Statement to Corpus Christi Police Department (Apr. 17, 1986). [7]

D. Gonzalez, Corpus Christi Police Officer, CCPD Arrest Report (Jan. 21, 1987). [9]

Google Maps, http://goo.gl/Pgpxk (last visited May 11, 2012). [9]

Google Maps, http://maps.google.com/maps?q=808+South+19th+Street+Corpus+Christi&oe=utf-8&rls=org.mozilla:en-US:official&client=firefox-a&um=1&ie=UTF8&hq=&hnear=0x86685e48f32c4399:0xa02aec9f6861e6ce,808+S+19th+St,+Corpus+Christi,+TX+78405&gl=us&ei=KZ6-TpWWEOLqoQHWhPzCBA&sa=X&oi=geocode_result&ct=image&resnum=1&ved=0CBwQ8gEwAA (last visited May 11, 2012). [13]

Google Maps, https://maps.google.com (search "1014 Seventh Street Corpus Christi Texas") (last visited Mar. 25, 2012). [17]

Google Maps, http://maps.google.com/maps?saddr=2602+South+Padre+Island+Dr.%2C+Corpus+Christi%2C+TX+78415+&daddr=3215+South+Padre+Island+Dr.%2C+Corpus+Christi(last visited May 3, 2012). [5]

Google Maps, South Carrizo St, Corpus Christi, TX 78401 Map, http://goo.gl/fzkJf (last visited May 12, 2012). [8]

Google Maps, South Carrizo St, Corpus Christi, TX 78401 Map, http://goo.gl/JLIvk (last visited May 12, 2012). [8]

Google Maps, South Carrizo St, Corpus Christi, TX 78401 Map, http://goo.gl/
    OB6aI (last visited May 12, 2012). [8]

Grand Jury Indictment, Texas v. DeLuna, No. 83-CR–194-A (Nueces Cty., 28th
    Dist. Tex. Feb. 17, 1983). [11]

Grand Jury Indictment of Timoteo Clark and Carlos Hernandez, Grand Jury of
    Nueces County (May 25, 1972). [6]

J. Granger, Corpus Christi Police Officer, CCPD Arrest Report (July 29, 1978). [9]

Web Site for Attorney Grant Jones, http://www.grantjones.net (last visited
    May 11, 2012) [17]

Handwritten Note on Manila File Folder in District Attorney's File. [3]

D. G. Harrison, Corpus Christi Police Officer, Corpus Christi Police Department
    Arrest Sheet for Carlos DeLuna (Jan. 12, 1979). [5]

Alvina Hernandez and Maria Ramirez, Untitled Witness Report, Statement to
    Corpus Christi Police Department (1980). [5]

Carlos Hernandez and Carlos DeLuna Time Line, 1951–1999. [9]

Carlos Hernandez Arrest Record, Nueces County District Attorney's Office, Of-
    fense No. 20229123 (Feb. 29, 1972). [6]

Carlos Hernandez Criminal Record Transcript, Texas Department of Public
    Safety (Jan. 31–Oct. 3, 1972). [6]

Carlos Hernandez Complete On-Line Criminal Record, Criminal History Sys-
    tem. [8, 9]

Carlos Hernandez, Statement to Corpus Christi Police Department (Apr. 15,
    1989). [17]

Carlos Hernandez, Suspect in Murder of Dahlia Sauceda, Statement to Corpus
    Christi Police Department (Dec. 10, 1979). [7]

D. Hewparch, Corpus Christi Police Officer, CCPD Arrest Report (Aug. 19,
    1978). [9]

Holdings of the Texas State Archives, Transcript of Conference Call Re: Clem-
    ency for Carlos DeLuna Between Ryder Strong, Advisor to Governor William
    Clements, Jr., Kristen Weaver, Lawyer for Carlos DeLuna, and William Za-
    palac, Lawyer for the State of Texas (Dec. 6, 1989). [16]

Indictment, Texas v. Carlos Hernandez, No. 89-CR–957-H (Nueces Cty., 105th
    Dist. Tex. Apr. 21, 1989). [17]

Joel Infante, Corpus Christi Police Identification Technician, Field Investigation
    Report (Feb. 4, 1983). [3, 4, 9, 10, 15]

Inmate Release Report for Carlos Hernandez, Texas Board of Pardons and Parole
    (May 30, 1997). [17]

Investigator's Report of Custodial Death of Carlos Hernandez, TDCJ No. 539060, Texas Department of Criminal Justice Internal Affairs Division (May 6, 1999). [P, 17]

Irvington High School Transcript for Carlos Hernandez (1971). [6]

Jail Release Form with Fingerprints, Corpus Christi Police Department (Apr. 17, 1989) . [17]

Sergeant J. D. Johnson, Corpus Christi Police Officer, Supplementary Report (June 20, 1978). [5]

Judgment, DeLuna v. Lynaugh, No. C–89–336 (S.D. Tex. Dec. 2, 1989). [15]

Judgment, Texas v. DeLuna, No. 83-CR–194-A (Nueces Cty., 28th Dist. Tex. at Sept. 12, 1983). [15]

Judgment, Texas v. Manuel DeLuna, No. 80-CR–147-C (Nueces Cty., 94th Dist. Tex. May 20, 1980). [5]

Judgment, Texas v. Manuel DeLuna, No. 95-CR–4273-G(81) (Nueces Cty., 319th Dist. Tex. Feb. 17, 1998). [5]

Judgment of Conviction, Texas v. Hernandez, No. 14–986 (Nueces Cty., 105th Dist. Tex. Sept. 28, 1972). [6]

Judgment on Plea of Guilty, Texas v. Carlos Hernandez, No. 89-CR–957-H (Nueces Cty., 105th Dist. Tex. Apr. 21, 1989). [17]

Juvenile Call Sheet for Carlos DeLuna, Juvenile Department, Case No. 7147 (Sept. 23, 1977). [5]

Juvenile Call Sheet for Carlos DeLuna, Juvenile Department, Case No. 7147 (June 1, 1978). [5]

Juvenile Call Sheet for Carlos DeLuna, Juvenile Department, Case No. 7147 (July 19, 1978). [5]

Juvenile Call Sheet for Carlos DeLuna, Juvenile Department, Case No. 7147 (Sept. 9, 1978). [5]

Juvenile Call Sheet for Case No. 9699, Corpus Christi Police Department (Mar. 21, 1971). [6]

Juvenile Face Sheet for Carlos DeLuna, Probation Department (Feb. 28, 1978). [5]

Juvenile Face Sheet for Carlos Hernandez, Case No. 71-9699, Probation Department (Feb. 11, 1971). [6]

Juvenile Field Interrogation Report for Carlos DeLuna, Sgt. Askarst, Arresting Officer (Mar. 28, 1978). [5]

Juvenile Field Interrogation Report for Carlos DeLuna, I. Loa and Sgt. Bible, Arresting Officers (June 19, 1978) (p. 12 of set). [5]

Juvenile Record for Carlos Hernandez (Case No. 9699), Corpus Christi Police Department (Mar. 21, 1971). [9]

[First Name Unknown] Kearney, Corpus Christi Police Officer, Supplementary Report (Apr. 15, 1989). [1]

Dr. Joel Kutnick, Psychiatrist, Psychiatric Evaluation of Carlos DeLuna (June 14, 1983). [5, 11, 13]

R. S. Lara, Corpus Christi Police Officer, Offense Report (July 19, 1978). [5]

James Lawrence, Affidavit (Aug. 8, 1983). [15]

James R. Lawrence's Application for Payment of Statutory Fee and Order Granting Application, Texas v. DeLuna, No. 83-CR-194-A (Nueces Cty., 28th Dist. Tex. July 26, 1983). [11]

[First Name Unknown] Lee, Corpus Christi Police Department Officer, Supplementary Report (May 19, 1982). [5]

Letter from Richard A. Anderson to Judge Dunham (Oct. 7, 1986). [15]

Letter from Richard Banks, Executive Administrator, to Attorneys in DeLuna v. State, No. 16,436–01 (Tex. Crim. App. Oct. 13, 1986). [15]

Letter from William Belford to James Liebman (Aug 3, 2005). [5]

Letter from Roland J. Brauer, Ph.D., to Martineau Juvenile Shelter Regarding Carlos DeLuna (June 27, 1978). [5]

Letter from Jesus M. Chávez, Superintendent of Schools, Corpus Christi Ind. Sch. Dist., to William Belford (Aug. 3, 2004). [5]

Letter from Carlos DeLuna to Judge Dunham (Nov. 17, 1983). [11, 15]

Letter from Carlos DeLuna to Noel Gutierrez, Nephew of Carlos DeLuna (Nov. 10, 1988). [16]

Letter from Carlos DeLuna to Vicky Gutierrez, Half-Sister of Carlos DeLuna (July 27, 1983). [15]

Letter from Carlos DeLuna to Vicky Gutierrez, Half-Sister of Carlos DeLuna (Aug. 9, 1983). [15]

Letter from Carlos DeLuna to Vicky Gutierrez, Half-Sister of Carlos DeLuna (Sept. 17, 1983). [15]

Letter from Carlos DeLuna to Vicky Gutierrez, Half-Sister of Carlos DeLuna (Jan. 21, 1984). [15]

Letter from Carlos DeLuna to Vicky Gutierrez, Half-Sister of Carlos DeLuna (May 24, 1984). [15]

Letter from Carlos DeLuna to Vicky Gutierrez, Half-Sister of Carlos DeLuna (May 27, 1988). [15]

Letter from Carlos DeLuna to Vicky Gutierrez, Half-Sister of Carlos DeLuna (June 30, 1988). [15, 16]

Letter from Judge Walter Dunham, Jr., to Judge Robert Barnes (Sept. 27, 1983). [11]

Letter from Judge Walter Dunham, Jr., to Hector De Peña, Jr., Texas v. DeLuna, No. 83-CR–194-A (Nueces Cty., 28th Dist. Tex. Feb. 28, 1983). [11]

Letter from Jack Hunter, Acting District Attorney, to Hector De Peña, Trial Lawyer for Carlos DeLuna, Texas v. DeLuna, No. 83-CR–194-A (Nueces Cty., 28th Dist. Tex. Feb. 28, 1983). [11]

Letter from Jack Hunter, Acting District Attorney, to Hector De Peña, Trial Lawyer for Carlos DeLuna, Texas v. DeLuna, No. 83-CR–194-A (Nueces Cty., 28th Dist. Tex. Mar. 4, 1983). [11]

Letter from Jack Hunter, Acting District Attorney, to Hector De Peña, Trial Lawyer for Carlos DeLuna, Texas v. DeLuna, No. 83-CR–194-A (Nueces Cty., 28th Dist. Tex. Mar. 16, 1983). [11]

Letter from Oscar Soliz, Nueces County District Court Clerk, to James Lawrence, Trial Lawyer for Carlos DeLuna (Jan. 6, 1984). [15]

Letter from James F. Waller, Jr., Texas Department of Public Safety, to Jesse Cervantes, Corpus Christi Police Sergeant (Offense Date Mar. 15 1994). [9]

Letter from James F. Waller, Jr., Supervisor, Texas Department of Public Safety Chemistry Laboratory, to Charles J. Parker, Identification Analyst (Feb. 16, 1983). [10]

Letter from James F. Waller, Jr., Supervisor, Tex. Department of Public Safety, to Olivia Escobedo, Corpus Christi Police Detective in Wanda Lopez and Dahlia Sauceda Cases (Feb. 17, 1983). [3, 10]

James S. Liebman, Important Info upon JSL's Brief Perusal of Recently Obtained Nueces County District Court Records in CDL's 2/4/83 Murder Case (internal memo) (July 27, 2004). [11]

James S. Liebman, Memorandum to File 22 and 23—District Attorney Records (Feb. 25, 2005). [11]

James S. Liebman, Outline of the DeLuna Investigation (Nov. 5, 2005). [8, 11]

List of State's Exhibits, Attached to Motion to Withdraw Exhibits, Texas v. DeLuna, No. 83-CR–194-A (Nueces Cty., 28th Dist. Tex. July 22, 1983). [15]

Wanda Lopez Medical Chart, Memorial Medical Center (Feb. 4, 1983). [3]

State of Texas Death Certificate for Wanda Lopez, Nueces County Medical Examiner (Feb. 4, 1983). [1, 4]

MapQuest, http://www.mapquest.com/maps?city=Corpus%20Christi&state=TX (last visited Oct. 22, 2011). [6]

Officers R. McCollum and H. G. Cunningham, Statement of Witnesses, Untitled Witness Reports, Corpus Christi Police Department (1980). [5]

Bruno Mejia, Corpus Christi Police Officer, Supplementary Report (Feb. 4, 1983). [2, 4, 9, 10, 11, 13]

Memorandum of Law on Application for Stay of Execution, DeLuna v. Lynaugh, No. 89–6262 (5th Cir. Dec. 4, 1989). [15]

Memorandum of Law on Application for Writ of Habeas Corpus, DeLuna v. Lynaugh, No. 83-CR–194-A (S.D. Tex. Nov. 30, 1989). [15]

Memorandum of Law on Application for Writ of Habeas Corpus, Ex Parte De-Luna, No. 83-CR–194-A (Nueces Cty., 28th Dist. Tex. Nov. 2, 1989). [15]

Memorandum on Miguel A. Ortiz (Sept. 21, 2004). [8]

Memorial Medical Center Records, Multidisciplinary Assessment of Carlos Hernandez (July 28, 1995). [15]

Miscellaneous Criminal Records of Carlos Hernandez (1980–1996). [6]

Motion for a New Trial, Texas v. DeLuna, No. 83-CR–194-A (Nueces Cty., 28th Dist. Tex. Aug. 9, 1983). [15]

Motion for Discovery and Inspection of Evidence Texas v. DeLuna, No. 83-CR–194-A (Nueces Cty., 28th Dist. Tex. Feb. 25, 1983). [11]

Motion for Discovery and Inspection of Evidence, Texas v. DeLuna, No. 83-CR–194-A (Nueces Cty., 28th Dist. Tex. May 6, 1983). [11]

Motion for Hearing on Voluntariness of Any Admission or Confession Whether Written or Oral, Texas v. DeLuna, No. 83-CR–194-A (Nueces Cty., 28th Dist. Tex. June 1, 1983). [11]

Motion for Identification Hearing, Texas v. DeLuna, No. 83-CR–194-A (Nueces Cty., 28th Dist. Tex. June 3, 1983). [11]

Motion for Jury List, Texas v. DeLuna, No. 83-CR–194-A (Nueces Cty., 28th Dist. Tex. June 1, 1983). [11]

Motion for New Counsel, Texas v. DeLuna, No. 83-CR–194-A (Nueces Cty., 28th Dist. Tex. June 17, 1983). [15]

Motion for Reduction of Bond, Texas v. Hernandez, No. 86-CR–1032-B (Nueces Cty., 117th Dist. Tex. 1986). [7]

Motion for Relief from Order, Motion for Certificate of Probable Cause, and Notice of Appeal, DeLuna v. McCotter, No. C–86–234 (S.D. Tex. June 2, 1988). [15]

Motion for Relief from Order, Motion for Certificate of Probable Cause, and Notice of Appeal, DeLuna v. Lynaugh, No. C–89–336 (S.D. Tex. Dec. 2, 1989). [15]

Motion for Stay of Execution, Ex Parte DeLuna, No. 16,436–01 (Tex. Crim. App. Oct. 9, 1986). [15]

Motion to Attach Affidavits and Evidentiary Matters to Previously Filed Pleadings, DeLuna v. McCotter, No. C–86–234 (S.D. Tex. July 12, 1988). [15]

Motion to Dismiss, State v. Hernandez, No. 86-CR–1032-B (Nueces Cty., 117th Dist. Tex. Dec. 22, 1986). [15]

Motion to Disqualify Counsels and for Appellant to Proceed by Himself as Counsel, Texas v. DeLuna, 83-CR–194-A (Nueces Cty., 28th Dist. Tex. Aug. 30, 1983). [15]

Motion to Produce Exculpatory and Mitigating Evidence, Texas v. DeLuna, No. 83-CR–194-A (Nueces Cty., 28th Dist. Tex. Feb. 25, 1983). [11]

Motion to Suppress Identification, Texas v. DeLuna, No. 83-CR–194-A (Nueces Cty., 28th Dist. Tex. June 3, 1983). [11]

Motion to Withdraw Exhibits, Texas v. DeLuna, No. 83-CR–194-A (Nueces Cty., 28th Dist. Tex. July 22, 1983). [9, 15]

Thomas Mylett, Corpus Christi Police Officer, Supplementary Report (Feb. 6, 1983). [2, 3, 5, 11]

Nueces County Sheriff's Department, Jail Card for Carlos DeLuna (Feb. 8, 1983). [9]

Nueces County Sheriff's Department, Re-Arrest Report for Carlos Hernandez (May 6, 1980). [9]

Pedro Olivarez, Witness Against Jesse Garza in Trial for Murdering Dahlia Sauceda, Statement to Corpus Christi Police Department (Nov. 29, 1979). [7]

Oral Argument on June 20, 1983 Motion for Continuance, Texas v. DeLuna, No. 83-CR–194A (Nueces Cty., 28th Dist. Tex. June 20, 1983). [5]

Order, DeLuna v. Lynaugh, No. C–89–336 (S.D. Tex., Dec. 4, 1989). [15]

Order, Ex Parte DeLuna, No. 83-CR–194-A (Nueces Cty., 28th Dist. Tex. Oct. 9, 1986). [15]

Order, Juvenile Court of Nueces County (Sept. 23, 1971). [6]

Order Appointing an Attorney, State v. Hernandez, No. 86-CR–1032 (Nueces Cty., 117th Dist. Tex. Nov. 13, 1986). [7, 15]

Order Appointing Attorney James Lawrence, Texas v. DeLuna, No. 83-CR–194A (Sept. 12, 1983). [15]

Order Denying Defendant's Motion for Continuance, Texas v. DeLuna, No. 83-CR–194-A (Nueces Cty., 28th Dist. Tex. June 10, 1983). [11]

Order Denying Motion for a Continuance (handwritten), Texas v. DeLuna, No. 83-CR–194-A (Nueces Cty., 28th Dist. Tex. June 17, 1983). [11]

Order Denying Motion for Stay of Execution, DeLuna v. Lynaugh, 890 F.2d 720 (5th Cir. 1989). [15]

Order Denying Motion of Appellant to Recall the Mandate and Stay the Setting of an Execution Date, DeLuna v. Lynaugh, 890 F.2d 720 (5th Cir. 1989). [15]

Order Denying Petitions for Habeas Corpus and Stay of Execution, DeLuna v. Lynaugh, No. C–89–336 (S.D. Tex., Dec. 2, 1989). [15]

Order Granting Motion to Dismiss, State v. Hernandez, No. 86-CR–1032 (Nueces Cty., 117th Dist. Tex. Dec. 31, 1986). [7, 15]

Order Granting Motion to Withdraw Exhibits, Texas v. DeLuna, No. 83-CR–194-A (Nueces Cty., 28th Dist. Tex. July 22, 1983). [15]

Order Granting Statutory Attorney Fee for Hector De Peña, Jr., Texas v. DeLuna, No. 83-CR–194-A (Nueces Cty., 28th Dist. Tex. Aug. 24, 1983). [15]

Order Granting Statutory Attorney Fee for James Lawrence, Texas v. DeLuna, No. 83-CR–194-A (Nueces Cty., 28th Dist. Tex. July 26, 1983). [15]

Order and Notice of Withdrawal of Pre-Revocation Warrant of Arrest, Texas Department of Criminal Justice (May 23, 1980). [9]

Order of Assignment, Texas v. DeLuna, No. 83-CR–194-A (Nueces Cty., 28th Dist. Tex. May 26, 1983). [11]

Order of Assignment, Texas v. DeLuna, No. 83-CR–194-A (Nueces Cty., 28th Dist. Tex. June 1, 1983). [11]

Order of Assignment, Texas v. DeLuna, No. 83-CR–194-A (Nueces Cty., 28th Dist. Tex. June 27, 1983). [11]

Order of Examination, Texas v. DeLuna, No. 83-CR–194-A (Nueces Cty., 28th Dist. Tex. May 16, 1983). [11]

Order on Habeas Corpus Application from Nueces County, Ex Parte DeLuna, No. 16,436–02 (Tex. Ct. Crim. App., Nov. 29, 1989). [15]

Order on Motion for Court Appointed Co-Counsel, Texas v. DeLuna, No. 83-CR–194-A (Nueces Cty., 28th Dist. Tex. Apr. 15, 1983). [11]

Order on Petitioner's Motion for Stay of Execution and Application for Writ of Habeas Corpus, Ex Parte DeLuna, No. 16,436–01 (Tex. Crim. App. Oct. 13, 1986). [15]

Marcia Packer, Corpus Christi Police Department, Field Investigation Report (Feb. 5, 1983). [10]

James R. Peters, Corpus Christi Ranger, Progress Report in Dahlia Sauceda Investigation (Nov. 20, 1979). [7]

Petition for a Writ of Certiorari, DeLuna v. Lynaugh, 493 U.S. 999 (1989) (cert. denied Aug. 2, 1989). [15]

Petition for Divorce, In the Matter of the Marriage of Rosa Anzaldua Hernandez and Carlos Hernandez, No. 83–5525-H (Nueces Cty., 347th Dist. Tex. Nov. 7, 1983). [6]

Petitioner's Objections to State's Proposed Findings of Fact and Conclusions of Law, Ex Parte DeLuna, No. 83-CR–194-A (Nueces Cty., 28th Dist. Tex. Nov. 17, 1989). [15]

Petitioner's Objections to Trial Court's Findings of Fact and Conclusions of Law, Ex Parte DeLuna, No. 83-CR–194-A (Nueces Cty., 28th Dist. Tex. Nov. 22, 1989). [15]

Petitioner's Response to Respondent's Motion for Summary Judgment, DeLuna v. McCotter, No. 86-cv–234 (S. D. Tex. Jan. 23, 1987). [15]

David Petrusaitis, Former Corpus Christi Sheriff's Deputy, Signed Notarized Statement (Mar. 3, 2005). [9]

Plaintiff's Exhibit 4, Vargas v. Diamond Shamrock, No. 84–4951-D, 86–5900-D (Nueces Cty., 105th Dist. Tex. 1988). [11]

Plaintiff's Exhibit 6, Vargas v. Diamond Shamrock, No. 84–4951-D, 86–5900-D (Nueces Cty., 105th Dist. Tex. 1988). [3, 10]

Plaintiff's Exhibit 7, Vargas v. Diamond Shamrock, No. 84–4951-D, 86–5900-D (Nueces Cty., 105th Dist. Tex. 1988). [3, 10]

Plaintiff's Exhibit 8, Vargas v. Diamond Shamrock, No. 84–4951-D, 86–5900-D (Nueces Cty., 105th Dist. Tex. 1988). [3, 10]

Plaintiff's Exhibit 9, Vargas v. Diamond Shamrock, No. 84–4951-D, 86–5900-D (Nueces Cty., 105th Dist. Tex. 1988). [10]

Plaintiff's Exhibit 11, Vargas v. Diamond Shamrock, No. 84–4951-D, 86–5900-D (Nueces Cty., 105th Dist. Tex. June 3, 1988). [1]

Plaintiff's Exhibit 13, Vargas v. Diamond Shamrock, No. 84–4951-D, 86–5900-D (Nueces Cty., 105th Dist. Tex. 1988). [11]

Plaintiff's Exhibit 15, Vargas v. Diamond Shamrock, No. 84–4951-D, 86–5900-D (Nueces Cty., 105th Dist. Tex. June 3, 1988). [1]

Plaintiff's Exhibit 16, Texas v. DeLuna, No. 83-CR–194-A (Nueces Cty., 28th Dist. Tex. July 18, 1983). [2]

Plaintiff's Exhibit 22, Vargas v. Diamond Shamrock, No. 84–4951-D, 86–5900-D (Nueces Cty., 105th Dist. Tex. 1988). [11]

Plaintiff's Exhibit 26, Vargas v. Diamond Shamrock, No. 84–4951-D, 86–5900-D (Nueces Cty., 105th Dist. Tex. 1988). [11]

Plaintiff's Exhibit 29, Vargas v. Diamond Shamrock, No. 84–4951-D, 86–5900-D (Nueces Cty., 105th Dist. Tex. 1988). [4, 11, 13]

Plaintiff's Original Petition, Martinez v. De Pena, No. 83–4893-E (Nueces Cty., 148th Dist. Tex. Oct. 14, 1983). [11]

Plaintiff's Second Request for Production, Vargas v. Diamond Shamrock, No. 84–4951-D, 86–5900-D (Nueces Cty., 105th Dist. Tex. Mar. 25, 1987). [11]

Dr. James R. Plaisted, Clinical Psychologist, Psychological Evaluation of Carlos DeLuna (June 15, 1983). [5, 11, 15]

Plea Bargain Agreement, Texas v. DeLuna, No. f80–8598mq (Nueces Cty., 28th Dist. Tex. June 19, 1980). [5]

Plea of Nolo Contendere, Texas v. DeLuna, No. f80–8598mq (Nueces Cty., 28th Dist. Tex. Sept. 25, 1980). [5]

Police 911 Recording, Trial Transcript, Texas v. DeLuna, No. 83-CR–194-A (Nueces Cty., 28th Dist. Tex. July 18, 1983). [1, 2]

Police Dispatch Tape, Corpus Christi Police Department (Feb. 4, 1983). [1, 2, 3, 5, 13]

Pre-Disposition Investigation for Carlos DeLuna, Al. R. Reyna, Intake Coordinator, Probation Department (June 27, 1978). [5]

Proposed Findings of Fact, Conclusions of Law, and Order, Ex Parte DeLuna (Nueces Cty., 28th Dist. Tex. Nov. 15, 1989). [15]

Protective Order, In re Fidela Gonzalez Hernandez and Javier Hernandez, No. 87–6919-H (Nueces Cty., 347th Dist. Tex. Jan. 27, 1988. [7]

PublicData.com Results for Carlos Ortiz (undated). [8]

D. G. Pulido, Corpus Christi Police Officer, CCPD Arrest Report (Jan. 10, 1980). [9]

Reception of Carlos DeLuna at Ellis Unit of the Texas Department of Corrections (July 26, 1983). [15]

Records of the Nueces County District Attorney's Office Regarding Prosecution of Carlos DeLuna for Murder of Wanda Lopez (Set A Provided by NCDA to Douglas Tinker, Esq., Feb. 24, 2005). [11]

Records of the Nueces County District Attorney's Office Regarding Prosecution of Carlos DeLuna for Murder of Wanda Lopez (Part 1 of Set B Provided by NCDA to James S. Liebman Feb. 25, 2005). [11]

Records of the Nueces County District Attorney's Office Regarding Prosecution of Carlos DeLuna for Murder of Wanda Lopez (Part 2 of Set B Provided by NCDA to James S. Liebman Feb. 25, 2005). [11]

Records of the Nueces County District Attorney's Office Regarding Prosecution of Carlos DeLuna for Murder of Wanda Lopez (Part 3 of Set B Provided by NCDA to James S. Liebman Feb. 25, 2005). [11]

Records of the Nueces County District Attorney's Office Regarding Prosecution of Carlos DeLuna for Murder of Wanda Lopez (Part 4 of Set B Provided by NCDA to James S. Liebman Feb. 25, 2005). [11]

Reindictment, Texas v. Hernandez, No. 86-CR–1032-B (Nueces Cty., 117th Dist. Tex. 1986). [7]

Respondent's Motion for Summary Judgment, DeLuna v. McCotter, No. C–86–234 (S.D. Tex. Nov. 10, 1986). [15]

Respondent's Motion to Dismiss for Abuse of the Writ and, Alternatively, Answer, Motion for Summary Judgment, and Supporting Brief, DeLuna v. Lynaugh, No. C–89–336 (S.D. Tex. Nov. 30, 1989). [15]

Respondent's Motion to Expedite, DeLuna v. Lynaugh, No. C–86–234 (S.D. Tex., Feb. 3, 1988). [15]

Respondent's Original Answer to Application for Writ of Habeas Corpus, Application for Writ of Habeas Corpus, Ex Parte DeLuna, No. 83-CR–194-A (Nueces Cty., 28th Dist. Tex. Nov. 13, 1989). [15]

Report of Vocational Training Completion for Michael Ortiz, Texas Department of Corrections (Aug. 5, 1991). [8]

Review Committee, Corpus Christi Ind. Sch. Dist., Special Education: Admission, Review and Dismissal Committee Report on Carlos DeLuna (Apr. 9, 1976). [5]

Paul Rivera, Corpus Christi Police Detective, CCPD Arrest Report (May 4, 1980). [9]

Paul Rivera, Corpus Christi Police Detective, Supplementary Report (Nov. 30, 1979). [7]

Paul Rivera, Corpus Christi Police Detective, Supplementary Report (Dec. 14, 1979). [7]

Paul Rivera, Corpus Christi Police Detective, Supplementary Report (July 16, 1986). [7]

Ruben Rivera, Nueces County Deputy Constable, Supplementary Report (Feb. 7, 1983). [2, 10, 11]

Ruben Rivera, Nueces County Deputy Constable, Supplementary Report (Feb. 8, 1983). [2, 10, 11]

[First Name Unknown] Rodriguez, Corpus Christi Police Officer, Supplementary Report (undated, June 19 or 20, 1978). [5]

Dr. Joseph C. Rupp, Postmortem Examination upon the Body of Dalia Sauceda (Nov. 20, 1979). [6]

Duncan Ryan, Teacher, Corpus Christi Independent School District, Student Referral for Special Services for Carlos DeLuna (Undated). [5]

Governor George Ryan, Speech at Northwestern University College of Law (Jan. 11, 2003), http://www.stopcapitalpunishment.org/ryans_speech.html. [E]

Mark Schauer, Corpus Christi Police Officer, Supplementary Report (Feb. 8, 1983). [2, 3, 10, 11, 13, E]

Mark Schauer, Corpus Christi Police Officer, Supplementary Report (Undated). [1, 2, 3, 10, 11, 13]

Schedule A, In re Hector De Pena, Voluntary Case: Debtor's Petition, No. 84-D2129-C–4 (Bankr. S.D. Tex. Dec. 12, 1984). [11]

Steve Schiwetz Law Offices, Yellow Pages, http://www.yellowpages.com/corpus -christi-tx/mip/steve-schiwetz-law-offices–15648527 (last visited Mar. 30, 2012). [E]

L. Scrna, Corpus Christi Police Officer, CCPD Arrest Report (Apr. 3, 1983). [9]

Sentence, Texas v. DeLuna, No. f80–8598mq (Nueces Cty., 28th Dist. Tex. Sept. 25, 1980). [5]

Sentence After Mandate, Texas v. DeLuna, No. 83-CR–194-A (Nueces Cty., 28th Dist. Tex. July 23, 1986). [15]

Shamrock Inventory "Re-check" Photo P2170097, Vargas v. Diamond Shamrock, No. 84–4951-D, 86–5900-D (Nueces Cty., 105th Dist. Tex. Feb. 5, 1983). [4]

M. Shedd, Corpus Christi Police Sergeant, Supplementary Report (Feb. 6, 1983). [2, 3, 11]

Social and Criminal History for Carlos Hernandez, Texas Department of Corrections (Mar. 15, 1990). [6, 17]

State's Announcement of Ready, Texas v. Hernandez, No. 86-CR–1032-B (Nucccs Cty., 117th Dist. Tex. 1986). [7]

State's Exhibit 4, Trial Transcript, Texas v. DeLuna, No. 83-CR–194-A (Nueces Cty., 28th Dist. Tex. July 18, 1983). [11, 13]

State's Exhibit 5, Trial Transcript, Texas v. DeLuna, No. 83-CR–194-A (Nueces Cty., 28th Dist. Tex. July 8, 1983). [13]

State's Exhibit 9, Trial Transcript, Texas v. DeLuna, No. 83-CR–194-A (Nueces Cty., 28th Dist. Tex. July 18, 1983). [13]

State's Exhibit 10, Trial Transcript, Texas v. DeLuna, No. 83-CR–194-A (Nueces Cty., 28th Dist. Tex. July 18, 1983). [13]

State's Exhibit 11, Trial Transcript, Texas v. DeLuna, No. 83-CR–194-A (Nueces Cty., 28th Dist. Tex. July 15, 1983). [13]

State's Exhibit 20, Trial Transcript, Texas v. DeLuna, No. 83-CR–194-A (Nueces Cty., 28th Dist. Tex. July 15, 1983). [2]

State's Exhibit 21, Trial Transcript, Texas v. DeLuna, No. 83-CR–194-A (Nueces
    Cty., 28th Dist. Tex. July 15, 1983). [2]
State's Exhibit 23, Trial Transcript, Texas v. DeLuna, No. 83-CR–194-A (Nueces
    Cty., 28th Dist. Tex. July 15, 1983). [2]
State's Exhibit 25, Trial Transcript, Texas v. DeLuna, No. 83-CR–194-A (Nueces
    Cty., 28th Dist. Tex. July 18, 1983). [13]
State's Exhibit 26, Trial Transcript, Texas v. DeLuna, No. 83-CR–194-A (Nueces
    Cty., 28th Dist. Tex. July 15, 1983). [13]
State's Exhibit 30, Trial Transcript, Texas v. DeLuna, No. 83-CR–194-A (Nueces
    Cty., 28th Dist. Tex. July 18, 1983). [13]
State's Exhibit 31, Trial Transcript, Texas v. DeLuna, No. 83-CR–194-A (Nueces
    Cty., 28th Dist. Tex. July 18, 1983). [13]
State's Exhibit 32, Trial Transcript, Texas v. DeLuna, No. 83-CR–194-A (Nueces
    Cty., 28th Dist. Tex. July 18, 1983). [13]
State's Exhibit 33, Trial Transcript, Texas v. DeLuna, No. 83-CR–194-A (Nueces
    Cty., 28th Dist. Tex. July 18, 1983). [13]
State's Exhibit 35, Trial Transcript, Texas v. DeLuna, No. 83-CR–194-A (Nueces
    Cty., 28th Dist. Tex. July 18, 1983). [13]
Statement of Financial Affairs for Debtor Engaged in Business, In re Hector De
    Pena, Voluntary Case: Debtor's Petition, No. 84-D2129-C–4 (Bankr. S.D. Tex.
    Dec. 12, 1984). [11]
Stipulation, Texas v. DeLuna, No. 83-CR–194-A (Nueces Cty., 28th Dist. Tex.
    July 15, 1983). [2]
Stipulation of Evidence, Texas v. DeLuna, No. f80–8598mq (Nueces Cty., 28th
    Dist. Tex. Sept. 25, 1980). [5]
Subpoena of Estella Flores Jimenez, Texas v. DeLuna, No. 83-CR–194-A (Nueces
    Cty., 28th Dist. Tex. Sept. 9, 1983). [15]
Suggestion for Rehearing En Banc, DeLuna v. Lynaugh, 890 F.2d 720 (5th Cir.
    1989). [15]
Summary of Debts and Property, In re Hector De Pena, Voluntary Case: Debtor's
    Petition, No. 84-D2129-C–4 (filed Dec. 12, 1984). [11]
Summary of Efrain Hernandez Death Record at Nueces County Clerk's Office
    (July 7, 2005). [6]
Supplementary Call Card, Corpus Christi Police Department (Feb. 4, 1983). [11]
Temporary Orders, In re the Marriage of Rosa Anzaldua Hernandez and Carlos
    Hernandez (Nueces Cty., 347th Dist. Tex. Dec. 13, 1983). [8]

Texas Department of Criminal Justice, Board of Pardons and Paroles, Certificate of Parole for Carlos Hernandez (Dec. 7, 1977). [9]

Texas Department of Criminal Justice, Board of Pardons and Paroles Division, Minutes from Feb. 26, 1975 to May 18, 2000, Carlos Hernandez. [9]

Texas Department of Criminal Justice, Board of Pardons and Paroles Division, Minutes of Carlos Hernandez (May 27, 1980). [9]

Texas Department of Criminal Justice, Board of Pardons and Paroles, Notice of Alleged Violation of Release, Carlos Hernandez, List of Court Records (Dec. 6, 1983). [9]

Texas Department of Criminal Justice, Clemency and Parole System, Minutes Browse Screen, Name: Hernandez, Carlos (Aug. 13, 2004). [9]

Texas Department of Criminal Justice, Clemency and Parole System Records for Carlos Hernandez (Aug. 13, 2004). [9, 17]

Texas Department of Criminal Justice, Crime Summary for Carlos DeLuna (July 26, 1983). [11]

Texas Department of Criminal Justice, Executed Offenders, http://www.tdcj.state. tx.us/death_row/dr_executed_offenders.html (last visited Mar. 30, 2012). [E]

Texas Department of Criminal Justice, Offender Information Last Statement for Carlos DeLuna (Dec. 7, 1989), http://www.tdcj.state.tx.us/death_row/dr _info/delunacarloslast.html. [E]

Texas Department of Criminal Justice, Prison Admission Record, Texas Department of Corrections Bureau of Records and Identification (July 26, 1983). [9]

Texas Department of Public Safety, Criminal History for Carlos DeLuna (1982). [5]

Texas Legislature, SCR 14, 69th Regular Session (signed into law June 13, 1985). [P]

Texas Senate Res. No. 386, In Memory of Edward S. Garza (Mar. 5, 2007). [E]

Texas v. DeLuna Docket, Texas v. DeLuna, No. 83-CR–194-A (Nueces Cty., 28th Dist. Tex. Feb. 17, 1983). [11]

Texas v. Plaisted, Cases No. 92-CR–1926-H, 92-CR–1927-H, 92-CR–1928-H, 92-CR–025-H (Dec 7, 1995). [5]

Tocayo—Definition, Merriam-Webster.com, http://www.merriam-webster.com/ spanish/tocayo (last visited Jan. 30, 2012). [8]

Transcript of Wanda Lopez's Phone Call to Corpus Christi Police Department on Feb. 4, 1983, at 8:09 (Feb. 10, 1983) (version that appears in Corpus Christi Police Department records). [1, 2, 11, 13]

Transcript of Wanda Lopez's Phone Call to Corpus Christi Police Department on Feb. 4, 1983, at 8:09 (Feb. 10, 1983) (version that appears in Nueces County district attorney's records). [1, 11, 13]

True Bill of Indictment, Texas v. DeLuna, No. f80–8598mq (Tex. Dist. Ct. July 7, 1980). [5]

B. T. Uhler, Corpus Christi Police Officer, CCPD Arrest Report (July 16, 1987). [9]

Unit Classification Review Form for Carlos DeLuna, Texas Department of Corrections (Apr. 3, 1984). [14, 15]

United States Department of Justice, Federal Bureau of Investigation, Identification Division, Identification Record for Carlos De Luna Based on FBI or SID Identification Number (May 25, 1983). [5]

Signed Statement of Louis Richard Vargas, Brother of Wanda Jean Vargas Lopez (June 2006). [E]

R. Vasquez, Corpus Christi Police Sergeant, CCPD Arrest Report (May 9, 1985). [9]

R. H. Veregara, Corpus Christi Police Officer, CCPD Arrest Report (May 25, 1996). [9]

Voluntary Statement of Clara Carson, Store Clerk at Circle K Allegedly Robbed by Carlos Hernandez, Corpus Christi Police Department (Apr. 5, 1972). [6]

Waiver of Indictment, Texas v. DeLuna, No. f80–8598mq (Nueces Cty., 28th Dist. Tex. Sept. 25, 1980). [5]

What does the Spanish word "tocayo" or "tocallo" mean in English?—Question, Yahoo! Answers, http://answers.yahoo.com/question/index?qid=20080517113 451AA5AQ24 (last visited Jan. 30, 2012). [8]

Witness Subpoena for Carlos Hernandez, No. 83-CR–194-A (Nueces Cty., 28th Dist. Tex. July 6, 1983). [9]

R. Yatu, Investigating Officer, City Vehicle Accidents (Jan. 13, 1980). [5]

Dina Ybañez, Neighbor of Carlos Hernandez, Statement to Corpus Christi Police Department (Apr. 16, 1989). [17]

W. H. Yeager, Corpus Christi Police Officer, CCPD Arrest Report (May 5, 1987). [9]

## VIDEOTAPE AND AUDIOTAPE INTERVIEWS

Transcribed Videotape Interview with Janie Adrian, Neighbor of Carlos Hernandez, in Corpus Christi, Texas (Dec. 5, 2004). [6, 8, 9]

Transcribed Audiotape Interview with Kevan Baker, Eyewitness to Attack on Wanda Lopez, in Jackson, Mich. (Nov. 22, 2004). [2, 3, 10]

Transcribed Videotape Interview with Mary Ann Perales Benavides, Witness Against Carlos DeLuna, in Corpus Christi, Texas (Feb. 23, 2005). [11]

Transcribed Videotape Interview with Karen Boudrie-Evers, Corpus Christi Television Reporter, in Dallas, Texas (Feb. 28, 2005). [P, 5, 9, 10, 11, 12, 13, 14, 15, 16, E]

Transcribed Videotape Interview with Marcella Brown, Friend of Carlos Hernandez, in Corpus Christi, Texas (Feb. 24, 2005). [6, 7, 8]

Transcribed Videotape Interview with Eddie Cruz, Private Investigator for Defendant Jesse Garza in Dahlia Sauceda Case, in Corpus Christi, Texas (Feb. 25, 2005). [6, 7]

Transcribed Videotape Interview with Hector De Peña, Jr., Trial Lawyer for Carlos DeLuna, in Corpus Christi, Texas (Feb. 23, 2005) [2, 6, 11, 12, 14, 15, E]

Transcribed Videotape Interview with Rosie Esquivel, Girlfriend of Carlos DeLuna While He Was on Death Row, in Garland, Texas (Feb. 27, 2005). [5, 11, 15, 16, E]

Transcribed Videotape Interview with Eddie Garza, Corpus Christi Police Detective (Retired), in Corpus Christi, Texas (Dec. 6, 2004). [P, 5, 6, 9, 10, 11, 12]

Transcribed Videotape Interview with Diana Gomez, Girlfriend of Carlos Hernandez, in Corpus Christi, Texas (Dec. 7, 2004). [6, 7]

Transcribed Videotape Interview with Vicky Gutierrez, Half-Sister of Carlos DeLuna, in Garland, Texas (Feb. 27, 2005). [5, 11, 15, 16, E]

Transcribed Videotape Interview with Pricilla Jaramillo, Niece of Carlos Hernandez, in Corpus Christi, Texas (Dec. 4, 2004). [6, 8]

Transcribed Videotape Interview with Jon Kelly, Lawyer for Carlos Hernandez, in Corpus Christi, Texas (Dec. 9, 2004). [P, 5, 6, 7, 9, 10, 11, 12, 15]

Transcribed Videotape Interview with Becky Nesmith, Cousin of Wanda Lopez, in Corpus Christi, Texas (Dec. 8, 2004). [1, 4, 13]

Transcribed Videotape Interview with Yolanda Ortiz, Owner of Casino Club, in Corpus Christi, Texas (Dec. 5, 2004). [5, 6, 8]

Transcribed Videotape Interview with Albert Peña, Lawyer for Jesse Garza in Dahlia Sauceda Case, in Corpus Christi, Texas (Feb. 25, 2005). [6, 7, 8, 11, 12]

Transcribed Videotape Interview with Rev. Carroll Pickett, Texas Death House Chaplain, in Huntsville, Texas (Feb. 26, 2005). [P, 15, 16, E]

Transcribed Videotape Interview with Rose Rhoton, Sister of Carlos DeLuna, in Houston, Texas (Feb. 26, 2005). [3, 5, 6, 9, 11, 12, 13, 15, 16, E]

Transcribed Videotape Interview with Ruben Rivera, Nueces County Deputy Constable, in Robstown, Texas (Dec. 7, 2004). [2]

Transcribed Videotape Interview with Rene Rodriguez, Lawyer for Wanda Lopez's Family in Suit Against Diamond Shamrock, in Corpus Christi, Texas (Dec. 8, 2005). [1, 11]

Transcribed Videotape Interview with Gloria Sanchez, Girlfriend of Carlos Hernandez, in Corpus Christi (Feb. 23, 2005). [6, 7, 9]

Transcribed Videotape Interview with Freddy Schilling, Brother-in-Law of Carlos Hernandez, in Corpus Christi, Texas (Feb. 24, 2005). [P, 6, 7, 8, 9, E]

Transcribed Videotape Interview with Robert Stange, Shamrock Gas Station Manager, in Fredericksburg, Texas (Feb. 24, 2005). [1, 2, 3, 4, 10]

Transcribed Videotape Interview with Beatrice Tapia, Neighbor of Carlos Hernandez, in Corpus Christi, Texas (Dec. 9, 2004). [6, 8]

Transcribed Videotape Interview with Mary Margaret Tapia, Girlfriend of Carlos Hernandez, in Corpus Christi, Texas (Dec. 4, 2004). [6, 8]

Transcribed Videotape Interview of Richard Louis Vargas, Brother of Wanda Lopez, in Corpus Christi, Texas (Dec. 4, 2004). [1, 11, 13, 15, 16, E]

Transcribed Videotape Interview of Kristen Weaver, Posttrial Lawyer for Carlos DeLuna, in Dallas, Texas (Feb. 28, 2005). [15, 16]

Transcribed Videotape Interview with Dina Ybañez, Neighbor of Carlos Hernandez (Dec. 7, 2004). [6, 7, 8, 15, 17]

Videotaped Interview Exhibit A. [9]

Videotaped Interview Exhibit B. [9]

Videotaped Interview Exhibit C. [9]

### NOTES FROM OTHER INTERVIEWS

Bruce Whitman's Notes on Interview with Janie Adrian, Neighbor of Carlos Hernandez (Sept. 23–24 and 27, 2004). [6, 7, 8]

Lauren Eskenazi and Sita Sovin's Notes on Interview with Janie Adrian, Neighbor of Carlos Hernandez (Oct. 29, 2004). [6, 8]

James S. Liebman's Notes on Interview with Janie Adrian, Neighbor of Carlos Hernandez (Dec. 4, 2004). [6, 8]

Peso Chavez's Notes on Attempt to Interview Rosa Anzaldua (Feb. 18, 2005). [E]

Susan Montez's, Notes on Interview with Mary Arredando, Half-Sister of Carlos DeLuna (July 26, 2004). [5]

Bruce Whitman's Notes on Interview with Johnny Arsuaga, Cousin of Carlos Hernandez (Nov. 3, 2005). [6, 8, 17, E]

Peso Chavez's Notes on Interviews with Linda Perales Ayala, Stepmother of Pricilla Hernandez Jaramillo and Ex-Wife of Manuel DeLuna (Feb. 22–26, 2004). [8, 11]

Susan Montez's Notes on Interview with Linda Perales Ayala, Stepmother of Pricilla Hernandez Jaramillo and Ex-Wife of Manuel DeLuna (July 20, 2004). [5, 6, 8]

James S. Liebman's Notes on Bruce Whitman's Interview with Linda Perales Ayala, Stepmother of Pricilla Hernandez Jaramillo and Ex-Wife of Manuel DeLuna (Aug. 11, 2004). [8]

Sita Sovin and Lauren Eskenazi's Notes on Interview with Linda Perales Ayala, Stepmother of Pricilla Hernandez Jaramillo and Ex-Wife of Manuel DeLuna (Sept. 14, 2004). [8]

Peso Chavez's Notes on Interviews with Mary Ann Perales Benavides, Witness Against Carlos DeLuna (Feb. 22–26, 2004). [11]

Susan Montez's Notes on Interview with Mary Ann Perales Benavides, Witness Against Carlos DeLuna (July 16, 2004). [8]

Lauren Eskenazi and Sita Sovin's Notes on Interview with Mary Ann Perales Benavides, Witness Against Carlos DeLuna, and Ruben Benavides, Mary Ann's Husband (Sept. 15, 2004). [6, 9]

James S. Liebman's Notes on Interview with Linda Carrico, Corpus Christi Newspaper Reporter (Sept. 2004). [11, 15, E]

Sita Sovin and Lauren Eskenazi's Notes on Interview with Beatriz Castro, Friend of Fidela Hernandez (Oct. 23, 2004). [6, 7, 8]

Peso Chavez's Notes on Interview with Shirley Curric, Friend of Carlos Hernandez (Aug. 17, 2004). [9]

Bruce Whitman's Notes on Interview with Manuel DeLuna, Brother of Carlos DeLuna (Aug. 11, 2004). [8, E]

James S. Liebman's Notes on Bruce Whitman Interview with Manuel DeLuna, Brother of Carlos DeLuna (Aug. 11, 2004). [8, 9, 16]

James S. Liebman's Notes on Interview with Manuel DeLuna, Brother of Carlos DeLuna (Aug. 17, 2004). [5, 6, 8]

James S. Liebman's Notes on Interview with Hector De Peña, Trial Lawyer for Carlos DeLuna (Dec. 3, 2004). [11, 15]

James S. Liebman's Notes on Sita Sovin's Interview with Mary Ellis, Friend of Carlos Hernandez (Oct. 22, 2004). [9]

Tamara Theiss's Notes on Interview with Olivia Escobedo, Corpus Christi Police Detective in Wanda Lopez and Dahlia Sauceda Cases (Feb. 27. 2005). [P, 2, 3, 4, 5, 7, 9, 10, 11]

James S. Liebman's Notes on Sita Sovin and Lauren Eskenazi Interview with Jesse Escochea, Corpus Christi Police Dispatcher (Feb. 11, 2005). [2]

Peso Chavez's Notes on Interview with Rosie Esquivel, Girlfriend of Carlos De-Luna While He Was on Death Row (Aug. 18, 2004). [11, 16]

Bruce Whitman's Notes on Interview with Richard Garcia, Brother-in-Law of Margie Tapia (July 22, 2005). [6]

Bruce Whitman's Notes on Interview with Eddie Garza, Corpus Christi Police Detective (Aug. 23, 2004). [11]

Bruce Whitman and James S. Liebman's Notes on Interview with Eddie Garza (Aug. 25, 2004). [6, 8, 9, 10, 11]

Bruce Whitman's Notes on Interview with Jesse Garza, Defendant in Dahlia Sauceda Killing (Aug. 12, 2004). [6, 7]

Peso Chavez's Notes on Interview with Michelle Garza, Friend of Carlos Hernandez (Aug. 28, 2004). [7, 8]

Bruce Whitman's Notes on Interview with Pete Gonzalez, Shamrock Gas Station Area Supervisor (Sept. 23, 2004). [3]

Bruce Whitman's Notes on Interview with Fidela Hernandez, Mother of Carlos Hernandez (Aug. 7, 2004). [6, 7]

Sita Sovin and Lauren Eskenazi's Notes on Interview with Fidela Hernandez, Mother of Carlos Hernandez (Sept. 14, 2004). [8]

Sita Sovin and Lauren Eskenazi's Notes on Interview with Fidela Hernandez, Mother of Carlos Hernandez (Sept. 15, 2004). [P, 6, 8]

Sita Sovin and Lauren Eskenazi's Notes on Interview with Fidela Hernandez, Mother of Carlos Hernandez (Sept. 16, 2004). [6]

Lauren Eskenazi and Sita Sovin's Notes on Interview with Sylvia Hernandez, Sister-in-Law of Carlos Hernandez (Oct. 27, 2004). [6]

Sita Sovin and Lauren Eskenazi's Notes on Interview with Joe Hinajosa, Former Assistant Manager at Sigmor Station (Oct. 25, 2004). [4]

James S. Liebman and Peso Chavez's Notes on Interview with Rita Hull, Friend of the Hernandez Family (July 22, 2004). [6, 7, 8]

Sita Sovin and Lauren Eskenazi's Notes on Interview with Rita Hull, Friend of the Hernandez Family (Sept. 14, 2004). [6, 7, 8]

James S. Liebman's Notes on Interview with Rita Hull, Friend of the Hernandez Family (Nov. 4, 2005). [6, 8]

Bruce Whitman's Notes on Interview with Joel Infante, Corpus Christi Police Identification Technician (July 25, 2005). [10]

Bruce Whitman's Notes on Interview with Mary Jackson, Mother of Cindy Maxwell (Aug. 9, 2004). [8]

Bruce Whitman's Notes on Interview with Pricilla Hernandez Jaramillo, Niece of Carlos Hernandez (Aug. 9, 2004). [6, 8, E]

Sita Sovin and Lauren Eskenazi's Notes on Interview with Pricilla Hernandez Jaramillo, Niece of Carlos Hernandez (Sept. 16, 2004). [7, 8, 9]

Sita Sovin and Lauren Eskenazi's Notes on Interview with Priscilla Hernandez Jaramillo, Niece of Carlos Hernandez (Oct. 29, 2004). [7, 8]

James S. Liebman's Notes on Interview with Pricilla Hernandez Jaramillo, Niece of Carlos Hernandez (Dec. 3, 2004). [6, 7, 8, E]

Peso Chavez and James Liebman's Notes on Interview with Jon Kelly, Lawyer for Carlos Hernandez (Aug. 16, 18, 20, 2004). [5, 6, 7, 8, 9, 11, 12]

James S. Liebman and Bruce Whitman's Notes on Interview with Jon Kelly, Lawyer for Carlos Hernandez (Aug. 24, 2004). [10, 11]

James S. Liebman's Notes on Interview with Jon Kelly, Lawyer for Carlos Hernandez (Jan. 21, 2005). [9, 15]

James S. Liebman's Notes on Interview with James Lawrence, Trial and Appellate Lawyer for Carlos DeLuna (July 12, 2004). [11]

James S. Liebman's Notes on Interview with James Lawrence, Trial and Appellate Lawyer for Carlos DeLuna (Feb. 25, 2005). [11, 12]

Peso Chavez's Notes on Interview with Gilbert Limon, Acquaintance of Carlos Hernandez (Aug. 12, 2004). [6]

James S. Liebman's Notes on Peso Chavez Interview with Gilbert Limon, Acquaintance of Carlos Hernandez (Aug. 12, 2004). [6]

James S. Liebman's Notes on Interview with Bea Martinez, Sister of Fidela Hernandez (Nov. 3, 2005). [6]

Bruce Whitman's Notes on Interview with Maria Martinez, Neighbor of Carlos Hernandez (July 22, 2005). [6, 8]

Peso Chavez's Notes on Interview with Maria Martinez, Neighbor of Carlos Hernandez (Dec. 2, 2005). [8]

Susan Montez's Notes on Interview with Cindy Maxwell, Girlfriend of Carlos Hernandez (July 22 and 26, 2004). [8, 17]

Bruce Whitman's Notes on Interview with Cindy Maxwell, Girlfriend of Carlos Hernandez (Aug. 8, 2004). [8]

James S. Liebman's Notes on Interview with Bill May, Corpus Christi Criminal Defense Lawyer and Former Assistant District Attorney (July 13, 2004). [5, 6, 7, 11, 15]

Bruce Whitman, Notes on Interview with Robert Mayorga, Corpus Christi Police Officer Who Dated Wanda Lopez (Nov. 18, 2004). [1]

Bruce Whitman's Notes on Interview with Becky and Jesse Nesmith, Cousins of Wanda Lopez (Sept. 28, 2004). [4, 13]

Sita Sovin and Lauren Eskenazi's Notes on Interview with Becky Nesmith, Cousin of Wanda Lopez (Oct. 26, 2004). [4, 13]

Bruce Whitman's Notes on Interview with Pedro Olivarez, Witness Against Jesse Garza in Trial for Murdering Dahlia Sauceda (Aug. 20, 2004, and Mar. 1, 2005). [6, 7]

Bruce Whitman's Notes on Interview with Yolanda Ortiz, Owner of Casino Club (Sept. 21, 2004). [6, 7, 8]

Susan Montez's Notes on Interview with Toni Peña, Half-Sister of Carlos DeLuna (July 25, 2004). [5, 16]

James S. Liebman's Notes on Interview with Cruz Perez and Lisa Garza, Neighbors of Carlos Hernandez in the Mid-1980s (Nov. 3, 2005). [6, 8]

James S. Liebman's Notes on Interview with Rev. Carroll Pickett, Texas Death House Chaplain (July 11, 2004). [16]

Susan Montez's Notes on Interview with Rev. Carroll Pickett, Texas Death House Chaplain (July 24, 2004). [16]

James S. Liebman's Notes on Interview with Rose Rhoton, Sister of Carlos De-Luna (July 11, 2004). [5]

Susan Montez's Notes on Interview with Rose Rhoton, Sister of Carlos DeLuna (July 17, 2004). [5]

James S. Liebman's Notes on Interview with Paul Rivera, Corpus Christi Police Detective (July 14, 2004). [6, 7, 8, 9]

James S. Liebman and Bruce Whitman's Notes on Interview with Paul Rivera, Corpus Christi Police Detective, and Elmer Cox, Nueces County Sheriff's Deputy (Aug. 25, 2004). [9, 10]

Bruce Whitman's Notes on Interview with Glenda Ruggles, Corpus Christi Police Department 911 Operator (Nov. 17, 2005). [10]

Peso Chavez's Notes on Interview with Gloria Sanchez, Girlfriend of Carlos Hernandez (July 21 and 23, 2004). [6, 7, 8]

James S. Liebman's Notes on Peso Chavez's Interview with Gloria Sanchez, Girlfriend of Carlos Hernandez (July 22 and 26, 2004). [9]

Peso Chavez and James S. Liebman's Notes on Interview with Gloria Sanchez, Girlfriend of Carlos Hernandez (Aug. 16, 2004). [6, 7, 9]

Bruce Whitman's Notes on Interview with Eddie Schilling, Nephew of Carlos Hernandez (Aug. 8–9, 2004). [6]

Peso Chavez's Notes on Interview with Freddy Schilling, Brother-in-Law of Carlos Hernandez (Aug. 5, 2004). [P, 6, 7, 8, 9, E]

James S. Liebman's Notes on Peso Chavez's Interview with Freddy Schilling, Brother-in-Law of Carlos Hernandez (Aug. 5, 2004). [9]

Peso Chavez's Notes on Interview with John Michael Schilling, Son of Freddy and Paula Schilling (Aug. 12, 2004). [6, 7, E]

James S. Liebman's Notes on Peso Chavez's Interview with John Michael Schilling, Son of Freddy and Paula Schilling (Aug. 11, 2004). [6]

Danalynn Recer's Notes on Interview with Elias Sissamis, Half-Brother of Louis Sissamis (Aug. 20, 2004). [6]

Bruce Whitman's Notes on Interview with Aida Sosa, Girlfriend of Carlos De-Luna (Sept. 27, 2004). [5]

Bruce Whitman's Notes on Interview with Beatrice Tapia, Neighbor of Carlos Hernandez (Sept. 28, 2004). [8]

Bruce Whitman's Notes on Interview with Mary Margaret Tapia, Girlfriend of Carlos Hernandez (Sept. 24 and 26, 2004). [6, 8]

Lauren Eskenazi and Sita Sovin's Notes on Interview with Mary Margaret Tapia, Girlfriend of Carlos Hernandez (Oct. 28, 2004). [6]

Sita Sovin and Lauren Eskenazi's Notes on Interview with Carmen Taylor, Former Employee of Shamrock Gas Station (Oct. 24, 2004). [1, 4]

James S. Liebman's Notes on Sita Sovin and Lauren Eskenazi's Interview with Carmen Taylor, Former Employee of Shamrock Gas Station (Nov. 7, 2004). [4]

Kate Wagner McCoy's Notes on Interview with James J. Vanacek, Fire Department Emergency Medical Technician (Mar. 31, 2005). [2]

Bruce Whitman's Notes on Interview with Richard Louis Vargas, Brother of Wanda Lopez (Nov. 21, 2004). [E]

James S. Liebman's Notes on Bruce Whitman's Interview with Carolyn Vargas (now Vasquez), Nueces County Constable (Nov. 23, 2004). [2]

Kate Weisburd's Notes on Interview with Teresita Perez Vela, Wife of Beto Vela (May 13, 2005). [8]

James S. Liebman's Notes on Interview with Robert Veregara, Corpus Christi Police Officer (Nov. 2, 2004). [3, 9]

Peso Chavez's Notes on Interview with Andres Ybañez, Neighbor of Carlos Hernandez (Aug. 4, 2004). [6]

Peso Chavez's Notes on Interview with Dina Ybañez, Neighbor of Carlos Hernandez (June 14 and 15, 2004). [6, 7, 8, 15, 17]

James S. Liebman's Notes on Interview with Dina Ybañez, Neighbor of Carlos Hernandez (July 13, 2004). [6, 8, 15, 17]

James S. Liebman's Notes on Steve Mills's Interview with Dina Ybañez, Neighbor of Carlos Hernandez (Nov. 3, 2005). [7, 8, 17]

Peso Chavez's Notes on Interview with Johnny Ybañez, Neighbor of Carlos Hernandez (Aug. 4, 2004). [6, 7, 15, 17]

Bruce Whitman's Notes on Interview with Lina Zapata, Friend of Carlos Hernandez (Nov. 20, 2004). [6, 8]

### NEWSPAPER AND MAGAZINE ARTICLES, TELEVISION BROADCASTS, AND DOCUMENTARIES

*Acquitted Man Hopes Arrest of Another Man Will Help Clear His Name*, Corpus Christi Caller-Times, July 25, 1986. [7, 15]

Anderson Cooper 360° (CNN television broadcast Mar. 10, 2005) (transcript http://transcripts.cnn.com/TRANSCRIPTS/0503/10/acd.01.html). [2]

Ken Armstrong and Steve Mills, *Death Penalty Support Erodes*, Chi. Trib., Mar. 7, 2000, http://articles.chicagotribune.com/2000-03-07/news/0003070315_1_death-penalty-tribune-poll-illinois-voters. [E]

Ken Armstrong and Steve Mills, *Death Row Justice Derailed: Bias, Errors and Incompetence in Capital Cases Have Turned Illinois' Harshest Punishment into Its Least Credible*, Chi. Trib., Nov. 14, 1999, http://articles.chicagotribune.com/1999-11-14/news/9911150001_1_death-row-capital-cases-capital-punishment. [E]

Ken Armstrong and Steve Mills, *Inept Defenses Cloud Verdicts: With Their Lives at Stake, Defendants in Illinois Capital Trials Need the Best Attorneys Available. But They Often Get Some of the Worst*, Chi. Trib., Nov. 15, 1999, http://articles.chicagotribune.com/1999-11-15/news/9911150176_1_new-trial-or-sentencing-illinois-supreme-court-sentencing-hearing. [E]

Associated Press, *Inmate Gains Stay 12 Hours Before Set Execution*, Oct. 15, 1986. [15]

Associated Press, *Inmate Given Reprieve Hours Before Execution*, Dallas Herald Times, Oct. 15, 1986. [15]

Associated Press, *Parolee Given Death Penalty for Murder*, July 22, 1983. [14]

Associated Press, *Texan Is Put to Death by Injection for Killing Woman in a Robbery*, N.Y. Times, Dec. 8, 1989, http://www.nytimes.com/1989/12/08/us/texan-is-put-to-death-by-injection-for-killing-woman-in-a-robbery.html. [13, 15, 16]

Allen Ault, *I Ordered Death in Georgia*, Daily Beast, Sept. 25, 2011, http://www.thedailybeast.com/newsweek/2011/09/25/ordering-death-in-georgia-prisons.html. [E]

Libby Averyt, *City Man Is Jailed in 7-Year-Old Murder Case*, Corpus Christi Caller-Times, July 25, 1986. [7, 15]

Raymond Bonner and Sara Rimer, *A Closer Look at Five Cases That Resulted in Executions of Texas Inmates*, N.Y. Times, May 14, 2000, http://partners

.nytimes.com/library/politics/camp/051400wh-bush-cases.html?scp=1&sq =%22david%20spence%22&st=cse. [E]

Karen Boudrie, Report (NewsWatch 10 broadcast). [11]

Karen Boudrie, Transcribed Television Reports on DeLuna/Lopez Case (1984–1985). [13, E]

Ethan Bronner, *Lawyers, Saying DNA Cleared Inmate, Pursue Access to Data*, N.Y. Times, Jan. 3, 2013, http://www.nytimes.com/2013/01/04/us/lawyers-saying -dna-cleared-inmate-pursue-access-to-data.html? [E]

Linda Carrico, *City Man Gets Execution Date for '83 Slaying*, Corpus Christi Caller-Times, July 24, 1986. [11, 15]

Linda Carrico, *Death Row Inmate Misses Appointment with Death*, Corpus Christi Caller-Times, Oct. 15, 1986. [11]

Linda Carrico, *DeLuna Guilty, Could Be Given Death Sentence*, Corpus Christi Caller-Times, July 21, 1983. [13]

Linda Carrico, *DeLuna Is Scheduled to Be Executed Tomorrow*, Corpus Christi Caller-Times, Oct. 14, 1986. [11, 12, 15, E]

Linda Carrico, *Judge Grants DeLuna Stay of Execution*, Corpus Christi Caller-Times, Oct. 15, 1986. [13, 15]

Linda Carrico, *Judge Sentences DeLuna to Die*, Corpus Christi Caller-Times, July 22, 1983. [14]

Cindy V. Culp, *Lake Waco Murders: Efforts Underway to Exonerate Man Convicted of Famed Slayings*, Waco Tribune-Herald, May 5. 2011, http://www.wacotrib .com/registration/subscription-landing/?rurl=http%3A%2F%2Fwww.waco trib.com%2Fnews%2FLake-Waco-murders-Efforts-underway-to-exonerate -man-convicted-of-famed-slayings.html. [17, E]

Bryan Dakss, *Urban Shootout Raises Eyebrows: Police Use of Firearms in Focus After Gun Battle*, The Early Show, May 10, 2005, http://www.cbsnews.com/ stories/2005/05/10/earlyshow/main694133.shtml?tag=mncol;lst;1. [2]

Kathy Fair, *Condemned Man Appeals Case to Supreme Court*, Hous. Chron., Dec. 6, 1989. [10, 15]

Kathy Fair, *DeLuna Waits for Execution in '83 Murder*, Hous. Chron., Dec. 6, 1989. [11, 15, 16]

Kathy Fair, *Each Tick of Clock Increases Terror of Condemned Killer*, Hous. Chron., Nov. 30, 1989. [15, 16]

Kathy Fair, *Executed Murderer Asks Forgiveness, Chaplain Says*, Hous. Chron., Dec. 8, 1989. [11, 16]

Kathy Fair, *Murderer DeLuna is Put to Death*, Hous. Chron., Dec. 7, 1989. [16]

Sara Lee Fernandez and Mike Baird, *Cases Not Closed: Police Continue Homicide Investigations*, Corpus Christi Caller-Times, June 20, 2005, http://www.caller.com/news/2005/jun/20/cases-not-closed/. [9]

Sandra Forero, *Judge Frees Man Charged in Murder*, Jan. 1, 1987. [15]

Terry Ganey, *After Execution, Case Is Reopened*, St. Louis Post-Dispatch, July 12, 2005, http://business.highbeam.com/435553/article-1G1-133964265/after-execution-case-reopened. [E]

John Gonzalez, *Texans Await Execution Ruling*, Dallas Morning News, Oct. 14, 1986. [15]

David Grann, *Trial by Fire*, The New Yorker, Sept. 7, 2009, http://www.newyorker.com/reporting/2009/09/07/090907fa_fact_grann. [E]

Karen Boudrie Greig, *Last Call from Death Row: Seeking the Truth During a Final Conversation*, New Orleans Mag., Aug. 2012, http://www.myneworleans.com/New-Orleans-Magazine/August-2012/Last-Call-From-Death-Row/. [E]

Bob Herbert, *The Wrong Man*, N.Y. Times, July 25, 1997, http://www.nytimes.com/1997/07/25/opinion/the-wrong-man.html. [E]

Michael Holmes, *Mystery Still Surrounds Last Woman Executed in Texas*, Abilene Rep., Jan. 26, 1998, http://www.texnews.com/1998/texas/last0126.html (last visited Oct. 11, 2011). [P]

Christy Hoppe, *County Grand Jury Indicts Man for Beating Death of Woman*, Corpus Christi Caller-Times, Dec. [date unknown] 1979. [7]

Grant Jones and Sam Milsap, *Legislature Should Seriously Reconsider the Death Penalty*, Hous. Chron., Dec. 13, 2012, http://www.chron.com/opinion/outlook/article/Legislature-should-seriously-reconsider-the-death-4116758.php. [E]

Steve James and Peter Gilbert, At the Death House Door (Kartemquin Films & IFC Docs, Uncut 2008). [E]

Jay Jordan, *Man Being Held in Beating Death*, Corpus Christi Caller-Times, Nov. 30, 1979. [7]

Jay Jordan, *Nude Woman Found Dead in Van*, Corpus Christi Caller-Times, Nov. 21, 1979. [7]

Frank Klimko, *State Appeals Court Refuses to Block Texan's Execution*, Hous. Chron., Oct. 14, 1986. [11, 14, 15]

KZTV Channel 10, Feb. 4, 1983 Archive Tape on Wanda Lopez Homicide, Vargas v. Diamond Shamrock, No. 84-4951-D, 86-5900-D (Nueces Cty., 105th Dist. Tex. 1988). [2, 3, 13]

Dave Mann, *DNA Tests Undermine Evidence in Texas Execution*, Tex. Observer, Nov. 11, 2010, http://www.texasobserver.org/cover-story/texas-observer-exclusive-dna-tests-undermine-evidence-in-texas-execution. [E]

Ruel McDaniel, *The Day They Hanged Chipita*, Texas Parade, Sept. 1962. [P]

Anne Michaud, *Inmate Executed at Walls*, The Huntsville Item, Dec. 7, 1989. [16]

Steve Mills and Ken Armstrong, *Convicted by a Hair*, Chi. Trib., Nov. 18, 1999, http://articles.chicagotribune.com/1999-11-18/news/chi-991118deathillinois5 _1_hair-evidence-death-penalty-cases-amy-schulz. [E]

Steve Mills and Ken Armstrong, *The Inside Informant*, Chi. Trib., Nov. 16, 1999, http://articles.chicagotribune.com/1999-11-16/news/9911180109_1_murder -confessions-court-and-police-records-hours-of-tape-recordings. [E]

Steve Mills and Ken Armstrong, *A Tortured Path to Death Row*, Chi. Trib., Nov. 17, 1999, http://articles.chicagotribune.com/1999-11-17/news/chi-991117deathilli nois4_1_confession-stanley-howard-jon-burge. [E]

Steve Mills and Maurice Possley, *About the Chicago Tribune Special Report: Did This Man Die . . . for This Man's Crime?*, Chi. Trib., June 24, 2006, http:// www.chicagotribune.com/news/chi-tx-1-story,0,653915.story. [E, 8]

Steve Mills and Maurice Possley, *"I Didn't Do It But I Know Who Did," New Evidence Suggests a 1989 Execution in Texas Was a Case of Mistaken Identity, First of Three Parts*, Chi. Trib., June 25, 2006, http://www.chicagotribune.com/news/ chi-tx–1-story,0,653915.story. [2, 3, 4, 5, 11, 12, 13, E]

Steve Mills and Maurice Possley, *Man Executed on Disproved Forensics*, Chi. Trib., Dec. 9, 2004, http://www.chicagotribune.com/news/nationworld/chi-04120 90169dec09,0,1173806.story. [E]

Steve Mills and Maurice Possley, *A Phantom, or the Killer?, A Prosecutor Said Carlos Hernandez Didn't Exist. But He Did, and His MO Fit the Crime, Second of Three Parts*, Chi. Trib., June 25, 2006, http://articles.chicagotribune.com/2006-06-26/ news/0606260189_1_jurors-hernandez-home-gas-station. [12, 13, E]

Steve Mills and Maurice Possley, *The Secret That Wasn't: Violent Felon Bragged That He Was Real Killer*, Chi. Trib., June 27, 2006, http://www.chicago tribune.com/services/newspaper/eedition/chi-tx-3-story,0,761635.htmlstory. [3, 4, 8, 9, 10, 12, 13, 17, E]

Steve Mills and Maurice Possley, *Sidebar: Co-Prosecutor Knew of Hernandez*, Chi. Trib., June 26, 2006, http://articles.chicagotribune.com/2006-06-26/ news/0606260190_1_new-trial-murder-case-real-killer. [12]

Terry Moran, *The Wrong Carlos: Did Texas Execute an Innocent Man?*, ABC Nightline, July 18, 2013, at 7:18–7:44, available at http://abcnews.go.com/ Nightline/video/wrong-carlos-texas-execute-innocent-man-19708635. [11]

*Murder Victim Found In Park*, Robstown Record, May 24, 1979. [6]

Lise Olsen, *Did Texas Execute an Innocent Man?*, Hous. Chron., July 24, 2006, http://www.chron.com/disp/story.mpl/front/3472872.html. [E]

Robert Patrick and Heather Ratcliffe, *Review Defends Execution, Prosecutor's Finding*, St. Louis Post-Dispatch, July 12, 2007, http://business.highbeam.com/435553/article-1G1-166337396/review-defends-execution-prosecutor-finding-new-witness. [E]

Steve Ray, *Chipita's Execution Haunts Local Memory*, Corpus Christi Caller-Times, Feb. 2, 1998, http://www.caller2.com/newsarch/news10471.html (last visited Feb. 13, 2012). [P]

John Schwartz, *Changes to Police Lineup Procedures Cut Eyewitness Mistakes, Study Says*, N.Y. Times, Sept. 18, 2011, http://www.nytimes.com/2011/09/19/us/changes-to-police-lineup-procedures-cuteyewitness-mistakes-study-says.html. [E]

Suzanne Smalley, *Police Update Evidence Gathering: Suspect Identification Is Focus of Changes*, Boston Globe, July 20, 2004, http://www.psychology.iastate.edu/~glwells/boston_globe_july_2004.pdf. [E]

Carlton Stowers, *Final Passages: The Reverend Carroll Pickett Leaves a Grim 15-Year Legacy of Very Personal Ministry*, Hous. Press, Nov. 2, 2000, http://www.houstonpress.com/2000-11-02/news/final-passages/. [16]

David Teece, *Judge Lifts Stay of Execution for DeLuna*, Corpus Christi Caller-Times, July 20, 1988. [11, 15]

*Texas Clerk Killer Executed, as Father, Stepmother Watch*, Palm Beach Sun Sentinel, May 15, 1985, http://articles.sun-sentinel.com/1985-05-15/news/8501190637_1_rosa-store-clerk-la. [15]

*Three Held in Two Homicides*, Corpus Christi Caller-Times, May 26, 1979. [6]

Transcribed Videotape of Television Station Archive Tapes on Wanda Lopez Homicide (July 17, 1983). [13]

Cindy Tumiel, *Convicted Killer Executed After Court Rejects Appeals*, Corpus Christi Caller-Times, Dec. 7, 1989. [2, 11, 15, 16, E]

United Press International, *Full Court Denies Stay of Execution: DeLuna Scheduled to Die*, Oct. 10, 1986. [11, 15]

*Wrecks Kills Six in South Texas*, Corpus Christi Caller-Times, Jan. 1, 1971. [6]

Kate Zernike, *Executed Man May Be Cleared in New Inquiry*, N.Y. Times, July 19, 2005, http://www.nytimes.com/2005/07/19/national/19death.html?page wanted=1&th&adxnnl=1&emc=th&adxnnlx=1310932831-BuJo%20E5HvBsbbbcnhl68CA. [E]

## OTHER SECONDARY SOURCES

Anthony G. Amsterdam, *In Favorem Mortis: The Supreme Court and Capital Punishment*, 14 Hum. Rts. 14 (1987). [15]

Craig A. Anderson, *Abstract and Concrete Data in the Perseverance of Social Theories: When Weak Data Lead to Unshakeable Beliefs*, 19 J. Experimental Soc. Psychol. 93 (1983). [E]

Rebecca Averbeck, *Super Glue to the Rescue*, Law Enforcement Tech., Aug. 1998, http://www.detectoprint.com/article.htm (last visited May 12, 2012). [10]

Biography of Mark Skurka, Texas A&M University at Corpus Christi, http://rattler.tamucc.edu/Syllabi_Courses/CV/Skurka_Mark.pdf (last visited May 12, 2012). [17]

Julia E. Boaz, *Note, Summary Processes and the Rule of Law: Expediting Death Penalty Cases in the Federal Courts*, 95 Yale L.J. 349 (1985). [15]

Amy L. Bradfield, Gary L. Wells, and Elizabeth A. Olson, *The Damaging Effect of Confirming Feedback on the Relation Between Eyewitness Certainty and Identification Accuracy*, 87 J. Applied Psychol. 112 (2002). [E]

Kenneth S. Broun et al., McCormick on Evidence, 6th ed. (St. Paul: Thomson/West, 2005). [13]

George W. Bush, A Charge to Keep (New York: Morrow, 1999). [16]

John M. Butler, Fundamentals of Forensic DNA Typing (Burlington, MA: Academic Press, 2010). [11]

Corpus Christi City Directory (1983). [2, 13]

Jonathan I. Creamer, et al., *Attempted Cleaning of Bloodstains and Its Effect on the Forensic Luminol Test*, 20 Luminescence 411 (2005). [10]

Brian L. Cutler and Steven D. Penrod, Mistaken Identification: The Eyewitness, Psychology, and the Law (New York: Cambridge University Press, 1995). [E]

Martin F. Davies, *Belief Persistence After Evidential Discrediting: The Impact of Generated Versus Provided Explanations on the Likelihood of Discredited Outcomes*, 33 J. Experimental Soc. Psychol. 561 (1997). [E]

Death Penalty Information Center, *Charlie Brooks*, http://www.deathpenaltyinfo.org/charlie-brooks (last visited May 12, 2012). [11]

Death Penalty Information Center, *Executions by County*, http://www.deathpenaltyinfo.org/executions-county (last visited May 12, 2012). [E]

Death Penalty Information Center, *Executions in the U.S. from 1976–1986*, http://www.deathpenaltyinfo.org/executions-us-1976-1986 (last visited May 12, 2012). [P, 16]

Death Penalty Information Center, *Executions in the U.S. from 1987–1990*, http://www.deathpenaltyinfo.org/executions-us-1976-1986 (last visited May 12, 2012). [P]

Death Penalty Information Center, *State Data for Texas*, http://www.deathpenaltyinfo.org/state_by_state (last visited Jan. 14, 2014). [P]

Alyson Dinsmore, *Clemency in Capital Cases: The Need to Ensure Meaningful Review*, 49 UCLA L. Rev. 1825 (2002). [16]

Jesse Escochea—Biography, TV.com, http://www.tv.com/jesse-escochea/person/207061/summary.html (last visited May 12, 2012). [2]

Jesse Escochea—Filmography, IMDb.com, http://www.imdb.com/name/nmo260383/ (last visited May 12, 2012). [2]

Brandon L. Garrett, Convicting the Innocent: Where Criminal Prosecutions Go Wrong (Cambridge, MA: Harvard University Press, 2011). [E]

Andrew Gelman et al., *A Broken System: The Persistent Pattern of Reversals of Death Sentences in the United States*, 1 J. Empirical Legal Stud. 209 (2004). [11, E]

Alan M. Gershel, *A Review of the Law in Jurisdictions Requiring Electronic Recording of Custodial Interrogations*, 16 Rich. J.L. & Tech. 1 (2010). [E]

Gary Goodpaster, *Trial for Life: Effective Assistance of Counsel in Death Penalty Cases*, 58 N.Y.U. L. Rev. 299 (1983). [11, 14]

Dashiell Hammett, The Thin Man (New York: Vintage, 1989) (1934). [E]

Kevin Jon Heller, *The Cognitive Psychology of Circumstantial Evidence*, 105 Mich. L. Rev. 241 (2006). [E]

Randy Hertz and James S. Liebman, Federal Habeas Corpus Practice and Procedure, 6th ed. (San Francisco: LexisNexis, 2011). [15]

History of Corpus Christi Housing Authority, Corpus Christi Housing Authority Web Site, http://www.hacc.org/index.php?option=com_content&view=article&id=81&Itemid=28 (last visited May 12, 2012). [5]

Irwin A. Horowitz et al., *Chaos in the Courtroom Reconsidered: Emotional Bias and Juror Nullification*, 30 Law & Hum. Behav. 163 (2006). [11]

Elizabeth R. Jungman, *Beyond All Doubt*, 91 Geo. L.J. 1065 (2003). [14]

Katherine R. Kruse, *Instituting Innocence Reform: Wisconsin's New Governance Experiment*, 2006 Wis. L. Rev. 645 (2006). [E]

Richard O. Lempert et al., A Modern Approach to Evidence: Text, Problems, Transcripts, and Cases, 4th ed. (St. Paul: Thomson/West, 2011). [14]

James S. Liebman, *The New Death Penalty Debate: What's DNA Got to Do with It?*, 33 Colum. Hum. Rts. L. Rev. 527 (2002). [E]

James S. Liebman, *Overproduction of Death*, 100 Colum. L. Rev. 2030 (2000). [11, E]

James S. Liebman et al., A Broken System, Part II: Why There Is So Much Error in Capital Cases, and What Can Be Done About It (2002), http://www2.law.columbia.edu/brokensystem2/index2.html 15. [E]

James S. Liebman et al., *The Evidence of Things Not Seen*, 98 Iowa L. Rev. 577 (2013). [E]

James S. Liebman and Peter Clarke, *Minority Practice, Majority's Burden: The Death Penalty Today*, 9 Ohio St. J. Crim. L. 255 (2011). [15, E]

James S. Liebman and David Mattern, *Correcting Criminal Justice Through Collective Experience Rigorously Examined*, 87 So. Cal. L. Rev. (forthcoming 2014). [E]

Martindale-Hubbell Law Directory (St. Paul: Thomson/West, 1994). [11]

E. Roland Menzel, Fingerprint Detection with Lasers, 2d ed. (New York: Dekker, 1999). [10]

Victoria Nourse, *Passion's Progress: Modern Law Reform and the Provocation Defense*, 106 Yale L.J. 1331 (1997). [17]

Narina Nuñez et al., *The Testimony of Elderly Victim/Witnesses and Their Impact on Juror Decisions: The Importance of Examining Multiple Stereotypes*, 23 Law & Hum. Behav. 420 (1999). [11]

Office of Governor Rick Perry, Gov. Rick Perry Issues One Pardon for Innocence (Dec. 20, 2006), http://governor.state.tx.us/news/press-release/2320/. [16]

The Old Farmer's Almanac, www.almanac.com (last visited May 12, 2012). [3, 10]

Rev. Carroll Pickett, with Carlton Stowers, Within These Walls: Memoirs of a Death House Chaplain (New York: St. Martin's, 2002). [P, 16, E]

The Pulitzer Prizes, The 2000 Pulitzer Prize Winners: Public Service, jttp://www.pulitzer.org/citation/2000-Public-Service (last visited May 12, 2012). [E]

The Pulitzer Prizes, The 2001 Pulitzer Prize Winners: National Reporting, http://www.pulitzer.org/citation/2001-National-Reporting (last visited May 12, 2012). [E]

The Pulitzer Prizes, The 2007 Pulitzer Prize Winners: National Reporting, http://www.pulitzer.org/citation/2007-National-Reporting (last visited May 12, 2012). [E]

The Pulitzer Prizes, The 2008 Pulitzer Prize Winners: Investigative Reporting, http://www.pulitzer.org/citation/2008-Investigative-Reporting (last visited May 12, 2012). [E]

*Chipita Rodriguez*, Wikipedia, http://en.wikipedia.org/wiki/Chipita_Rodriguez (last visited May 12, 2012). [P]

Zandieh Saeid et al., *Using Luminal Solution for Identification Washing Blood and DNA Typing*, 14 Sci. J. Forensic Med. 143 (2008). [10]

Austin Sarat and Nasser Hussain, *On Lawful Lawlessness: George Ryan, Executive Clemency, and the Rhetoric of Sparing Life*, 56 Stan. L. Rev. 1307 (2004). [16]

Vernon Smylie, A Noose for Chipita (Corpus Christi: Texas News Syndicate Press, 1970). [P]

Tracy L. Snell, Bureau of Justice Statistics Tables, Capital Punishment 2009 (Dec. 2010), http://bjs.ojp.usdoj.gov/content/pub/pdf/cp09st.pdf. [15]

Elizabeth Anne Stanko, *The Impact of Victim Assessment on Prosecutors' Screening Decisions: The Case of the New York County District Attorney's Office*, 16 Law & Soc. Rev. 238 (1981). [11]

Carol S. Steiker and Jordan M. Steiker, *A Tale of Two Nations: Implementation of the Death Penalty in "Executing" Versus "Symbolic" States in the United States*, 84 Tex. L. Rev. 1869 (2006). [E]

Thomas P. Sullivan, *Police Experiences with Recording Custodial Interrogations*, 88 Judicature 132 (2004). [E]

Raul Sutton and Keith Trueman (eds.), Crime Scene Management: Scene Specific Methods (New York: Wiley, 2009). [10]

Texas Board of Pardon and Paroles, Clemency: What Is Clemency?, http://www.tdcj.state.tx.us/bpp/exec_clem/exec_clem.html#WHAT_IS_EXECUTIVE_CLEMENCY (last visited May 12, 2012). [16]

Sandra Guerra Thompson, *Beyond a Reasonable Doubt? Reconsidering Uncorroborated Eyewitness Identification Testimony*, 41 U.C. Davis L. Rev. 1487 (2008). [E]

Adam Thurschwell, *Federal Courts, the Death Penalty, and the Due Process Clause: The Original Understanding of the Heightened Reliability' of Capital Trials*, 14 Fed. Sent'g Rep. 14 (2001). [15]

Jennifer R. Treadway, *"Residual Doubt" in Capital Sentencing: No Doubt It Is an Appropriate Mitigating Factor*, 43 Case W. Res. L. Rev. 215 (1992). [14]

Marylyn Underwood, *The Ghost of Chipita: The Crying Woman of San Patricio*, in Legendary Ladies of Texas, ed. Francis E. Abernethy (Denton: University of North Texas Press, 1981). [P]

Marylyn Underwood, *Rodriguez, Josefa [Chipita]*, Handbook of Texas Online, http://www.tshaonline.org/handbook/online/articles/fro50 (last visited May 12, 2012). [P]

http://www.mediation.com/memberprofile/steve—schiwetz-78401-8c.aspx. [15]

Ned Waplin, *Why Is Texas #1 in Executions?*, Death Penalty Info. Ctr. (Dec. 5, 2000), http://www.deathpenaltyinfo.org/node/583. [E]

Gary L. Wells, *Eyewitness Identification: Systemic Reforms*, 2006 Wis. L. Rev. 615 (2006). [E]

Gary L. Wells and Elizabeth A. Olson, *The Other-Race Effect on Eyewitness Identifications: What Do We Do About It?*, 7 Psychol., Pub. Pol'y & L. 230 (2001). [E]

David Wong, Salivary Diagnostics (New York: Wiley, 2008). [10]

Limin Zheng, *Actual Innocence as a Gateway Through the Statute-of-Limitations Bar on the Filing of Federal Habeas Corpus Petitions*, 90 Cal. L. Rev. 2101 (2002). [16]

Numbers in italics refer to pages on which figures appear.